Asia-Pacific and a New International Order: Responses and Options

ASIA-PACIFIC AND A NEW INTERNATIONAL ORDER: RESPONSES AND OPTIONS

PURNENDRA JAIN,
FELIX PATRIKEEFF
AND
GERRY GROOT
EDITORS

Nova Science Publishers, Inc.
New York

Copyright © 2006 by Nova Science Publishers, Inc.

All rights reserved. No part of this book may be reproduced, stored in a retrieval system or transmitted in any form or by any means: electronic, electrostatic, magnetic, tape, mechanical photocopying, recording or otherwise without the written permission of the Publisher.

For permission to use material from this book please contact us:
Telephone 631-231-7269; Fax 631-231-8175
Web Site: http://www.novapublishers.com

NOTICE TO THE READER

The Publisher has taken reasonable care in the preparation of this book, but makes no expressed or implied warranty of any kind and assumes no responsibility for any errors or omissions. No liability is assumed for incidental or consequential damages in connection with or arising out of information contained in this book. The Publisher shall not be liable for any special, consequential, or exemplary damages resulting, in whole or in part, from the readers' use of, or reliance upon, this material.

Independent verification should be sought for any data, advice or recommendations contained in this book. In addition, no responsibility is assumed by the publisher for any injury and/or damage to persons or property arising from any methods, products, instructions, ideas or otherwise contained in this publication.

This publication is designed to provide accurate and authoritative information with regard to the subject matter cover herein. It is sold with the clear understanding that the Publisher is not engaged in rendering legal or any other professional services. If legal, medical or any other expert assistance is required, the services of a competent person should be sought. FROM A DECLARATION OF PARTICIPANTS JOINTLY ADOPTED BY A COMMITTEE OF THE AMERICAN BAR ASSOCIATION AND A COMMITTEE OF PUBLISHERS.

Library of Congress Cataloging-in-Publication Data

Asia-Pacific and a new international order : responses and options / Purnendra Jain, (editor).
    p. cm.
Includes index.
ISBN 1-59454-986-9
1. Asia--Foreign relations. 2. Pacific Area--Foreign relations. 3. Security, International. I. Jain, Purnendra.
JZ1980.A82   2006
327.5--dc22   2006001937

Published by Nova Science Publishers, Inc. ✣ New York

Contents

Preface		vii
About Authors		xi
PART I.	**THE CHANGING ENVIRONMENT IN THE ASIA PACIFIC**	1
Chapter 1	The Pacific Century and the Post-Cold War World *Felix Patrikeeff and Purnendra Jain*	3
Chapter 2	Asia-Pacific Political and Economic Circumstances in an Era of Global and Regional Transformation *Purnendra Jain and Peter Mayer*	13
Chapter 3	Strategic Resets, Security Ripples and US Interests in the Asia-Pacific *Satu P. Limaye*	39
Chapter 4	Soft Power in the Asia-Pacific Post 9/11: The Cases of Japan, China and India *Gerry Groot*	53
Chapter 5	'Islamic Fundamentalism' in the Asia-Pacific Region: Failures of Civil Societies or Backlash Against the US Hegemony? *Shamsul Khan*	71
PART II.	**RESPONSE AND OPTIONS THE COLD WAR SUPERPOWERS**	89
Chapter 6	Post-Cold War US Foreign Policy in Asia *William T. Tow*	91
Chapter 7	Redefining Ideology: Russia and Asia in the Putin Era *Felix Patrikeeff*	109
Chapter 8	Japan and a New International Order: A Case for an East Asian Community *Eiichi Katahara*	121
Chapter 9	Peaceful Rise: China's 'Policy of Assurance' *Jia Qingguo*	133

Chapter 10	South Korea *Vis-À-Vis* the International Disorder: Internal Split and External Initiatives *Myongsob Kim and Yongho Kim*	145
Chapter 11	Indonesia Transforming *Malcolm Cook*	165
Chapter 12	Malaysia and the Changing Regional Security Environment: Responses and Options *Kamarulnizam Abdullah*	181
Chapter 13	The New International Order in the Asia-Pacific Region: Thailand's Responses and Options *Chookiat Panaspornprasit*	195
Chapter 14	India's Quest for Strategic Space in the 'New' International Order: Locations, (Re)Orientations and Opportunities *Sanjay Chaturvedi*	207
Chapter 15	Pakistan and the Bush Doctrine: Consensual Foreign Policy? *Samina Yasmeen*	227
Chapter 16	The Middle East: An Overview *Andrew Vincent*	243
Chapter 17	Iran's Security Perspectives and the Greater Middle East Initiative *Hossein Seifzadeh*	249
Chapter 18	Back to the Future: A 'Colonial' Australia in the 21st Century? *John Bruni*	267
Index		285

PREFACE

In 2005, the security challenges faced by nations in the Asia Pacific region are complex and compounding. From the late 1980s, three sudden, unprecedented and unanticipated developments have had particularly significant impact across the world, including in the nations of Asia-Pacific. The dismantling of the Berlin Wall in 1989 with the subsequent disintegration of the Soviet Union in 1991 was a major turning point in world politics. It led to the end of the bipolar Cold War world order and much speculation about what new international order might emerge. One widely touted possibility was that the Asia-Pacific would come to dominate world affairs through a framework of benign multilateral institutions. This hope faded with Japan's economic downturn from the early1990s and was finally shattered by the Asian economic crisis of 1997, the second major turning point.

Even before the crisis-afflicted Asian nations could recover from the economic upheaval and political instability that followed, world politics again changed dramatically with the third major development, the so-called '9/11' attacks on United States commercial and political establishments in September 2001. The George W. Bush administration cast its bellicose response as America's 'Global War on Terrorism' (GWOT) – invading Afghanistan in 2002 and Iraq in 2003. The strategic posturing of the US has reshaped world politics and strategically realigned nations in major and unexpected ways, particularly as US President George W. Bush sought to coerce international support by declaring a binary 'with us or against us' option.

These three major turning points have profoundly influenced Asia-Pacific. However, other significant changes within the region have made the politico-strategic environment even more complex. First, the rising political and economic weight of China over the last decade alongside the relative decline in Japan's economic clout, together with the all-time high political tensions between China and Japan, are reshaping both regional and international relations. Second, since the 1997 financial downturn and resultant political and economic turmoil in Indonesia, Southeast Asia no longer has a strong and united voice, let alone a capacity for agenda-setting in the region.

Third, the nations of South Asia, which the 'Pacific' Asian nations had kept deliberately outside the 'Asian' process of building regional institutions (e.g., the Asia Pacific Economic Cooperation forum (APEC) and the Asian Regional Forum (ARF), are now emerging as key players. Particularly from the start of the new century, India has become a major economic driver in Asia and India's political voice is now heeded much more than ever before in international forums. In the wake of 9/11, Pakistan has emerged as a key ally in America's

GWOT. Fourth, Australia, which had played a central role in the late-1980s to the mid-1990s promoting Asia-Pacific community building, has tended to turn more towards the US and away from Asia. As part of its new strategic posturing while following the US closely and at times apparently without question, Australia has involved itself further as a protection provider in the nation-building process in the South Pacific. Fifth, and perhaps even more importantly, unforeseen developments in Central and West Asia that concern particularly the region's oil riches have come to play a central role in Asia-Pacific affairs, affecting the options and responses of nations in the region.

In light of these major developments, I organized an international symposium, 'Asia-Pacific and a New International Order: Responses And Options', held at the University of Adelaide in January 2005. Leading strategic analysts from across Australia and the Asia-Pacific came together for in-depth discussion of the security challenges faced by nations in the region. Their brief was to examine the responses of national governments within Asia Pacific to the current security environment, and the options available to these governments for the future.

The term 'Asia-Pacific' broadly includes a range of nations in and on the Pacific rim, including some Latin American countries, the western reach of the US and Canada in North America, and the countries of Oceania including Australia and New Zealand on the Pacific's southern edge. However, for the Symposium we limited the scope of discussion to focus on countries of Northeast, Southeast and South Asia plus the two former superpowers and Australia. We also included the Middle East due to its centrality in the current regional security environment and its strategic importance to the Asia Pacific region and to the world at large.

Most of the papers presented at the Symposium are included in this volume. All contributors revised, updated and refined their papers to the satisfaction of external reviewers for publication purposes. My purpose in this Preface is not to summarise papers and instead I discuss briefly a number of key themes that surfaced in the Symposium discussion and consequently in this volume.[1] First, despite the end of the Cold War, the United States has maintained its central place in regional security considerations. This has led Asia-Pacific nations to develop pragmatic policies in their attempts to balance external issues, such as the preferences of the United States and their own moves towards greater regionalisation, with internal issues that include careful accommodation of religious tensions and potentially potent nationalism. Second, the rise of China and India as increasingly powerful nations has precipitated geopolitical realignments that will continue to shape the region as both nations become more powerful. This volume explores these matters and the inevitably complex web of sub-themes within the ambit of 'Asia-Pacific and a New International Order'.

The Symposium that gave birth to this volume was generously supported by several institutions. The Japan Foundation provided financial assistance under its Intellectual Exchange program. Mr Masaki Baba of the Japan Foundation Sydney office offered helpful advice and Ms Catherine Maxwell attended the symposium representing the Foundation. The Faculty of Humanities and Social Sciences at the University of Adelaide provided me with funding through a Strategic Research Initiative grant to organise and support the Symposium.

---

[1] A detailed summary of papers and emerging themes are available in Glen Stafford and Purnendra Jain, 'Asia-Pacific and a New International Order: Responses and Options', *Australian Journal of International Affairs*, 59:3, September 2005, pp. 375-81.

The Australian Research Council Asia Pacific Futures Network also provided financial support to enable a number of postgraduate and early career researchers to participate in the Symposium. To all three bodies, I express my deep gratitude for their generosity and support.

I very much appreciate the efforts of all the authors whose work appears in this volume; they have cooperated generously in preparing their work and meeting our publication deadlines. I understand that all authors have also appreciated the useful comments and feedback provided by discussants at the Symposium and drawn from these discussions in revising their papers for this volume. My thanks to Andrew MacIntyre, Michael Wesley, Robin Jeffrey, Richard Leaver, Tim Doyle, Michael Innes, David Lundberg, Maryanne Kelton and Roxanne Marcotte for providing insightful comments and constructive criticisms that helped authors to tighten their arguments and improve their papers for publication. It was a great pleasure to work on this project with my colleagues from the Politics and Asian Studies sections of our Faculty (Humanities and Social Sciences), especially Felix Patrikeeff and Gerry Groot who helped me with many aspects of the Symposium and in editing the revised papers. Their intellectual input and cooperation has enriched my own involvement in the project and enabled the project to progress to publication in timely fashion. Many thanks, Felix and Gerry.

I thank Glen Stafford and Shoo Lin Siah who helped with organising the symposium and liaising with authors during the publication process, and Niki Pavlidis who provided necessary administrative support. I thank Cally Guerin who meticulously copyedited all the papers for this volume, and Maya Columbus of Nova Science Publishers for her interest in this project and support at every stage of preparing this publication. Finally, I acknowledge with deep gratitude the relentless support, the care and patience – and the proofreading contributions – of my family, without which neither I nor this book would be in their present form. Sam has been particularly helpful with computer assistance for this volume and in helping me with research and useful comment on my paper.

Purnendra Jain
Centre for Asian Studies
The University of Adelaide
December 2005

ABOUT AUTHORS

Kamarulnizam **Abdullah** is Associate Professor at the School of History, Politics and Strategic Studies, Universiti Kebangsaan Malaysia. His main research areas are political violence, religious militancy and national security issues in relation to Malaysia and Southeast Asia. He has published numerous books, book chapters and international journal articles. He was a Visiting Lecturer in several institutions/universities, such as the Oxford Diplomatic Council, United Kingdom, Muhammadiyah University and Universitas Pembangunan Nasional in Indonesia. He is currently editing a book on *The Nusantara Connection: Malaysia-Indonesia Relations in a Globalized World* to be published by Marshall Cavendish of Singapore.

John **Bruni** is Adjunct Lecturer in the Centre for Asian Studies at the University of Adelaide and has worked on Australian defence and regional security issues in various capacities for over 18 years. Dr Bruni's publications include the book *On Weapons Decisions: How Australia Chooses to Arm Itself (1963-96)* (Southern Highlands Publishers, 2002). His most recent work (co-authored) is 'Japan, Australia and the US—Mini NATO or Shadow Alliance?' *International Relations of the Asia Pacific: A Journal of the Japan Association of International Relations* (Oxford University Press, 2004).

Sanjay **Chaturvedi** is Reader in Political Science and Honorary Director, Centre for the Study of Mid-West and Central Asia at Panjab University in India. He is the author of *Polar Regions: A Political Geography* (1996); co-author of *Partitions: Reshaping Minds and States* (2005); and co-editor of *Geopolitical Orientations, Regionalism and Security in the Indian Ocean* (2004); *Energy Security and the Indian Ocean Region* (2005); and *Globalization: Spaces, Identities and Insecurities* (2005). He has also published in such journals as *Environment and Planning D: Society and Space*, *Journal of Economic and Social Geography*, *Ocean Yearbook* and *Third World Quarterly*.

Malcolm **Cook**, Program Director Asia Pacific Region at the Lowy Institute for International Policy, has a PhD in international relations from the Australian National University, an MA in international relations from the International University of Japan and an honours degree from McGill University in Canada. Malcolm recently published a policy brief on Indonesia's political transition for the Foreign Policy Centre in London and has commented frequently in the Australian and international media on Australia-Indonesia relations. Before joining the Institute in November 2003, he ran his own risk analysis consulting practice on Southeast Asian politics and economics.

Dr Gerry **Groot** is a Senior Lecturer in the Centre for Asian Studies, University of Adelaide where he teaches Chinese politics, religion and society, as well as Asian Studies. Dr Groot spent several years studying and working in China teaching English. In the early 1990s he worked on a PhD on the Chinese Communist Party's united front work with minor political parties. This has subsequently been published as the book *Managing Transitions* (Routledge, 2004). Some of the matters it covers stimulated his interests in ideas of legitimacy and soft power.

Purnendra **Jain** is Professor and Head of Asian Studies at the University of Adelaide in Australia. He is the author, editor and co-editor of 10 books and has published more than four dozen book chapters and scholarly articles in international journals. His most recent book is *Japan's Subnational Governments in International Affairs* (London and New York: Routledge, 2005).

Jia Qingguo is Professor and Associate Dean of the School of International Studies of Peking University. He received his PhD from Cornell University in 1988 and has taught at the University of Vermont, Cornell University, University of California at San Diego and University of Sydney in Australia, as well as Peking University. He is a member of the editorial board of several international academic journals. He has published extensively on U.S.-China relations, relations between the Chinese mainland and Taiwan, Chinese foreign policy and Chinese politics.

Eiichi **Katahara** is Professor and Senior Research Fellow at the National Institute for Defense Studies of the Defense Agency of Japan. His recent publications include 'Japan as a Civilian Peacekeeper', in Graeme Cheeseman and Lorraine Elliott (eds) *Forces for Good* (Manchester: Manchester University Press, 2004), and 'Japan: From Containment to Normalization', in Muthiah Alagappa (ed.) *Coercion and Governance* (Stanford: Stanford University Press, 2001).

Satu P. **Limaye** is Director, Research and Publications, Asia-Pacific Center for Security Studies (APCSS) in Honolulu. APCSS is a unit reporting directly to the US Pacific Command. Dr Limaye works on US relations with Asia. His recent publications include *Asia's China Debate* (APCSS, 2004) and the forthcoming *Japan in a Dynamic Asia* (Rowman and Littlefield, 2006). The views expressed are entirely those of the author and do not represent the views of APCSS, US Pacific Command, the US Department of Defense or any US government department or agency.

Shamsul **Khan** teaches international and Asian studies and is the Director of the honours and postgraduate programs at the School of International Studies, University of South Australia. Shamsul has written extensively in research journals and contributed articles in books on issues related to security, foreign policy, democratisation and economic restructuring and gender issues. He is currently working on a book on the correlation between alienation and political extremism.

Myongsob **Kim** was an Associate Professor in Hanshin University until 2003. He is currently an Assistant Professor at Yonsei University and Public Relations Director of the Korean Political Science Association in 2005. He has published many articles and several books, most recently *The History of Atlantic Civilization* (in Korean), and 'On Huntington's Civilizational Paradigm', *Issues and Studies* (June 2005).

Yongho **Kim** is Associate Professor and Chair of the Department of Political Science, Yonsei University, and Associate Director of Yonsei Institute for Korean Unification Studies in Seoul. He has authored or co-authored six books and has published dozens of scholarly articles in Korean and international journals. His most recent book, co-authored with Professor Chin Wee Chung, is *North Korea, Inter-Korean Relations and Unification* (Seoul: Yonsei University Press, 2003) and his most recent article is 'The Russo-North Korean Relations in the 2000s: Russia's Continuing Search for Regional Influence', *Asian Survey*, 44:6, 2004.

Peter **Mayer** is Associate Professor in Politics at the University of Adelaide. He is the author of *India* (Sydney: Australia-Asia Institute, 1992) and co-author of *Capitalism and Colonial Production* (London and Canberra: Croom Helm, 1982) and of many journal articles. His recent work examines a diverse range of issues including: why the proportion of women in the Indian population has been steadily declining since 1901; the role played by civic engagement and social capital in the human development performance of the Indian states; the introduction of e-governance in the Indian states; and a major study of the sociology of suicide and homicide in India.

Chookiat **Panaspornprasit** is Assistant Professor in the Department of International Relations, Faculty of Political Science at Chulalongkorn University in Bangkok. Currently he is also the Director of the Institute of Security and International Studies (ISIS). His most recent publication is *US-Kuwaiti Relations, 1961-1992: An Uneasy Relationship* (London: Routledge, 2005).

Felix **Patrikeeff** is a Senior Lecturer in the School of History and Politics at the University of Adelaide. He has also taught at the universities of Warwick, Oxford and Sydney. His publications include the book *Mouldering Pearl: Hong Kong at the Crossroads* (London: Hodder and Stoughton, 1990) and numerous essays on Russia and East Asia.

Hossein **Seifzadeh** is Professor of Politics at Tehran University. He specialises in international and developmental theory and has a keen interest in Iran's post-revolutionary politics, both foreign and domestic. He is the author of twelve books and has translated three books into Persian. Two of his new works to be published soon are 'International Theory in a Globalized International Relations' and 'Foreign Policy of Iran'. He has also written over 100 articles in English and Persian.

William T. **Tow** is Professor of International Security in the Department of International Relations, The Australian National University. He is the author of many books and articles on Asian security politics including *Asia-Pacific Strategic Relations—Seeking Convergent*

Security (Cambridge: Cambridge University Press, 2001). He is Editor of the *Australian Journal of International Affairs*.

Andrew **Vincent** is the Director of the Centre for Middle East and North African Studies at Macquarie University and Chairman of the NSW Chapter of the Australia Arab Chamber of Commerce and Industry. As a political scientist, his academic interests include the interaction of religion and politics in the Middle East.

Dr Samina **Yasmeen** is Director of the Centre for Muslim States and Societies at the University of Western Australia, Perth. She has also worked as Executive Director of the Indian Ocean Centre for Peace Studies at UWA and Curtin Universities (1995) and as Senior Research Fellow in a UNESCO-funded project at the Ministry of Education, Government of Pakistan (1977-79). Dr Yasmeen has published articles on the position of Pakistani and Middle Eastern women, the role of Muslims in Australia and Indo-Pakistan relations. Her current research focuses on the role of Islamic groups in Pakistan's foreign policy.

Part I. The Changing Environment in the Asia Pacific

Chapter 1

THE PACIFIC CENTURY AND THE POST-COLD WAR WORLD

Felix Patrikeeff and Purnendra Jain

With the dissipation of the Cold War after 1991 (a major event triggered by the reforms and radical foreign policy of Mikhail Gorbachev in the Soviet Union, which were then followed by the country's dramatic collapse in December 1991), a number of scholarly International Relations orthodoxies came into question. One idea in particular began to gain momentum. With increasing authority, both scholars and business communities began painting an image of the post-Cold War twenty-first century as a 'Pacific Century'.[1] In the 1980s there had been a good deal of evidence to indicate that the centre of economic gravity in the global system was indeed shifting to the Pacific (Adler *et al.*, 1986; Chan, 1993; Borthwick, 1992; Linder, 1986; World Bank, 1993). A litany of new terms and concepts became associated with Pacific Asia and the rapid economic changes taking place there. These ideas ranged from such sober notions as 'Developmental State' and 'Newly-Industrialising Economy' (NIE) (Amsden, 1989; Chowdhury and Islam, 1993), to more exotic concepts, including 'flying geese', 'Tiger Economies' and 'Four Little Dragons', the latter designations depicting the economies of South Korea, Taiwan, Hong Kong and Singapore (Shibusawa *et al.*, 1992). An ascendant Northeast Asian regional economy rapidly expanded, with Southeast Asian economies appearing to seamlessly assume the growth patterns and integrate the economic forms generated by the Japanese-led post-war economic development (Shibusawa *et al.*, 1992). Despite the fact that the Pacific region was still firmly locked in a Cold War architecture, the latter's political dimensions seemed to impede neither the pace nor the forms delivering economic progress. If anything, these patterns suggested that economic growth could overcome strong political enmities and ideological suspicions. As

---

[1] This wasn't the first time that the Pacific was singled out as an emblem of growth and development. As early as 1892, the term 'Pacific Age' was coined in Japan (see Korhoven, 1996: 41-70) in order to depict the exceptional nature of the region. However, at its height, the notion of a 'Pacific Century' seemed to capture the imagination of the region, to the point that a major telecommunications firm in Hong Kong was renamed Pacific Century Cyberworks (PCCW), blending Asia's 'arrival' with the 'brave new world' of high technology.

the *Economist* summed it up so succinctly in early 1990s: 'The peoples of Asia have never had it so good. From mighty China to micro Singapore, the 1980s was [sic] a decade of growth, trade and increasing prosperity. Then came the peace dividend' (1993: 13). States such as Malaysia and Indonesia (with early post-colonial histories of political instability and fears of communist interference and subversion), could now, with measured confidence, contemplate relations even with implacable adversaries such as the People's Republic of China and the Soviet Union. In the immediate post-Soviet period, this economic development and confidence-building was at its height, with state-driven policies broadening to incorporate even the previously unthinkable: open relations with the region's socialist behemoth, China. There were hiccoughs, of course. In recasting its regional and global role, China's relations with the United States had, by the mid 1990s, spiralled downward, leading some observers to note the emergence of the spectre of a new Cold War (*Asiaweek*, 1995: 24-28). Then there was the Stalinist state of North Korea. In 1994, Pyongyang threatened to upset the regional balance by insisting on pursuing the development of its nuclear program. The immediate result was a dramatic confrontation with the US. Yet the region absorbed the impact of the crisis, and instead focused on how North Korea could be enticed to increased openness and economic integration. Thus, while the nuclear stand-off was in progress, attention focused on other developing projects. The more ambitious of these was a multilateral initiative known as the Tumen River Strategic Action Project, centring on the Rajin-Sombong Free Economic and Trade Zone (involving North and South Korea, China, Russia, Japan and Mongolia). This project was an economy-driven confidence-building measure that, it was hoped, might create peaceful lines of multilateral relations at the heart of an historically troubled confluence of powers.[2] Moreover, it was clear that even China, long a friend of Pyongyang, was playing a responsible and even-handed role in tempering this rogue regime.

However, at the core of this regional formation, replete as it was with 'miracle economies' and aspiring NIEs, was a major, yet essentially simple, problem. The security of individual states was largely built upon the understanding that each had a common focus on an overriding target: economic growth. This has been reflected by the fact that the positive policy initiatives of the period were those centred on the regional economy and the formation of bodies such as the Pacific Economic Cooperation Conference (PECC) and the Asia-Pacific Economic Cooperation (APEC) forum to facilitate regional economic cooperation (Harris, 1991: 17). Even the Association of Southeast Asian Nations (ASEAN), founded in the face of a communist threat, had steadily transformed into an organisation that regarded a successful regional balance as one that was built on mutual understanding and common purpose. ASEAN was looking increasingly to facilitate cooperative economic development among its members. The appropriateness of such an approach appeared to be strongly reinforced by the rapid opening up of China. The latter was banking on the global economy to vouchsafe its long-term well-being as a nation-state, rather than its former preoccupations with radical politics and liberationism, preoccupations which had for so long defined features of its presence on the international stage. In place of radicalism, China instead turned sharply towards making responsible contributions as an international player and the greater use of 'soft power'; these themes are explored by Jia Qingguo and Gerry Groot in their essays in the present volume. Neutralised, too, had been the communist superpower, the Soviet Union.

---

[2] For full coverage of the parameters of this project, see Asian Perspective (1995), which has a number of articles devoted to the Tumen River initiative.

Long suspected of harbouring plans for global hegemony and advocating an aggressive ideology, the Soviet Union had been a key to understanding the politics of the region in the post-war period, a perspective that stretched as far as the Island Pacific. With its virulent communist essence gone, the new post-Soviet Russia was suddenly a far more benign political presence, having renounced radical ideology and cut economic lifelines to former allies, such as the socialist regimes of Vietnam and North Korea. The overriding impression of the political architecture for the post-Cold War period was, therefore, one of a structure-by-default. Sturdy, booming economies were matched by measured political policies of pragmatic regimes that placed economic success well ahead of pursuing political differences. With socialism a spent force both in political terms and as an economic rival, such a perspective appeared to be reinforced by the eagerness of the socialist states of Vietnam and Laos to join the ranks of ASEAN, and the remarkable speed and ease with which they were accepted (the former in 1995 and the latter in 1997).

Where, then, was the problem? Arguably, this architecture-by-default lacked any refined alternative political structures and strategies to go forward into the post-Cold War era. As one commentator observed in the early 1990s, while the United States and its allies were steadily elaborating clear lines of policy in anticipation of a post-Cold War Europe, they had no such contingency or outlook for the Asia-Pacific region (Harris, 1991: 16-17). This omission was a considerable concern, given *inter alia* that the United States was involved in a number of close political relationships within the region. After all, it was directly contributing to the politico-military security of Japan, South Korea and Taiwan in Northeast Asia, and through an intricate network of cooperation with, and reinforcement of, a number of west-leaning states in Southeast Asia. Its place was also prominent in the South Pacific, where it had a key security alliance in Australasia (ANZUS) and a prominent role with states in the Island Pacific. But here again was a problem: with the Soviet Union despatched to its political grave and China on balance becoming more an economic partner than an overt political opponent, the United States' role within the region was itself in need of reassessment. How this role was to be re-shaped remained a puzzle. The US lay at the core of the region, but at the same time, how was it to release itself from the straitjacket of the Cold War political framework? There were indications that, no longer having a clear-cut overarching role to play in the Asia-Pacific region, the US might begin to disengage from it. Indeed, at a grassroots level within the region, there was often considerable support for such an outcome, as the essay by Yongho Kim and Myongsob Kim indicates with regard to the Korean political stalemate and South Korean popular attitudes. But in reality, this disengagement was an option only in relation to the Island Pacific, where the US could comfortably leave matters of a geopolitically less perplexing sort in the hands of its close middle-power ally, Australia (the relationship between Australia and the US is explored by William Tow). To remove itself from the heart of Pacific Asia was arguably far more complicated for the US. For a start, its active treaty obligations and the persistence of a highly charged political atmosphere in various pockets of the region demanded/ensured the sole superpower's continued presence. Ironically, it needed this presence to remain largely in its traditional Cold War form.

Thus, with no fresh blueprint, the US's role is an ongoing one. Satu Limaye in his paper observes that the Pacific Asia was already in some respects perched precariously and hence was vulnerable. Reflecting this, Purnendra Jain's and Peter Mayer's chapters show that, with the end of the Cold War, the region's arms purchases have persisted, and at high levels in some countries. Moreover, Japan's economy, the engine of growth and economic alignment in the broader region, had been vulnerable since the 1980s, but the absence of workable, clear-sighted reform saw the country slowing down, a situation which seemingly persists even today. The impact of this stagnation had (and has) been buffered to a degree because China's fresh 'Open-Door' economy enlarged the regional economic pie. In addition, despite the fraught political relationship between China and its so-called 'rogue province' Taiwan, the economic relationship between the two Chinas grew apace, in many ways both validating, and to a measure even reinforcing, the appropriateness of growth-oriented security. The eagerness of other former antithetical states and those formerly on the region's political margins (Vietnam, Cambodia, Laos and Burma) to join ASEAN suggested that even Southeast Asia was willing to put economic prosperity above lines of political difference. And this despite the Cold War conflicts played out in them over the previous 40 years. So, the Cold War political architecture was still very much intact and working, even within the context of the post-Soviet world order.

The first major test for this system by default came with the currency crises of 1997-1998. The subsequent economic downturn bit hard into the Asia-Pacific region as a whole, not just Thailand, Malaysia and Indonesia where it had developed. The consequences undermined a number of key aspects of the region's security. First and foremost, it gave the lie to the notion that Pacific Asia could rely solely on its economic growth as a foundation for its political well-being. For countries that had been so impressive in economic development, these years of turmoil showed them to be remarkably vulnerable in political terms.[3] And while the affected states did weather the economic storm, and have in most cases now resumed rapid and sustained growth, the political lessons of the 1997-98 crash remain profound for them.[4]

Second, China benefited from the post-crisis downturn in Southeast Asia, Hong Kong, South Korea and Taiwan. It allowed China to enjoy accelerated economic development and had the effect of making it more prominent internationally. Of course, the PRC was

---

[3] Nowhere was this better demonstrated than in Malaysia, where the then Prime Minister Mahathir Mohammad not only found himself having to deal with the severe effects of an intense economic crisis, but also having to fend off his Deputy Prime Minister, Anwar Ibrahim, from promoting his own credentials as the aspiring leader. Mahathir, in a rare display of uncontrolled pique, lashed out at 'moron' currency speculators, and particularly George Soros, with whom he engaged in an extended and virulent spat. So pervasive was the crisis that even an advanced economy such as Hong Kong's was not immune. In a television interview with Sir Donald Tsang (then the HKSAR's Financial Secretary, and now its Chief Executive) in late August 1997, he was asked to comment on the exchange between Mahathir and Soros. He chose to avoid direct comment on this, instead confidently predicting that the Asian economies would bounce back, and that Hong Kong's economy, with its impeccable fundamentals, would not succumb to the region's problems (Business Sunday, 1997). He was proven wrong, as Hong Kong slid into one of its most prolonged periods of economic downturn. This became enmeshed with Hong Kong's own political problems, notably its relationship with China, to whose sovereignty it had returned just a few weeks earlier.

[4] Malcolm Cook's contribution to this book raises the valuable point that there were positive as well as negative results of the economic crisis. Without it, he argues, there was little likelihood of Indonesia enjoying such a dramatic shift into a more open political system, as President Suharto would not have been forced out of office so easily. Such a perspective notwithstanding, the link between sharp economic decline and political unease is one that has long characterised the region. As a result of the last major regional economic downturn in the mid-1980s, a leading article in the London Times observed: 'The resulting nervousness has become visible in the internal politics of the countries concerned: a growing sensitivity to opposition, problems of political succession, difficulties in finding a new tack' (1985: 11). While these symptoms were all prominent again after the 1997-98 crisis, it must also be observed that the underlying political impact of the latter was far more profound, and enduring.

meticulous in avoiding being seen to take advantage of the regional economic troubles in any obvious way (such as, for example, devaluing its currency at the time, thereby driving still greater levels of investment away from its Southeast Asian neighbours' export-driven economies, and into its own rapidly expanding manufacturing sector). Yet China benefited if only by showing that it was seemingly rock-solid as an investment destination and manufacturing base. In contrast, its competitor states in Southeast Asia looked decidedly fragile.[5] Perhaps the most intriguing outcome of this, however, was with regard to the regional geopolitical balance. As a result of China's rise in economic stature, it has emerged as a clearer rival to Japan's subtle regional preponderance—a role that the former has further developed in recent times (Golub, 2003). Given the tensions between the two powers, the implications of this change are significant, particularly for Japan in the longer term. With few strategies to counter this shift, Japan surely faces a major dilemma as to how to re-shape its foreign policy to accommodate the pretender. By extension, important too is the issue of the US's role in the relationship. After all, it is locked into defence arrangements with Japan and Taiwan, while at the same time finding China a rather prickly counterpart to negotiate with.

Third, having been shaped by a history of tensions and conflicts rather than clear-sighted plans for political transition and restructuring, the issue for Pacific Asia becomes whether or not any reorganisation is possible. Southeast Asia has a shape and structure, largely achieved via the expansion and elaboration of ASEAN, not only as a general vehicle for regional confidence-building, but also as a forum within which specific security issues can be broached and tamed. However, sovereignty and nationalism are sacrosanct concepts there (Beeson, 2003: 364). In contrast, there has been no sign of even an ASEAN-like body emerging in Northeast Asia. Nor does there seem to be any likelihood of such a body being created in the short to medium term. Given that two of the preponderant powers are in the North East and there are tensions between them, and that these stresses have the potential to shake Pacific Asia as a whole (if not, in fact, well beyond the region), the complexity of how to achieve universally acceptable common ground becomes in itself a major security issue. In addition, there is the perennial issue of North Korea, and how that petulant state is to be politically tempered towards moderation and economically rescued. Given that both China and Japan have a vested interest in reaching a peaceful outcome there on the Korean Peninsula, but have in the meantime experienced fraught relations themselves, the broader matrix of political relations in the Northeast Asian region becomes even more complicated.

And finally, what of Russia? The political topography of Pacific Asia was, as discussed earlier, formed largely as a result of countering the spread of its perceived attempt to establish hegemony in the region. The fact that Russia's influence has waned since 1991, and that it has not shown any ideological pretensions since, does not remove it entirely from consideration, given that it shares borders with the major powers in the key Northeast Asian region, and has expanded working relations—and arms sales—with the Southeast Asian states. Any shift in the nature of the broader region's political structure will have consequences for this former superpower—given that it still produces some of the most technologically advanced weaponry in the world, and its eastern borders have long been seen by Russians as being vulnerable to destabilisation and intrusion.

---

[5] Robert N. McCauley has calculated that China's current account balance leapt from $US 4.4 billion in 1995-1996, to $US 20.8 billion in 1999-2000 and $US 26.4 billion in 2001-02. The Southeast Asian economies showed a far more erratic set of results over period in question (2003: 42).

Where, then, is the broader region in political terms? From an economic powerhouse, with fully industrialised states leading aspirants along the path to full development, Pacific Asia has not only failed to thus far make the twenty-first century its own, but threatens to provide a good deal of world's future political instability and sense of uncertainty.

In broad geopolitical terms, these factors have made the search for a clear framework for Pacific Asia all the more important, as this would potentially provide the region with a hitherto unprecedented coherence, as well as common foundations for building sustained political security (a theme that is so adroitly broached by Eiichi Katahara's essay in the present volume). However, for the Northeast Asian states to draw closer to regional organisations farther south and adopt the equivalent of an 'ASEAN spirit' is unlikely. Meanwhile the prospect of creating a Northeast Asian security network is, as has already been suggested, even more remote. And even if one or the other were to come into being, it is likely that there would still be no ready-made answer to the overarching question of 'whither Pacific Asia?' It is, as Barry Buzan prosaically puts it, likely to be a situation of 'more of the same' (Buzan, 2003: 143).

Muddying the waters further is, of course, the fact that the region has been caught up in the United States' own vision for the post-9/11 world—a world that has seen the focus shift to the imperative of eradicating global terrorism, backed by that state's ability (and increasing readiness) to adopt unilateral means to further this process. The pursuit of this seemingly ever-retreating goal in itself leaves many of the region's countries in a state of considerable discomfort, as Chookiat Panaspornprasit argues in his perspectives on Thai-US relations after 9/11. But the American global political imperative also carries a renewed emphasis on the need for states to democratise;[6] however, this is not a proposition that has been welcome to all in the region. After all, most of the states of Pacific Asia achieved their early successes through single-minded state-driven economic development, in which the notion of promoting genuine democratic reform was seen not only as a luxury, but also something that might dilute strong leadership and unnecessarily hinder pragmatic policies (which looked to economic outcomes as the essential driving force of societies, not the *desiderata* of their citizenry's political life and outlook). In the old international order, the United States had appeared to quietly accept benign, and at times even overt, authoritarian regimes, as long as they 'delivered the goods' to their populations and overseas investors, and remained on-side politically. However, with the assault on America in 2001, this perspective altered. Authoritarian regimes are now being subjected to increased scrutiny and shrill riposte. In the context of this new outlook, one state in Pacific Asia (North Korea) quickly earned a place in George W. Bush's 'Axis of Evil', and others found themselves on a watching brief regarding their political credentials. At the core of America's post-9/11 policies is not only a strong sense of moral purpose, but also the clear sanction of the use of power politics and zero-sum games, as so vividly portrayed by President George W. Bush himself in his stark post-9/11 ultimatum to the international community: 'either you're with us or you're against us' (*Shanghai Star*, 2001). Power politics is a manifestation quite familiar to the states of Pacific Asia, and notably in its northern portion. It has also been a form that has lately (in many key

---

[6] Democratisation was, in the early 1990s, already an important political issue (it was a prerequisite for aid from the World Bank, for example), but rarely has it been as pointed or as stark as it is today (Secretary of State Condaleezza Rice's call for democratisation in Egypt in June 2005 drew the following comment from Tangi Salaun in French right-of-centre newspaper Le Figaro: 'Egypt cannot completely hide the irritation it feels about America's ambitions in the region and what it considers to be unbearable "interference"' (2005).

respects) been studiously eschewed by these countries. These are states that had had the frequent experience of big power rivalry for well over a century, drawing in as it did the pernicious aspects (and after-effects) of colonialism (Beeson, 2002: 550), internal and global conflicts, invasions and counter-invasions. All these influences had been part-and-parcel of achieving geopolitical goals in an uncompromising fashion. In this specific sense, the focus on economic growth and benign political cohabitation has been a highly successful strategy for the states of Pacific Asia, allowing them to justify positions of political compromise for the sake of maintaining economic momentum. Arguably, getting the formula right for rapid economic development is itself a major imposition on a population (witness, for example, South Korea's breakneck development plan under President Park Chung Hee [Harvie and Lee, 2003: 260-261], and the social costs that accompanied the remarkable strides of the economy as a whole). But this overriding need to maintain political openness and allow a 'hundred flowers [to] bloom' (to adapt Mao Zedong's motto from his abortive attempt to generate open political debate in China) adds burdens which many of the leaders of these strictly governed states can neither entirely accept philosophically at present, nor deal with in operational terms if they are to devote their attention to maintaining high levels of economic growth. They therefore face a major dilemma, the resolution for which is not readily apparent, nor is success assured.

But even if Pacific Asia does resume a more forceful drive towards a 'Pacific Century', will it do so with the very definition of the region having become ambiguous?[7] With the collapse of the Soviet Union, India no longer felt its interests restricted to either the South Asian region or the Indian Ocean, as it had in the course of the Cold War. Indian Prime Minister Atal Bihari Vajpayee underlined such thinking in a lecture delivered to the Institute of Southeast Asian Studies in 2002, when he noted that his country's earlier reticence had not been a willing one; rather, it

> was a consequence of the divergences in economic ideology, political outlook and security assumptions[,] much of which the Cold War imposed on us. Fortunately, we have emerged from this straitjacket. The end of the Cold War removed the hurdles to close India-ASEAN cooperation. (Vajpayee, 2002)

India's own choices and strategies will have a considerable impact on Pacific Asia, and how we look upon it. India is, after all, the second most populous state in the world, is a nuclear power, and one with an economy that is already of considerable weight and prominence internationally. As with China, it has a burgeoning middle class, showing signs of prosperity and consumption that make it a magnet for investors and sellers alike. India, as Sanjay Chaturvedi's illuminating essay on its geopolitics shows in the present volume, is a state that must juggle alliances, links, the all-important aspect of self-interest and its own international prestige in a changing environment. Alongside this, another power in South Asia, Pakistan (discussed by Samina Yasmeen) has been thrust onto the international stage in a different, and potentially negative, way. It has found itself as an economically vulnerable

---

[7] In early 1987, the respected Far Eastern Economic Review focused one of its issues on the question 'What is Asia?' The conclusion to the lead article (written by the journal's Deputy Editor Philip Bowring) was an interesting one: 'Maybe dominant civilisations will always be defined by what they are, while others are given common identity by what they are not. In which case, as some nations in Asia rise to global ascendancy the notion of Asia will fade away' (1987: 7).

nuclear power, sitting uncomfortably near the heart of the globalised 'War on Terror', and still very much at odds with its nemesis India (especially so over the intractable Kashmir problem). Its Muslim majority represents something of a causeway between the Muslim states and minorities of Pacific Asia and those of West Asia. As such, it must observe the increasing militancy of some sectors of Islam in the East and the deeply troubled (and some might say western-inspired) situation in Central and West Asia. The growing focus internationally on so-called 'Islamic Fundamentalism' to a less critical observer's eyes brings the negative political processes of these other states much closer to Pacific Asia and its own Muslim majorities/minorities. At the crossroads of this worrying nexus is Pakistan. The uncertainty of how politics will develop in the latter, and its unfortunate status as the country from which the families of a number of those involved in the London bombings of July 2005 had originally migrated, leaves that state more open to scrutiny and, to its critics, its possible role in (or grassroots influence on) the Pacific region.

The Pacific Century may still come to pass (albeit, to use Hobsbawm's depiction of the twentieth century, perhaps in the form of a 'short century'), but almost certainly not in the form envisioned by the optimists of the 1980s and early 1990s. Rather than the orderly pattern of Japanese-led economic development envisaged then, it may well be characterised by an economic balance between technologically-rich developed economies, such as those of Japan and South Korea, and the emergence of a greater China (drawing as it does from the technology and advanced manufacturing techniques of Taiwan, and the management/financial/service acumen of Hong Kong). But the balance here will also be marked by political rivalry that, in earlier analyses of an emerging Pacific Asia, few commentators would have recognised. Whether this remains an entirely peaceful balance remains to be seen, but in the meantime Pacific Asia must also realign itself with the politically redefined notion of globalisation—one that not only has a core technological-economic component, but also a very pointed post-9/11 political dimension. The way in which the core regions of Northeast and Southeast Asia lock into this reconfigured notion of globalism is an important aspect of how the twenty-first century will unfold for them. Equally, it is also important to see how bordering states and regions deal with this new political topography (explored in the context of the troubled Middle East by papers from Andrew Vincent and Hossein Seifzadeh). Post-Soviet Russia has been surprisingly adept in integrating itself into this new environment, as Felix Patrikeeff's essay argues.

Significant, too, is the way in which the Island Pacific re-aligns itself with Pacific Asia, a topic examined by John Bruni. Australia, as the dominant force in the Island Pacific region, has already seen the difficulties entailed in such a realignment, being linked (often seemingly inextricably) with the US's politico-military project as a founding member of the so-called 'Alliance of the Willing'. But at the same time, Australia is deeply involved in economic terms with Japan and, increasingly, China. Political consequences invariably flow from the latter relations, although the importance of a firm alliance with the United States remains. Alignments and re-alignments are torturous in a unipolar world as the defining line between bowing to hegemony and charting an independent path is difficult to divine.

The authors of the essays in this book explore many dimensions of the key issues discussed above, and in so doing give form to the broader complexities confronting Pacific Asia in the early years of the twenty-first century. The book charts the problems of, and in some cases the options open to, individual countries and sub-regions. Some of these are familiar issues, such as coping with colonial pasts, the maintenance of multiculturalism and the blending of multilateral approaches with individual needs. In addition, however, there are the new issues confronting Pacific Asia: how are countries with Muslim majorities to accommodate the increasingly hostile positions adopted in countries of the Western world on the question of 'Islamic Fundamentalism'? As Shamsul Khan points out, there are no ready-made answers to this. Indeed, much of the debate—insofar as it exists—is based on skewed views taken by critics who neither fully understand the nature of Islam, nor the make-up of the societies dominated by Islam in the Asia-Pacific region, a case reinforced in great measure by Kamarulnizam Abdullah's discussion of post-9/11 politics in Malaysia. In some ways, states like Malaysia represent important weather vanes in the new Asia Pacific and international political climate: solidly committed to globalisation and the requirements of the international marketplace, with complex societies (based in strongly-rooted cultural and religious traits, but needing to accommodate many cultural perspectives). Yet its political processes reflect great-power politics, past and present, and complicate the ability to shape a robust region for the twenty-first century. As the developments over a single constitution, broadening of the membership base and the conduct of regional economic policies in Europe have shown in the course of 2005, the elaboration of a powerful, unified region is one that is painfully dependent on the ability of its member states to temper individual needs for the sake of a common goal. Perspectives on region in the Asia-Pacific have, on the other hand, been defined largely by the building on economic success on an individual basis, rather than aspiring to any broader identity for the region, beyond the one that has come from being associated with vibrant economic growth.

REFERENCES

Adler, N. *et al.* (1986) 'From the Atlantic to the Pacific Century: Cross-Cultural Management Reviewed'. *Journal of Management*, 12(2): 295-398.

Amsden, A. (1989) *Asia's Next Giant: South Korea and Late Industrialisation*, Oxford: Oxford University Press.

Asian Perspective (1995) 19(2).

Asiaweek (1995) 21(29): 24-28.

Beeson, M. (2002) 'Southeast Asia and the Politics of Vulnerability'. *Third World Quarterly*, 23(3): 549-564.

Beeson, M. (2003) 'Sovereignty under Siege: Globalisation and the State in Southeast Asia'. *Third World Quarterly*, 24(2): 357-374.

Borthwick, M. (1992) *Pacific Century: The Emergence of Modern Pacific Asia*, Boulder: Westview Press.

Bowring, P. (1987) 'What is Asia?' *Far Eastern Economic Review*, 135(7) 12 February.

Business Sunday (1997) Channel Nine, Australia (broadcast on 31 August).

Buzan, B. (2003) 'Security Architecture in Asia: The Interplay of Regional and Global Levels'. *The Pacific Review*, 16(2): 143-173.

Chan, S. (1993) *East Asian Dynamism: Managing Growth, Order, and Security in the Pacific Region*, Boulder: Westview Press.

Chowdhury, A. and I. Islam (1993) *The Newly Industrialising Economies of East Asia*, London: Routledge.

Economist (1993) 327(7805).
Golub, P.S. (2003) 'China: The New Economic Giant: World's Trade and Manufacturing Centres Shift East'. *Le Monde diplomatique*, October, http://www.globalpolicy.org/socecon/crisis/2003/10chinagiant.htm, accessed 18 August 2005.
Harris, S. (1991) 'The Political and Strategic Framework in Northeast Asia'. In S. Harris and J. Cotton (eds) *The End of the Cold War in Northeast Asia*, Boulder: Lynne Rienner Publishers.
Harvie, C., and H.H. Lee (2003) 'Export-Led Industrialization and Growth: Korea's Economic Miracle, 1962-1989'. *Australian Economic History Review*, 43(3): 256-286.
Korhoven, P. (1996) 'The Pacific Age in World History'. *Journal of World History*, 7(1): 41-70.
Le Figaro (2005) 21 June.
Linder, S.B. (1986) *The Pacific Century: Economic and Political Consequences of Asian-Pacific Dynamism*, Stanford, California: Stanford University Press.
McCauley, R.N. (2003) 'Capital Flows in East Asia since the 1997 Crisis'. *BIS Quarterly Review*, June: 41-55.
Shanghai Star (2001) 'No Lip Service'. 8 November, http://app1.chinadaily.com.cn/star/2001/1108/cn9-1.html, accessed 3 August 2005.
Segal, G. (1990) *Rethinking the Pacific*, Oxford: Clarendon
Shibusawa, M. *et al.* (1992) *Pacific Asia in the 1990s*, London: Routledge.
Times (1985) 9 August: 11.
Vajpayee, A.B. (2002) 'India's Perspective on ASEAN and the Asia Pacific Region'. ASEAN Annual Singapore Lecture, 9 April, http://www.aseansec.org/2787.htm, accessed 21 August 2005.
World Bank (1993) *The East Asian Miracle*, Oxford: Oxford University Press.

In: Asia-Pacific and a New International Order
Editors: Purnendra Jain et al. pp. 13-37
ISBN 1-59454-986-9
© 2006 Nova Science Publishers, Inc.

Chapter 2

ASIA-PACIFIC POLITICAL AND ECONOMIC CIRCUMSTANCES IN AN ERA OF GLOBAL AND REGIONAL TRANSFORMATION[1]

Purnendra Jain and Peter Mayer

From the end of the 1980s, much of the Asia-Pacific region continued to be marked by the prospect of transformation in various forms, from diverse sources and with varying consequences. The region has never been uniform, given the diversity of historical experience, geography, resource endowments, and the populations, cultures and traditions of the nations within this region. Indeed, at times the strongest link unifying the Asia-Pacific nations has been their inclusion within the continental title, 'Asia'. Towards the end of the twentieth century, developments were under way to open new possibilities for some types of unity, particularly through economic interdependence—between these Asia-Pacific nations as a region, and between some of these nations forming their own sub-regions. But there were also developments creating fissures at bilateral and sub-regional levels. Three flashpoints—tensions across the Taiwan Straits, North Korea's nuclear brinkmanship and the sporadic India–Pakistan standoff threatening nuclear war—come straight to mind.

The Asia-Pacific surely presents a complex and continuously evolving matrix of political and economic development. It is therefore a real challenge to assess its political and economic circumstances, especially during what appears to be an era of global and regional transformation that is reconfiguring not just the politico-economic circumstances of independent nations, but also the relationships between these nations bilaterally and multilaterally. In this chapter we survey some of the key indicators of this terrain to identify what some apparently 'transformative' developments have actually meant for Asia-Pacific nations over the last 15 years, through the 1990s and the first half of the decade beginning in 2000.

Difficult questions inevitably confront us in approaching this task. What are valid indicators of actual, rather than anticipated or expected, circumstances? How do we identify where there is change and attribute this change—if indeed there is any—to its sources. We

---

[1] We thank Shoo Lin Siah for her research assistance.

approach this task recognising a need to distinguish between what has been expected or anticipated by the various luminaries who prognosticate upon the region, and what has actually transpired. We have chosen to inform our assessment through statistical data, derived from the most reliable, independent sources we could access. We recognise that we can work only at a general rather than a specific level of analysis, given the geographic and temporal scope of our investigation in this chapter.

We begin this overview with an assessment of the region's major contextual influences, which have generally inspired the expectation of a more liberal political and economic environment developing in the region. We turn first to the transformative factors of globalisation and the rise of China as soon to be a great power in the region, and then to the three more specific, one-off developments that are also expected to have profoundly influenced the context here: the end of the Cold War, the Asian Financial Crisis and the '9/11' terrorist attacks on American sites. We consider the expected influences of these developments as a guide to what we need to look at in the nations under survey here, and also to the possible explanations of trends evident in the data. We then consider data to assess the state of the region in terms of the political and economic openness and security that many have expected in light of the five major contextual developments. Our final area of discussion is generational change among national leaders, to round out the analysis and add almost literal flesh to the bones of the hard data.

Overall, we find signs of both continuity and change in the institutional and structural arrangements of the nations we examine. We also find that expectations can be misleading, deceptive or simply unmet. Hard data suggest some trends consistent with—but some trends clearly countering—the expected consequences of the region's transformative influences and specific developments. The data reveal signs of a very uneven mix of outcomes: greater political and economic openness and peace in some national instances, but outcomes quite different in others, and in some cases a failure to align political, economic and 'peace' outcomes. These results indicate how apparently global and regional transformations become localised in different national contexts under the influence of a complex interplay of national circumstances and concerns.

CONTEXT: DEVELOPMENTS AND EXPECTATIONS

To appreciate what has happened in the Asia-Pacific since 1990, we turn first to the developments expected to have altered the region significantly. We have identified two categories. In one category we recognise two portentous developments taking place over time with global and regional transformative capacities. These are economic globalisation and China's rise towards great power status. Both are seen to have inevitable consequences for the pace and style of economic development and the nature of politico-strategic development in all Asia-Pacific nations, especially since China appears to be moving towards a pivotal position within the Asia-Pacific economy.

In the second category we see specific developments that, despite the suddenness of their occurrence, may also have a long-term influence upon economic and politico-strategic development in Asia-Pacific. Here we place the end of the Cold War (1989), the Asian Financial Crisis (1997) and the terrorist attacks on American sites on September 2001. Only one of these three developments, the 1997 financial crisis, played out primarily inside Asia, but all three had consequences that have reached worldwide and all three were abrupt and unanticipated.

Expectations of what would follow from these developments are not universal. But while economists, political pundits and other observers do not all refract through the same lens, nor foresee the same likely outcomes, certain expectations have dominated the regional and international discourses. These expectations have shaped views held by many in the general public, whether accurate or not.

Globalisation

Advocates of globalisation have expected that its bounty will be more than economic—the global spread of free market principles, liberal economic institutions and unregulated trade. They have claimed that economic globalisation will produce a flow-on of liberal principles into the political marketplace, with democracy, rule of law and political transparency becoming the preferred behaviour of nations. In this thinking, autocratic or other authoritarian regimes and closed economic and political systems have been expected to free-up by degrees, to be replaced eventually by democratic liberalism. The consequences were expected to reach beyond national borders with successful transitions to democracy reducing security tensions and leading to a 'peace dividend', which would further enhance the prospects of economic growth and prosperity across the board (Friedberg, 1993/94; IMF, 2001). This logic sees a world where cooperation is possible on a global scale and major conflict is avoided because democracies do not go to war with each other.[2]

China's Rise as a Great Power

China's move towards marketisation under the economic reform program begun in the late 1970s has seen the national economy strengthen at extraordinary speed. Demand for raw materials to sustain China's production boom and supply of affordable products to overseas markets has been expected to spur economic growth across Asia-Pacific. The increasing dependence of some nations upon their economic engagement with China has also triggered expectations of a reconfiguration of power relations within the region, while China continues to build its military capacity and quietly positions itself strategically for long-term leverage in the region.

---

[2] Observers such as Russett (1993) and Friedman (2000) have argued this case. Friedman observed that one of the positive consequences of globalisation is that no two nations with a McDonald's franchise had ever gone to war with each other, a theory he called the 'The Golden Arches Theory of Conflict Prevention' (pp. 248-275).

The End of the Cold War

The crumbling of the Berlin Wall and subsequently of the Soviet Union and the bipolar world order of the Cold War generated expectations about the spread of economic and political liberalism and ensuing peace similar to those that globalisation has inspired. The end of the Cold War was recognised as the demise of communism and command economies, and the triumph of democracy and the market economy. It was to herald the ascendency of liberal trading regimes and freer movement of goods and services across national boundaries in the name of globalisation, facilitated by the forces of political liberalism. Here, too, some spoke of a 'peace dividend' resulting from the ending of more than four decades of strategic bipolarity (*Fortune*, 1990: 145; *Economist*, 1993: 7805). The dominant expectations were an end to the arms race and to the constant 'security dilemma' that characterised much of the Cold War era.

The Asian Financial Crisis

Explanations for the Asian Financial Crisis present a range of causes and likely outcomes for the economic drama that first appeared in Thailand as a currency crisis and rapidly afflicted a number of East Asian economies in 1997. Many observers agreed that 'illiberal regimes', lack of transparency and cronyism, as key features of the political economies of countries that suffered the crisis, were largely responsible for it. Dominant expectations after 1997 were that the lessons taught powerfully by the crisis would compel countries to strive for democratic institutions, transparency and rule of law in order to build robust political and economic systems and avert future crises (see various essays in Jain, O'Leary and Patrikeeff, 2002).

The September 11 Attacks on the United States

What has been popularised under the label 9/11 symbolises another turning point in world history that, in time, has greatly affected the region. The US administration under George W. Bush mounted what it labels a 'War on Terror' purportedly in response to 9/11, to root out terrorism by Muslim fundamentalists—not just through 'war' characterised by 'state violence', but also by instituting democratic governance through the ballot box. One of the Bush administration's stated strategies is to establish liberal political and economic institutions in place of dictatorships and Islamic fundamentalism, in order to bring stability to a volatile region, under a US government design (Tucker *et al.*, 2002). This 'war' has destabilised much of Asia (especially West, Central, South and parts of Southeast Asia), which is home to the largest Muslim populations in the world, and is now the main theatre where the war against terrorism is waged. The 'new world order' of unprecedented peace and cooperation, of which George W. Bush's father spoke at the start of the period, could hardly be further from this picture.

In these five far-reaching developments, we recognise the transformative capacity that was expected to usher into Asia-Pacific a new era of liberalism. Democracy, greater transparency and market-oriented economic frameworks would prevail and (until the US administration pursued war abroad, claiming it was a response to 9/11) a peace dividend would further enhance regional prosperity. With this in mind, let us now consider the hard data on regional performance from 1990. We have chosen data to indicate actual economic, political and strategic outcomes in Pacific Asian countries in terms of: 1) economic liberalism and the economic influence of China's ascendance; 2) political liberalism; and 3) a 'peace dividend' for the region. On most of the indicators, data are sub-regionalised into East Asia, Southeast Asia and South Asia. Trends evident from the data examined enable us to assess progress towards the expected outcomes and also help to explain actual outcomes in the light of the contextual developments considered above.

PROGRESS TOWARDS ECONOMIC LIBERALISM AND FREE TRADE

Here we use the Economic Freedom Index.[3] We also consider data on directions of international trade to identify movements in regional/global trade and what they mean for the region's future. The expectations are that globalisation has driven international economic integration and that the Asian Financial Crisis has worked effectively as an accelerator towards economic openness in the region.

Economic Openness

In East Asia there is movement towards, and away from, opening domestic economies (Figure 1; n.b. the higher the score, the lower the economic openness). As may be expected, North Korea remains fairly firmly closed and immobile on this front while Hong Kong is still the most open. China has made the most progress towards openness, but remains the second most closed economy in East Asia. The most striking trend seems counter to the expected outcome of the Asian Financial Crisis, with *decreased* openness in the original tiger economies of Japan, Taiwan and South Korea.

---

[3] The Heritage Foundation/Wall Street Journal Index of Economic Freedom (past scores): http://www.heritage.org/research/features/index/index.html

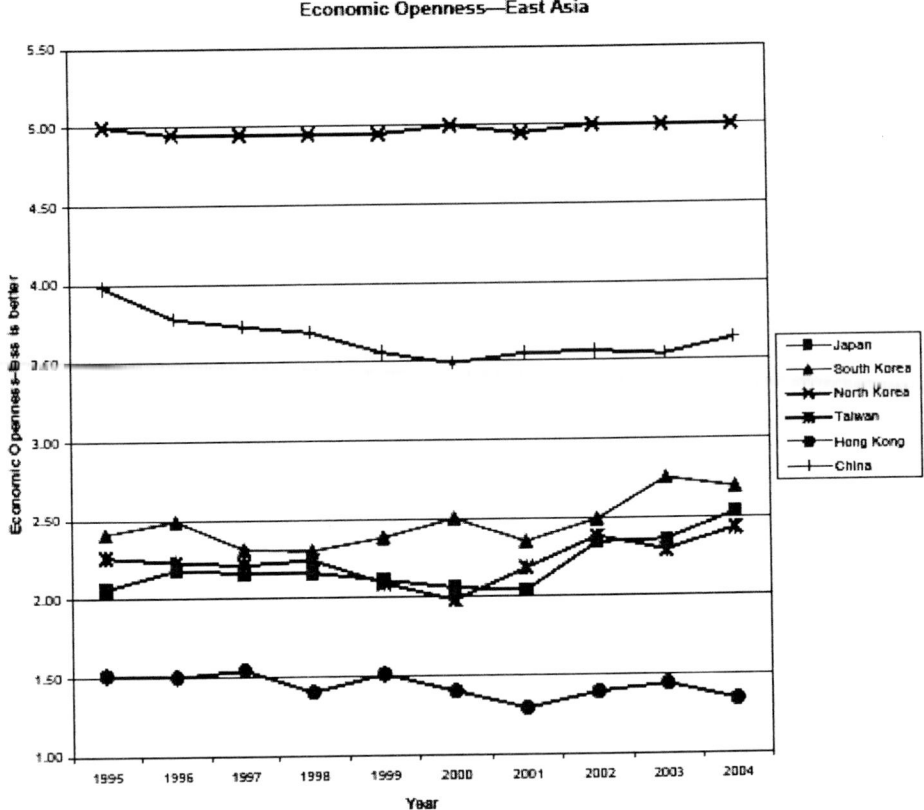

Figure 1.

In Southeast Asia three distinct categories are evident (Figure 2). The least open economies are those of the present and former socialist nations Laos, Vietnam and Myanmar, although Vietnam has undergone significant economic opening that has brought it almost into the range of the major ASEAN economies. In the middle category we see the most striking trend. Indonesia, Malaysia, the Philippines and Thailand show clear signs of closure after initial stagnation or decline in the first few years from 1995 and for a few years after the Asian Financial Crisis. Only Cambodia, like Vietnam, has steadily increased the openness of its economy. Singapore is in the third category, the most open economy of the region by far and with only minimal change over the period.

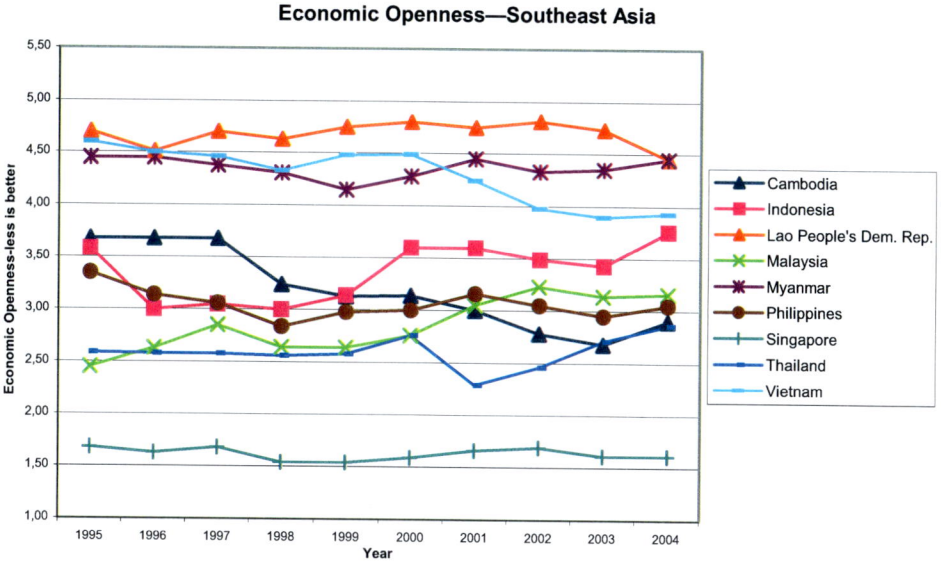

Figure 2.

The insularity of the subcontinent is clearly evident in Figure 3. Pakistan and Sri Lanka were no more open in 2004 than they were a decade earlier. India and Nepal had opened their economies somewhat, and Sri Lanka, which began the period on a path towards openness, ended back in the same position.

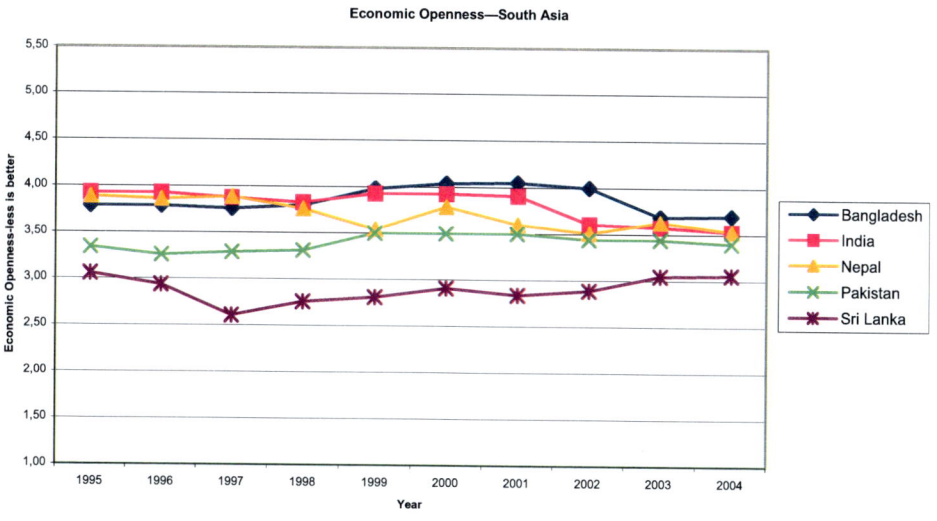

Figure 3.

Overall, the trends evident in data for the three regions do not indicate strong movement towards economic opening. This is counter to expectations that economic globalisation and the Asian Financial Crisis would inspire more liberal approaches to economic management in

Asian countries. Indeed, we must conclude that not only have the forces driving economic liberalisation had relatively little impact, but also that in Southeast Asia there is firm evidence that economies are being made more, not less, restrictive. Only the former command economies of China, Vietnam and Cambodia have sustained significant programs of opening to the international economy.

The Economic Influence of China's Emergence as a Great Economic Power

Media reports speak constantly of China's economic resurgence, and the performance of the Chinese economy, particularly from the 1990s, has been spectacular. However, although China's trade has increased considerably through the period, the volume of trade with Central and South Asia is still very low (Figure 4), and even including Southeast Asia it is still only a fraction of the level of trade with East Asia (Figure 5), the USA (Figure 6) and the EU (Figure 7).[4] These data suggest that China's economic resurgence has certainly spurred economic growth in Asia-Pacific, although a major share of the trade driving the Chinese growth is still with partners outside Asia.

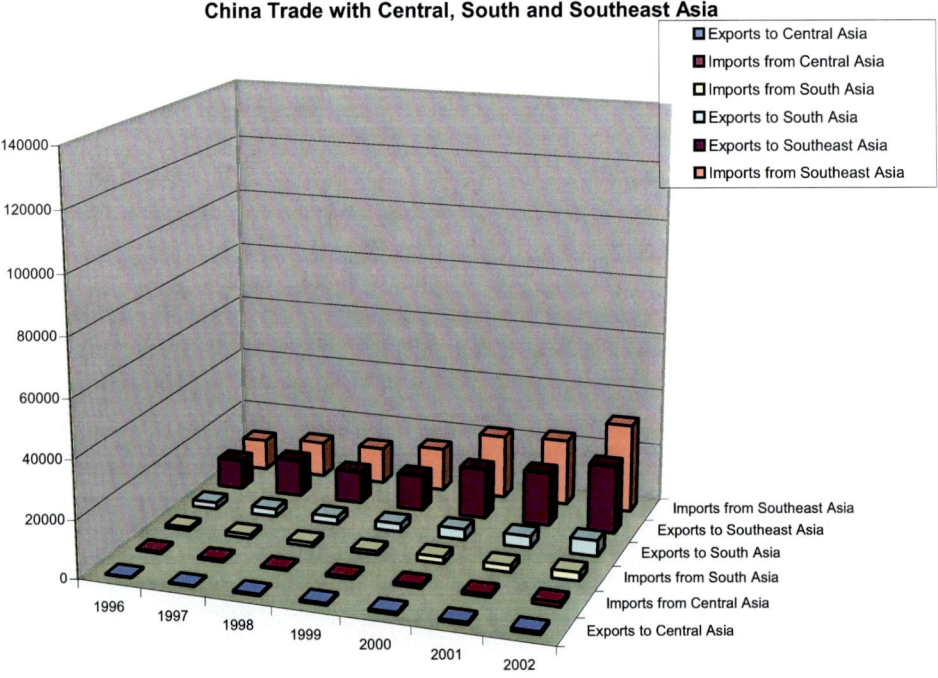

Figure 4.

---

[4] Trade between India and China has grown phenomenally in the last two to three years. In the late 1990s two-way trade was worth about $US 1 billion, which rose to about $US 13 billion in 2004-05. All figures on Direction of Trade are taken from the annual IMF publication, *Directions of Trade Statistics Year Book*, published by International Monetary Fund: 2003, 2004.

China's Trade with East Asia

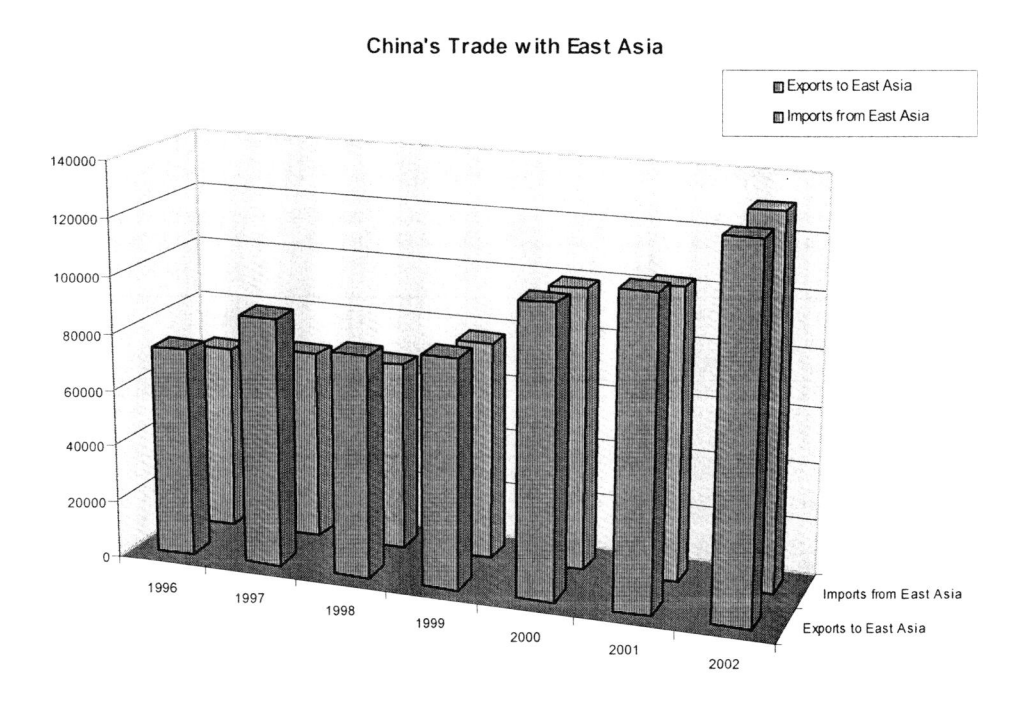

Figure 5.

China's Trade with USA

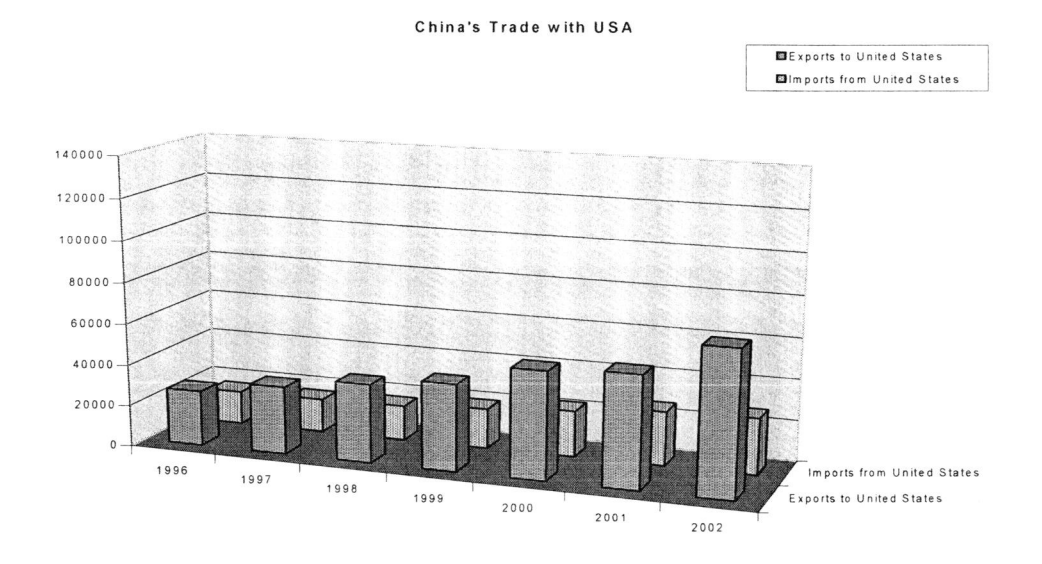

Figure 6.

China's Trade with the European Union

☐ Exports to European Union
☐ Imports from European Union

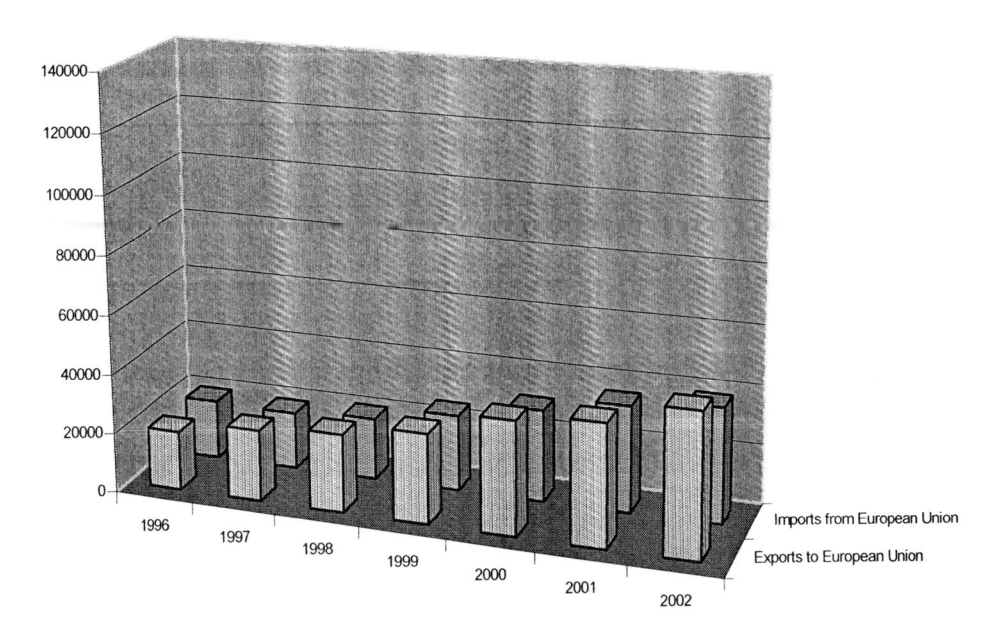

Figure 7.

PROGRESS TOWARDS POLITICAL LIBERALISM AND DEMOCRACY

For insights into political development in Pacific Asian nations we consider data on levels of corruption, civil liberties and political rights.

Corruption

Corruption is one useful indicator of government transparency and its absence when quantified data offer no direct measure. We use the Corruption Perception Index where, we must note, higher scores indicate lower levels of perceived corruption.[5] Figure 8 indicates modest improvement in perceptions of corruption in East Asia. Although there was relatively little change in Japan and South Korea, there were noticeable gains in China.

---

[5] These data on perception of corruption are produced by Transparency International and are available at http://www.transparency.org/surveys/index.html#cpi.

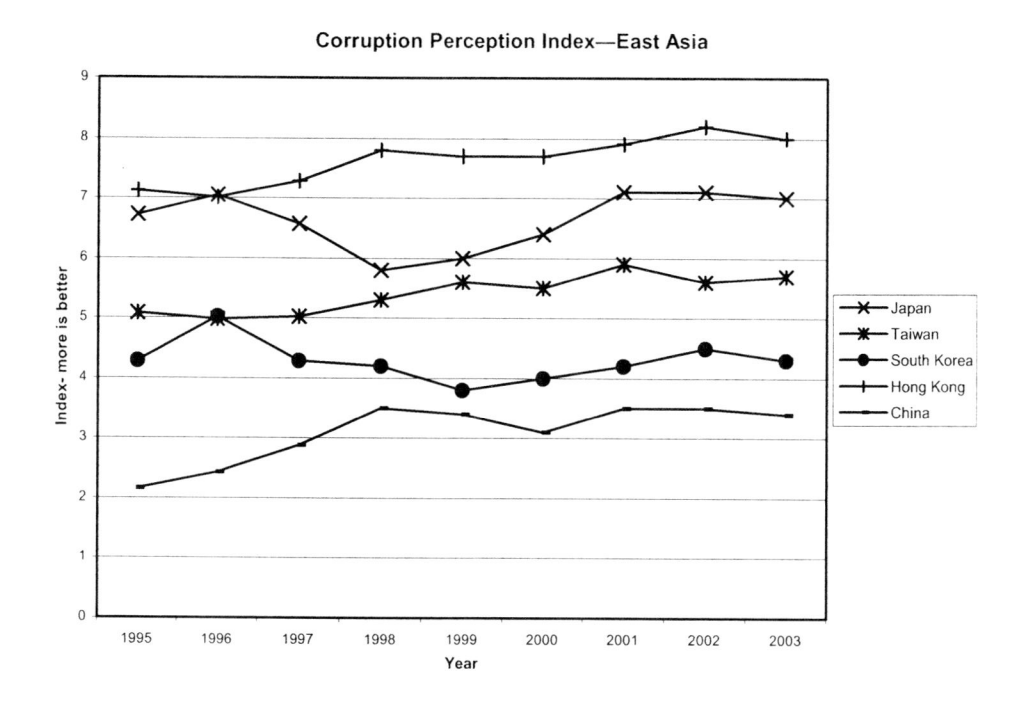

Figure 8.

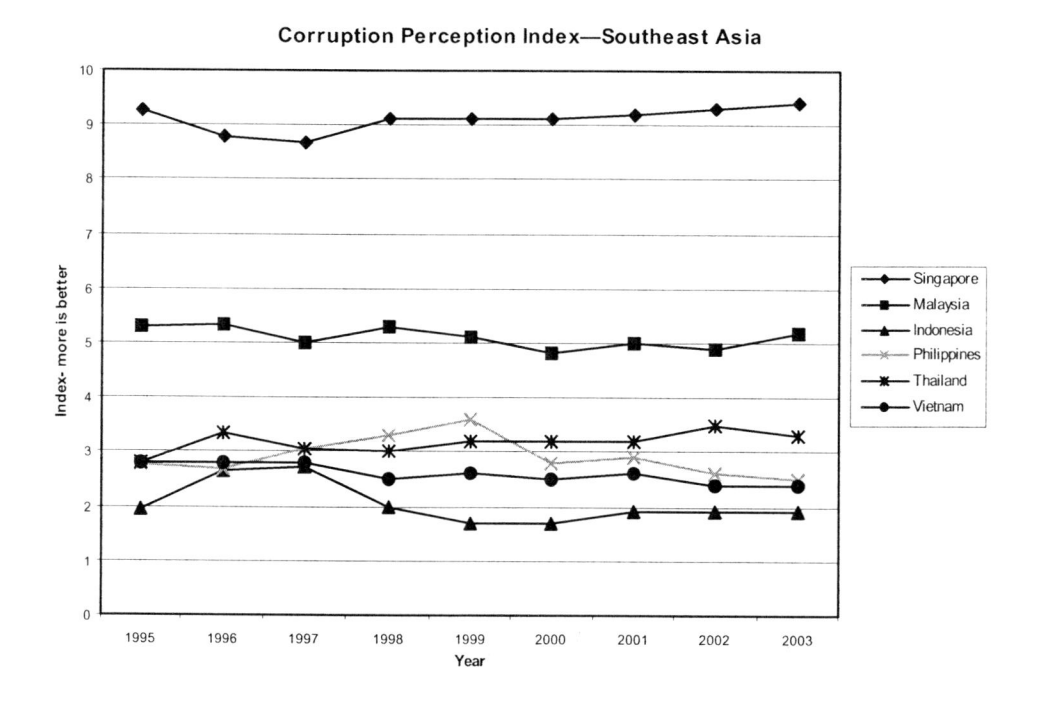

Figure 9.

In Southeast Asia there appears to be very little change over time. Data in Figure 9 reveal some improvement in 1996 and 1997 in Indonesia, which ranks lowest among the six nations itemised, but by the end of the 1990s the standard had slipped to that of 1995. Here we see nothing to indicate sustained movement towards lower corruption and, by extension, towards greater transparency in government.

In South Asia we see relatively high levels of perceived corruption (Figure 10). There is minimal overall change in India and Pakistan. Data are missing for Sri Lanka and Bangladesh in the middle years of the decade, but we do see a sharp rise in Sri Lanka towards the end of the period. With Sri Lanka perhaps being an exception, data for South Asia do not indicate increased government transparency through lower perceived levels of corruption.

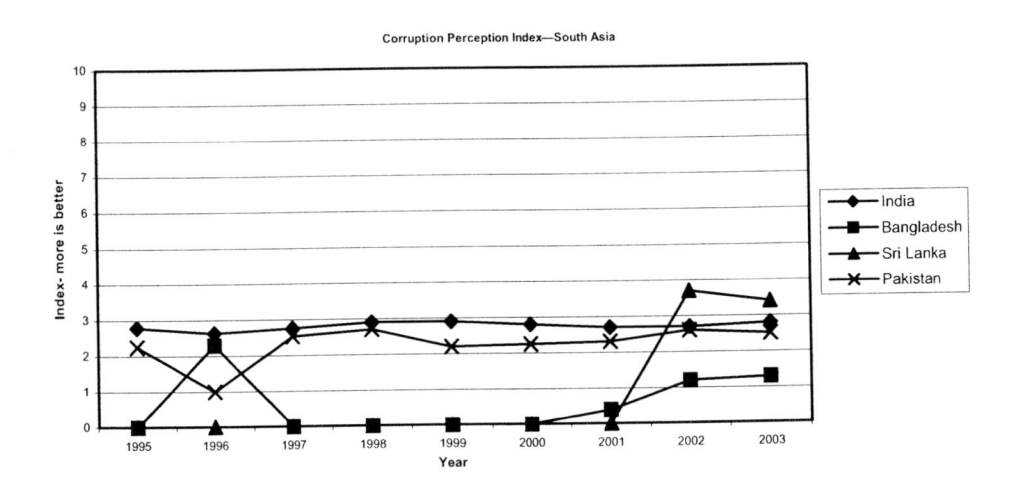

Figure 10.

Civil Liberties

Recognising that in this case 'less is better', these data signal some observable improvement in human rights in East Asia (Figure 11). China's high level indicates relatively large-scale violations of civil liberties, although sustained improvement is noticeable from 1998. Taiwan also shows sustained improvement after initial unsteadiness. The limited data for South Korea reveal improvement from 1993, but data are not available from 1997 onwards, that is, after the financial crisis struck.

Civil Liberties—East Asia

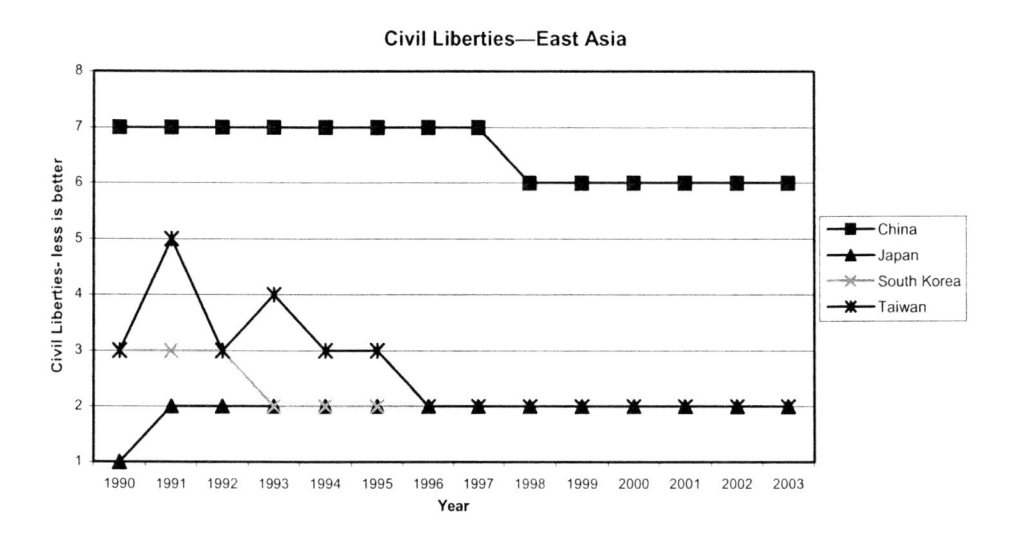

Figure 11.

Civil Liberties—Southeast Asia

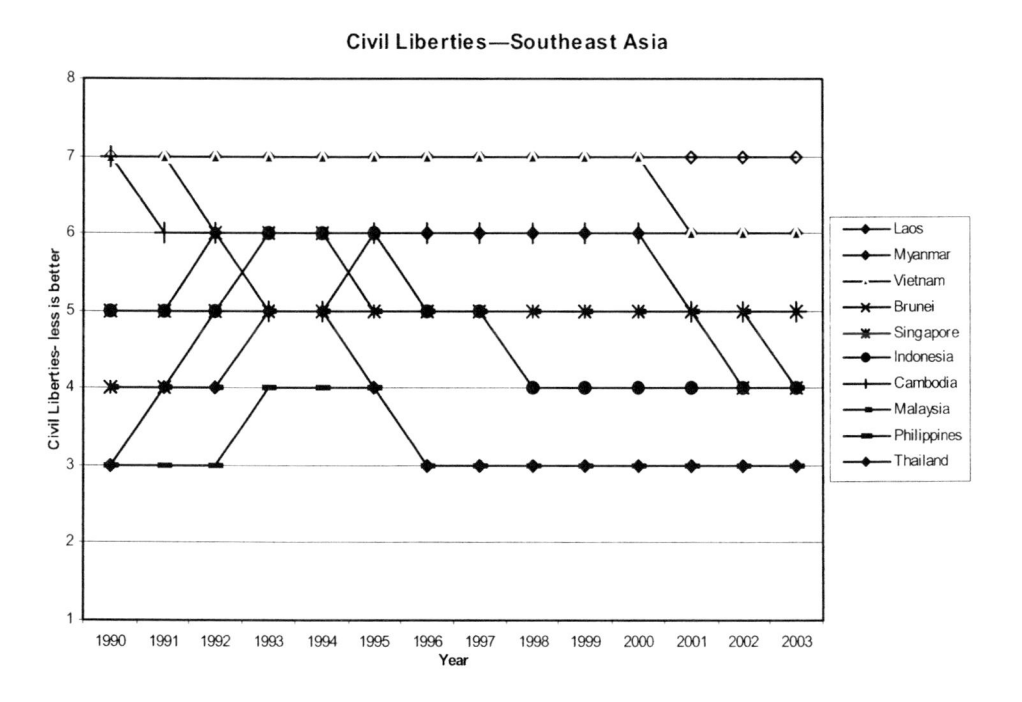

Figure 12.

Trends in civil liberties are distinctly mixed in Southeast Asia (Figure 12). At the beginning of the decade, Myanmar, Laos, Cambodia and Vietnam had the worst records. Myanmar remained unreconstructed throughout the decade, and Cambodia and Laos made early (if small) improvements, to be followed by Vietnam in recent years. Several other countries here experienced periods of worsened civil liberties. In Thailand, conditions went seriously backward around 1993, returning to 1990 levels only in 1996. In Brunei, Singapore, the Philippines, Malaysia and Indonesia civil liberties were restricted for periods of several years, but all five countries had returned to their 1990 levels by the end of the decade. Only in Indonesia did civil liberties improve overall.

As in Southeast Asia, civil liberties advanced little in South Asia (Figure 13). All countries experienced periods of regression. In Pakistan, Bangladesh and Nepal there was no recovery. In India there was a return to the previous state by the end of the decade. Sri Lanka alone experienced steady gains in civil liberties over the period.

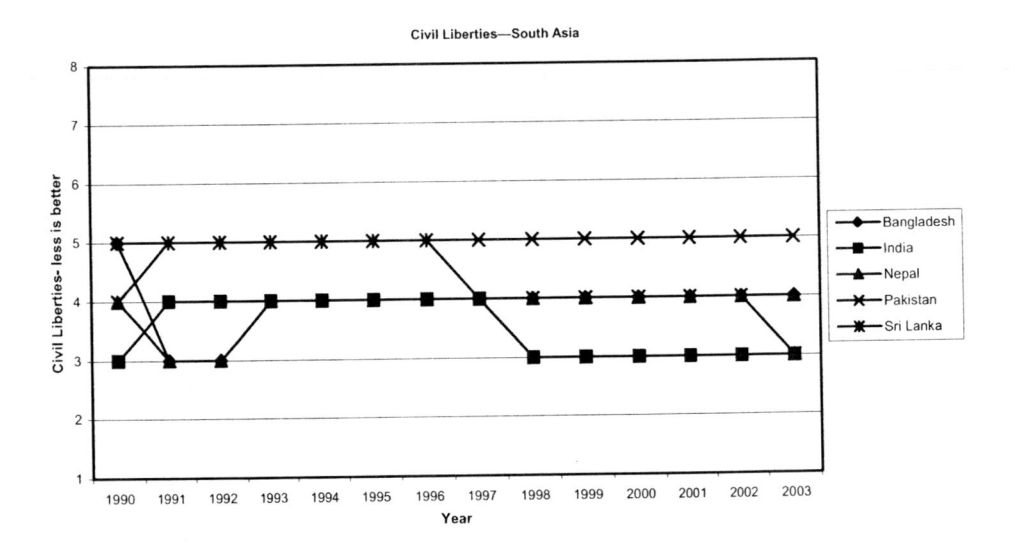

Figure 13.

Political Rights

There was minimal change in political rights in East Asia over the decade (Figure 14). China maintained its poor record throughout the period and South Korea—better than Taiwan but worse than Japan—also registered no change. Japan recorded minor regression in 1993 and 1994, while Taiwan recorded uneven progress, but was better placed at the end of the period than at the start.

Political Rights—East Asia

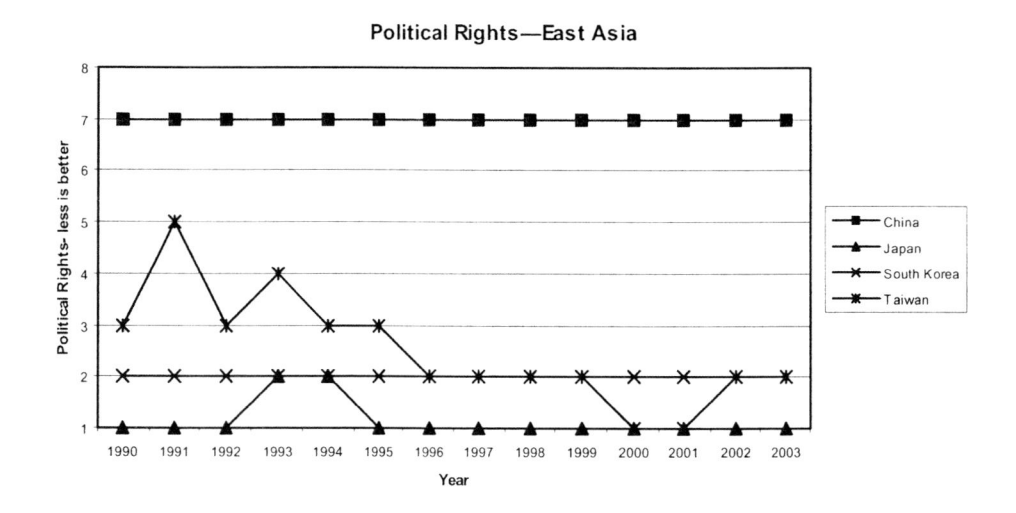

Figure 14.

Political rights in Southeast Asia as a whole saw few improvements (Figure 15). There was no change in Myanmar and Vietnam and only slight improvement in Cambodia. In Laos, Brunei and Singapore conditions deteriorated. Despite short-term regression in Thailand and the Philippines, both had regained their status as the Southeast Asian states with the strongest political rights. The most remarkable gains were made in Indonesia, following the end of the regime of long-standing president Suharto.

Political Rights Index—Southeast Asia

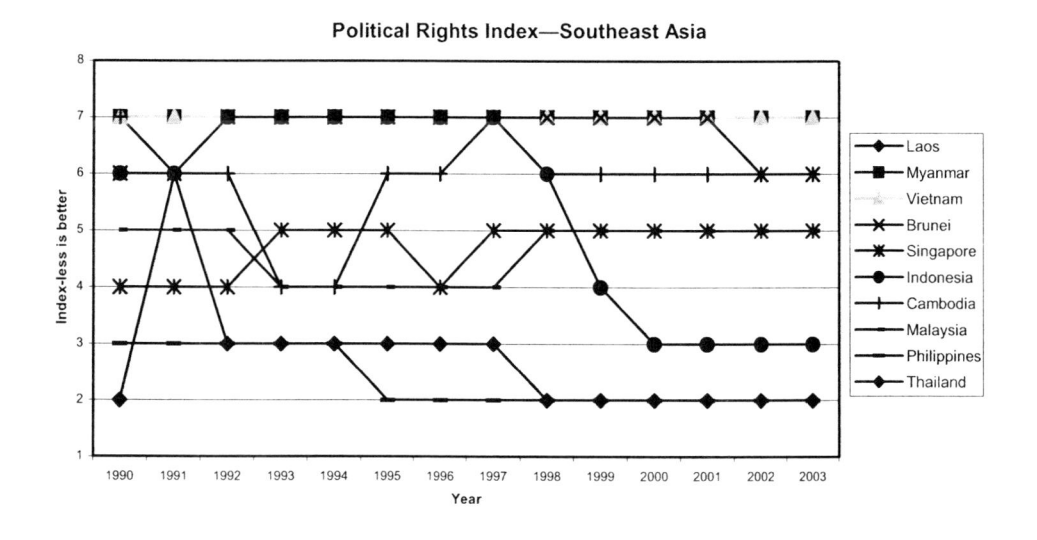

Figure 15.

In South Asia, as in Southeast Asia, regression predominated over gains (Figure 16). Pakistan lost what it gained in the early 1990s, especially following the coup by General Pervez Musharraf in 1999. Bangladesh and Nepal also lost political rights from the peaks achieved early in the decade. Having gone backwards after the 1992 destruction of the Babri

Masjid,[6] India returned to its previous place as South Asia's most politically liberal nation. Sri Lanka made modest gains after 1996.

Political Liberties Index—South Asia

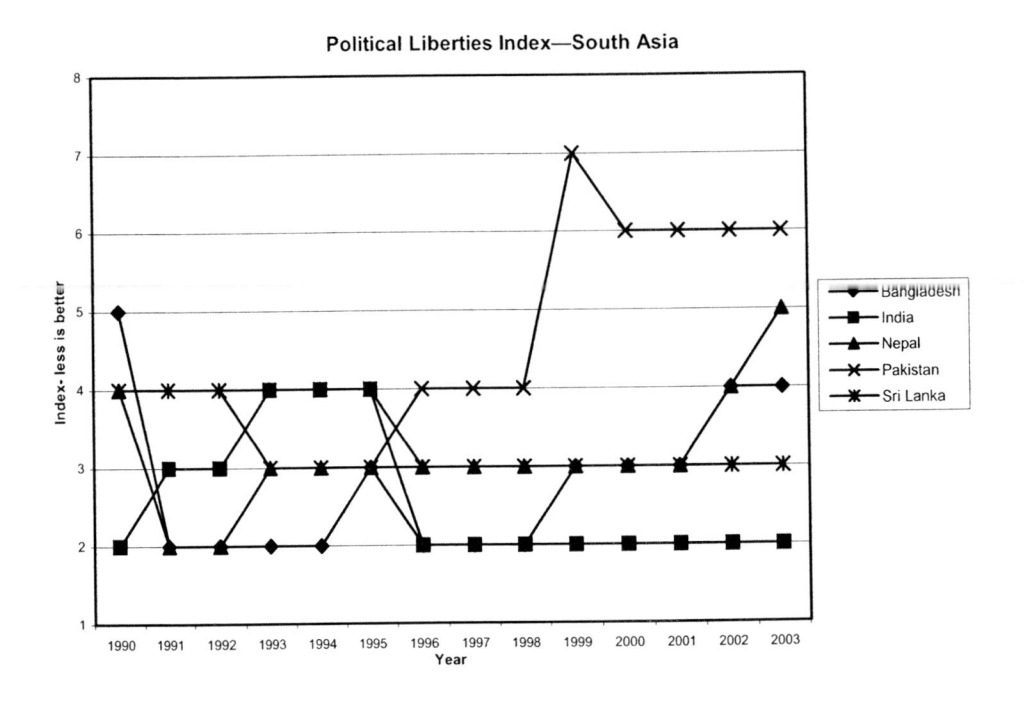

Figure 16.

On the whole, the trends evident in these data present little evidence of the liberalising effects that were expected to flow across the region's political landscape as a consequence of greater integration with the global economy. With the exception of Indonesia, there were no substantial gains in political liberties and a dismaying number of nations where civil liberties and political rights were lost. Rising corruption suggests growing government opacity rather than transparency.

A POST-COLD WAR 'PEACE DIVIDEND'

The early expectation was that the end of the Cold War confrontation between communism and capitalism would halt a potential arms race in Asia. As discussed earlier in this chapter, globalisation and the end of the Cold War were expected to produce economic liberalisation, that would in turn nurture political liberalisation and in its wake a 'peace dividend'—this from the belief that countries across the region interlocked through economic linkages such as trade, and sharing domestic political stability born of democratisation, would not attack others in a similar state. However, the regional data considered above have not indicated the economic and political liberalisation anticipated by the liberalisation advocates.

---

[6] This was the site of communal rioting in 1992 when the Babri Masjid (mosque) was wrecked. Rioters held that the site had earlier housed a Hindu temple, which a Moghul emperor had destroyed in order to erect the Babri

What does this mean for regional peace, if the circumstances that were to deliver it have not evolved as expected. Are there signs of 'loss of peace' after 9/11?

To assess peace in the region we turn to patterns of defence spending, since there is no clear measurement of 'peace' appropriate for this comparative study. Data are from the International Institute for Strategic Studies.[7] We believe that these defence data provide a useful indication of how national governments perceive their need for national security, and their assessment of threat to the nation. But first we must note some caveats on the utility of these data. First, they indicate for comparison only the share of a nation's GNP spent on defence, rather than the actual amount spent or what it was spent on. This narrow understanding of GNP proportion limits what the figures can reveal. For example, in East Asia, although Japan has one of the highest defence expenditures in the world, defence is but a small share of a relatively huge GNP. By contrast, North Korea actually spends much less than Japan on defence, but continuously recorded defence spending at roughly a 25 times greater share of GNP than Japan, because North Korea's GNP is relatively miniscule. Still, the proportional data do provide some indication of the national priority of defence spending. Second, while we assume that defence spending is in response to national security assessment, we need to appreciate that sometimes defence spending can be partly motivated by other factors that concern domestic politics, such as the bureaucratic need to clear budgets or a national leader's urge to demonstrate a militarily strong leadership style. Recognising these limitations on the data, they are nonetheless useful for our purposes here as an indicator of peace dividend or, indeed, its absence.

Defence Spending

Data on defence spending in East Asia (Figure 17) yield two striking observations. First is the utterly disproportionate and crippling burden that defence spending places on the struggling economy of North Korea. The national government continued to spend roughly 25 percent of GDP on defence through the period until 1998, when the figure plummeted aberrantly to just below 15 percent of GDP. Relative to the size of its economy, North Korea was spending about five times more on defence than the other economies in East Asia (except Japan, which generally holds to a steady 1 percent of GDP). Second is the relative consistency of defence spending by East Asian nations throughout the period. There is no indication of decline (apart from the North Korean one-off plummet) that suggests a post-Cold War fall-off in defence spending on a gradual path towards a peace dividend. The minimal downward shift in spending evident in 1998 seems more likely to relate to economic pressures forced by the Asian Financial Crisis, than to the expected peace-yielding consequences of economic and political liberalisation.

Masjid.

[7] All figures on defence spending are taken from the International Institute for Strategic Studies annual publication, *The Military Balance*, published by Oxford University Press: 1990/91, 1992/93, 1994/95, 1995/96, 1996/97, 1998/99, 2000/01, 2001/02, 2002/03.

Defence Spending—East Asia (% GDP)

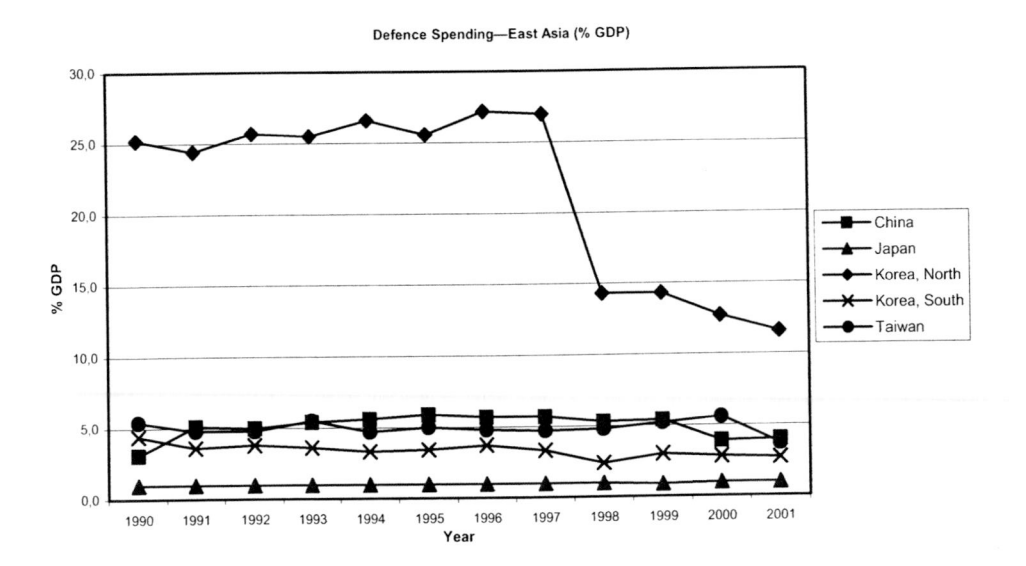

Figure 17.

Data for Southeast Asian nations present a somewhat different picture (Figure 18). Here Vietnam's spending is most dramatic, with a three-quarter fall from 1990 to 1993, and only slight changes either way from the 1993 figure for the rest of the period. Brunei, too, reduced by more than half in 1993, but quickly rose and maintained a level of about three quarters of the 1990 figure. Laos rose notably from 1991, but, after peaking two years later, continued downward to end in second lowest position. Myanmar was erratic, marked by rises and falls. Laos almost doubled over the first four years, but then fell, ending with the second lowest expenditure. Thailand and the Philippines both maintained fairly even and comparatively low expenditures through the period, as did Indonesia, which began and ended with the lowest levels of all the Southeast Asian countries.

As might be predicted, given the largely introspective nature of interstate relations in South Asia, there is little evidence of a response to the ending of the Cold War. The data in Figure 19 indicate how each country in the sub-continent has followed an idiosyncratic trajectory. The largest declines were in Pakistan, which in 1991 was spending nearly 8 per cent of GDP on defence. By 2000 military spending had been halved to 4 per cent. Spending in Nepal, which had been quite steady during the 1990s at around 1 per cent, rose dramatically to a still-modest 3 per cent in 2001 as a response to worsening insurgency in the west of the country. A similar internal crisis is likely to explain the gradual increase in military spending in Sri Lanka during the second half of the 1990s.

Defence Spending—Southeast Asia (% GDP)

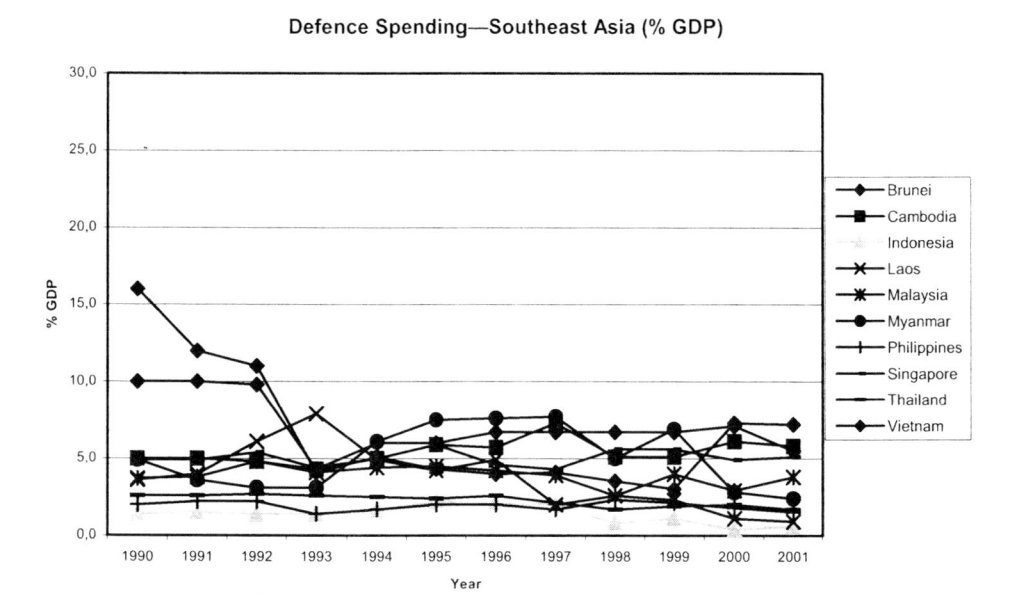

Figure 18.

Defence Spending—South Asia (% GDP)

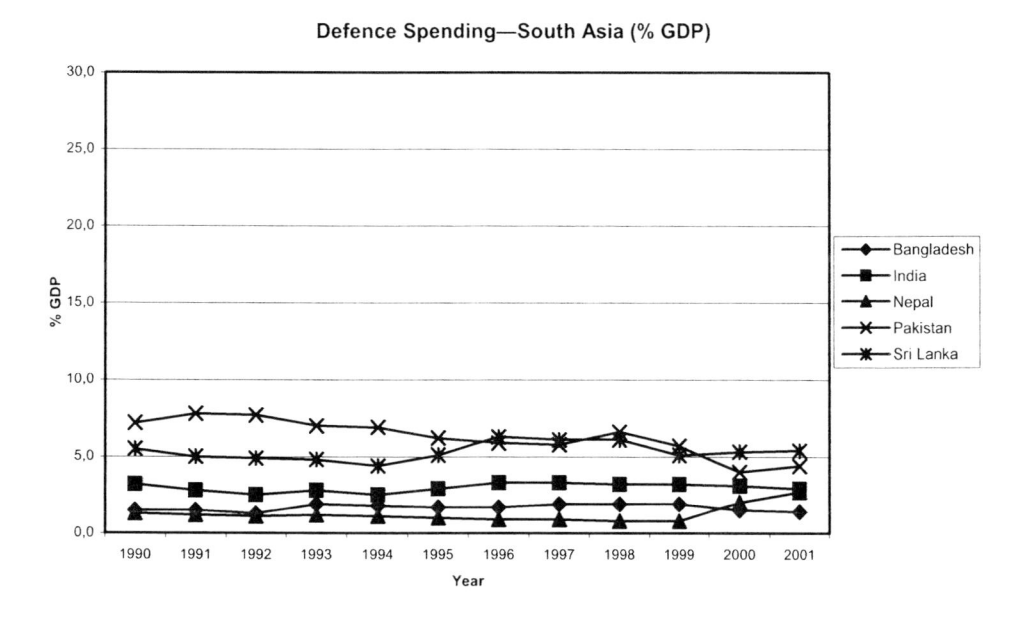

Figure 19.

In general, then, the data considered here indicate that the end of the Cold War and the economic and political liberalisation that was expected to follow have not yielded a 'peace dividend' for the region. There were very few dramatic changes in the defence expenditures of Asia-Pacific nations through the 1990s. To the contrary, many nations are marked by relative consistency in their defence spending through the period.

From Figure 20 we see that the greatest changes occurred in those countries where democratic accountability was lowest and ruling elites had the greatest ability to commit relatively large portions of national income to military spending during the Cold War. These countries, which include Brunei, experienced the greatest year-to-year percentage changes in military spending. We should also note Vietnam's erratic outcomes, sliding to the lowest in 1993, but then jumping to the highest in 2000. On the whole, significant declines have outnumbered increases, the most dramatic being the huge reductions in military spending in North Korea in 1998, but with return to a position close to 'the usual' for the following years.

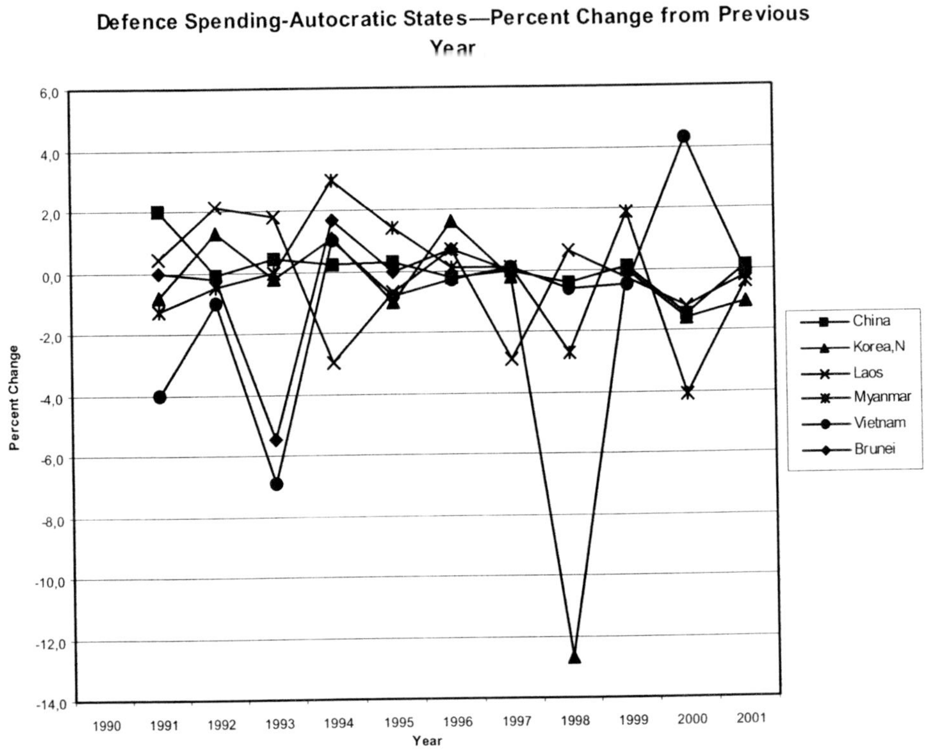

Defence Spending-Autocratic States—Percent Change from Previous Year

Figure 20.

Data on military spending in Figures 17 to 20 do not extend to beyond 2001 to suggest the possible impact of 9/11. Since 9/11 in 2001, the US has flexed its military muscle more forcefully than before in the name of the War on Terror, with US military spending leaping dramatically from $US 296 billion in 1997 to $336 billion in 2002 and $379 billion in 2003 (Deen, 2004). Reliable reports suggest that defence spending is increasing across Asia and globally as perceptions of military threat induce a spiralling military build-up. For example, in 2004 China increased its military spending by 12 percent over the previous year to make total military spending that year close to $US 25 billion.[8] Clearly, the Asia-Pacific has shown no sign of moving into an era of peace induced by the end of the Cold War. To the contrary, by the middle of the 2000s, the region is marked again by military build-up, with prospects

---

[8] BBC news< http://news.bbc.co.uk/2/hi/asia-pacific/3538343.stm> accessed 7 September 2005.

for peace palpably diminished and national and sub-regional tensions still inspiring considerable military and 'defence' expenditure. The expected 'pacifying' consequences of the five major developments influencing the region from 1990 are nowhere in sight.

Political Succession

Having considered data on economic, political and strategic circumstances, we turn to our final area of discussion to consider the political landscape of Asia-Pacific in terms of generational change among national leaders and what this may mean for the future. This is an important consideration for our assessment, since across the region we find a number of changes in leadership that have inducted a new, younger generation of leaders whose visions and approaches may induce a national policy landscape somewhat different from the past—perhaps more liberal in politics and economics—in regional as well as domestic terms.

What appears to be the most important leadership change in the region took place in an increasingly powerful China, through a process of transferring full power incrementally from former president Jiang Zemin to current president Hu Jintao. President Hu officially took the reins of the Chinese Communist Party (CCP) in 2002, was appointed China's president in 2003, and finally replaced the former president as Chairman of the CCP Central Military Council in September 2004. The former president's decision to stand down surprised many observers, since there were increasingly obvious disagreements between the two leaders, particularly on issues of foreign and economy policy (*Australian*, 2004). For example, Hu's concept of China's 'peaceful rise' to international power was seen to have adopted a 'soft' attitude towards Taiwan. How President Hu handles China's relationships with Taiwan, North Korea and Japan is very likely to have a considerable impact upon the geopolitics of the region. Although contested, it is generally regarded that Hu Jintao is liberal-leaning in the tradition of his mentor, Hu Yaobang, who presided over a radical overhaul of the CCP structure and personnel in the first half of the 1980s. Hu Jintao has ruled out western-style democracy as a 'blind alley' for China, but he is pushing ahead solidly with marketisation of the economy, while trying to manage astutely the consequences of huge rural unemployment and social dislocation. His foreign policy philosophy is to consolidate political and economic power through a network of closer relations in the region—including free trade agreements with countries such as Australia.

Japan has operated as a fully democratic nation with liberal institutions since the 1950s, yet the Liberal Democratic Party has retained its hold on government almost without let-up. Prime Minister Koizumi, an LDP 'new leader' who took office in 2001, is conservative, nationalistic and an advocate of neo-liberal reforms such as privatisation. The actions of his government in censoring school history textbooks and his own actions in flagrantly visiting Yasukuni Shrine where Class A war criminals are buried have fanned tensions with China to levels unprecedented in the post-war period, while Koizumi leads Japan into an ever-closer alliance with the US, including military support for the Bush administration's invasion of Iraq. Koizumi's administration is therefore moving Japan away from an East Asian bloc and positioning it strategically with the US and towards a constitution that will allow Japan the full international engagement in war that the present constitution prohibits.

Southeast Asia has seen recent leadership changes in some semi-authoritarian political systems such as those of Malaysia and Singapore, and with these changes are some prospects for further liberalisation of political institutions and processes. In October 2003 Abdullah Badawi succeeded Mahathir Mohamad, Malaysia's long-serving prime minister. Badawi's political platform includes clean government (e.g., re-examining large-scale public projects and the process of tendering), and he is generally supported by the Malay middle class. Various actions, such as the release from prison of Mahathir's political nemesis Anwar Ibrahim, signal that rule of law is replacing arbitrary executive decisions in some instances, although over time Badawi is proving to be more of the Mahathir style of illiberal leader than many had originally expected.[9]

In Singapore, Goh Chok Tong retired as prime minister in August 2004 after 14 years in office. Lee Hsien Loong assumed the position, which his father Lee Kuan Yew held for over 30 years from 1959 when Singapore became an independent state. Lee Hsien Loong is from the next generation after his father, whose authoritarian rule guided Singapore's transformation from an economic backwater into a thriving maritime trading state. It is anticipated that the new prime minister will retain some of his father's disciplinarian approach, but generally favour some reform of political life towards a more liberal disposition, particularly to the extent that this may now be required to sustain the economic liberalism that his father championed.

Indonesia saw the peaceful transition of power from Megawati Sukarnoputri to Susilo Bambang Yudhoyono through the ballot box in September 2004. This was seen as a remarkable democratic development for a country ruled for 30 years until 1998 by General Suharto, whose 'New Order' regime held the army as the nation's dominant political institution. Suharto's fall saw bloody scenes in Jakarta and elsewhere in Indonesia and led to a period of political turmoil with three different presidents in six years. President Yudhoyono, like the string of short-term presidents before him, struggles to address complex and sometimes irreconcilable needs: rebuilding confidence to restore the national economy which is yet to recover from the 1997 crisis; maintaining political stability while keeping the military in check; maintaining national unity in the face of separatist bids; and, particularly in recent years, trying to strategically manage hostile Muslim fundamentalism expressed in targeted bombings that drag this nation with the world's largest Muslim population closer to the destructive geopolitics played out as the War on Terror.

A respected Japanese scholar of Southeast Asia observed of these leadership changes that 'the era of developmental authoritarianism is over and the age of democracy has arrived' (Shiraishi, 2004). Certainly, we see signs of democratic development institutionally, with elections and other procedures indicating that some governments in Southeast Asia are more truly representative of the nation's people, and more freedom and information are available to the people in registering their political views. The further democratisation of parts of Southeast Asia appears to have produced new, more liberal leaders with the political and personal will to shed some of the authoritarian style of their predecessors, though only time will tell how firmly these democratic developments are entrenched.

In South Asia the results are mixed. The 2004 general elections in India, the world's most populous democracy, saw a smooth democratic transition from Atal Bihari Vajpayee's ardently reform-minded government led by the Bharatiya Janata Party (BJP) to the Congress-

---

[9] William Case's (2005) appraisal of Badawi's first year as prime minister found that, contrary to popular expectation, Badawi has made only minor adjustments to some key institutions; e.g., he has restored some independence to the judiciary, but has maintained the firm controls on civil liberties for which Mahathir was renowned.

led government of Manmohan Singh. Singh is keen to pursue the major plans for India's economic liberalisation and infrastructure development introduced under the previous government's 'India Shining' program. But whereas that program focused primarily on the urban middle class, Singh's government is pursuing a wider allocation of resources to include the rural population and the underprivileged masses. One of those most ambitious programs was announced in July 2005, guaranteeing jobs for millions of rural poor.

Other South Asian nations present less reason for optimism. Pakistan continues to be ruled by a former military general with little improvement in the nation's economy or its political processes, instability from close proximity to the heartland of Al Qaeda and other terrorist organisations that act in the name of Muslim fundamentalism, and the nation's newest struggle—responding to the tragedy of human loss and physical devastation from the October 2005 earthquake. Political instability also undermines national capacity for economic and political progress elsewhere in the region, with periodic ethnic violence in Sri Lanka, ongoing tensions in Bangladesh and Maoist insurgency in Nepal, although 'globalisation', 'liberalisation' and 'more democratic process' continue to flavour political rhetoric.

CONCLUSION

In this chapter we have attempted to provide a broad overview of the political and economic landscape of Asia-Pacific nations in relation to five transformative factors with great potential to influence the region's development. However, in an era when these global and regional developments are thought to be transforming Asia-Pacific, our findings from quantified data suggest that this transformation may be less profound, or simply slower, than liberal advocates had anticipated.

Overall, there are signs of a shift in the economic landscapes of many nations across the region, with reforms that have begun to induce a more liberal ethos in economic management. This is evident not just in the rise of the middle class and a stream of entrepreneurs, but also in more liberal policy approaches to opening markets, loosening trade policies and generally creating more open national economies in much of the region. It is evident in China, where the push towards marketisation has produced striking economic growth. Flow-on to the Asian economies that trade with China is helping to make this nation a potentially powerful engine of economic growth for other Asian nations. Yet it is still the case that China's largest trade partners lie mostly outside Asia, with only Japan near the league of the EU and the US.

Data indicating the state of the region's political landscape reveal even less indication that the expected economic liberalisation has induced a more liberal political ethos as well. In some of the nations, particularly Indonesia, there are clear signs that democratic procedures have been more firmly institutionalised; for Indonesia this has occurred to the point of yielding the nation's first democratically elected president. But on other counts, such as civil liberties and political rights, some of the nations (China, for example) have regressed. As to political transparency, the rises in levels of perceived corruption across parts of the region also do not bode well for a liberal political environment spreading across the region. The election of a new generation of leaders may help to induce more liberal political environments in countries such as Malaysia and Singapore, but it will inevitably take time to dissociate national polities and national administrations from firmly embedded authoritarian traditions.

Finally, on the presence or absence of peace in the region, findings from the data surveyed here indicate that a peace dividend did not evolve quickly from the end of the Cold War. To the contrary, developments across the region associated particularly with the US administration's post 9/11 War on Terror from 2001 have raised fear, insecurity and defence build-up across Asia-Pacific, rather than easing in a period of international cooperation and peace.

Overall, we find signs of both continuity and change in the economic and political circumstances of the Asia-Pacific nations we have examined. The five transformative factors of economic globalisation, China's resurgence as a great power, the end of the Cold War, the Asian Financial Crisis and the so-called 9/11 terrorist attacks on the US have aroused considerable expectations about the type of liberalised future that may ensue for the nations of Asia-Pacific and beyond. But expectations can be simply expressions of hope. They can be misleading, unmet or a guide to long-term prospects. By 2005 there are indications of greater political and economic openness in some Asia-Pacific nations, but there are quite different outcomes in other national circumstances. Even in an era of apparent global and regional transformation, national sovereignty remains predominant. Our survey indicates that the behaviour of nations of the Asia-Pacific is more a product of domestic conditions than the frequently predicted domination of global and regional influences. Detailed country-based studies which explore how global influences are resisted or become localized, such as those presented in this rest of this volume, will be essential to understand the security environment in the Asia-Pacific for the foreseeable future.

REFERENCES

Australian (2004) 21 September.

Case, William (2005) 'How's My Driving? Abdullah's First Year as Malaysian PM'. *The Pacific Review*, 18(2): 137-158.

Deen, Thalif (2004) 'Military Spending Nears $1 trillion'. *Asia Times Online*, http://www.atimes.com/atimes/Global_Economy/FH19Dj01.html, accessed 7 September 2005.

Economist (1993) 327: 7805.

Fortune (1990)'What We Can Expect from the Peace Dividend'. 26 March, 121(7): 145.

Friedberg, Aron (1993/94) 'Ripe for Rivalry: Prospects for Peace in a Multipolar Asia'. *International Security*, 18(3).

Friedman, Thomas L. (2000) *The Lexus and the Olive Tree*, London: HarperCollins Publishers.

International Monetary Fund (IMF) (2001) Staff Papers, *Military Spending, the Peace Dividend, and Fiscal Adjustment*, Hamid Davoodi; Benedict Clements; Jerald Schiff; Peter Debaere, June 48: 2.

Jain, Purnendra, Greg O'Leary, Felix Patrikeeff (eds) (2002), *Crisis and Conflict in Asia: Local, Regional and International Responses*, New York: Nova Science.

Russett, Bruce (1993) *Grasping the Democratic Peace: Principles for a Post-Cold World*, Princeton, NJ: Princeton University Press.

Shiraishi Takashi (2004) 'Election Year in East Asia'. *Japan Spotlight*, July/August.

Tucker, Robert, Michael Howard; Gary Schmitt; John J. Mearsheimer; Josef Joffe; James Chace; Wang Gungwu; Charles A. Kupchan; Pierre Hassner (2002) 'September 11th One Year On: Power, Purpose and Strategy in U. S. Foreign Policy'. *The National Interest*, 69: 5-34.

In: Asia-Pacific and a New International Order
Editors: Purnendra Jain et al. pp. 39-52
ISBN 1-59454-986-9
© 2006 Nova Science Publishers, Inc.

Chapter 3

STRATEGIC RESETS, SECURITY RIPPLES AND US INTERESTS IN THE ASIA-PACIFIC

Satu P. Limaye[1]

INTRODUCTION

The debate about the evolving Asia-Pacific security environment is quite rich and mixed at present. Recent writings on the Asia-Pacific suggest widely varying views of the region's security future. Some of the titles of these publications are quite dramatic: *Asia Rising* (Rohwer, 1995), *The New Asian Renaissance* (Godemont, 1996), *Thunder from the East* (Kristof and WuDunn, 2000), and *Fire in the East* (Bracken, 2000) are just a few examples. The different views on the Asia-Pacific's evolving security environment are in some senses to be expected, given the range of sometimes contradictory developments now taking place. To simplify, there are two broad 'schools' of thinking about the regional security environment. One school, represented by scholars such as Aaron Friedburg, tend to view the regional security environment as being on the cusp of major rivalries, as he argued in his important articles 'Struggle for the Mastery of Asia' and 'Ripe for Rivalry'. Others, such as Amitav Acharya, are more optimistic that regional states can work out accommodations that do not imperil their future. These accommodations include a combination of overlapping mechanisms, including bilateral relationships and regional multilateral arrangements.

Another way of assessing the regional security environment is to think of the range of challenges it faces, and the level of danger or manageability of each set of challenges. Under this construction, the Asia-Pacific today faces two broad sets of challenges.

The first, which I term *Strategic Resets*, are challenges that:

- pose a threat of major war among key regional states;

---

[1] Satu P. Limaye is Director of the Research & Publications Program at the Asia-Pacific Center for Security Studies (APCSS) in Honolulu, HI. APCSS is a direct reporting unit of US Pacific Command. The views expressed here are entirely personal and do not reflect the views of APCSS, PACOM, the US Department of Defense or any other US government agency.

- sustain persistent national-level political, diplomatic and military involvement from the major powers;
- potentially could fundamentally alter state-to-state relationships and the balance of power in the Asia Pacific;
- could seriously affect the economic health of the entire region;
- and, possibly, could shape future US commitments to the region, including alliances.

In short 'strategic resets' are those challenges that have the potential to fundamentally change the prevailing Asia-Pacific security order.

In my view, at least six potential developments could reset the present, largely manageable, strategic order in the Asia-Pacific:

1. a sudden unexpected change in United States' alliances, forward basing and bilateral relationships in the region;
2. conflict on the Korean peninsula;
3. miscalculation in the Taiwan Straits;
4. a breakdown of the US-Japan alliance;
5. sudden, dramatic changes in the power trajectories and national identities of China, Japan and India;
6. outside of northeast Asia, possible miscalculation between India and Pakistan—though this flashpoint is much less likely to be a strategic reset for the wider Asia-Pacific region than the Cross-Straits or Korean Peninsula.

Fortunately, the prospects of any of these strategic resets occurring remain relatively low, but require regular attention. However, the changing structural nature of regional flashpoints presents especially serious mid- and long-term challenges to regional security managers. Therefore, these structural changes in regional flashpoints are considered in more detail below.

A second category of Asia-Pacific challenges are what I term 'security ripples'. These are challenges that:

- are unlikely to result in large-scale, state-to-state war, though smaller-scale military actions might be necessary to address them;
- require multilateral engagement and solutions;
- might involve militaries, but are more the provenance of law enforcement and other elements of a country's security apparatus;
- erode the socio-economic and physical health of citizens and states alike, but do not threaten state survival, borders or the regional balance of power.

Some of the key Asia-Pacific security ripples include:

Transnational threats that include illicit activities like drugs and human trafficking. These 'seams of lawlessness', as Admiral Blair labelled them, have the ability to erode the sovereignty and control of governments and exacerbate social and economic tensions.

Terrorism is of course one of the key security challenges in the Asia-Pacific region—particularly in South and Southeast Asia. Admiral Fargo, recently retired Commander of Pacific Command, has stated that: 'we see Southeast Asia as a primary fault line in the War on Terrorism. But the JI's capabilities and goals extend far beyond Indonesia. Jemaah Islamiyah wants to establish a pan-Islamic state that would extend from Indonesia through Malaysia to Mindanao in the Philippines. It intends to achieve this goal by destabilizing, through terrorism, the democratic, legitimate governments of the region' (2004).

The proliferation of weapons of mass destruction (WMD), such as nuclear, biological and chemical weapons, and particularly the possibility that they could be acquired by terrorists correctly haunts security planners in all countries.

Maritime security continues to be an important need in the region. Addressing maritime security cooperatively will diminish the dangers posed by transnational threats such as terrorism and trafficking in WMD, humans, drugs and piracy.

Energy security—including both the availability of actual resources and the safe means for their delivery—will be critical in a region whose energy demands are rapidly growing. Indeed, energy issues are now occupying an increasingly prominent role in bilateral relations.

Transnational diseases represent another facet of the unwelcome side of globalisation. The spread of SARS and Avian 'Flu are just two examples of the dangers that directly, immediately affect the physical, economic and psychological health of citizens and countries alike.

ASSESSING THE STRATEGIC RESETS

While security ripples will persistently engage regional security sectors, it is the strategic resets that could fundamentally re-order the regional environment in terms of balance of power and relationships, and it is for this reason that they deserve considerably more focus. Of particular importance are the evolving structural changes in regional flashpoints.

There is unlikely to be a sudden, unexpected change in United States' alliances, forward basing and major relationships in the region. To be sure, the US is in the process of adjusting its 'footprint' in the region (and elsewhere), but its commitment to its alliances and relationships remain unchanged. Indeed, the consultative process to address footprint issues is part of a wider effort to adjust, adapt and update alliances that date from the last century. In the end, the net effect on many existing relationships between the US and the region, not to mention new ones, is that they will be strengthened and made more productive and active. Hence, this potential strategic reset is unlikely to occur any time soon. It is true that changes in US alliances, basing arrangements and relationships occasionally cause discomfort to partners as well as adversaries, but there are no indications that the US is reducing its commitment to the security of the Asia-Pacific region, as is often feared by countries located there.

Also, there is little prospect of a breakdown in the US-Japan alliance. Structural factors are actually working to shore up the alliance, and, along with it, more political and security activism by Tokyo. Japan's growing international role within the context of the US-Japan alliance is to be welcomed. However, Japan's security 'normalisation' should not be exaggerated—there still remain formidable international and domestic obstacles to Japan's emergence as a major security player. On the international side, Japan's relations in its own neighbourhood remain quite constrained, and Japan is far from a domestic consensus about its own more active international role. Indeed, Japanese debates regarding their country's role in the world tend to play out within the box of the alliance relationship, rather than as alternatives to the alliance.

As for the changing power trajectories of the major Asian players (China, India and Japan), they are unlikely to be so swift is to make it difficult to manage the change. Indeed, there is room and time to engage and manage China's rise. Japan, as already noted, is clearly rethinking its security and foreign policy, but it is far from a military state acting independently to the detriment of the region. In fact, Japan's role is on the whole positive for regional peace and prosperity. India, too, has shown signs of increased activism and dynamism in terms of its regional role and economic and military modernisation. Nevertheless, it faces enormous obstacles to its rise and, in any case, needs regional relationships (not to mention global ones) in order to succeed. Hence, its interest in undertaking destabilising behaviour appears to be low. It is the case that nationalism in these three countries is growing, but there are few signs of a fervid, chauvinistic nationalism that would cause severe disruptions in regional relationships.

The situations in the three flashpoints, the Korean peninsula, the subcontinent (Kashmir dispute), and in the Cross-Straits, are perhaps the most important challenges facing the strategic stability of the Asia-Pacific. And, what is more, the underlying dynamics and structural aspects of the flashpoints are changing. Though there are profound differences in these three 'flashpoints', there are at least five common variables that have the potential to shape peace and security outcomes in the future.

First, today the central role of the US is acknowledged by not only the parties to particular disputes, but also by the surrounding states and the international community generally. Parties to these disputes look to the US not only to protect their interests, but also, increasingly, to intervene. To some extent this constitutes an important change from past practices, in that it increases the onus on the US, as well as its leverage. For example, in the past, India has been strongly resistant to US 'mediation' in the Kashmir dispute. However, India today is somewhat more receptive to a US role there, primarily because it sees such a role as putting pressure on Pakistan to halt its support for the militants operating across the line of control. Similarly, while China would no doubt prefer a bilateral solution to the situation with Taiwan, and is opposed to what it regards as US support that emboldens some in Taiwan to seek independence, it also realises that this very US engagement with Taiwan can also exert a constraining effect on the latter's moves toward independence. And, finally, in the Korean case, while many in Seoul view the US as problematic in dealings with the North, sober-minded analysts realise that the US is the target of North Korea's diplomacy, and therefore Washington has leverage to help manage the situation—not to mention assist in ensuring South Korea's security. The net effect is that US leverage in all of the regional flashpoints has increased and is likely to remain high over the coming years.

A second important, emerging structural adjustment in regional flashpoints is military balance. As military balances in the potential flashpoints change, they cause increasing anxiety. The factors that affect military balances include economic/resource capacity changes (e.g., the PRC's military modernisation is stoked by a fast-growing economy), US realignment and roles (e.g., $US 11 billion plus for US Force in South Korea–USFK, possible arms sales to Pakistan with simultaneous offers of sales, and cooperation with India), along with other factors, such as the competitive arms market and indigenous military and technological modernisation. The point here is that it is difficult to assess what the outcome of evolving military modernisation will be. But, if military balances are seen as effective mechanisms of stability, then it will be important to address what appear to be some changing situations in the three flashpoints.

A third notable structural development is the increasing relevance of economic interactions in shaping choices in the diplomacy and management of flashpoints. These economic interactions apply not only to the specific parties to the dispute, but also to their neighbours and, more widely, the international community. To take but one example, the growing economic interchanges between Taiwan and China, between China and the US, and China and the region, as well as the rest of the world, create a fundamentally different context for the handling of the cross-straits relationship from even a decade ago. On the whole, the effect of economic considerations has been to place a premium on the management of these disputes.

A fourth element of structural change in the three flashpoints is the changing nature of democracies and civil societies (with the possible exception of North Korea). In each case, of course, the situation surrounding domestic demographic, societal and political changes are extraordinarily complex. However, in each of the cases it is possible to the say that the situation has changed to the extent of 'opening space' for nongovernmental pressures on the handling of the respective flashpoints. The net effect of this change is that it complicates decisionmaking through the requirement to address often competing constituencies. On the one hand, this could lead to some dangerous pressures, but on the other hand it makes quick, decisive action more difficult, as numerous stakeholders in the disputes jockey to have influence. In effect, a certain degree of constraint is engineered into the management of the flashpoints.

A fifth factor constraining any major changes in the flashpoints is their internationalisation. In a globalise world, the outcomes of these flashpoints are seen as having potentially important implications well beyond the parties to the dispute. In each case the drivers that have led to internationalisation are different. In the case of India and Pakistan's, the acquisition of nuclear technology has affected the dispute's internationalisation. The nuclear dimension is important in the Korean case too. In the cross-straits scenario, Taiwan's democratisation and China's rise are factors in the issue's increasing internationalisation. The point is that these regional flashpoints are now even more important to the international community than in the past, and this will mean that a number of actors beyond the traditional players will seek to have an influence on the management of the issue. This has already occurred in the North Korean case, as several new players have sought to influence Pyongyang's decisionmaking while it normalises diplomatic relations with certain countries. The net effect is to bring another layer of activism, and hence constraint, into the management of these flashpoints.

The overall assessment I would make about these strategic reset variables is that they are undergoing change. But I am perhaps more optimistic than others that these changes are manageable, to some extent necessary and part of the evolution of the regional security environment, rather than a fundamental, dangerous break.

THE CASE FOR CAUTIOUS OPTIMISM

Asia-Pacific 'strategic resets' and 'security ripples' are serious potential and real challenges. Complacency must not displace vigilance and persistent efforts to build even better regional outcomes. But the view that Asia's security future will mimic Europe's bloody twentieth-century past is, to my mind, excessively pessimistic. There are several reasons for cautious optimism.

First, if we compare today's Asia-Pacific region with just the post-independence period, we find many improvements in terms of peace, prosperity and stability. The Cold War has left legacies, but does not overshadow the region. Extremist ideologies are clutched by either isolated regimes or small minorities, rather than advocated by large states or movements. Some insurgencies persist, but many others have been resolved or are being managed.

Second, as noted earlier, the key developments that could reset the Asia-Pacific's strategic order are manageable. Most of these strategic challenges have been with us for 50 years, parties to them appreciate their intricacies as well as their overall frameworks and the parties themselves are well known to each other. These challenges are, to borrow Secretary Rumsfeld's phrase, 'known unknowns'. This does not mean miscalculation is impossible, but steady, persistent engagement in these very serious challenges means that surprises are unlikely.

Third, despite outstanding historical, nationalistic, territorial and border disputes in the region, great power cooperation exists, and several important regional bilateral relationships have either improved or disputes in them are being managed—not least due to economic compulsions. Unlike in times past, Asia's major countries are at peace with each other. What is more, old intra-regional relationships are in the process of being redefined, and new ones being established. This is just one example of the region's dynamism and changing security texture.

Fourth, despite setbacks such as the Asian financial crisis, or the spates of SARS and Avian 'Flu, regional economic interdependence has increased and countries are focusing their priorities on socio-economic improvements with a great deal of success. The fundamentals for economic prosperity, such as openness and legal frameworks, are improving across much of the region. Even holdout states are slowly reconsidering their self-imposed isolation and poverty.

Fifth, despite the dizzying diversity of the Asia-Pacific and the presence of different types of regional governments, the overall trends point toward more political openness and more robust civil societies. It is stunning to note that nearly a dozen elections have been or will shortly be held across the Asia-Pacific's vast expanse. Aspirations for a voice in the affairs of one's country are not isolated to any culture, faith, economic level, educational level or social condition.

Sixth, the Asia-Pacific's efforts at building multilateral institutions and regional integration, though they ebb and flow, do continue. East Asia's efforts in this area are distinctive, and unlikely to look like Europe's or any other region's. Any humanly constructed architecture must be suitable to its surroundings or it will not stand. The dynamics, norms and pace of Asia's regional institutions reflect the comfort-level and consensus of the region. This multilateral, integrative effort offers an opportunity to manage disputes and build cooperation in ways that were nearly unimaginable just a decade ago. But by the same token, one should not expect these multilateral institutions to solve bilateral disputes, nor reconfigure the regional balance of power any time soon.

Finally, and importantly, the positive role of the United States is a baseline for the Asia-Pacific's hopeful outlook.

THE UNITED STATES IN THE ASIA-PACIFIC

US interests and equities continue to grow in the Asia-Pacific region. Not only are five of seven of its treaty partners (Japan, ROK/South Korea, Thailand, Philippines and Australia) in this region, but also the US is now building new relationships for the twenty-first century with a number of other regional countries. The US has reinvigorated ties with India, Pakistan, Malaysia, Singapore and Vietnam, just to mention a few examples. On the economic front, two regional states, China and Japan, are the largest foreign holders of US debt. Trade with the region steadily climbs—and the importance of the US as a trading partner for countries like China continues to grow, even as intra-Asian economic links expand.

US engagement and presence is viewed as useful not only by formal treaty allies and close friends, but also by other regional countries who appreciate the contributions that the US makes to peace and prosperity in the Asia-Pacific. Countries that were previously critical of America's regional role, such as India, have become less so.

US priorities, given its national interests and the views of its regional role, are manifold. The most important of these priorities from the perspective of dealing with the possibility of strategic resets and on-going security ripples is to maintain our alliances, friendships, relationships and forward presence of American forces—what Admiral Fargo characterised as 'reinforcing the constants'.

The US is in the process of working with allies, friends and partners in the region to adjust bilateral relationships to take into account the challenges of this century, rather than being stuck in the static postures created in the last one. Hence, the US is working with alliance partners such as South Korea and Japan to meet not only the initial needs for which they were formed, but also to provide essential and growing contributions to the regional and global security picture. In Southeast Asia the US is working with Thailand and the Philippines, among others, to combat terrorism, piracy, drugs and other transnational threats both through bilateral cooperation and building regional capacities. The US is also building forward-looking, productive relationships with countries in South Asia. President Bush has stated his intention to transform relations with India into a 'strategic relationship' and much progress has been made. Meanwhile, the US is in close cooperation with Pakistan. Australia is an ever-closer ally and discussions on a Strategic Framework between the US and Singapore signals a new era of partnership. Pacific Command takes the lead in many exchanges and activities with friends in the South Pacific countries. Relations with China are candid and complex, and the US welcomes its constructive engagement in the region. The Korean Peninsula is just one of the areas where the US and China are working together.

The US also welcomes expanding regional cooperation and integration in East Asia. These efforts are critical to addressing transnational and other challenges. But the US also seeks an East Asia that is open and inclusive, and will work for a regional architecture that allows states to build partnerships with each other as well as partnerships with the United

States. The US is an active contributor to the ASEAN Regional Forum (ARF), Assocation of Southeast Asian Nations (ASEAN) and Asia-Pacific Economic Cooperation (APEC). The US wishes to work with these institutions to foster partnerships to solve problems, not just to talk about them.

Initial Bush Administration Policies Towards Asia

The Bush administration took office with several planned policies towards Asia. The first priority was revitalising relations with 'allies and friends'. The first of four goals identified in the Quadrennial Defense Review (QDR)—much of which was written prior to 9/11 and released two weeks after the attack—is concerned with 'Assuring allies and friends of the United States' steadiness of purpose and its capacity to fulfill its security commitments' (Department of Defense, 2001: 11). This emphasis was calculated to signal a divergence from the Clinton administration, which the Bush administration perceived as having neglected America's key partnerships. Hence, the Bush administration initially sought to focus on the Republic of Korea (ROK or South Korea) over the Democratic Peoples' Republic of Korea (DPRK or North Korea), Taiwan over China, and, most importantly, Japan.[2] Australia, too, received considerable administration attention. With slightly less emphasis, the Bush administration revived consideration of a number of Southeast Asian friends, including Singapore[3], Thailand and the Philippines, and sought restored but limited military links with Indonesia. Indeed, the concept of an 'East Asian littoral', articulated in the QDR, gives importance to Asian friends beyond the traditional allies Japan and ROK.

Other than to distinguish itself from the preceding administration, the emphasis on 'allies and friends' was designed to reinforce ideological components of US foreign policy (i.e., democracies, open markets), American primacy in the region based on politico-military relationships with welcoming partners rather than engagement through weak multilateral organisations, a revised regional threat assessment, and a distinction between those countries the US considers like-minded, cooperative and non-threatening, and those it does not. Whether 'allies and friends', for their part, desired the level of attention, interaction and expectations that the administration seemed keen to provide is another matter. For example, Japan's ability to meet the bold and expectant milestones that some in the administration desire was (and is) an open question. Moreover, the emphasis on 'allies and friends' did not appear to have been very well coordinated with them. This was especially the case on the Korean peninsula where the administration initially undertook a lengthy and ominous-sounding policy review regarding North Korea, causing considerable anxiety in Seoul—identified as a key ally. Nor were other administration emphases and initiatives necessarily

---

[2] The top Asia hands in the Bush Administration were and/or are Japan rather than China 'hands' (e.g., Under Secretary Armitage, Assistant Secretary Kelly, and the National Security Council's Patterson. Dr Green, a Japan hand, is now senior director for Asia at the NSC and Mr Kelly has been replaced with Ambassador Christopher Hill, an experienced Asia hand. Under Secretary Armitage has been succeeded by Robert Zoellick, another expert on Asia, including Japan.

[3] Assistant Secretary of State for East Asian and Pacific Affairs James A. Kelly noted at his confirmation hearings that 'Singapore, a longtime friend that is not a treaty ally, recently completed new port facilities specifically designed to accommodate visits by US aircraft carriers'.

helpful to revitalising 'alliances and friendships'. A case in point was the administration's early approach to China.

The Bush administration's emphasis on allies and friends was partly reflective of its apparently contradictory views of China. The first was to regard China, in Secretary Colin Powell's words, as a 'competitor, a potential regional rival' (2001), and second to treat it as a less central player in US Asia policy. Both approaches deviated sharply from the Clinton administration's formulation of China as a 'strategic partner' and *de facto* treatment of it as the centrepiece of the US-Asia relationship. Secretary Powell's statement that the US would 'treat China as she merits' (2001) appeared to refer not only to competition and rivalry, but also to its proper weight relative to other regional countries. A pattern of statements and contacts were further evidence of an intention to take China off the centre-stage of US-Asia policy.[4] But the attitude of treating China both as a 'potential rival' and as 'peripheral' was not really a contradiction. By treating China as a less integral and determinative country to Asia's international relations, the administration was again reinforcing China's distinctiveness from America's allies and friends, while simultaneously highlighting its potential threat. Notwithstanding the administration's nod that 'Japan, South Korea, Australia, and our other allies and friends in the region have a stake in this process of nurturing a constructive relationship [with China]...And we will want to work with them' (Powell, 2001), the fact is that some significant gaps existed initially between 'allies and friends' and the US in dealing with China (Montaperto and Limaye, 2001).

A third characteristic of early Bush administration policy in the Asia-Pacific was resistance to South Korean President Kim Dae-jung's 'Sunshine Policy' or engagement with North Korea. The administration immediately halted official contacts with the North. There was to be no follow-up on Secretary of State Albright's visit to Pyongyang and there most emphatically was not going to be a presidential visit, as had been contemplated during the waning days of the Clinton administration. Apart from the launch of a policy review, one immediate and substantive divergence from the Clinton administration's approach towards the peninsula was the new administration's complaints about North Korea's conventional force posture—in addition to concerns about missiles and 'unconventional weapons'. The administration's DPRK policy complicated the emphasis on 'allies and friends'—particularly with the ROK (and to a lesser extent with Japan).

A fourth and much-missed facet of the Bush administration's Asia-Pacific policies was an intention to 'transform' relations with India. Interestingly, this policy was the most consistent carry-over from the Clinton administration. An improvement of relations with India was predicated on a number of factors, of which two specifically involved East Asian considerations.[5] The first factor was the rise of China. Though both countries officially reject an improvement of relations based on third-party considerations, at least some in India and the US see possible threats from China as a basis for enhanced relations. A second driver of improved relations with India, especially in the military field, was the intended adjustment of

---

[4] Despite the administration's desire to calibrate China's place in the region, it was difficult to do so. The first country to which then Secretary of State-Designate Powell turns his attention in his confirmation hearings is China. A couple of months later, in a prepared statement at his confirmation hearings, Assistant Secretary of State Kelly makes a brief reference to Japan but immediately turns to China—perhaps understandable in the aftermath of the EP3 incident three weeks earlier.

[5] India's perceived role in the wider Asia-Pacific context was evident in the fact that the 'Bush administration reorganised the National Security Council staff, such that India is now the responsibility of the Senior Director for Asia, rather than the Middle East' (Harding, 2001).

US military forces in the Asia-Pacific. India was seen as a possibly promising partner for military cooperation.

In the military and defence realm, several elements comprised the Bush administration's initial approach to the Asia-Pacific. The first element was a greater emphasis on Asia. Of the five 'critical areas' described in the QDR, three encompass Asia (Northeast Asia, the East Asian littoral—'stretching from south of Japan through Australia and into the Bay of Bengal'—and Southwest Asia).[6] The administration initiated numerous studies as part of a planned process to re-allocate US resources, personnel and attention to the region. Second, the QDR articulated plans to redeploy military assets to East Asia and to increase 'access' for US forces in the region. Specifically, '[t]he QDR...calls for an increase in aircraft carrier presence in the region..., increased contingency stationing for the US Air Force..., and the possibility that three or four more surface combatants..., and a yet to be converted Trident-class SSGN (with capability for "stealthy" cruise missile strikes), could be forward stationed in East Asia' (McDevitt, 2001). Third, 'theatre engagement' was replaced by 'theatre security cooperation', indicating an emphasis on access, interoperability and intelligence cooperation. Both the proposed redeployments and the move from military-to-military engagement to security cooperation suggested a more military-oriented approach to regional security based on repeated administration warnings that war in Asia was more probable than in Europe. Fourth, there was to be a continued commitment to forward-stationed forces—though these forces were to be adjusted in scale and location to meet a range of missions and respond to technological innovations. Finally, the commitment to missile defences was in part aimed at 'undermining China's growing strategic capability' (Harding, 2001), as well threats from rogue countries with weapons of mass destruction.

The Bush administration's scepticism about regimes, treaties and multilateral organisations was another major feature of the early approach towards Asia—and elsewhere. The Bush administration's objective was a US foreign and security policy built on self-reliance—itself based on unrivalled (and not to be rivalled) power, assured self-defence (e.g., through missile defence), flexibility (fewer regime and treaty commitments) and key bilateral relationships around the globe. The Director of Policy Planning at the State Department, Richard Haass, famously spoke of '*a la carte* multilateralism'—a formulation apparently designed to suggest that multilateralism was not rejected out of hand, but would be engaged only as and when the United States chooses to participate. The favoured phrase in President Bush's White House for more than one country working with the US was 'coalition of the willing'.

In its tone, rhetoric and style, the early approach of the Bush administration to security in the Asia-Pacific gave the appearance of being a major departure from the Clinton administration's policies. But within just a few months of taking office, and before the events of September 11, adjustments were already beginning to be made. In the post-9/11 environment these trends waxed further.

---

[6] Europe and the Middle East were the other regions identified in the QDR.

US-Asia Relations Post-9/11

There are several notable developments in US-Asia relations over the past half decade. First, relations with allies and friends generally have been strengthened. This is especially so of US relationships with Japan, Australia, and the Philippines. Japan, for example, adopted new legislation allowing the Self Defense Forces (SDF) to provide support to US and other forces participating in Operation Enduring Freedom (OEF). Japan has also sent a reconstruction team to Iraq. The US is now conducting a level of cooperation with the Philippines, including recently signing a logistics agreement, that would have been unlikely prior to 9/11. With Singapore, Malaysia and Thailand, too, US security ties have increased. The Philippines and Thailand have been accorded Major Non-Nato Ally status. The Indonesia case is more complicated, but considerable (and successful) efforts are being made to work with Jakarta in counter-terrorism. But 9/11 in at least two cases, with Japan and Australia, helped improve earlier troubled relations.[7] US relations with ROK have been more complicated due to domestic changes in South Korea and differences between Washington and Seoul regarding North Korea. However, Seoul and Washington are currently participating in the Six Party Talks designed to end the nuclear crisis created by North Korea, and success on this front could reduce a number of challenges to US-ROK relations.

This is not to suggest that there are no concerns and constraints in US relations with friends and allies in the region regarding the war against terrorism. The level of priority given to military solutions, the asymmetry of resources and capabilities between the US and regional states, and the delicate domestic balances required in counter-terrorism require close, consistent dialogue with 'allies and friends'. The administration has mostly been mindful of these challenges. There is recognition in the US that countries will cooperate with the US at levels and in ways that they can afford to—sometimes openly, sometimes not. The US will also need to continue to be sensitive to the impact of US decisions (e.g., warnings to US citizens that they might face dangers in certain parts of Asia) on the economies and societies of Asia. Nevertheless, on the whole, US relations with 'allies and friends' have been strengthened in the wake of 9/11 and the GWOT.[8]

Second, US-China relations, though still highly complex and fragile, generally have become less confrontational, too. Most obviously, the administration's early attention to China has ebbed as the demands of counter-terrorism and Iraq have taken top place on the American agenda. Every indication is that this development is not unwelcome to China. Even before the events of 9/11, and especially after the EP3 incident in April 2001 was settled, Washington and Beijing fashioned a less prickly relationship. Stability and a certain pragmatism in US-China relations has not diminished all of the administration's concerns about China—such as 'Chinese involvement in the proliferation of missile technology and equipment' (Powell, 2002) and human rights. The Taiwan issue also continues to be a constraint to US-China relations, but even here both sides have sought to walk a fine line.

---

[7] The US-Japan alliance was dealing with the Ehime Maru accident. US-Australia relations were complicated by 'Canberra's lukewarm response to Deputy Secretary of Defense Richard Armitage's [sic] comments that the test of a faithful ally was its willingness to shed blood on behalf of the United States' (Harding, 2001).

[8] 'In leading the campaign against terrorism, we are forging new, productive international relationships and redefining existing ones in ways that meet the challenges of the twenty-first century' (Bush, 2001: 7). An excellent review of US efforts with Asian partners may be found in the 'Statement of James A. Kelly' (2002).

Third, US-India relations are improving. The July 2005 visit of India's Prime Minister Manmohan Singh to Washington was successful, and has likely cleared the way for civilian nuclear cooperation between the two countries. However, the road to improvement has not been entirely smooth nor will it be in the future. Differences regarding Pakistan, infiltration of terrorists into Kashmir, and, most important, structural problems in US-India relations (such as poor trade and investment ties) continue to constrain any overnight transformation of US-India relations.

Fourth, changes in US military and defence policies towards Asia that had initially been contemplated, though not abandoned, remain further downstream. Other changes may be sped up, and changes not envisioned two years ago might yet occur. For example, the GWOT has simultaneously increased attention to Southeast Asia (or the East Asian littoral), while diminishing overall the importance of Asia as the war on terrorism has gone global and the US is fighting wars in Afghanistan and Iraq. Pre-QDR speculation that the United States would shift its strategic focus from Europe to Asia has faded. Indeed, while it is common to speak of Southeast Asia as a 'second front' in the war on terrorism, US defence officials such as Deputy Secretary of Defense Paul Wolfowitz have insisted that the problem of terrorism is global (it is even within the United States) and not restricted to a particular region or country (Wolfowitz, 2002). The July 2005 London and Sharm el-Sheikh bombings have illustrated the global activities of terrorists. And, interestingly, the American public now regards Europe, and US partners in Europe, 'more important to the United States than Asia, and more see the countries of the European Union as reliable partners in the war on terrorism than any other country asked about'.[9] Whether such attitudes will persist is unclear. In any case, the attention now being given to Asia, especially Southeast Asia, is more negative than positive. Third, the GWOT has had the effect of speeding up the transition from military 'engagement' to military 'security cooperation' as the US works with a number of partners in Asia on counter-terrorism. Indeed, capacity-building of partners in the fight against terrorism is now an important activity in relations with Asia and countries across the globe. In the current environment, it is unlikely that any dramatic steps will be taken regarding US forward stationed forces, though the US government continues to examine force structure and footprint in Asia (and elsewhere) as part of the effort to 'transform' the US military and respond to a range of contingencies.

Fifth, US commitment to multilateralism has increased in the context of the GWOT. Much has been said and written about a retreat from multilateralism by the US But at least in terms of the war on global terror, multilateralism has been an important component of US policy. The US has worked with ASEAN as a whole, in addition to member countries individually, on counter-terrorism. With the ASEAN Regional Forum (ARF), for example, the US has launched workshops on financial counter-terrorism measures for senior officials. Similarly the US is working through APEC on a number of initiatives, including aviation and maritime security and customs enforcement. Still, the utility of regional institutions to the GWOT will be mixed, and not the prime focus of US policy. This is because most Asia-Pacific countries will focus on local dimensions of the problem and there are disagreements as to what the problem is, and how it should be dealt with. Hence, while still somewhat sceptical of multilateralism, the GWOT has led the Bush administration to try and pursue its

---

[9] See Chicago Council on Foreign Relations, *Worldviews 2002*.

counter-terrorism efforts with the support of and through, rather than against, these multilateral mechanisms—without ceding the right to act unilaterally.

The net effects of the events of 9/11 and the ensuing GWOT on the United States' evolving approaches to Asia-Pacific security, as initially outlined by the administration, have not been transforming and are generally sound.[10]

CHALLENGES AHEAD

There are at least six challenges confronting the management of US relationships in the region. First, there is the challenge of calibrating and coordinating policy priorities. For the US government right now, and for the American public (according to recent polling data), terrorism and stemming the proliferation of weapons of mass destruction top the agenda. But in Asia, internal and external priorities encompass, but do not rest on, these US priorities. One shared priority among Asian states is what might be called the 'US factor' (both keeping good relations with the US and using the US to meet its own objectives), but this is buffeted by these other priorities.

Second, there is the substantial challenge of managing expectations. A case in point is some US expectations regarding Japan. The recalibrated US-China relationship comes with its own set of mutual expectations that have implications for the cross-straits situation.

Third, there is the management of relationships moving from traditional deterrence alliances to what might be called 'alliances of the willing'. Japan and Australia are particular examples of this phenomenon. This shift has potential implications for inter-operability, presence (whether forward deployed or other forms) and defence acquisitions among others.

Fourth, there are challenges emanating from what might be called 'unintended consequences of alliances, new friendships'. Changes in one relationship have ripple effects for others. There are many examples. In the context of the cross-straits situation, improvements in the US-Japan relationship affect Japan-Taiwan relations, as they do Sino-Japan relations; so, too, improvement in US-Australia relations has had spillovers for Australia's relations with both Taiwan and China.

Fifth, there continues to be a need to manage various security approaches simultaneously. Asia's new bilateralism, both between the US and regional states, and within the region itself, has potentially significant implications for a regional order that is also experimenting with different forms of institution-building and regional multilateral arrangements.

A sixth challenge is growing public/government divides regarding relations with the United States. Government to government ties between the US and the region are quite sound, but public attitudes about the US have shown a downturn. The US needs to improve its image in the region, and Asian governments need to do a much better job of explaining to their publics the rationale and gains from cooperation with the US.

---

[10] For more details by the same author, see Limaye, 2003.

REFERENCES

Bracken, Paul (2000) *Fire in the East: The Rise of Asian Military Power and the Second Nuclear Age,* New York: HarperCollins.

Bush, George W. (2001) *'Strengthen Alliances to Defeat Global Terrorism and Work to Prevent Attacks Against Us and Our Friends'.* Delivered at the National Cathedral (Washington, DC), 14 September.

Chicago Council on Foreign Relations (2002) Worldviews 2002: *American Public Opinion and Foreign Policy,* November.

Department of Defense (2001) *Quadrennial Defense Review Report,* 30 September.

Fargo, Thomas, Admiral (ret.) (2004) *Speech to the Singapore Armed Forces Institute* (SAFTI), February.

Friedburg, Aaron (1993/1994) *'Ripe for Rivalry: Prospects for Peace in a Multipolar Asia'.* International Security, 18(3): 5-33.

────── (2000) *'The Struggle for the Mastery of Asia'.* Commentary, November.

Godemont, Francois (1996) *The New Asian Renaissance: From Colonialism to the Post-Cold War,* London : Routledge.

Harding, Harry (2001) *'The Bush Administration's Approach to Asia: Before and After September 11',* Speech to the Asia Society, Hong Kong, 12 November.

Kelly, James A. (Assistant Secretary of State for East Asian and Pacific Affairs) (2001) *Confirmation Hearing.*

────── (2002) *'Statement of James A. Kelly, Assistant Secretary of State for East Asian and Pacific Affairs before the House International Relations Committee's East Asia and Pacific subcommittee',* 14 February.

Kristof, Nicholas D. and Sheryl WuDunn (2000) *Thunder in the East: Portrait of a Rising Asia,* New York: Alfred A Knopf.

Limaye, Satu P. (2003) *'Almost Quiet on the Asia-Pacific Front: An Assessment of Asia-Pacific Responses to US Security Policies'.* Special Assessment: Asia-Pacific Responses to US Security Policies, Asia-Pacific Center for Security Studies, Honolulu, March.

Montaperto, Ronald and Satu Limaye (2001) *'Asians on America: Real Problems Don't Get US Attention'.* International Herald Tribune, 26 July.

McDevitt, Michael (2001) *'The Quadrennial Defense Review and East Asia'.* PACNET 43, 26 October.

Powell, Colin L. (2001) Prepared Statement of Secretary of State-Designate, 17 January.

────── (2002) *'Remarks at Asia Society Annual Dinner'*, New York, 10 June.

Rohwer, Jim (1995) *Asia Rising,* New York: Simon and Schuster.

Wolfowitz, Paul (2002) *Interview with CNN International,* 5 November.

In: Asia-Pacific and a New International Order
Editors: Purnendra Jain et al. pp. 53-69
ISBN 1-59454-986-9
© 2006 Nova Science Publishers, Inc.

Chapter 4

SOFT POWER IN THE ASIA-PACIFIC POST 9/11: THE CASES OF JAPAN, CHINA AND INDIA

Gerry Groot

INTRODUCTION

Power is a slippery concept to define, let alone quantify. Judging relative power balances between states is therefore necessarily fraught with difficulty. Two types of power—military and economic—have at least the advantage of being reasonably easy to quantify; soldiers, tanks, ships and planes can be calculated in more-or-less objective ways, even if quality and likely effectiveness can not. Economic power, the power to buy and to sell, can also be assessed in relatively clear (albeit coarse) ways using indices such as Gross Domestic Product (GDP) (see Jain and Mayer in this volume). On the basis of these measures, it is clear that many states in the Asia Pacific are strong and growing stronger and, in the cases of China and India, quite quickly. It is even possible that China will become the world's single largest economy by 2025 should growth continue at present rates of 8-9 per cent (ChinaNews, 2005). India, too, is growing rapidly at around 7-8 per cent (BBC News, 2005). Commensurate with this economic growth is growing military capacity (see Jain and Mayer).

Yet it is also clear that there are other aspects of power, such as the ability to persuade others to do as one wants, to be able to expect others to do as you wish, and to have others emulate your actions and systems. These forms, which Joseph Nye famously labelled as 'soft power', are harder to define and even harder to quantify, encompassing as they do the admiration of wealth and institutional/systemic efficiency, legitimacy, morality and the like (Nye, 2002, 2004). Nye's insights and his terminology have certainly caught the attention of those seeking evidence of an increased general Asian influence in world affairs commensurate with its economic strength. China, for example, has been called 'a trade-driven soft power without military threat' by one European Union analyst (Liu, 2005), and official Chinese news sources began using related terms for the first time in 2005, with one writer waxing lyrical about the potential of China's 'soft strength' (Wang, 2005). In Japan, the apparent success of cultural exports in the late 1990s even led to the official coining of the term 'Gross National Cool' as a term reflecting increased soft power (McGray, 2002). The recent success of South Korean movies and television soap operas has also been interpreted as boosting Korean soft power (Onishi, 2005). In India's case, too, there has been discussion of the apparent rise of Indian soft power influence and one writer has even gone so far as to claim it was India's greatest asset in the twenty-first century (Tharoor, 2003).

One result of the increased economic prominence of Asia is a growing perception that Asian soft power is growing in tandem with economic success, a growth reflected in the increased success or at least visibility of Asian cultural exports. The fact that Nye highlighted the potential for cultural exports as a key feature of soft power has encouraged this idea (Nye, 2004a). It is certainly one message that many Asian academics and leaders have taken from Nye's work. It is also true that cultural exports from Japan, China, Korea and particularly India have been growing rapidly, sold primarily to their closest neighbours, but also to the rest of the world.

As Jain and Mayer in this volume make clear, Asian hard power has continued to grow over the last fifteen or so years but this chapter takes a necessarily more speculative approach to assess Japan, China and India's soft power potential, particularly as reflected through cultural exports. This examination indicates that it is by no means clear that the rising influence of China and the other Asian states also means any immediate increase in soft power. The main limitation seems to be a general absence of one of its key features, universal values, an absence currently obscured by the attractiveness of economic success.

To substantiate these claims, this chapter discusses some of the key definitional aspects of soft power and then examines them in relation to Japan, China and India. This approach highlights the centrality of universal values to soft power: hence we see the weaknesses of Japan and China and understand why India is perhaps best placed to eventually become a 'super soft power.'

SOFT POWER

A key problem with invoking the idea of soft power is that it is easily misunderstood and misused. It is also much more than international cultural exchange or public diplomacy as practised by government foreign affairs services, even if these can be a part of it. One key problem is that many aspects of the concept depend on degrees of subjective judgement and few scholars have tried to quantify it systematically. Indeed, soft power may be near impossible to quantify with any great accuracy, but the attempt to do so is important as it allows some assessment of key aspects of power that we intuitively know are important. Nevertheless, it needs to be remembered that, in order to be useful, soft power needs to be shown to *exert power*, to somehow influence the ways in which people/governments act *or do not act* as they might otherwise reasonably have been expected to.

According to Joseph Nye, the developer and great populariser of the concept, soft power is something apart from hard power (i.e., economic and military: it is not the buying or coercing of action); it is when

> A country may obtain the outcomes its wants in world politics because other countries—admiring its values, emulating its example, aspiring to its level of prosperity and openness—want to follow it. In this sense, it is also important to set the agenda and attract others in world politics, and not only to force them to change by threatening military force of economic

sanctions. This soft power—getting others to want the outcomes you want—co-opts people rather than coerces them.... Soft power rests on the ability to shape the preferences of others. (Nye, 2004a: 5)

One of the great attractions of soft power is its potential to reduce the cost of actions because, if one country can get others to willingly follow its agenda, the cost of forcing change by unilateral use of military and economic strength can be avoided or much reduced. Hence, attracting others to one's causes is of central importance (Nye, 2005: 12). It is precisely the Bush administration's limited success in getting allies to support its war in Iraq in particular, which gives substance to claims of a decline in American soft power (Nye, 2004b).

There are three key bases for a country's soft power:

- its culture, in places where it is attractive to others;
- its political values, when it lives up to them at home and abroad; and
- its foreign policy, when they are seen as legitimate and having moral authority. (Nye, 2005: 12)

Central to understanding the increasing interest in Nye's ideas is his identification of culture, particularly popular culture, as being of great importance. In his books, *The Paradox of American Power: Why the World's Super Power Can't Go it Alone* (2002) and *Soft Power: The Means to Success in World Politics* (2004a), two polemics calling for greater official American emphasis on public diplomacy, Nye highlighted the potential of popular culture as a transmitter of soft power, alongside the attractions of American higher education, the exemplary nature of American institutions, state foreign policy, listening to others and the promotion of the altruistic and universal values of democracy, as well as human rights (Nye, 2002: 10).

Yet it is this pop culture aspect in particular that has been picked up and used by other scholars, often with little relation to the other aspects of Nye's thesis. The result is to conflate all popular culture as somehow equating to soft power in-and-of-itself. What is left unclear, but which might be inferred from Nye's emphases, is which audiences are influenced and by which aspects of soft power. The emphasis on popular culture can easily be taken as meaning soft power will influence individuals whose subsequent preferences will somehow shape state policy. At other times the implication is that state organs might be those being influenced, but how these might relate to the universal values that Nye stresses remains unclear.

Nye is also not very strong on explaining how something as amorphous as popular culture might embody universal values, although his examples do give us some indication. In *Soft Power* (2004a), Nye discusses examples such as how egalitarianism was communicated by Hollywood and how popular music forms such as rock music communicated ideas of freedom. Other examples include how the economic successes of American sport stars reflected the ability of individuals to become rich and successful. Another example, and one likely to appeal to the hearts of academics, was how academic exchanges helped promote the notions of openness and democracy (2004a: 44-55).

These messages are notable for the fact that they were readily discernible from pop culture products of a liberal democratic and capitalist/consumerist west. Far less obvious is that the power of Nye's examples was contextually dependent despite Nye himself making this point clearly (2004a:12). Pop culture messages were discernible when seen from the perspective of subjects of authoritarian, generally socialist dictatorships with rigid hierarchies, sharp ideological boundaries, rationing of essentials and shortages consumer goods. The soft power of western pop culture in Eastern Europe resulted from it acting as an alternative to current reality and was enhanced by the efforts of dictatorships to quash it. Thus, in Czechoslovakia before the Velvet Revolution of 1989, merely listening to Frank Zappa's avant-garde rock music could become in-and-of-itself a political statement (Gillespie, 2005).

Significantly, these messages with their latent political power were also products of consumer markets and not generally disseminated via official international cultural exchange programs or public diplomacy. Nevertheless, 'western' values of individual freedom, freedom of expression and hence 'democracy' could be found in music. It was easy to deduce that such music could exist despite official disapproval because it arose out of a free market and democratic political systems, not a state Bureau of Culture in a centrally planned economy. The material success of the western system was the ultimate material 'proof' of its superior values and is vital for encouraging emulation and attraction; this culture market is one more natural outlet for the largely unconscious expression of those values. On this basis, Asian economic successes might also increase their soft power and Japan, as the most developed, should display this most of all.

SOFT POWER AND JAPAN

Theoretically, Japan should be a super soft power as well an economic power, despite negligible growth over the last decade. Japan has the world's second largest economy ($US 4.6 trillion in 2004), almost four times greater than China's (World Bank, 2005), and hence enormous hard power. Moreover, unlike China, Japan has been strong for decades and is the world's most technologically advanced economy. It is also a democracy, has very high standards of living and very high attainments in education. Moreover, befitting its status, Japan was, after 1992, the world's largest foreign aid donor for nearly a decade until it was again overtaken by the United States. However, as a proportion of its wealth and as a result of the manner of its aid distribution, Japan is significantly less generous than the other major industrialised nations (*Economist*, 2004).

Since the 1990s, Japan has also become an increasingly obvious exporter of popular culture, both to its near neighbours and the rest of the world, particularly its cartoons (*manga*), animated movies (*animé*) and computer games. This recent success partially mirrors the success of Japanese firms in shaping popular culture everywhere through their success in miniaturising consumer electronics, from first popularising the transistor radio to the mass marketing of affordable, high quality electronics and innovations such as the Walkman. Most recently, the Japanese firms Nintendo and Sony have been at the forefront of producing incredibly successful computer game consoles. The commercial beauty of these products is matched by the potentially useful (for soft power) fact that the computer games themselves are platforms for other iconic pop culture products such as manga and animé characters like Hello Kitty and Super Mario.

Other products and concepts like karaoke, the 'anti-orchestra' singing to a video screen phenomenon, have also been exported around the world, together with the requisite technology. These successes are in addition to the success world wide of much older cultural forms such as ikebana, martial arts (e.g., judo, karate, aikido, jujitsu), reiki massage, food styles (such as sushi and sashimi), haiku poetry and Zen Buddhism. Japan also attracts tens of thousands of foreign students and the government sponsors many more individuals to teach at Japanese schools through programs like the Japan Exchange Teaching Scheme (JET). As result of all these factors, Nye believes that Japan 'has more potential soft power resources than any other Asian country' (Nye, 2004a: 85). Yet the promise has not materialised.

Despite Japan's apparent strengths and its sources of potential soft power, being able to 'get the outcomes it wants' has proved difficult. Between 14 and 16 September 2005, for example, a special United Nations summit failed to approve a proposal to expand the Security Council from 15 to 24 members and to include Japan as a permanent member. Japan's Foreign Ministry failed to win Japan a seat, despite highlighting Japan's contributions to world peace, disaster relief and foreign aid amounting to 'one fifth of the world's overseas development aid over the last ten years' (Machimura, 2005).

This failure was one more significant example of the failure of Japanese bureaucrats to turn Japan's apparent hard (economic/aid contributions and the like) and soft power potentials into real power: gaining acceptance for Japan's official positions and validating Japan's contributions to international forums. This result was despite a British Broadcasting Commission (BBC) poll early in 2005 having found strong public support for United Nations reform and a Security Council seat for Japan in particular. The average support over 23 countries was 69 per cent in favour of reform. Japan was favoured for inclusion by majorities in 20 countries (BBC World Service, 2005). There was background level support for official Japanese aspirations, but clearly not enough.

Where Japan's case failed, at least in part, was because its bureaucrats and leaders had failed to win support for their position from Japan's neighbours. Even early in the year when the BBC poll was taken, the majority of Chinese polled opposed Japan's proposals while in Korea 32 per cent were opposed (BBC World Service, 2005). China's official English language mouthpiece, *China Daily*, had in May already indicated potential problems for Japan with the headline: 'Japan's Security Council dreams clouded with neighbours wary' (*China Daily*, 2005a). The *China Daily*'s underlying message was that the Chinese government was opposed to Japan's ambitions. Yet the fact that a majority of Chinese also opposed Japan, and that it had so little support in South Korea, has important implications for Japanese soft power because elements of potential soft power attraction are particularly relevant to these two countries.

According to Nye, Japan's relative weakness in international affairs can be largely explained by the failure of Japanese governments to properly atone for the crimes committed by the Japanese military in the course of their imperial expansion into Asia between 1931 and 1945. Other factors, including Japan's inwardness, the difficulty of learning Japanese and an aging population, 'continue to limit' Japan's capacity to turn potential resources into soft power. As a result, admiration of Japan's successes by the publics and elites of its neighbours has limits (Nye, 2004a: 87). The recent attempts of the Koizumi government to revise the pacifist constitution imposed on Japan after 1945, and the appointment of conservative hardliners to cabinet positions after the 2005 election, merely serve to reinforce suspicions of Japanese trustworthiness among its nearest neighbours (see *Korea Herald*, 2005).

It is true that officials in Russia, Korea and especially China opposed Japan's Security Council aspirations and turned a blind eye to, if not actively encouraged, anti-Japanese demonstrations and petitions in the lead up to the United Nations votes (see, for example, Lague, 2005). This explanation does not go far enough but Nye's own criteria for soft power perhaps offer some guidance. For example, although Japan does have many foreign students, they amount to only 4 per cent at the tertiary level—and it took two decades to surpass the target of 100,000 set in 1983. In 2004 there were still only 117,302 international students (Web-Japan, 2004). Significantly, while the vast majority are from Japan's closest neighbours—China, Korea and Taiwan—very few of them go to Japan to learn about its institutions in order to adopt them at home.

This is not to say that Japan has lacked exemplary ideas, systems and organisations worth being emulated by others. When Japan's economy was growing well from the 1960s to the early 1990s, factors behind that success, such as just-in-time management, product quality control methods and the like, were promoted abroad and indeed were copied extensively outside of Japan (see, for example, Ezra Vogel's 1979 *Japan as Number 1 Lessons for America*). Japanese experts also played a key part in helping Cambodia develop a constitution along Japanese lines (Sim, 2003). However, it would seem that there has been very little to emulate since.

Japan has few political or bureaucratic institutions that readily spring to mind as world class or easily and profitably transferred to other contexts. The key attraction of Japan remains the fact that, despite only now recovering from a decade of economic stagnation (Koll, 2005), it still has the world's second largest economy. Students are studying Japanese in order to work more effectively in trade or to learn about world-class Japanese technology. These are the areas where ideological content is least important and where Japan also tends to abide by established international, or even more particularly American, norms, rather than setting them.

It is true that Japanese pop culture, in particular, has in the last decade radiated out from Japan to its nearest East Asian neighbours and beyond in recognisably 'Japanese' forms. Moreover, this expansion has often occurred despite overt resistance, as in Korea and Taiwan (Lent, 2004: 41). In one important example, a 2002 Chinese survey found that six out of ten children preferred Japanese animé and only two liked Chinese cartoons (China Daily, 2005b). In 2001 only 10 per cent of cartoon-related sales in China were domestic publications (China Daily, 2001). Moreover, anecdotal reports in China indicate that Japanese and, to a lesser extent, Korean commercial products are major contributors to student choices for overseas study (*Eastday.com*, 2001). Such has been the success of Japanese youth culture in China, the *Beijing Review* felt compelled to ask whether Japanese and Korean influences should be a cause of concern. It asked specifically whether some sort of soft power was at work, perhaps tapping into Chinese Communist Party concerns about harmful foreign influences and fears of peaceful evolution promoted by hostile outsiders (*Beijing Review*, 2005). One Chinese response to this potential threat has been to try to co-opt Japanese animé producers to jointly produce cartoons that are both more appealing to Chinese audiences and have Chinese content (*Tokyo Animé Headline*, 2005; *Taipei Times*, 2005). Implicit in such co-option, of course, is that content will conform to Communist Party requirements and a fear that without such control it may indeed contain dangerous ideas.

It is now also common to find Japanese pop culture dispersed widely throughout South East Asia and most recently in the youth consumer markets of America, Europe and Australia. In Japan, this unexpected development gave some Japanese officials what would seem to be false cause for hope for expanding what they saw as Japan's 'gross national cool' and hence soft power influence (McGray, 2002; Sekiguchi, 2003). The desire of Japanese foreign ministry officials to promote this 'coolness' was in itself a consequence of the popularisation of Nye's ideas. Unfortunately for its promoters, though, there are quantitative and qualitative problems with seeing Japanese popular culture (or even more elite cultural forms) as important or useful in the struggle to expand Japanese soft power and these have implications for China's position also.

Quantitatively, exports of commercial Japanese cultural product are but a tiny proportion of the $US 2.2 trillion estimated for creative industries in 1999 (Howkins, 2001: 116). In America in 2004, manga sales made up a mere 1 per cent (albeit growing) of book sales (interestingly, sales in France were 3 per cent) and large publishers such as Random House were entering the market (MacDonald, 2004: 29). Yet, though they are often very obvious when sold alongside domestic product, the Japanese forms make up only a tiny part of the market and are insignificant compared to American cultural exports. Tsutomu Sugiura, director of the Marubeni Research Institute, calculated that, while total Japanese exports of culture-related products did triple to $US 19 billion between 1994 and 2004, after patent royalties and photographic related materials were subtracted there were only $US 1.5 billion of other, presumably manga, animé, movie exports and the like (Sugiura, 2005: 4). It must be admitted, though, that quantifying sales numbers is very difficult. America's *Publishers Weekly*, for example, claimed in October 2004 that manga sales in America were expected to reach $US140 million and animé was already worth some $US 4.2 billion (*Publishers Weekly*, 2004).

Qualitatively, there is an even bigger problem with Japanese culture as potential soft power—the lack of underlying universal values to give it substance and a basis for political thought and action. For any aspect of culture to have soft power potential requires that relevant values can be read into or taken from it. This assumes that such messages are present, that they can be discerned and that these are salient to the audience. It is then another large leap whether any section of the audience, particularly one with some actual or latent political influence, will then act on such ideas.

In the case of Japanese pop culture there has been inherent and, in hindsight, sometimes unsubtle ideas informing it. In the 1960s and 1970s such pop culture began to make its way to the west via cartoons such as Kimba the White Lion. Even a superficial analysis can now reveal strong pacifist and/or Buddhist undertones with Kimba advocating peace, never eating his helper gazelles, and seeking understanding between man and beast. Yet there is no evidence that Kimba persuaded anybody to become a vegetarian, for instance. In 2003, though, *Time Magazine* declared that, 'Japan's Cool. OK!' and went on:

> Pokémon has supplanted Astroboy in the hearts of schoolkids in more than 65 countries, and 60 per cent of the world's animated-cartoon series are made in Japan. Games running on PlayStation 2 and (to a lesser degree) Nintendo's Game Cube rule the video-game universe just as tightly as before ... (Sekiguchi, 2003)

In 2005, it would seem that *Time's* claim reflected little more than what was, if not merely a fad, something far from substantial. As far as soft power is concerned, it seems that 'J-pop' in all its forms is simply an easily consumed and readily forgotten commercial product.

This enigma of Japanese cultural power, a lack of relevance despite growing ubiquity, can be explained by the lack of any appropriate sets of currently salient altruistic or universal values among the nation's political elite and culture creators, or at least ones over which Japan can claim some sort of ownership. At the elite level, Japanese commentator and former diplomat, Ogoura Kazuo, who, while seemingly dismissing soft power as crude cover for the exercise of military power, recognised this fundamental problem when he bewailed the fact that Japan had no clear national goals and hence ideals to convey to the world via public diplomacy (Kazuo, 2004). He suggested that 'Japanese spirit', peaceful mediation and the philosophy of coexistence which allowed tradition and modernity to coexist were appropriate ideals upon which to base public diplomacy (Kazuo, 2004: 29).

Yet soft power wields influence in large part because it is not state directed and emanates from broader societal values. Kazuo's analysis is accurate in that there is no consensus on such values and neither are these conveyed through official diplomacy, but he also wants any such values to serve state interests in very direct ways. For this to work with soft power, and pop culture in particular, would require forcing Japan's creative industries to submit to external supervision, if not control, a position that harks straight back to the type of militarism that marked Japan until 1945 and which its neighbours find so hard to forgive and forget. Such official values are unlikely to appeal to many outside Japan.

Another major crimp in Japan's appeal is that many of the values its leaders, and in the 1980s and 1990s many western scholars and pundits, touted as key to its economic success—self sacrifice, commitment to both the group and employer over family and the like—are now just as often seen as factors behind the economic stagnation Japan faced after the collapse of its bubble economy in the early 1990s.

Moreover, it was the sudden rise to prominence of the individuals behind 'Gross National Cool' who were lauded as breaking the mould of conformity in favour of individualism, creativity and business entrepreneurialism. The contradiction was that these entrepreneurs with these values, now seen as important in helping the economy grow again, are often producing products with ideological content at odds with that desired by the state. Sony, for example, once considered Ken Kutaragi, the inventor of its hugely successful PlayStation computer console game (190 million sales world wide and climbing) as 'mad' and blacklisted him (Davis, 2005: 29). Kutaragi only succeeded because he ignored some key Japanese values. China faces similar problems.

SOFT POWER AND CHINA

As the Chinese communist government revealed in its desire to control the content of Japanese anime for Chinese youth, culture remains a key battleground for ideas and political support. The material basis for China becoming a 'soft' super power is clear: a large, growing economy and an increasingly obvious cultural presence among its neighbours and overseas. This economic success is certainly attracting students from around the world—some 86,000 in 2004, with a target of 120,000 by the time of the Beijing Olympics in 2008. In context, this is almost 15 per cent of the number going annually from China to America. Qualitatively though, few students in China are graduate students doing research, although an increasing number are doing bachelor degrees. The pull of the big neighbour is reflected by the fact that more than 60,000 are Asian—notably South Koreans (35,000), Japanese (16,000) and the remainder from South East Asia. In 2003-04 there were only some 7,000 American and 6,000 European students (*China Daily*, 2004, Sept 29). To complicate matters, a substantial number of these students are of Chinese descent and many seem to be in China at the behest of parents anxious to instil a sense of 'Chineseness' in them.

Before the 1980s, the handfuls of foreign students who went to China, particularly during the 1960s, were indoctrinated with ideas designed to support a worldwide communist revolution along Maoist lines. In the case of third world students, however, this effort often failed in the face of the unreflective racism of Chinese unaccustomed to foreigners and resulted in many students returning home disillusioned and far from happy to extol Chinese revolutionary values (Brady, 2003: 127). With the discrediting of Maoist socialism, the post-1978 economic reforms along capitalist lines and the subsequent collapse of the Eastern bloc in 1989-91, there is now little communist ideology that might be remotely relevant to the interests of the new waves of students.

Of course, for those with as yet unformed opinions or knowledge of many issues, the opportunity exists to use teaching content intended to win over students to official Chinese views on sensitive issues like human rights and the status of Tibet and Taiwan. Yet it is on precisely these sorts of issues, grounded as they are in universal values relating to individual human rights, sovereignty and national independence, that reveal the limits of potential Chinese soft power. Whether we take Chinese institutions, policies, culture or values, the keys to Nye's formulation, there is very little likely to be attractive in-and-of-itself, and little which individuals might use to stake out a moral or ethical position against coercion elsewhere. Foreign governments though, can.

Perhaps the most significant principles that the post-Mao leaderships have endorsed and promoted are the 'five principles of peaceful coexistence' first enunciated at the Non-Aligned Movement's Bandung Conference of 1955. These are: mutual respect for territorial integrity and sovereignty; non-aggression; non-interference in the internal affairs of others; mutual equality and benefit; and peaceful co-existence. Allowing as they do unfettered action over subjects, these policies are very attractive to dictators and authoritarian regimes. As state-centred principles they privilege state interests as defined by national leaders and these national interests always trump those of individual citizens and groups. For these ideas to have wide appeal requires other publics also to see the interests of their state as paramount.

The CCP leadership has also set economic development, social stability and its own continued domination of the state as the key principles underlining domestic policy. It is this combination of privileging its own position and reification of national interests which has justified the CCP's ability to work with, and even support, any other regime, no matter how much the policies of the leaders of those regimes harm their citizens or subjects. One consequence of this policy is that China has very good relations with states in inverse proportion to their commitment to human rights, democracy, freedom and political and economic openness. Burma, North Korea, Sudan, Cuba, etc., all have excellent and ever-closer relations with the People's Republic.

This relationship of egregiousness with closeness to Beijing is particularly stark when contrasted with the difficulties other states encounter when they attempt to promote human rights within China. For example, hen criticised, or likely to be, Chinese diplomats are often quick to apply pressure to critics, particularly by threatening access to Chinese markets. In 1997, for example, Chinese authorities threatened such retaliatory measures for Danish attempts to sponsor a United Nations resolution criticising Chinese human rights infringements. Denmark eventually caved in and the episode was a salutary lesson for others; there was, moreover, nothing soft about the official Chinese response (Human Rights Watch, 1998).

The fear of exclusion from Chinese markets is potent because the promise seems so great. However, this growth also fails to provide much useful material for soft power development. The evolution of enterprise in China since 1978 has produced unique forms of businesses, but it is not obvious that any of these are easily applicable elsewhere. Much of the success is being driven by the enormous amounts of Foreign Direct Investment; many of the most successful firms are foreign and/or many of those managing them are foreign trained, particularly American trained. Furthermore, despite the successes, the economy is still beset with fundamental problems of state-owned enterprise reform, banking reform, an underdeveloped taxation system and, above all, endemic corruption. At times it seems much more the case that China succeeds *despite* the systems in place, rather than because of them, as the *Economist* recently reminded us (*Economist*, 2005). At a more basic level, much of what passes for necessary knowledge for doing business in China consists of learning to become sensitive to the supposedly central role of *guanxi* ('insider connections') to get things done.

Nor can it be said that arguably the world's most successful Bolshevik political system is necessarily worth emulating. It is, after all, also responsible for disasters like the Great Leap Forward of the late 1950s in which tens of millions died (Becker, 1996) and the Cultural Revolution of the 1960s. Although the Party-state is judged to have successfully reformed China's economy since 1978, this process has also given rise to a society of obvious haves and have-nots. The CCP's systemic inability to address corruption even after this contributed to the violently suppressed demonstrations in 1986 and 1989, underline some fundamental flaws in its system. Indeed, the vision of the brutal suppression of students and bystanders in 1989 is emblematic of the real values of the CCP.

The Party's material success hitherto is a result of reforms that have made China's economy increasingly capitalist in essence; but problems of corruption, rising social unrest, income disparities and pollution are also direct consequences of its leaders' desires to maintain power at any cost. This is justified by their view of the Chinese state as the ultimate good, rather than merely the means of protecting the interests of individual citizens. Validity aside, this is a difficult principle to incorporate readily into cultural products.

This inability to reform the political system in order to address obvious problems while simultaneously preserving CCP domination explains why Chinese theoreticians have been unable to articulate any comprehensive and cohesive alternative values or ideology to the West. It also explains why recent increases in Chinese cultural exports are likely to have only minimal soft power potential.

The current popularity of many forms of Chinese popular culture throughout the world, however, does suggest that a substantial basis exists for the development of Chinese soft power. From feng shui to daoism, kung fu and tai chi to yum cha, moxibustion, acupuncture and Chinese slimming teas, Chinese cultural influences have become common. Chinese movies, movie makers and actors have increasingly made their presence felt in foreign markets since the 1980s and have been assimilated and welcomed to the extent that notable American director, Quentin Tarantino, is spending 2005-2006 in China making, 'Inglorious

Bastards,' a homage to past Chinese martial arts greats (Rose, 2004). More revealingly, Hollywood studios are intending to set up studios in China (Jin, 2005).

Yet the problem facing any Chinese product is similar to that facing Japan; there is no real ideological agenda with inherently appealing universal values to help give the potential real substance. Moreover, as Chinese sensitivity to Japanese anime suggested, the CCP wishes to maintain tight control over any ideas in any products or pronouncements. State sanctioned ideas revolve around preservation of the Party's dominance and the interests of the state, thus limiting their appeal considerably. Some critics have claimed that one recent and successful Chinese film, *Hero*, does have a substantial ideological undercurrent: no matter how bad or even evil the ruler is, to assassinate him when he is key to holding the empire (i.e., the CCP party-state) together is immoral (Eng, 2004). Such a message is not one likely to inspire many outside of China to somehow support the CCP.

The obvious bases for any soft power values are Chinese philosophical and religious traditions, Buddhism, Daoism and especially Confucianism. Indeed, the recent Chinese government initiative to launch Confucius Institutes around the world in the manner of Germany's Goethe Institute, the British Council or Alliance Française, is indicative of the CCP's awareness of the need for national promotion. It therefore purposely invokes a name synonymous with not only China, but also profound culture, ethics and philosophical substance. Yet the CCP spent decades trying to eradicate so-called Confucian and feudal thinking in the interests of ensuring total loyalty to the party-state. Any widespread propagation of Confucian ideas would unavoidably encounter the problem of insistence on the right to overthrow bad rulers, not a principle the CCP would want applied to itself.

Similarly, the promotion of Admiral Zheng He's early fifteenth century voyages around the Asia Pacific are also potentially dangerous. A Foreign Ministry official declared that Zheng He both 'fully displayed traditional Chinese diplomatic culture' and, more importantly, that 'the Chinese never established their own stability and development by exploiting and enslaving other countries' (York, 2005). Moreover, a lead editorial in *China Daily* went even further, claiming Zheng He's voyages as 'evidence that China chose to be a bringer of peace when it had the potential to be a bully' (York, 2005). And this despite Zheng's 10,000 marines and reorganisation of kingdoms in the Malay Archipelago (York, 2005). What was notable in this instance was the willingness of leaders in South East Asia to acquiesce to this official version of Zheng's exploits, a willingness best explained by a desire to maximise good relations with an eye to China's increasing hard power.

Nevertheless, this obvious official use/manipulation of the past to serve the present is just one more problem that Chinese soft power faces. An amazing article published in October 2005 by Wang Xiaohui, an editor for China News Service, neatly highlighted the emptiness of CCP desires for soft power. In an article entitled 'Let China's Soft Strength Be Real Strength', Wang, clearly invoking Nye, declared that China's soft strength surge was already in sight and he equated its importance with hard power. However, in evoking 'putting the people first' and valuing peace in the context of 'constructing' soft power, he merely reiterated the Marxist, statist and instrumentalist conception of the world unlikely to appeal to many Chinese, let alone any visitors to the Chinese Culture Exhibition in the United States that it was addressing (Wang, 2005). Meanwhile, China's giant neighbour, India, is also becoming much more prominent and, while its cultural exports are presently limited, it would seem to have much greater potential for soft power development.

SOFT POWER AND INDIA

India, for long periods past a great centre of learning and prosperity, has suffered in modern times from being associated with poverty and backwardness, a reputation gained while a British colony. This status did not change significantly after Independence in 1947 but as a new independent power in the 1950s and 1960s, India did succeed in having democratic elections in a populous country with numerous opportunities for national disintegration. Indian leaders also tried to carve a third, non-aligned way between the capitalist west and the communist east. However, Indian governments failed to achieve rapid development by pursuing a socialist-type economic independence, a failure which encouraged millions to emigrate in search of opportunities elsewhere. The resultant inefficient and backward sectors of the economy dragged down the rest, and it was only after the economic reforms of 1991 that India's economy began to grow rapidly. It has since become internationally significant because so much of its success is based around modern information technology, computer software, high-level research capacity and similar factors. This contemporary India has enormous soft power potential.

The keys to India's future soft power success are its current achievements and the myriad of ideas that can be developed from its rich religious, philosophical and cultural traditions. Indian thinkers can draw on the legacies of the key religions of Buddhism, Hinduism, Jainism, Zoroastrianism, Islam and others in addition to thousands of sects. India's six main schools of philosophy are another major resource developed over the course of several millennia and almost certainly contain numerous potentially useful insights. Some, such as non-violence, combined with Indian political successes, have already wielded influence.

The manner in which India won independence and the subsequent success of Indian democracy are powerful exemplars. One key idea that emerged from India's struggle for independence and one that shaped worldviews was Mahatma Ghandi's concept of non-violent resistance. Ghandi's thoughts and example went on to shape events in Denmark in the Second World War, the southern states of America during the civil rights movement of the 1950s and 1960s, South Africa and even, perhaps, the Chinese student movement of 1989.

India's success in carrying out regular and competitive elections since 1947, despite the attractiveness of dictatorship as a simplistic solution to India's many problems, is also notable. When Indira Gandhi attempted to move towards authoritarianism in the 1970s, she lost the election she had nevertheless called. Assisting India's position is that its political parties lack the CCP's self-preservation agenda and the restrictions resulting from Japan's cultural inwardness precisely because India already is an extensive and intensive democracy. If Indians can manage democracy with its implicit stress on individualism despite having more than a billion people divided by geography, religion and language, who could not?

Looking to Indian sources for inspiration is not new of course. For westerners it began with the Oriental Renaissance of the 1700s, recurred with the Theosophists of the late nineteenth and early twentieth centuries, and the Beatniks and so-called counter-culture/hippy movements of the 1950s and 1960s. Like those before them, the beatniks and hippies explored Hindu, Buddhist and other teachings in search of new insights and approaches to life and living. However, any sympathy for Indian policies they took home in addition to yoga and transcendental meditation never became influential, owing to the exigencies of Cold War politics. In the twenty-first century, though, many factors have shifted in favour of Indian governments. These factors include the growing prominence of Indian thinkers, the large Indian Diaspora and the synergies between Indian high-tech and creative industries that combine to allow the rapid global dissemination of any new Indian ideas.

More than ever, Indians are able to speak for themselves in world forums and its intellectual base means that it is producing numerous intellectuals with international status, from Nobel Prize winners poet Tagore and economist Amartya Sen, to writers Arundhati Roy, Salman Rushdie and Vikram Seth. These thinkers are not only increasingly prominent, with their books selling well around the world, but also their ideas are often at odds with western orthodoxy. The Diaspora also has growing influence through its economic might, both as a market that allows Indians a foreign foothold, as well as a source of expertise able to be tapped by Indian firms and governments. Often highly educated, India's migrants also provide more opportunities to disseminate Indian ideas, products and culture into host societies.

Key to this increased cultural dissemination is the success of Indian high-tech industries, especially those related to information technology. Nye saw American domination of these sectors as key to American soft power influence, but India is rapidly developing these areas (Nye, 2004a: 30-34). India's software industry, for example, a key purveyor of content in the new era, is currently worth some $US 20 billion but is expected to more than triple in size to some $US 67 billion by 2008 (Unctad, 2004: 8). New Indian multinational companies like Infosys have been central to this success, and raise India's international profile as modern and at the cutting edge of technology. One consequence of this success, and relevant to any assessment of soft power, is the growing reputation of aspects of Indian education. In Pakistan, India's *bête noire*, for example, the Indian Institute of Technology is regarded by many youths as the most desirable place to study (Sinha, 2005).

The increasing integration of software, Internet and information technology in general will also work in India's favour as it develops its soft power resources. With an annual production of anywhere between 800 and over 1000 films, India's 'Bollywood' film industry has an obvious synergistic future when combined with new modes of information technology and distribution. In 2008, India's domestic entertainment industry is expected to double to over $US 9 billion (Unctad, 2004: 7). Even the animation industry is developing, although it is far from challenging Japan's animé phenomenon (Adiga, 2004).

The sites of greatest soft power influence are initially amongst those culturally closest, so the role of Indian success and ideas will likely influence its South Asian neighbours first; there are indications that Indian music was used as a form of resistance to the Taliban in Afghanistan, for example (*Times of India*, 2005). But in India's case, numerous ideas and products, from yoga to curry, have already become common around the world more generally. Bollywood and other forms of Indian pop culture have also started making their presence felt in the west via movies like *Lagaan* and *Monsoon Wedding*. Events like Australia's annual Bollywood Masala festival attract tens of thousands of non-Indian viewers (Arora, 2005), while singers like Alisha have also successfully crossed over (Bhushan, 1999). Nevertheless, whatever commercial success Indian pop culture might have, much more important for effective soft power is that this contains or attracts the buyers to important underlying values. It is much more significant then, that in March 2005, India's Minister for Human Resource Development opened a Mahatma Gandhi Centre for Values and Thoughts in Singapore. This was in addition to establishing a node centre for Indian curriculum and signing a cooperative agreement between the Indian Institute of Technology and the National University of Singapore (Bhalla, 2005).

Conclusions

Soft power is more than simply that which is not hard power. Popular culture, while potentially a potent form of power, requires an ethical-moral base and particular circumstances for it to influence choices and shape political action. Without this precondition, popular culture is merely a consumed luxury.

China now has rock music and punk rockers, but rock music in a China with a developing market economy has little relevance as political statement. Japan has singularly failed to gain any advantage from its relatively successful cultural exports because they lack any discernible message apart from 'consume!' China under the CCP is also unlikely to develop any substantial alternative ideas because the Party's narrow agenda is inimical to the development of new values: these might well undermine it. State-centric ideas like peaceful coexistence can be important for winning support from other regimes, but such ideas are not China's alone (India supported them in Bandung also); they are unlikely to become imbedded in pop culture. In the long term it seems that India is by far the best placed to develop ideas that could become soft power and to be able to diffuse these through its developing cultural industries. The keys to American soft power dominance, ownership of ideas and the size of its creative industries, will decline relative to Asian capacities with each passing year as long as Asian economies continue to grow. The lead-time advantage that America has also enjoyed will also diminish over time. The potential for new Asian ideas to supplant those currently common in the world is therefore growing by the day.

However, if no Asian society develops any substantial variations of the current values underpinning our ideas of modernity and formulated in the Universal Declaration of Human Rights, or economic alternatives to opening markets to capitalism and international trade, then Francis Fukayama's 'end of history' thesis will be vindicated (Fukayama, 1989). That would also be the ultimate vindication of Nye's soft power thesis.

References

Adiga, Aravind (2004) 'The Next Big Draw for India'. *Time Asia*, 5 July.
Arora, Akash (2005) 'Bollywood Adds Spice to the Mix'. *The Australian*, 9 November.
Bhalla, Shobha Tsering (2005) 'Region's First Mahatma Gandhi Centre Unveiled'. Todayonline.com www.todayonline.com/articles/42395print.asp
BBC World Service (2005) 'Twenty-Three Country Poll Finds Strong Support for Dramatic Changes at UN'. 21 March
http://www.bbc.co.uk/pressoffice/pressreleases/stories/2005/03_march/21/un.shtml
BBC News World Edition (2005) 'Sharp Rise in India's Growth Rate'. http://news.bbc.co.uk/2/hi/business/4297050.stm
Becker, Jasper (1996) *Hungry Ghosts: Mao's Secret Famine*, New York: Free Press.

Beijing Review (2005) 'Shall the Chinese Worry about Japanese and South Korean Pop Culture?' May, http://www.bjreview.com.cn/En-2005/05-27-e/zm-1.htm

Brady, Anne-Marie (2003) *Making the Foreign Serve China: Managing Foreigners in the Peoples Republic* (Lanham : Rowman and Littlefield).

Bhushan, Nyay (1999) 'Indipop Still Evolving in Indian–and Globally'. *Billboard*, 111(39).

China Daily (2001) 'Chinese Cartoons Struggle to Attract More Interest'. 21 August, http://www.china.org.cn/english/2001/Aug/17944.htm

—— (2002) 'Chinese Kids Prefer Foreign Cartoons'. 21 August http://www.china.org.cn/english/2002/Aug/39978.htm

—— (2004) 'China Expects Influx of Foreign Students'. 29 September, http://www.chinadaily.com.cn/english/doc/2004-09/29/content_378812.htm

—— (2005a) 'Japan's Security Council Dreams Clouded with Neighbors Wary'. 8 May, http://www.chinadaily.com.cn/english/doc/2005-05/08/content_440128.htm

ChinaNews (2005) 'China to Become 2nd Largest Economy by 2025'. http://www.chinanews.cn//news/2005/2005-10-11/12191.html

Davis, Johnny (2005) 'Play Money'. *The Weekend Australian Magazine*, 24-25 September.

Desai, Meghnad, Sakiko Fukuda-Parr, Claes Johansson and Fransisco Sagasti (2002) 'Measuring the Technology Achievement of Nations and the Capacity to Participate in the Network Age'. *Journal of Human Development*, 3(1): 95-106.

Eastday.com (2001) 'Cartoons, Big Influence on Study Abroad'. 14 December, http://www.china.org.cn/english/SO-e/23713.htm

Eng, Robert (2004) 'Is HERO a Paean to Authoritarianism?' AsiaMedia, July 7, http://www.asiamedia.ucla.edu/article.asp?parentid=14371

Economist (2005) 'Chinese Industry and the State: The Myth of China Inc'. 1 September.

Economist (2004) 'Japan's Foreign Aid: Not So Nice'. 6 May.

French, Howard and Norimitsu Onishi (2005) 'Economic Ties Binding Japan to Rival China'. *New York Times (online)*, 31 October.

Fukayama, Francis (1989) 'The End of History?' *The National Interest,* Summer.

Gillespie, Nick (2005) 'Rock and Roll Entrepreneur: Frank Zappa's True Legacy'. *Reason Online*, April (www.reason.com/0504/cr.ng.rock.shtml)

Howkins, John (2001) *The Creative Economy*, London: Penguin Press.

Human Rights Watch (1998) *Human Rights Watch World Report 1998*, http://www.hrw.org/worldreport/Intro97.htm

Jin, Liwang (2005) 'Hollywood See the Chinese Film Market a Rising Star'. *China Daily*, 4 July.

Kazuo, Ogoura (2004) 'Sharing Japan's Cultural Products as "International Assets"'. *Japan Echo*, 31(6).

Koll, Jesper (2005) 'Japan is Back, For Real This Time'. *Far Eastern Economic Review*, October.

Korea Herald (2005) 'Putting the Brake on Japan'. 3 November.

Lague, David (2005) 'In China, Tensions Inflame Festering War Wounds'. *International Herald Tribune*, 15 August.

Lent, John A. (2004) 'Far Out *and* Mundane: The Mammoth World of Manga'. *Phi Kappa Phi Forum,* 84(3).

Liu, Melinda (2005) 'China: Soft Power, Hard Choices'. *Newsweek*, 7 March, http://msnbc.msn.com/id/7038182/site/newsweek/

MacDonald, Heidi (2004) 'Manga Sales Grow; So Do Worries'. *Publishers Weekly*, 15 March.
Machimura, Nobutaka (2005) Address by H.E. Mr. Nobutaka Machimura, Minister for Foreign Affairs of Japan at the Sixtieth Session of the General Assembly of the United Nations, 'A New United Nations and Japan'. New York, 17 September, http://www.mofa.go.jp/policy/un/assembly2005/state_fm3.html
McGray, Douglas (2002) 'Japan's Gross National Cool'. *Foreign Policy*, May/June.
Nye, Joseph S. 2002, *The Paradox of American Power: Why the World's Super Power Can't Go it Alone*. Oxford: Oxford University Press.
—— (2004a) *Soft Power: The Means to Success in World Politics*, New York: Public Affairs.
—— (2004b) 'The Decline of America's Soft Power: Why Washington Should Worry'. *Foreign Affairs*, 83(3).
—— (2005) 'Soft Power and Higher Education'. Publications from the Forum for the Future of Higher Education, Educause.edu.
Onishi, Norimitsu (2005) 'South Korea Adds Culture to Its Export Power'. *New York Times*, 29 June, http://www.iht.com/articles/2005/06/28/news/korea.php
Pocha, Jehangir (2002) 'The Rising 'Soft Power' of India and China'. *New Perspectives Quarterly*, Fall, http://www.digitalnpq.org/archive/2003_winter/pocha.html
Publishers Weekly (2004) 'Manga Sells Animé and Vice Versa'. 18 October.
Rose, Steve (2004) 'Tarantino Plans Old-Style Kung Fu Film—In Mandarin'. *The Guardian*, 2 November, http://www.guardian.co.uk/china/story/0,7369,1341355,00.html
Samdech Chea Sim (2003) Speech Made By a Senate President on the Occasion of the International Conference on 'The Cambodian Constitutionalism', 10-11 January, The Royal University of Law and Economics, http://www.rule.edu.kh/Speech.htm
Sen, Amartya (2005) *The Argumentative Indian: Writings on Indian History, Culture and Identity*, New York: Farrar, Straus and Giroux.
Sekiguchi, Toko (2003) 'Japan's Gross National Cool'. *Time Asia*, http://www.time.com/time/asia/2003/cool_japan/story.html
Sinha, Aditya (2005) 'Kashmiri Kids Have Indian Idols'. *Hindustan Times*, 3 April.
Sugiura, Tsumoto (2005) 'From Capitalism to Culturalism'. OECD Forum, *'Fuelling the Future'*.
Taipei Times (2005) 'In China Even Animé Transcends Politics'. 8 July: 17, http://www.taipeitimes.com/News/feat/archives/2005/07/08/2003262734
Tokyo Animé Headline (2005) 'China Establishes National Animé Industry Bases'. 2 February.
Tharoor, Shashi (2003) 'The New Global Mantra'. *The Hindu*, 28 September, http://www.thehindu.com/thehindu/mag/2003/09/28/stories/2003092800140300.htm
Times of India (2005) 'Editorial: Nations as Brands'. 11 October, http://timesofindia.indiatimes.com/articleshow/1259945.cms
Trans-Atlantic Trends 2004, A Project of the German Marshall Fund of the United State and Compagnia Di San Paolo.
Unctad (United Nations Conference on Trade and Development) (2004) *'Creative Industries Development'*. Eleventh Session, Sao Paulo, 13-18 June.
Vogel, Ezra (1979) *Japan as Number 1- Lessons for America*, Tokyo: Charles E. Tuttle and Co.

Wang Xiaohui (2005) 'Let China's "Soft Strength" Be Real Strength'. *People's Daily Overseas Edition*, 10 October, http://english.people.com.cn/200510/10/eng20051010_213610.html

Voice of America (2005) 'Highlights of Rice Testimony'. 18 January, http://www.voanews.com/english/2005-01-18-voa67.cfm

Web-Japan, 'Foreign Students in Japan (1991-2004)'. http://web-japan.org/stat/stats/16EDU61.html

World Bank (2005) *World Bank Development Indicators Database*, 15 July, http://www.worldbank.org/data/databytopic/GDP.pdf

York, Geoffrey (2005) 'Revisiting the History of the High Seas'. *The Globe and Mail*, 18 July.

In: Asia-Pacific and a New International Order
Editors: Purnendra Jain et al. pp. 71-88

ISBN 1-59454-986-9
© 2006 Nova Science Publishers, Inc.

Chapter 5

'ISLAMIC FUNDAMENTALISM' IN THE ASIA-PACIFIC REGION: FAILURES OF CIVIL SOCIETIES OR BACKLASH AGAINST THE US HEGEMONY?

Shamsul Khan

'We do not profess to be the champions of liberty, and then consent to see liberty destroyed.'
(Woodrow Wilson)

The events of 11 September 2001 and the Bali bombing of 12 October 2002 have pinpointed so-called 'Islamic terrorism', which has tended to be conflated with Islam, to make Islam as a religion an important focal point for analysing various contemporary political phenomena, including international terrorism and the security of the Asia-Pacific region. Four contested assumptions emanating from the predominant 'Islamic terrorism' bubble have made Islam the subject of hundreds of recent books and articles, many of which have provided new opportunities for some instant 'specialists' to add their 'expertise' to the ever-expanding subject area on the so-called 'Islamic militancy'.[1] These four contested assumptions are: (i) that Islam as a religion, and fundamentalist Islam, generally implying the militant Islamists, are monolithic;[2] (ii) that so-called fundamentalist Islam is inherently violent;[3] (iii) that the

---

[1] For some 'entrepreneurial' researchers, it seems, the issue of 'Islamic terrorism' provided the most convenient pathway to elevate, almost overnight, their terrorism 'expertise' from the obscure issues in the local arena to international security issues in the global arena; more so because, with the heightened media interest in possible terrorist threats (particularly in the western hemisphere), it became possible for these 'entrepreneurial' researchers to speculate almost anything without producing any shred of evidence, simply by referring to their personal interviews with some 'terrorists' or 'would be terrorists' or to secret intelligence reports as their main sources of information, the factuality of which could not be verified by anyone independently. Thereafter, when their unsubstantiated assertions were uncritically accepted and cited as 'facts' not only by the media but also by some 'information-hungry' academics, those assertions became self-perpetuating 'realities'. For an interesting reading, see Hughes (2003).

[2] This notion does not take into consideration the differences between those who try to interpret the 'Islamic foundations' (i.e., the Qur'an or hadith) and observe Islamic religious principles and values just as a personal vision of faith and do not necessarily insist on the establishment of a state based on Shari'a (Islamic law) and those who embrace Islam as a political ideology as much as a religion of faith and, therefore, propose and endeavour to establish Islam as a state religion, insisting on the strict implementation of Shari'a. It also fails to

intermingling of politics and religion is unique to Islam;[4] and, (iv) that the relationship between Islamic values and western Christian, particularly American, norms is essentially antagonistic.[5] While some of the contemporary writings on the real or perceived threats of 'Islamic militancy' in the Asia-Pacific region for the foreseeable future reflect the informed views of some seasoned western diplomats who have lived and worked with and among Muslims in South and Southeast Asia, there are other writings which are constructed more on the basis of certain geographical assumptions and cultural understandings (or misunderstandings for that matter) about places and populations in South and Southeast Asia than on the basis of the existing socio-political and cultural realities of the region.[6]

Of course, this is not a new phenomenon in the study of violence and conflict. Perceptions of a particular form of threat posed by a specific group of people in a certain geographic space—usually invented on the basis of cultural assumptions— have been offered in the past in various neo-Orientalist and new barbarism theses for explaining the symbolic violence in the Middle East.[7] For example, *The Arab Mind*, written by Raphael Patai, is a telling example of an approach where the imagined backwardness of the 'Arab mind' is offered as the root cause of irrational violence in the Middle East. 'The Arab', Patai writes, 'has a proclivity to blaming others for his own shortcomings and failure. Since the West is the most readily available scapegoat, it must take most of the blame, [and] with that goes inevitably most of the hate' (Patai, 1973: 85). Daniel Pipes and Jonathan Schanzer in *Militant*

---

distinguish between those who claim to be able to determine a politics for Muslim peoples, albeit within a legal political framework, and those who try to pursue that politics with revolutionary zeal and violent means. For some stimulating analyses on this whole debate, see: Roy, 2004; Halliday, 1994; Moghissi, 2000.

[3] Why is fundamentalist Islam inherently violent? Because, as it is assumed by some, but quite erroneously so, that 'terrorism is not a deviation but actually the norm for Islamic culture...from its seventh-century breakout from the Arabian peninsula until the late seventeenth century, Islam advanced at sword point, spreading from the Pyrenees to the Philippines. The tide was checked only at the gates of Vienna. From the decline of the Ottoman Empire until the 1970s, Islam ebbed. Today—fuelled by oil wealth, surplus, population, immigration and the rise of fundamentalism—Islam is resurgent. Instead of wild horsemen, its banners are carded by guerrillas, terrorists, theocrats and tyrants'. For a glimpse of such views, see Feder (2001: 22). However, this is a much-contested view in regard to the historical spread of Islam around the globe. Although the early Islamic empire, founded during the time of Prophet Muhammad, played a leading role in spreading Islam in the powerful neighbouring countries (namely, those of Byzantium, Egypt, Mesopotamia and Iran), and continued to do so for a century after the death of Muhammad, covering a huge area from the Indus in the east to Spain in the west, from 732 onward Islam started spreading primarily through trading activities, particularly in Southeast Asia and Africa. See Westerlund & Svanberg (1999: 1-37); Clarke (1988); Lapidus (1988).

[4] The most popular and powerful myth with regard to Islam is that one cannot separate religion as a faith from religion as a politics. The reasons for suggesting the existence of a close link between Islam and politics might be grounded on the general belief, as Katerina Dalacoura has explained in greater detail in Islam, Liberalism and Human Rights, that Muhammad, the Prophet of Islam, himself combined the roles of political and religious leader for the Arabs in his lifetime and that is why, in the years after him, the fortunes of religion and the Arab empire were also closely linked. Of course, the real situation must have been much more complex than the above-mentioned assumptions presuppose and it is extremely debatable to what extent the popular myth in regard to the bond between Islam and politics is historically real, and whether Islam is the exception among religions in this respect. See Dalacoura (2003: 39-68). See also Lewis (1988); Ayubi (1991); Pieterse (1994).

[5] Why is the relationship between Islamic values and the American norms antagonistic? Because, as it is explained in some popular American writings, 'their culture is backward and corrupt' and because 'they are envious of America's power and prestige'. It is further assumed that Muslims are jealous of American success and superiority, 'which springs neither from luck nor resources, genes nor geography', but from free market, free society, and, above all, its military might'. For details see Hanson (2002); see also Danner (2001); Gerecht (2002).

[6] For examples representing those varied viewpoints, see Millard (2003); Jones (2003); Abuza (2003); Devine (2001).

[7] Robert Kaplan's (1993) *Balkan Ghosts* is an example of such assumptions.

Islam's New Stronghold have also provided another glaring example of blurring at will the boundary between threat perceptions and cultural stereotypes, while trying to designate new flashpoints of the so-called Islamic terrorism in Indonesia, Bangladesh and Nigeria. What particular feature made these three countries militant Islam's new stronghold? For Pipes, who is, incidentally, the Director of the Middle East Forum in Washington, DC, and Schanzer, a Sorel Fellow at the Washington Institute of Near East Policy, the very fact that the 378 million Muslims who populate these three countries constitute about a third of the global Muslim community seems to be reason enough to designate them as militant Islam's new stronghold (Pipes and Schanzer, 2002: 13). This view is quite consistent with Pipes's earlier view that Muslim countries have the most terrorists and the fewest democracies in the world (cited in Sadowski, 1993: 14). For Pipes, the closest ideologies to Islam and Islamism are the radical utopianisms like fascism and Marxism-Leninism (2000: 92; 2001: 19-24). Pipes branded Dr Khaled Medhat Abou El Fadl, a professor of law at the University of California in Los Angeles and a visiting professor of law at the Yale Law School, a 'disguised protagonist of the militant Islam' simply because he suggested that it was possible to live by Islamic law and that *Shari'a* and Islam were inseparable (2004: 1-8). Of course, in the context of Bangladesh, Pipes and Schanzer went one step further to explain how, to their minds, the Muslim population of that country was turning Bangladesh into an extremist Islamic state and was oppressing its religious minorities:

> Islamists in this 83 per cent Muslim country in South Asia aspire to establish a true 'Islamic Republic of Bangladesh' with a constitution based on the Shari'a. The goal, says the head of one group, 'is to pursue a slow but steady policy towards Islamization of the country' much like Afghanistan under Taliban. Not surprisingly, Al-Qaeda has tentacles in Bangladesh. Harakat ul-Jihad Islami, Bangladesh was reportedly established with direct aid from Osama bin Laden in 1992 and calls itself the 'Bangladeshi Taliban'.... Meanwhile, members of minority religions have suffered from ghastly violence, including collective terror. The nation reports that some Buddhists and Christians were blinded, had fingers cut off, or had hands amputated, while others had iron rods nailed through their legs or abdomen... women and children have been gang-raped, often in front of their fathers or husbands. In addition, hundreds of temples were desecrated and statues destroyed; thousands of homes and businesses looted or burned. As for Hindus, the human rights organisation Freedom House reports they have been subject to 'rape, torture and killing, and the destruction of their cultural and religious identity at the hands of Muslims'. In one indicative step, Islamists sometimes force Hindu women to dress in the Islamist fashion. (Pipes and Schanzer, 2002: 13)

It did not matter to Pipes and Schanzer, who are not known to have ever visited Bangladesh, that they were making all of their assertions about the supposed extreme religiosity of the majority population of a small South Asian developing country either on the basis of an alleged statement of a 'leader' of an obscure radical party at the fringes or on the basis of vague and scanty evidence without any sort of cross verification.[8] What is interesting in this context is that another report on Bangladesh, published in the conservative US journal

---

[8] No information, whatsoever, was provided with regard to when and where those alleged crimes took place. Also, besides vague references to an undated *The Nation* and an undated report of the conservative organisation Freedom House, no other sources of information were provided in regards to their claims and, therefore, they could not be independently verified. Furthermore, as it seems, Pipes and Schanzer did not even care to crosscheck their information with the information provided in the yearly 'Country Reports on Human Rights Practices', published by the US Department of State (US Department of State, 2002; 2003).

New Republic, and just a few months before Pipes and Schanzer made their above-mentioned assertions, sketched a totally different picture. Joshua Kurlantzick, in his report in the *New Republic* entitled 'Civil Society: Dhaka Dispatch', wrote:

> Late one afternoon in Dhaka, capital of Bangladesh, men and women in an upscale district are hurrying home through tangled traffic when the tinny afternoon calls to prayer rings out. Paying little heed to the mosque across the street, numerous young men flock to a very different institution—Wimpy's, the British burger chain that has become one of the most popular local eateries, to enjoy some pre-dinner junk food. That so many young men would ignore the call to prayer might surprise a visitor to Dhaka, where nearly every major street contains at least one mosque. Indeed, in many respects, Bangladesh resembles nearby Pakistan, today a cauldron of poverty, nuclear weapons, and radical Islam. Like Pakistan, Bangladesh is overwhelmingly Muslim. Like Pakistan, Bangladesh is poor and overcrowded, with an annual per capita income of $350 and a population of 130 million packed into a territory smaller than Wisconsin. Like Pakistan, Bangladesh is ruled by a small, rich, Westernized elite that could be vulnerable to Islamic resentment. Yet democratic Bangladesh isn't home to a powerful fundamentalist movement. One sign: outside the capital, I visited a village where women gather to obtain small loans from the *Grameen Bank* in order to run businesses ranging from raising cows to renting mobile phones. In particular, the predominant domestic NGOs—with their liberal, and even feminist, agendas—have affected the status of Bangladeshi women... Most knowledgeable people in Bangladesh aren't overly worried about Islamism, and the Dhaka government has openly supported the U.S. campaign against the Taliban. (Kurlantzick, 2001: 20)

The image suggested here, and in contrast to the danger of Islamic militancy in Bangladesh suggested by Pipes and Kurlantzick in their work, is one in which the phenomenon of so-called Islamic militancy in the Asia-Pacific region is a much more complex issue than one can possibly address adequately in some sensationalist journalistic excursus. Or perhaps the writings of Raphael Patai and Daniel Pipes, cited above, basically betray the same ideological frame of mind as that of Robert Kaplan, who is firm in the belief that in places where western Enlightenment has not penetrated, and where there has always been mass poverty, people inevitably find liberation through fanaticism and violence (Kaplan, 2000: 45). It is no wonder, then, that the people with such an outlook would only be interested in conducting their 'intellectual exercises' on the basis of their own cultural assumptions, with a simple objective of designating the presence of violence or the propensity to violence in a given place to the prevailing predominant culture of that population, claiming that the traits of violence are embedded in that local culture or in the predominant ideology of that culture.[9] Of course, there is an accompanying benefit in resorting to such kinds of 'culture stereotypes' (implying that culture is the most reliable clue to people's politics): ascribing the violence of one's adversaries to their culture helps absolve oneself of any moral responsibility. However, a proper understanding of the phenomenon of terrorism in the Asia-Pacific region, particularly the Islamic militancy at the fringes, requires much more than engaging in blame games. It requires an understanding of the complex interplay of economic, social and political forces both in the local and the global arenas. The alternative to doing so

---

[9] Janet Tassel (2005), in her article 'Militant about "Islamism"' has elaborated in greater detail how the combative Daniel Pipes, motivated by "the simple politics of a truck driver", wages verbal war on what he describes as today's most threatening "totalitarian ideology".

would be, as Greg Barton has rightly pointed out in the context of Indonesia, 'falling into habitual errors of reductionism and essentialism when talking about Islam and Muslim society' (Barton, 2004:81).

Herein lies the point of departure for this essay: to explore, in the context of the Asia-Pacific region, whether or not is there any necessary correlation between an individual's, a group's or an organisation's efforts to reappropriate and reinvent concepts from its traditions for attaining its political objectives and its resorting to violence for the same purpose. If there is no necessary correlation, could there be any circumstances under which such a correlation might eventually emerge? The process of this investigation can begin with a content analysis of the most influential existing literature pertinent to the relevant issues.

CLASH OF CIVILISATION THESIS OR THE FRIEND/FOE DICHOTOMY AND ISLAM'S ALLEGED INCOMPATIBILITY WITH MODERNITY AND GLOBALISATION

Those western scholars who generally equate Islamic fundamentalism with the activities of various militant Islamist groups that propagate violence, and attribute the emergence of those groups to the absence of economic and political liberalisation/democratisation in certain parts of the Muslim world, can be divided broadly into two groups.

One group comprises those scholars who primarily agree either with the clash of civilisation thesis of Samuel P. Huntington (1993: 22-48; 1996), or the similar friend/foe dichotomy of Bernard Lewis (2001a, 2001b), Robert Kaplan (2000) and Francis Fukuyama (2001: 21). Huntington's (1996: 217-218) controversial 'clash of civilisations' argument posits *inter alia* that the extent of both domestic and international conflict between civilisations will increase with the end of the Cold War. This is expected to be especially true of clashes involving western and Islamic civilisations. It is precisely this line of reasoning that has convinced some American scholars such as Bernard Lewis (2003: 3) to claim that what preceded and produced the terrorist attacks like those of 11 September 2001 were neither the real motives of the planners and perpetrators of those horrible crimes nor the post-Cold War search for new enemies but, instead, the Muslim awareness that Christendom constitutes the only serious rival to Islam as a world faith and a world power.

In his *The Clash of Civilizations and the Remaking of the World Order* Huntington (1996) has discussed at length the possibility of conflict between the western and Muslim worlds as being one of the main faultlines of an inter-civilisational war, primarily because of the alleged incompatibility of Islam with both capitalism and secular western liberalism. Echoing Huntington's views, Robert Kaplan (2000: 26) also presented the possibility of future conflicts as the struggle between primitivism and civilisation, between the educated few and the uneducated but newly empowered millions whose borders are not those of national states, but those of culture and tribe. Although there are also many non-Muslim countries that have not made the transition to either capitalism or democracy, Francis Fukuyama (2001: 21), following Huntington and Kaplan, also came to the conclusion that Islam appeared to be particularly resistant to both. Islam is the only cultural system, he argues, 'that seems regularly to produce people like Osama bin Laden or the Taliban who reject modernity lock, stock and barrel'.[10] Huntington and the others generally identify the causes of the growth of Islamic militancy and fundamentalism as being located not only in the economic and military dominance of western societies, but also in the demographic changes of Muslim societies in the last few decades, which has produced a large number of mobile, unemployed and disaffected young men who are ideal recruits to Islamic fundamentalism.[11] They further argue that Islamic militancy has, so far, been mobilised by political grievances, not only against the US and its allies, but also against their own national governments that have failed.[12]

The main weakness in Huntington's thesis and other authors' friend/foe dichotomy is that neither religious groups nor civilisations are anything like as united and monolithic as their accounts logically require. The current conflicts in the Middle East, as well as elsewhere around the globe, often pit members of the same civilisations against one another, in both the Muslim and the non-Muslim worlds.[13] However, the main dangers with the civilisation thesis and the friend/foe dichotomy are that these views can become self-fulfilling, because their analyses can create exactly the kind of identities and, ultimately, the very foreign policy mindsets that bring such world orders into existence, a scenario which would be to the advantage of Osama bin Laden and others like him.[14]

The second group comprises those analysts who view the events of 11 September as an ultimate response to the secular modernisation of the west. Benjamin Barber, for example, much before 11 September, saw a world in which two forms of international order coexisted: the first rooted in race, holding out the grim prospect of a retribalisation of large swathes of human kind in which culture is pitted against culture, a *Jihad* against modernity itself (1996: 4). The second is a busy portrait of onrushing economic, technological, and ecological forces that demand integration and uniformity ... one McWorld tied together by communications, information, entertainment, and commerce (Barber, 1996: 5). In such a situation, Barber foresaw an inevitable clash between the universal consumer world (McWorld) and the tribal world of identity politics and particularities (Jihad). The reason for this is that Jihad and McWorld operate with equal strength in opposite directions, the first driven by parochial hatreds, the other by universalising markets; the first recreating ancient subnational and ethnic borders from within, the other making the national borders porous from without (Barber, 1996: 6). From this perspective, and in such a situation, if one understands and totally accepts a religion like Islam as a comprehensive and transcendental worldview that excludes the validity of all other systems and values, while serving as sort of an ideology capable of absorbing all scientific and technological innovations without being tainted with their philosophical substratum, then there can be a qualitative contradiction between western civilisation and the religion of Islam (Choueri, 1997: 123). If that happens, from this perspective (Bodansky, 1999: 389; Kurtz, 2002), the militant Islamists can, then, seek to use the tools that globalisation provides to subvert modernity and to seek to overthrow the

---

[10] Bryan S. Turner (2002: 103-119) has provided a detailed analysis of this friend/foe dichotomy.
[11] For an interesting overview of this kind of argument, see Bernard Lewis (2001b; 2002).
[12] Rushdie (2001), Buruma & Margalit (2002) and the *Economist* Special Report (2001) are further illustrations of such viewpoints.
[13] For further elaboration of this issue, see Henderson & Tucker (1999). See also Gerges (1999).
[14] Jürgen Habermas expressed the optimistic opinion that the Anglo-Saxon world would escape contagion from precisely this kind of foreign policy mindset that, in the past, sought to define sovereignty in terms of civilisational struggles between friend and foe in the European context. It seems his optimism may yet prove to be premature. See Habermas (1989: 135). See also Schmitt (1979: 26-28) and Wakim (2004).

perceived US hegemony, while extending its philosophy of all-Muslim resurgence on a global scale. However, so far, there is no empirical evidence whatsoever to support that this is actually happening.

BACKLASH AGAINST THE US HEGEMONY AND THE ISLAMIST 'CULT OF DEATH' AS THE NEO-NIHILISTIC TOTALITARIANS

There are, of course, others who see the contemporary Islamic resurgence, both in its violent and non-violent forms, as a legitimate response to western, particularly US, neo-colonialism. They, again, can be divided into two groups.

One group is made up of academics who see the events of 11 September primarily as a backlash again US global hegemony, essentially agreeing with the Chalmers Johnson's 'blowback' theory, which takes into account the costs and consequences of the 'American empire' (Johnson, 2000). Chalmers Johnson (2000: 224-238), writing exactly a year before the events of 11 September, after providing a critical analysis of the history of US economic, strategic and foreign policies in Asia, Latin America and the Middle East, had gloomily warned the American people that the world politics in the twenty-first century will, in all likelihood, be driven primarily by the unintended and unexpected negative consequences of US foreign policies in these regions. Further, these policies had been kept secret from the American people. The protagonists of this backlash theory view the events of 11 September primarily as a simple case of political terrorism.[15] Like political terrorism pursued in the past in other parts of the world, including Europe, the Middle East and Latin America, the events of 11 September are seen as having the purpose of turning the domestic or international conditions that the terrorists/revolutionaries perceive to be unjust into unstable revolutionary situations (Johnson, 2003: viii-ix). In other words, the suicidal killers of 11 September 2001 are not different from those left-wing revolutionaries of Latin America in the 1960s and 1970s, who were fighting the puppet US regimes and covert US operations in Nicaragua, Honduras and Peru.[16]

From this perspective, though the suicidal killers of 11 September 2001 have so far failed to disorient the US population by demonstrating, through their indiscriminate violence, that the supposedly omnipotent US state is incapable of protecting its citizens from its weak adversaries, they have at least succeeded in displaying the vulnerabilities of the US to a large section of the disgruntled people in the Islamic world who associate the US with the Israeli atrocities against Palestinians. Besides, according to this perspective, the terrorists also might have been successful in 'sucking' the US military forces into high-risk operations in Iraq, with the possibility of a quagmire and more body bags unloaded under television lights at Andrew Air Force Base, and possibly creating a new Vietnam syndrome in the US (Klein, 2005). However, according to the critics of this blowback theory, those involved in the suicide missions of 11 September have actually rendered a great disservice to the causes of the Islamic world. Instead of forcing the US population to demand US withdrawal from

---

[15] Dodds (2005: 202-212) elaborates on this issue.
[16] One of Noam Chomsky's most persistent accusations against successive American administrations has been that they have often covertly or overtly supported acts of terrorism against civilian populations throughout the Third World. See Chomsky (1991; 2001), and also Hersh (1998).

global hegemony, their actions have clouded the US population's understanding of Islam and the Arab World and generated popular support for a hardline policy of 'whatever it takes' against 'the enemies of freedom'.

The other group comprises those scholars who endeavour to interpret the violent manifestations of the so-called Islamic fundamentalism by tracing a genealogy of terror back to the nihilistic totalitarianisms whose varying death cults ravaged Europe in the first half of the twentieth century. According to Paul Berman (2003: 18-21), just as those nihilist movements threatened the future of capitalist liberal democracy in Europe in the early twentieth century, the emerging Islamist 'cult of death' is also now threatening western liberalism. Berman's analysis is based primarily on Camus's argument in *The Rebel* that to discover the roots of totalitarianism is also to discover the roots of terror.[17] For Berman, it is Camus's genealogy of the 'Promethean impulse to rebel' that allows us to see how the love of freedom and progress become caught up with an obsession with murder and death for what is perceived as a 'just cause', and it is this nihilism that the west has exported to the supporters of Al Qaeda (2004: 52-76).[18]

At the heart of each of these doctrines lies a peaceful and wholesome people whose lives had been undermined by others. Berman spells out that this is also the rhetoric adopted by Osama bin Laden, a person who exemplifies the hyphenated personalities of numerous Arab and Muslim leaders (2004: 17-21). From this perspective, Osama bin Laden's philosophy of a new pan-Arabism is a philosophy of overcoming, and the recovery of the Arab Empire of old from the days of Prophet Muhammad and the first Caliphs.

RELIGIOUS FUNDAMENTALISM AND VIOLENT MILITANCY? THE CONTESTED LINKS BETWEEN ISLAM AND TERRORISM IN THE ASIA-PACIFIC REGION

When one refers to the so-called Islamic fundamentalists, it becomes extremely difficult to pinpoint what it is to which one is referring. Does it refer to anyone who simply believes in religious conservatism in the context of the interpretation and the application of Islamic values and norms, both at individual and societal levels, without subscribing to any particular political ideology? Or does it refer specifically to those who believe in *Salafism*, the official corpus of Islamic doctrines, as practised in Saudi Arabia, which strictly enforces Shari'a? If the answer to the second question is yes, then how do the millions of Muslims from South and Southeast Asia fit into this category? Very few Muslims from this part of the globe are *Salafists* (sometimes known as *Wahabist*). Besides, all *Salafists* are not necessarily militant Islamists. *Salafism*, as a specific intellectual contribution to Sunni Islamic theology, basically proposes that its followers imitate their 'pious forefathers' (*Salaf*), the companions of the

---

[17] 'Freedom, "that terrible word inscribed on the chariot of the storm", is the motivating principle of all revolutions. Without it, justice seems inconceivable to the rebel's mind. There comes a time, however, when justice demands the suspension of freedom. Then terror, on a grand or small scale, makes its appearance to consummate the revolution' (Camus, 1951: 76).
[18] Berman further argues that those totalitarian movements of the first half of the twentieth century marked their rebellion against a perceived decadent old politico-economic order by establishing an ideal of submission. The path out of the devastation of the early twentieth century was through charismatic leaders promising delivery from the mistakes and injustices of the past. See Berman (2004: 52-76).

Prophet who led an exemplary life, and insists on the vigorous implementation of injunctions pronounced by medieval jurists (of whom the best known is Ibn Taymiyya).[19] Yes, this doctrine is inherently conservative. But does adherence to any particular conservative religious approach towards life, society and the state automatically make someone, or a particular group, militant? If the answer is yes, can the same line of reasoning convince someone to designate some part of the US 'an area of militancy' purely on the basis of the triumph of the Christian Right there in the last US presidential election? Of course, it goes without saying that no one is reasonably going to make such claims, because there is obviously no such danger, except perhaps risks that the Americans might run if, for example, the Republicans succeed in forcing some sort of 'judicial reforms' in light of the Terri Schiavo case.[20] Then, in a similar situation in future, an American citizen might be forced to allow the Governor and/or the Congressmen, instead of a competent doctor, to determine whether or not a life support system of his/her 'clinically dead' partner could be discontinued. This issue has been raised mainly to highlight the inherent danger in making any sweeping generalisation in regard to a particular religion or religiosity.

It is in this context that one can perhaps appreciate the concerns raised by the late Edward Said (2001:10) in regard to the danger of negating the plurality of the Islamic world in favour of a one-dimensional view of regions, cultures and people. His concerns seem quite pertinent, not only because it is extremely difficult to isolate and categorise different forms of religiosity prevalent among the Muslims of the Middle East, South and Southeast Asia and Africa, but also because Islam as a religion and Muslims as a cultural group are not synonymous. In fact, there is no single Muslim culture, as the Muslims are immersed in various ethnic cultures (for example, Bengali, Punjabi, Malay) around the globe. Here, one can perhaps legitimately accuse Huntington and Lewis of committing the 'cardinal sin' of not only providing an ahistorical analysis, but also of concocting and offering an *ad hoc* 'one size fits all' stereotyping template to hundreds of academic and media analysts. Moreover, this stereotyping template is built in the format of the Middle East, but it arbitrarily lumps together all the Muslims of the world, no matter whether they are Saudi, Egyptian, Palestinian, Indonesian, Malaysian, Pakistani, Nigerian, Turks or even Iranian Shias.

Furthermore, one could also look at Islamist groups that are increasingly using Islam as a political strategy in various states of the Asia-Pacific region, and doing so to attain certain domestic political goals, thereby turning Islam into a political ideology. Is there any danger that some members of these Islamic groups would eventually turn into fanatic militants, a kind of militant Islamist, so to speak? Work of scholars such as David Wright-Neville

---

[19] Kepel (2004: 152-196) has provided a detailed analysis on Salafism.
[20] Terri Schiavo, 25, was found unconscious and gasping for air at home by her husband early in the morning of 25 February 1990. She had suffered a full cardiac arrest and then went into coma. She was in a coma for approximately one month, which then evolved into a vegetative state. Four specialist neurologists in Florida, USA, consulting her on case repeatedly made diagnoses of PVS (Permanent Vegetative State) over the years. After Terri had been in a permanent vegetative state for a few years, prolonged legal battles broke out between Terri's husband, Michael Schiavo, and the parents of Terri in regard to the question of whether or not Terri's life-support system should be withdrawn. After the whole legal process was exhausted in Michael Schiavo's favour, various US 'right to life' groups, supported by the conservative politicians like Tom Delay, intervened, blaming the 'liberal judges' for 'legislating' through their decisions. As a result, trampled by the eleventh hour Congressional action, and President Bush's signing of it, were the broader principles of American government, such as separation of state and church, states' rights, and the checks and balances between the legislative branch and judicial branch of government. For further details, see Hoffmann (2005); Cranford (2005); Bergen *et al.* (2005).

suggests that the answer is 'no, not necessarily'. As Wright-Neville has pointed out, the overwhelming majority of the Islamic groups in the Asia-Pacific region work as legitimate political organisations, operating within the domestic-political framework of the land, and are dedicated to supporting or altering or replacing the political hierarchy and its policies in their respective countries (2004: 32).

It is important to bear in mind that Islam has historically played a key role (and particularly so in Indonesia and Malaysia), not only during the struggles for independence from colonial rule, but also in the processes of nation-building in the post-colonial period, including post-Suharto democratisation developments in Indonesia. As Kikue Hamayotsu (2002) has shown in some detail, in both Malaysia and Indonesia a variety of Islamic forces, working across a wide range of ideological spectrums, have fashioned their visions of nationhood on ideological and institutional fronts. In the process, while some Islamic groups have sought the creation of an 'Islamic state' (a state system based on narrowly-interpreted Islamic canons and tradition), others have adopted a less dogmatic approach, seeking to establish a moral order inspired by Islamic principles, but within a tolerant religious or even secular or quasi-secular political structure.

Currently, what most of the so-called radical Islamic Political Parties in Indonesia and Malaysia are trying to achieve is to turn their populations' focus on infusing national politics with a greater Islamic 'flavour' (Kadir, 2004). This includes *Partai Persatuan Pembangunan* (PPP) and *Partai Bulan Bintang* (PBB) in Indonesia, and *Parti Islam Se-Malaysia* (PAS) in Malaysia. Of course, whether the Islamic 'flavour' sought by these political parties would continue to remain compatible with western democratic ideas, or, conversely, turn more radical (including trying to impose Shari'a), would primarily depend on these parties' political margin of manoeuvrability within the legal frameworks of their countries. However, any such increase or decrease in this political margin of manoeuvrability might occur, as anyone who understands the nature of Indonesian and Malaysian politics would confirm, not because of the changes in the general level of religiosity of the Indonesian and Malaysian Muslims. Rather, it might occur because of the changing political perceptions, knowledge, values and attitudes of the Indonesian and Malaysian electorates centring on the Indonesian and Malaysian polities.

For the reasons suggested above, it would be difficult—indeed impossible—to attempt to draw a connection, as Zachary Abuza has tried to do, between any rise of the so-called Islamist militancy (or, for that matter, radical Islam) in Indonesia and Malaysia, either with the state facilitation of the *Hajj* (the pilgrimage to Mecca) programs, or with the number of pilgrims from Indonesia and Malaysia going to Mecca for *Hajj* each year (2003: 17). It would be equally difficult—indeed pointless—to attempt to link any rise in the so-called Islamist militancy with either the broadcasting (up to five times a day) of Islamic prayers on TV in Indonesia, Malaysia, the Southern Philippines and Singapore, or with the region's telecasting of Arabic language lessons based solely on the reading of the Qur'an (Abuza, 2003: 14). It should be pointed out here, however, that Abuza's approach to these issues is not an isolated one. As David Wright-Neville (2004: 28) has indicated, a new orthodoxy has begun to emerge in western literature on terrorism, which not only seeks to link terrorism with a 'dangerous dynamic' inherent within Southeast Asian Islam, but also attempts to put forward the notion that if this dynamic is not checked with a counter-response by a hitherto reticent moderate Muslim majority, well-organised militant minorities may eventually come to control the domestic political agendas in both Indonesia and Malaysia. From there, it is claimed that such well-organised militant minorities may try to exert a troublesome influence on neighbouring countries, where Muslim minorities are from time to time involved in violent conflicts with non-Muslim majorities (Wright-Neville, 2004: 28).

The main problem with this new orthodoxy, however, is that it is not only totally ahistorical in its approach, but it also fails to take into account the sociology of the complexities involved in Muslim politics in Indonesia and Malaysia. Equally, it also fails to take into cognisance the basic theological debate underlining the important relationship between the religion of Islam and Islamic religiosity. In fact, if militant minorities do eventually come to control the domestic political agendas in Indonesia and Malaysia, this will happen not because of the changes in the religious practices of the Muslims of these countries, or in other aspects of their religiosity, but because of the changes in these states' internal domestic political dynamics, including legitimacy crises in their existing political institutions (Singh, 2004; Derichs, 2001). In Malaysia, for example, there has been a direct correlation between fluctuations in support for the PAS and the ruling coalition of *United Malays National Organization* (UMNO), with a backlash against UMNO in the aftermath of the ousting and subsequent arrest of former Deputy Prime Minister Anwar Ibrahim, and a resurgence in support for UMNO after changes in its leadership (Liow, 2004).

If the existing political structure of a given country makes it impossible for those organisations to operate within a political system due to the nature of the governance there, or due to the appropriation of its Islamic agendas by the state in order to promote the narrow domestic political interests of the ruling elites (as happened in Indonesia under Suharto[21] or in Pakistan under Zia-ul-Haq[22]), there is a danger that in such a situation some of these organisations may feel tempted to use extra-constitutional means, including resorting to violence, in order to force the state to accommodate their grievances. Equally, institutional failures in various states can also create fertile grounds for militant groups, including the radical elements at the fringes of national politics, to emerge as successful political players, no matter whether they are the Maoist revolutionaries of Nepal, the Islamist militants of the Moro Islamic Liberation Front (MILF) in the Philippines, or of the Pattani United Liberation Organisation (PULO) in Southern Thailand.[23]

A fertile ground for breeding radical Islamists at the fringes can also be created if, or when, the perceived geopolitical interests of a superpower (particularly when those interests are viewed mostly through thick doctrinal lenses) intermixes with the domestic political games of a dictator of a client state, and does so during any ongoing crisis of democratic transition. US-Pakistan relations are an interesting illustration of such a phenomenon, particularly during the rule of Zia-ul-Haq and the Soviet occupation of Afghanistan in the early 1980s, and again during the current Pakistani military dictatorship of Pervaiz Musharraf and the so-called US 'War on Terror' in the post-11 September era. Dennis Kux, a retired US State Department South Asia specialist who served three tours as a diplomat in Pakistan and

---

[21] Douglas E. Ramage (1995: 55) has analysed this issue in the context of Indonesia.
[22] Haleem (2003: 470) has elaborated on this.
[23] It should be noted in this context that 'institutional failure' has been defined here not only in terms of the inability of the state to ensure meaningful and extensive competition among individuals and organised groups, e.g., political parties, for all effective positions of government power at regular intervals but also in terms of the inability of the state to maintain its domination over the larger domain of the state without providing material incentives and rewards and/or resorting to coercion.

India, has provided us with a fascinating insight into this phenomenon in his article 'The Pakistani Pivot':

> On September 10, 2001, Pakistan was a country of secondary interest to the United States. Although it had been America's 'most allied ally in Asia' in the 1950s and an indispensable partner in the struggle against the Soviets in Afghanistan in the 1980s, the relationship unravelled after the Soviets pulled out of Afghanistan. In October 1990, the United States suspended economic and military aid under the Pressler amendment because Pakistan had developed nuclear weapons. Its May 1998 nuclear tests and the army's overthrow of the civilian government of Nawaz Sharif in October 1999 led to further sanctions against the one-time US ally... With the country drifting toward national failure, the worst-case fear was that, like its neighbour Afghanistan, Pakistan might be engulfed by Islamic fundamentalism. A Pakistan ruled by religious extremists and armed with nuclear weapons posed a nightmare scenario with ramifications far transcending South Asia... Amid such concern, Clinton's inability to produce a better US relationship with Pakistan inevitably left the impression that the United States was "tilting" toward India ... The new leadership in Washington [the administration of Bush Jr] soon made clear that its top priority in South Asia was to continue the process of improving relations with India. The events of September 11 have changed all that. Geography and history have once more made Pakistan important to US interests. Islamabad's support is required in order to deal with Osama bin Laden, his Arab terrorist colleagues in Al-Qaeda and their Taliban hosts. (2001a: 49-50)

What is this 'history' that Kux has referred to here? Of course, one aspect of it is that the history of American foreign policy is one of incoherence *par excellence*. But is there more to it than meets the eye? How, for example, were Afghanistan and Pakistan engulfed by 'Islamic fundamentalism'? Who created those 'fundamentalists', and then supported them, increasing their effectiveness and strength with a substantial arsenal of weapons, including Stinger shoulder-launched missiles? The answer must surely include a reference to the US's attempts to check the global outreach of the Soviet Union in the course of the Cold War.

A short lesson from history may be pertinent in helping to explain the background here. After the Soviet invasion of Afghanistan in 1979, which arguably received impetus from the 'pull effect' of undercover CIA operatives working in Pakistan, and charged with the task of destabilising the then pro-Soviet government in Kabul,[24] a group of so-called *mujahideen* (freedom fighters) was created with the help of fractious Afghan tribal warlords to fight and overthrow the communist government in Afhganistan. The Americans knew very well, as a CIA Pakistan station chief would later recall, that these warlords were 'all brutal, fierce, bloodthirsty, and basically fundamentalist. There were no Thomas Jeffersons on a white horse among the Afghan resistance leaders' (Kux, 2001b: 275). Still, the CIA, in connivance with the Pakistani intelligence agency, Inter Services Intelligence (ISI), armed and financed them (Kux, 2001b: 275).

In time, Saudi Arabia was also brought into the alliance against the Soviet Union's presence in Afghanistan, and especially so because of its willingness to match US funds to the *mujahideen*. Indeed, this was seen by Saudi Arabia as an ideal opportunity for it to gain

---

[24] Carter's National Security Advisor, Zbigniew Brzezinski (1998), openly admitted this possibility during an interview with the French newsmagazine *La Nouvel Observateur*. He told the reporter of the magazine: 'We didn't push the Russians to intervene, but we knowingly increased the probability that they would. The secret operation ... had the effect of drawing the Russians into the Afghan trap'.

influence in the region. With American knowledge (and most probably with its tacit encouragement), it was even able to import its own brand of ultra-conservative Islam—or *Wahabism* (currently much maligned by the western press and analysts)—to the refugee camps it was funding in Afghanistan (Rashid, 1999: 23). Saudi Arabia was also allowed by the United States, with the complicity of the then Pakistani military regime, to bring in hundreds of Islamist fundamentalists, not only from the Arab region, but also from other parts of the world (including Chechnya) to fight the 'holy war' against the 'infidel' communists in Afghanistan (Hartman, 2002: 471). However, as soon as the Soviet forces withdrew from Afghanistan, the United States simply abandoned Afghanistan in the midst of a brutal civil war between the same Afghan warlords who had earlier helped the United States to resist the Soviet invasion and to overthrow the pro-communist government in Kabul. In 1994, the Taliban, a group of *madrasah* (Islamic school) students mainly from refugee camps in Pakistan, organised a campaign to cleanse Afghanistan of the fighting warlords. But as the Taliban set out to conquer the whole of Afghanistan, the movement in effect became just another warlord party, and its draconian interpretation of Islamic law isolated it from the international community, its neighbours and, indeed, many Afghans (Rashid, 2001: 396). Despite all of these characteristics of the Taliban, the United States, driven primarily by its anti-Iranian policy and the subsequent desire to build pipelines from Central Asia to the Persian Gulf through Afghanistan, supported the Taliban regime until the Clinton administration's response to attacks on US embassies in Africa in the late 1990s. This is the same Taliban regime that, it was belatedly acknowledged after US cruise missile attacks, gave shelter to Osama bin Laden (Howard and Kwon, 1998: 6). The late Professor Eqbal Ahmad, in a presentation at the University of Colorado at Boulder on 12 October 1998, provided a fascinating illustration of how the United States participated in creating a monster that eventually turned against it:

> In 1985, President Ronald Reagan received a group of bearded men. These bearded men I was writing about in those days in *The New Yorker*, actually did [sic]. They were very ferocious-looking bearded men with turbans looking like they came from another century. President Reagan received them in the White House. After receiving them he spoke to the press. He pointed towards them. I'm sure some of you will recall that moment, and said, 'These are the moral equivalent of America's founding fathers'. These were the Afghan *mujahideen*. They were at the time, guns in hand, battling the Evil Empire. They were the moral equivalent of our founding fathers!
>
> In August 1998, another American President ordered missile strikes from the American navy based in the Indian Ocean to kill Osama bin Laden and his men in the camps in Afghanistan. I do not wish to embarrass you with the reminder that Mr bin Laden, whom fifteen American missiles were fired to hit in Afghanistan [sic], was only a few years ago the moral equivalent of George Washington and Thomas Jefferson! He got angry over the fact that he has been demoted from 'Moral Equivalent' of our 'Founding Fathers'. So he is taking [out] his anger in different ways.

The situation described by Professor Ahmed is a classic instance of the 'chickens coming home to roost'. As a US diplomat in Pakistan pointed out a few years ago, 'You can't plug billions of dollars into an anti-communist jihad, accept participation from all over the world, and ignore the consequences' (cited in Rashid, 1999: 23). Ironically, Andrei Gromyko, the longest serving Soviet Foreign Minister, was quite prophetic when he termed the short-sighted US foreign policy in Afghanistan as being akin to 'lending your house to bandits to fire on the neighbours' (cited in Kux, 2001b: 270). Furthermore, it was not a lesson well learned by the US: there is every indication that another ideology-driven, short-sighted US foreign policy towards, and invasions of, Afghanistan and Iraq (in 2001 and 2003 respectively) may well have created more fertile soil for breeding Islamist militants in those states.[25] Of course, this may have happened on this occasion not because of the monsters created by the US, but because of the ongoing obstacles to the nation-building processes of these states, which have in effect been shattered by circumstances resulting from the implementation there of US foreign policy.

CONCLUSION

As the foregoing discussion suggests, a proper understanding of the phenomenon surrounding the rise of contemporary Islamic fundamentalism, particularly in its most violent forms, would become possible only if we could provide a judicious, but at the same time a concurrent, analysis of both the multi-dimensional crisis of the Muslim world, resulting from its supposed significant deficiencies in modernisation and democratisation, and existing geopolitics, and particularly so with regard to US global hegemony (no matter whether the latter is seen as benign or imperial), which is accused by many Muslims of perpetuating an unjust international order.[26]

However, it is also important to keep in mind in this context that the alleged deficiencies in modernisation and democratisation in many Muslim countries may have more to do with the inner dynamics of post-colonial nation-building than the political doctrines of Islam *per se*. Perhaps, in a post-colonial milieu, these Muslim states are experiencing (at times in similar and sometimes in dissimilar ways) the same tensions and conflicts that generally accompany the interactions between tradition and change in all societies in times of transition. As John Esposito has pointed out (1997: 13-15), the west and Christianity have also experienced centuries-long struggles as a result of the political revolutions that accompanied the emergence of modern western states and societies in the period of the Reformation (the latter, of course, including warfare as well as theological disputation).

Put in that perspective, there may not be any necessary correlation between an individual's, group's or organisation's efforts to reappropriate and reinvent concepts from its fundamental traditions for attaining its political objectives, and its resorting to violence to achieve that very same purpose. A correlation may, however, emerge if, for example, the relevant people perceive that their efforts have become severely restricted by a lack of freedom or autonomy, either in the national or in the global arena. It is precisely in this context that one has to take into consideration both the role of the civil society at the national level, and the impact of the unchecked power and influence of a hegemonic state at the global level.

---

[25] The 16-Nation Pew Global Attitudes Survey released on 23 June 2005 shows that anti-Americanism in Europe, the Middle East and Asia has surged as a result of the US-led war in Iraq. The United States remains broadly disliked in most countries surveyed. The magnitude of America's image problem is such that even popular US policies have done little to repair it. For details, see Pew Research Center (2005).

[26] For further elaborations on this issue, see Kevin Clements (2004); Nye (2004); Korb *et al.* (2005).

REFERENCES

Abuza, Zachary (2003) *Militant Islam in Southeast Asia: Crucible of Terror*, Boulder, Colorado: Lynne Rienner Publishers, Inc.

Ahmad, Eqbal (1998) *Terrorism: Theirs and Ours*, A Presentation at the University of Colorado, Boulder, 12 October, 1998http://www.sangam.org/ANALYSIS/Ahmad.htm

Ayubi, N. (1991) *Political Islam: Religion and Politics in the Arab World*, London: Routledge.

Barber, Benjamin (1996) *Jihad vs. McWorld: How Globalism and Tribalism are Reshaping the World*, New York: Ballantine Books.

Barton, Greg (2004) *Indonesia's Struggle: Jemaah Islamiyah and the Soul of Islam*, Sydney: UNSW Press.

Bergen, D.C. *et al.* (2005) 'The Terri Schiavo Case: An Exchange'. *The New York Review of Books*, 52(13): 323-327.

Berman, Paul (2004) *Terror and Liberalism*, New York: W.W. Norton and Company.

Bodansky, Yossef (1999) *Bin Laden: The Man Who Declared War on America*, New York: Forum.

Brzezinski, Zbigniew (1998) *La Nouvel Observateur*, 15-21 January.

Buruma, Ian and Avishai Margalit's (2002) 'Occidentalism'. *New York Review of Books*, 17 January.

Camus, Albert (1951) *L'Homme révolté*, Paris: Peregrine.

Chomsky, Noam (1991) *Deterring Democracy*, London: Verso.

—— (2001) *9-11*, New York: Seven Stories Press.

Choueri, Youssef (1997) *Islamic Fundamentalism*, London: Pinter.

Clarke, Peter (ed.) (1988) *Islam*, The World's Religions series, London: Routledge.

Clements, Kevin (2004) 'Response to Terrorism in America'. *Social Alternatives*, 23(2): 41-43.

Cranford, Ronald (2005) 'Facts, Lies, and Videotapes: The Permanent Vegetative State and the Sad Case of Terri Schiavo'. *Journal of Law, Medicine and Ethics*, 33(2): 363-371.

Danner, Mark (2001) 'The Battlefield for the American Mind'. *New York Times*, 16 October.

Dalacoura, Katerina (2003 Revised Edition) *Islam, Liberalism & Human Rights*, London: I. B. Tauris.

Derichs, Claudia (2001) 'A Step Forward: Malaysian Ideas for Political Change'. *JAAS*, 37(1): 43-65.

Devine, Frank (2001) 'Where is the Muslim Coalition Against Terrorism'. *The Australian*, 1 November.

Dodds, Klaus (2005) *Global Geopolitics: A Critical Introduction*, London: Pearson/ Prentice Hall.

Economist (2001) Special Report 'Islam's tensions'. 22-28 September.

Esposito, John L. (1997) 'Islam and Christianity Face to Face'. *Commonwealth*, 124(2): 11-16.

Feder, Don (2001) *Insight*, 5 November. Cited in Ziauddin Sardar and Merryl Wyn Davies (2002) *Why Do People Hate America?* Sydney: Allen and Unwin.

Fukuyama, Francis (2001) 'The West has Won'. *Guardian*, 11 October: 21.

Gerecht, Reuel (2002) 'The Future of bin Ladenism'. *New York Times*, 11 January.

Gerges, Fawaz A. (1999) *America and Political Islam: Clash of Cultures or Clash of Interests?* New York: Cambridge University Press.

Gunaratna, Rohan (2002) *Inside Al Qaeda: Global Network of Terror*, New York: Columbia University Press.

Habermas, Jürgen (1989) *The New Conservatism*, Cambridge: Polity Press.

Haleem, Irm (2003) 'Ethnic and Sectarian Violence and the Propensity Towards Praetorianism in Pakistan'. *Third World Quarterly*, 24(3): 463-477.

Halliday, Fred (1994) 'The Politics of Islamic Fundamentalism: Iran, Tunisia and the Challenge to the Secular State'. In Akbar S. Ahmed and Hastings Donnan (eds), *Islam, Globalization and Modernity*, London: Routledge: 91-113.

Hamayotsu, Kikue (2002) 'Islam and Nation Building in Southeast Asia: Malaysia and Indonesia in Comparative Perspective'. *Pacific Affairs*, 75(3): 355-375.

Hanson, Victor David (2002) 'Defending the West: Why the Muslims Misjudge Us'. *City Journal*, 25 (February).

Hartman, Andrew (2002) '"The Red Template": US Policy in Soviet-Occupied Afghanistan'. *Third World Quarterly*, 23(3): 467-489.

Henderson, Errol A. and Richard Tucker (1999) 'Clear and Present Strangers: The Clash of Civilisations and International Conflicts'. Paper presented at the annual conference of the American Political Science Association, Atlanta, 2-5 September.

Hersh, Seymour (1998) *The Dark Side of Camelot*, London: HarperCollins.

Gregg Hoffmann (2005) 'Symbolism and the Terri Schiavo Case'. *ETC: A Review of General Semantics*, 62(3): 323-326.

Howard, Lucy and Beth Kwon (1998) 'Costly Missiles Strikes'. *Newsweek*, 132(23): 6.

Hughes, Gary (2003) 'Analyse This'. *The Age* (Melbourne), 20 July.

Huntington, Samuel P. (1993) 'The Clash of Civilisations'. *Foreign Affairs*, 72(3): 22-48.

────── (1996) *The Clash of Civilizations and the Remaking of World Order*, New York: Simon and Schuster.

Johnson, Chalmers (2000) *Blowback: The Costs and Consequences of American Empire*, London: Time Warner Books.

────── (2003) *Blowback: The Costs and Consequences of American Empire*, Revised Edition, London: Time Warner Paperbacks.

Jones, David Martin (2003) 'Out of Bali: Cybercaliphate Rising'. *The National Interest*, Spring Issue: 75-85.

Kadir, Suzaina (2004) 'Mapping Muslim politics in Southeast Asia after September 11', *The Pacific Review*, 17(2): 198-222.

Kaplan, Robert (1993) *Balkan Ghosts*, New York: St Martin's Press.

────── (2000) *The Coming of Anarchy*, New York: Random House.

Kepel, Gilles (2004) *The War for Muslim Minds: Islam and the West*, Cambridge, Massachusetts: Harvard University Press.

Klein, Naomi (2005) 'You Break It, You Pay For It'. *The Nation*, 10 January.

Korb, Lawrence J., Robert O. Boorstin and the National Security Staff of the Center for American Progress (2005) *Integrated Power: A National Security Strategy for the 21st Century*, Washington, DC: Center for American Progress.

Kramer, Martin (2001) *Ivory Towers on Sand: The Failure of Middle Eastern Studies in America*, Washington, DC: Washington Institute of Near East Policy.

Kurlantzick, Joshua (2001) 'Civil Society: Dhaka Dispatch'. *New Republic*, 225(20): 20-21.

Kurtz, Stanley (2002) 'The Future of "History": Francis Fukuyama vs. Samuel P. Huntington', *Policy Review*, June/July: 43-58.

Kux, Dennis (2001a) 'The Pakistani Pivot'. *The National Interest*, Thanksgiving Issue: 49-59.

────── (2001b) *The United States and Pakistan, 1947-2000: Disenchanted Allies*, Washington, DC: Woodrow Wilson Center Press.

Lapidus, Ira M. (1988) *A History of Islamic Societies*, Cambridge: Cambridge University Press.

Lewis, Bernard (1988) *The Political Economy of Islam*, Chicago: University of Chicago Press.

────── (2001a) *Islam in History: Ideas, People, and Events in the Middle East*, London: Open Court.

────── (2001b) 'The Roots of Muslim Rage', *Policy*, 17(4): 17-28.

────── (2002) 'Targeted by a History of Hatred: The United States is Now the Unquestioned Leader of the Free World, also Known as the Infidels'. *The Washington Post*, 10 September.

────── (2003) *What Went Wrong? Western Impact and Middle Eastern Response*, London: Phoenix.

Liow, Joseph Chinyong (2004) 'Political Islam in Malaysia: Problematising Discourse and Practice in the UMNO-PAS "Islamisation Race"'. *Commonwealth & Comparative Politics*, 42(2): 184-205.

Millard, Mike (2003) *Jihad in Paradise: Islam and Politics in Southeast Asia*, London: M.E. Sharpe.

Moghissi, Haideh (2000) *Feminism and Islamic Fundamentalism: The Limits of Postmodern Analysis*, Dhaka: University Press Ltd.

Nye, Joseph S., Jr. (2004) 'Soft Power and American Foreign Policy'. *Political Science Quarterly*, 119(2): 255-270.

Patai, Raphael (1973) *The Arab Mind*, New York: Scribner.

Pew Research Center (2005) *American Character Gets Mixed Reviews: US Image Up Slightly, But Still Negative*, The Pew Global Attitudes Project, 16-Nation Pew Global Attitudes Survey, Washington, DC.

Pieterse, Jan N. (1994) 'Fundamentalism Discourses: Enemy Images'. *Women Against Fundamentalism Journal*, 5: 2-6. E-text at http://waf.gn.apc.org/j5p2.htm

Pipes, Daniel (2000) 'Islam and Islamism: Faith and Ideology'. *The National Interest*, Spring Issue: 87-93.

────── (2001) 'The Danger Within'. *Commentary*, November: 19-24.

────── (2004) 'Stealth Islamist: Khaled Abou El Fadl', *Middle East Quarterly*, Spring Issue, http://www.meforum.org/article/602

Pipes, Daniel and Jonathan Schanzer (2002) 'Militant Islam's New Stronghold'. *Human Events*, 58(42): 13-14.

Rabasa, A.M. (2003) 'Political Islam in Southeast Asia: Moderates, Radicals and Terrorists'. *Adelphi Paper* 358, London: International Institute for Strategic Studies.

Ramage, Douglas E. (1995) *Politics in Indonesia: Democracy, Islam and the Ideology of Tolerance*, London: Routledge.

Rashid, Ahmed (1999) 'The Taliban: Exporting Extremism'. *Foreign Affairs*, Nov/Dec: 22-35.

——— (2001) 'Afghanistan: Ending the Policy Quagmire'. *Journal of International Affairs*, 54(2): 395-410.
Roy, Olivier (2004), *Globalised Islam: The Search for a New Ummah*, London: Hurst and Company.
Rushdie, Salman (2001) 'Yes, This is about Islam'. *New York Times*, 2 November.
Sadowski, Yahia (1993) 'The New Orientalism and the Democracy Debate'. *Middle East Report*, 183: 14.
Said, Edward (2001) 'The Clash of Ignorance'. *The Nation*, 22 October: 9-12.
Sardar, Ziauddin and Merryl Wyn Davies (2002) *Why Do People Hate America*, Sydney: Allen and Unwin.
Schmitt, Carl (1979) *Der Begriff des Politischen*, Text von 1932 mit einem Vorwort und drei Corollarien von Carl Schmitt, Berlin: Duncker and Humblot.
Singh, Bilveer (2004) 'The Challenge of Militant Islam and Terrorism in Indonesia'. *Australian Journal of International Affairs*, 58(1): 47-68.
Stark, Jan (2004) 'Contesting Models of Islamic Governance in Malaysia and Indonesia'. *Global Change, Peace & Security*, 16(2): 115-131.
Strauss, Leo (1995) 'Jerusalem and Athens: Some Preliminary Reflections'. In S. Orr (ed.), *Jerusalem and Athens: Reason and Revelation in the Works of Leo Strauss*, Lanham, Maryland: Rowman and Littlefield: 179-208.
Tassel, Janet (2005) 'Militant about "Islamism"', *Harvard Magazine*, 107(3): 38-47.
Turner, Bryan S. (2002) 'Sovereignty and Emergency: Political Theology, Islam and American Conservatism'. *Theory, Culture & Society*, 19(4): 103-119.
US Department of State (2002) *Bangladesh: Country Reports on Human Rights Practices—2001*, Released by the Bureau of Democracy, Human Rights, and Labor, Washington, DC, 4 March.
——— (2003) *Bangladesh: Country Reports on Human Rights Practices—2002*, Released by the Bureau of Democracy, Human Rights, and Labor, Washington, DC, 31 March.
Wakim, Joseph (2004) 'To Bush, the Arab is Always the Villain'. *The Age* (Melbourne), 11 May.
Westerlund, D. and I. Svanberg (eds) (1999) *Islam Outside the Arab World*, London: Curzon.
Wright-Neville, David (2004) 'Dangerous Dynamics: Activists, Militants and Terrorists in Southeast Asia', *The Pacific Review*, 17(1): 27-46.

Part II. Response and Options
The Cold War Superpowers

In: Asia-Pacific and a New International Order
Editors: Purnendra Jain et al. pp. 91-107
ISBN 1-59454-986-9
© 2006 Nova Science Publishers, Inc.

Chapter 6

POST-COLD WAR US FOREIGN POLICY IN ASIA

William T. Tow

INTRODUCTION

During the past fifteen years, the United States' policy in the Asia-Pacific has been increasingly ambiguous and largely reactive to unexpected events that have shaped that region's security environment. As a result, American influence in the region may well have been undermined. While US power remains predominant in the 'hard power' sector of military strength, American politico-diplomatic and economic clout is now increasingly being contested by China's 'peaceful rise' and by regionally indigenous forces that view the United States' culture and values as less relevant to their own aspirations and visions for a future Asia-Pacific order. This outcome is far from what US President George H.W. Bush had in mind when he declared a 'new world order' after leading a successful coalition of forces to liberate Kuwait from Iraqi occupation (George H.W. Bush, 1991).

Why has this happened? During the Cold War, the US pursued a strategy of global containment against the Soviet Union with an Asia-Pacific component that was clear to all. Washington successfully underwrote Japan's economic reconstruction and the development of the region's newly industrialised economies. It extended bilateral security guarantees and ensured Asian allied access to the vast US marketplace. It led a United Nations force to defend South Korea following North Korea's June 1950 invasion of the South and China's intervention on Pyongyang's behalf six months later. Although the merit of America's subsequent military intervention in Indochina remains highly debatable, it did provide the rest of Southeast Asia with the time needed to forge its own economic and strategic future through the creation of the Association of Southeast Asian Nations (ASEAN). The Nixon Doctrine and US diplomatic overtures to China were decisive adaptations of US post-war strategy to produce regional and global structural change. They facilitated a gradual modification of Soviet economic and strategic behaviour that ultimately spelled the end of Soviet-American hegemonic competition.

Since the USSR's demise, however, American geopolitical objectives have been less clear and their results less evident. Much of the United States' military power has been redirected from the European and Asia-Pacific theatres to quell crises or fight wars in the Persian Gulf and Central Asia. This process intensified following September 11 and the launching of a Global War on Terror (GWOT) by the second President Bush. The 1997-1998 Asian financial crisis emerged at a time when many Asian elites and populaces were already questioning how US and western values could be reconciled with their own cultures and aspirations. A perceived hardline US response to their temporary economic plight reinforced this sense of alienation and prompted Asian initiatives to pursue more inclusive forms of institutionalisation and regional order-building. The December 2005 Asian summit in Kuala Lumpur can be regarded as a short-term culmination of this process.

This chapter will assert that the policies of the Clinton and George W. Bush administrations have produced a mixed record in terms of US influence in the Asia-Pacific region, but that it is possible for the United States to establish a more positive legacy over the next ten to fifteen years. First, it will briefly review key factors that have eroded US influence in the region since the advent of the Clinton presidency. This will be followed by an assessment of looming major challenges in the Asia-Pacific for current US policy interests and the United States politico-strategic role there. A final section will offer some regional policy recommendations for the future American administrations as they endeavour to identify and implement an 'end-game' to the U.S. occupation of Iraq and to define and implement US global strategy. The sustaining of American influence in what is arguably the world's most dynamic region cannot be overemphasised.

AMERICAN GEOPOLITICAL DECLINE?

The Soviet Union's demise at the end of 1991 spelled the end of the United States' post-war containment strategy and prompted American policy planners to revise their national security posture. Containment had been predicated on maintaining American strategic preponderance over its major Cold War competitor by exercising US military, economic and normative leadership over key allied states in Europe and Asia. Without a superpower rival, debate ensued over the degree to which strategic primacy was still relevant to US interests. Neo-conservative American advocates of 'unipolarity' argued that other 'large industrial nations' should be discouraged from contesting US global supremacy and leadership of the international order (Krauthammer, 1990/1991; Taylor, 1992). Critics argued, however, that the US would be better served by focusing on 'economic security' at home and economic interdependence abroad, and relying upon more conventional power balancing strategies to ensure international stability (Layne, 1993).

The Clinton administration embraced the second approach. In a definitive report on the US national security strategy released in October 1998, the president insisted that the US must 'harness the forces of global integration' by bolstering its own economic prosperity, promoting democracy abroad and ensuring its fundamental values remained intact. The United States' 'vital interests' would be pursued as a judicious combination of engagement strategies designed to underpin arms control agreements (especially against weapons of mass destruction [WMD] or their proliferation by 'rogue states'), by promotion of humanitarian causes and by application of the politics of 'human security' in response to the rising challenges of environmental degradation, resource distribution, terrorism and international crime (Clinton, 1998). In the Asia-Pacific, this strategy primarily translated into deterring hostile actions in 'critical localised areas' while maintaining capability for rapid major crisis response. A 'Comprehensive Engagement Presence Plus' posture for the region called for the retention of approximately 100,000 military personnel and an extensive US basing and access network within friendly states. Perhaps most importantly, it involved cultivating comprehensive engagement with China to facilitate its emergence 'as a stable, secure, open, prosperous and peaceful country' and its 'role as a responsible member of the international community'. Bill Clinton's summits with Chinese President Jiang Zemin in 1997 and 1998 underscored the centrality of comprehensive engagement in his administration's overall geopolitical strategy. By pursuing engagement in the Asia-Pacific, the Pentagon insisted, 'US security strategy in the...region reflects and supports our global security strategy' (US Department of Defense, 1998).

At least three developments emerged during Clinton's watch to seriously challenge its Asia-Pacific strategy and US regional influence: the Korean nuclear crisis in late 1994; the Asian financial crisis in 1997-98 and turbulence in Southeast Asia that was reflected by the East Timor crisis; and, more recently, by terrorist uprisings throughout the sub-region. Washington either failed to anticipate and respond sufficiently to these crises, or the US pursued its normative preferences far too rigidly. By the end of Clinton's second term of office, Republican campaign foreign policy spokespersons could claim with justification that rampant internationalism had superseded the pursuit of a well-articulated and clearly understood US national security strategy. They successfully postulated that 'multilateral agreements and institutions should not be ends in themselves...the Clinton administration has often been so anxious to find multilateral solutions to problems that it has signed agreements that are not in America's interest' (Rice, 2000).

The Korean Nuclear Crisis and 'Functional Multilateralism'

Bill Clinton's presidency was marked at the outset by a greater affinity than its predecessor had for US support for and involvement in East Asian regionalism (USIA, 1993). However, the new administration's initial optimism that bodies such as the ASEAN Regional Forum (ARF) or the Asia Pacific Economic Cooperation (APEC) summit would usher in a vigorous era of Asia-Pacific multilateralism was soon dashed. Requiring unanimity in its decision-making, and failing even to make use of ASEAN's own High Council to resolve regional disputes, the ARF soon became perceived in many quarters to be little more than a regional 'talk shop', while APEC became embroiled in protecting its economic agenda of 'open regionalism' against more exclusivist regional trade initiatives (Green, 2001, 35-36; Dorsch, 2003; Garofano, 1999; Green, 2001; Lim, 1998).

The Korean nuclear crisis, which intensified from 1994 onward, prompted the Clinton administration to favour 'functional multilateralism' as an approach to Asia-Pacific regional security. Michael Green has described functional multilateralism as 'multilateralism that achieves finite and clear objectives' (Green, 2001: 36). In responding to the nuclear crisis precipitated by the Democratic People's Republic of Korea (DPRK), the US and its security allies created the Korea Energy Development Organization (KEDO) in 1995 as an extension of the 'Agreed Framework' reached between Washington and Pyongyang the previous year: the US, Japan, South Korea and other concerned states would supply non-weapons grade nuclear energy, heavy oil deliveries and other energy-related capabilities to North Korea in return for the North's adherence to the nuclear non-proliferation regime. Other examples of multilateral or 'minilateral' initiatives relating to the Korean Peninsula included the US-Japan-ROK Trilateral Oversight Group created in 1998 after a North Korean missile launch and the Four Party Talks, convened intermittently between 1997 and 1999. In July 2000, the North Koreans were even induced to join the ARF and its foreign minister met US Secretary of State Madeline Albright at the ARF Ministerial Meeting in Bangkok for an informal discussion on her forthcoming visit to Pyongyang that October. US and North Korean officials held further discussions regarding missile production issues at another ARF conclave held in Kuala Lumpur in November, and came close to agreeing on a more permanent formula for limiting North Korean missile testing and missile exports.

In retrospect, however, functional multilateralism enjoyed no more success than other US policy approaches that have been previously employed for defusing North Korean hostilities. US sanctions against North Korea remained in place during most of Clinton's presidency. They were lifted only partially when the DPRK's incessant food shortages intensified into a fully-fledged famine precipitated by substantial flooding in that country during the latter 1990s. They were modified once again in 1999 in return for a North Korean promise to suspend long-range missile testing. Yet suspicion mounted during Clinton's last two years in office that, despite its economic doldrums and the resource disasters suffered by its populace, North Korea was systematically violating the Agreed Framework (Samore, 2003: 10-11). North Korean officials constantly attacked the US for delays in the construction of nuclear reactors authorised by the Agreed Framework and for delays in shipments of heavy fuel oil (although KEDO had overall supplied $US 167 million in fuel oil by early 2000). The Four Power Talks stalled over differences about what steps toward peace on the Korean Peninsula would be negotiated first: a US-North Korean bilateral peace treaty and the withdrawal of US forces from South Korea (North Korea's demands), or initial confidence-building measures that would lead to a peace agreement eventually replacing the 1953 Korean War armistice (the American position). The June 2000 bilateral summit between the North and South Korean heads of state generated a brief flurry of optimism that a political breakthrough was imminent. However, the initial euphoria and expectations flowing from South Korean President Kim Dae-jung's 'Sunshine Policy' were soon dampened by a new round of intra-Korean tensions and by the incoming Bush administration's unmitigated hostility toward the North Korean leadership.

Engagement is often cited as the Clinton administration's predominant strategy toward North Korea. Proponents of this approach have argued that it represented a far superior approach to coercion postures adopted by both the preceding and subsequent Bush administrations. They posit that it synthesised the pursuit of bilateral US-North Korean relations within a broader regional and international context via the Agreed Framework and KEDO, and achieved mutual accountability in the United States' and North Korea's behaviour toward each other through the Perry process. Desaix Anderson, Executive Director of KEDO from 1998-2001, has argued that: 'Although we had witnessed in the past sporadic cases of North Korean efforts to reach out to the international community, this was the first time where all efforts appeared to converge and suggested turning the DPRK from a dangerous wildcard into a less menacing and perhaps more constructive member of the community of Northeast Asia' (Anderson, 2003).

Opponents of the Clinton record on the DPRK countered that the administration's overall tendency to oscillate in its national security policy was clearly reflected in its approach to the North Korean problem. In late 1994 North Korea's offensive postures and insensitive bargaining tactics had pushed the US into a dangerous corner, and the US was only hours away from initiating a war with the North (Sigal, 1997). Following former President Jimmy Carter's last-minute intercession, the Framework Agreement was poorly negotiated and even more weakly enforced. This permitted North Korea to effectively undercut that accord and continue its covert pursuit of a nuclear weapons program. It also allowed the North to drive a wedge in the US-South Korean alliance, exacerbate Japanese feelings of abandonment by its American ally, and grind the Four Power Talks down toward an unsuccessful conclusion in 1999. These setbacks overshadowed the modest progress in US-North Korean bilateral ties following the implementation of the Perry process—progress that proved to be fragile and short-lived when the North Koreans responded so negatively to the new Bush administration's announcement to undertake a policy review on the US-DPRK relationship (Crispin and Shim, 1999; Mann, 2001).

The Asian Financial Crisis

Midway through 1997, the Asian financial crisis exploded onto the world scene. It was initially caused by the exposure of overvalued Asian currencies, such as the Thai baht and South Korean won, to unsustainable short-term foreign debt. The crisis soon threatened the region's overall security by undermining its social stability and economic growth. As a US Institute for Peace report warned in early 1998, the crisis tested the United States' 'long term capacity and willingness to extend its role in the region to that of [an] economic as well as [a] political and security stabilizer...' (Snyder and Solomon, 1998). The risk was that, if the United States failed to be sensitive to the region's 'dependence' and unpredictable global financial system it would be targeted, along with the International Monetary Fund (IMF) that it was seen to effectively control, by an embittered nationalist backlash. It would also be accused of putting the interests of US financial concerns ahead of regional economic recovery. As one critic of American economic liberalisation policies in the region observed, '[r]ather than trying to address the social costs of the crisis, Washington [was perceived as] focused on pursuing policy reforms that would enable US corporations to pick at the choice carcasses of Asia's economic crisis' (Gershman cited in Taylor, 2004: 468).

How well the Clinton administration responded to the crisis has been the subject of inconclusive debate. Administration spokespersons such as Stuart E. Eizenstadt, Undersecretary for Economic, Business and Agricultural Affairs, insisted that their efforts pursued the right course by supporting IMF packages for structural reforms 'to help the affected Asian economies recover' (Eisenstadt, 1998). The US initiated regular meetings of Asian financial ministers to implement surveillance measures against short-term currency flows. After initially declining to participate in the 1997 IMF relief package for Thailand, the US extended $US 1 billion in Export-Import Bank credits to Thailand. Washington also pressured international banks to reschedule South Korea's private debt loans along more generous lines (Dibb, Hale and Prince, 1998: 20; Scott and Solomon, 1998). Altogether, the IMF provided $US 35 billion of financial support for reform programs in Indonesia, Korea and Thailand during 1997. In tandem with the Clinton administration, it spearheaded $US 77 billion of additional financing. In July 1998, assistance for Indonesia was augmented by an additional $US 1.3 billion from the IMF and an estimated $US 5 billion from other sources (International Monetary Fund, 1999). Currency exchange rates in the region were substantially stabilised by mid-1998, interest rates began descending from record highs in Thailand and South Korea by the same time, and structural reforms encouraging macroeconomic stabilisation were well in place by the end of that year. By the end of 1998, many observers had concluded that the financial crisis had demonstrated that the United States remained 'the essential economic, political and security stabiliser in Asia' and that US Congressional support for economic and political transparency in IMF operations during the crisis was a constructive development within the overall US policy response (Snyder and Solomon, 1998).

Other analysts, however, took a more critical view of the US role in the crisis. They argued that relentless American pressure upholding the neo-liberal model of market deregulation and more globalisation was counter-productive. Regional political leaders such as Malaysia's Prime Minister Mahathir defied 'western' prescriptions for reform that he believed were integral to the IMF rescue packages. He instead implemented even greater capital controls in his country (including pulling the Malaysian ringgit from international markets) as a defence of 'Asian values' against those western currency traders he believed were undermining Asia's smaller economies (Taylor, 2004: 468). Perceptions of American efforts to prop up APEC's 'open regionalism' ethos at the expense of Asian economies were strengthened by Washington's refusal to support the 'Miyazawa Initiative' by Japan to create an Asian Monetary Fund (AMF). Many within the region opposed the Japanese proposal for historical and political reasons. This US position nonetheless served as a catalyst for the ten ASEAN members to invite Chinese, Japanese and South Korean delegates to ASEAN's leaders' summit in November 1997 to commence negotiations for a more exclusivist, intra-regional set of regional economic arrangements. Subsequent meetings of the 'ASEAN+3' led to the May 2000 'Chiang Mai Initiative', where measures were announced to advance East Asian cooperation in areas of finance and trade (Henning, 2002: 11-21). China's participation in this process was especially significant. Its 'holding of the yuan' during the financial crisis was viewed favourably by US policy officials. By comparison, Japan's failure to stimulate its own economic recovery during the early 1990s was viewed as a major reason for the region's economic crisis. Its proposal for an AMF was regarded as detrimental to Asia's need to engage in structural reform (Snyder and Solomon, 1998).

The Clinton administration approached the Asian financial crisis with two key assumptions: (1) US leadership was mandatory for containing the crisis in ways that were consistent with US values relating to sustaining open markets and modifying assertive nationalism in the region; and (2) there were two additional policy 'hazards' that had to be overcome: (a) regional political resentment against the US for bailing out foreign investors and political leaders who adhered to the 'Washington Consensus' of neo-liberal globalisation that went against predominant Asia-Pacific 'values'; and (b) the perception that only US businesses would ultimately gain from applying IMF-directed reforms (Eisenstadt, 1998; Snyder and Solomon, 1998; Shorrock, 1998).

In retrospect, the big winner in the crisis was not the United States but China. It only needed to exercise restraint on its currency valuation to assist other Asian states' export capabilities and extend minimal assistance to its regional neighbours ($US 1 billion to Thailand and a commensurate amount to Indonesia). Chinese leaders correctly viewed the financial crisis as an opportunity to enhance China's standing at small cost to itself and at the expense of the US-led global financial system (Halloran, 1998).

China was able to drive a wedge between US and regional economic philosophies and to underwrite Asian initiatives to pursue inclusive models of regional economic integration. This was hardly the outcome anticipated by Washington's economic policy planners. Contrary to the US reasserting its influence through the application of a neo-liberal economic strategy in Asia, the United States precipitated an exclusivist backlash by Malaysia and, to a lesser extent, by the other ASEAN member-states, an opportunistic Chinese posture of regional economic collusion, and a propensity by Japan to hedge its bets between the region's various economic players. The ultimate loser was APEC. It had been created in 1989 to institutionalise American prescriptions of open regionalism throughout Asia, but had been impeded from the outset by the impossible task of reconciling contending models of an exclusivist Asia—and American liberal internationalism. As the Clinton administration prepared to leave office, its vision of multilateralism was, ironically, giving way to America's own brand of exclusivism in the region: a strengthening of bilateral security alliances and a focus on bilateral trading arrangements.

Southeast Asian Turbulence: A Multilateral Remedy?

Along with the Korean nuclear crisis and the Asian financial crisis, the Clinton administration grappled with how the United States should respond to burgeoning East Asia's multilateral security politics. The president initially set a positive tone on this issue by endorsing the idea of a 'Pacific Community' in a speech at Waseda University, Tokyo, during July 1993. Multilateralism, along with more open regional economies and the evolution of more democratic Asia-Pacific governments, would constitute the Clinton administration's fundamental policy approach toward the Asia-Pacific (Clinton, 1993). While the president cited APEC as the key instrument for establishing regional multilateral dialogues, his Assistant Secretary of State for East Asian and Pacific Affairs, Winston Lord, earmarked the ARF as the major venue. The US Department of State website insists that the Clinton administration played 'an active role' in the establishment of the ARF during 1994 (US Department of State, 2004).

In retrospect, the Clinton administration's endorsement of multilateral security in Asia was part of a larger strategic decision—to engage China rather than to contain it. If China could be persuaded to participate in regional forums on the basis of 'accepting international norms of acceptable behaviour', a new cold war between Beijing and Washington might be avoided. Yet the main business in Sino-American relations was conducted at the bilateral level, with the Clinton-Jiang summits of 1997 and 1998 leading to the (somewhat hyperbolic) heralding of a new bilateral 'strategic partnership'. US bilateral alliances, moreover, were still designated as the key to sustaining the traditional American extended deterrence posture in the region. There were clear limits to how far multilateralism could be reconciled with bilateralism's traditional hub and spokes framework, which Evelyn Goh has termed 'unreconciled duality' (Goh, 2004). Yet the Clinton administration worked at finding the 'correct balance' between bilateral and multilateral components within that policy, even after the Korean nuclear crisis and the Taiwan Strait confrontations with China in 1994 and 1996 reaffirmed the centrality of the US extended deterrence strategy through its traditional bilateral alliance network. *Ad hoc* multilateralism was verbally endorsed and supported during that administration's later years.

Perhaps the most significant test for this approach was the East Timor crisis in 1999. Military intervention was authorised by the United Nations for humanitarian purposes, a decision fully commensurate with the Clinton administration's previous application of humanitarian intervention in Bosnia and Kosovo. Having never accepted Indonesia's occupation of East Timor as legitimate, and in possession of growing evidence of atrocities committed by pro-Indonesian militia forces after the East Timorese voted for secession from Indonesia, the UN overrode ASEAN's traditional aversion to interference in the internal affairs of member-states by outside parties (Cotton, 2001). The latter factor, however, resonated among various sectors of the US policymaking community. They were anxious not to alienate Indonesia as ASEAN's key player over a traditionally contested and geopolitically insignificant East Timorese separatist movement. Moreover, Bill Clinton was facing Congressional resistance to any further US force commitments to far-flung crisis points. The Republican Party was building a case that his past episodes of humanitarian intervention failed to equate to America's core national security interests (Bell, 2000: 173). The prevailing US sentiment was expressed by veteran Asian security analyst Douglas Paal: 'Timor is a speed bump on the road to dealing with Jakarta, and we've got to get over it safely. Indonesia is such a big place and so central to the stability of the region' (cited in Chomsky, 2000: 54). With Washington sustaining such calculations, initial Australian entreaties for the US to provide military 'boots on the ground' was a non-starter.

As the atrocities in East Timor intensified, ASEAN officials notified Indonesia's beleaguered President Habibie that other Southeast Asian states had neither the capacity nor willingness to form an ASEAN peacekeeping force. The US looked to other means for leveraging Jakarta and resolving the crisis. It found such a mechanism when the APEC heads of state summit convened in Auckland in September 1999. Although APEC itself lacked the formal mechanisms for organising and carrying out a military intervention, it provided the forum needed for Clinton, Australian Prime Minister John Howard and other regional leaders to forge a compromise that led to the creation of an Australian-led 'coalition of the willing'. To neutralise any Indonesian resistance to this intervention force in East Timor (INTERFET), Clinton dispatched top US defence officials to warn their Indonesian counterparts not to resist this operation. They were to 'remind' Jakarta that its own economy could hardly afford to subsidise an impoverished East Timor at a time when Indonesia's political instability and financial vulnerabilities emanating from the financial crisis were still pervasive. Resorting to tactics that must have appeared to be *déjà vu* for other ASEAN elites, the Americans caused the IMF and the World Bank 'to issue vague warnings about funds' (Bell, 2000: 171).

The immediate effect of the East Timor crisis on multilateralism's credibility in the region was positive. After an initial reluctance to join the intervention, most ASEAN states did so. They extended relatively substantial resources and commitments to both INTERFET and the UN Transitional Authority in East Timor (UNTAET) peacekeeping contingents. This helped defuse short-term criticism among elements within the US policy community that had been sceptical of ASEAN's relevance, viewing it as a superfluous 'talk shop'. Over the longer term, however, it raised questions about the ARF's or other multilateral bodies' will and capacity to impose crisis resolution in East Asia as compared to *ad hoc* coalitions or focused issue-oriented groupings. US regional engagement appeared still to be mostly focused on cultivating the China market and maintaining an American forward defence presence in the region's critical sea lanes of communication (SLOCs).

The Clinton administration's rhetoric about multilateralism 'complementing' its core bilateral security relationships was undercut by assigning responsibility for 'local' conflicts to friends or proxies who would spearhead 'coalitions of the willing'. This perception was reinforced by the Clinton administration frequently sending only a deputy secretary to the ARF's annual ministerial meetings. Many within ASEAN felt that such a US posture was a 'payback' for their previous insistence on sustaining 'Asian values' and their resistance to American pressure for the development of more 'western-style' democratisation in their region (Sukma, 2000: 13-14).

In summary, the Clinton administration began to implement the very critical step of shifting US strategy away from a containment mode predicated on 'finding an enemy out there somewhere'. A more sophisticated American approach to regional security was implemented. It sought avenues of security cooperation with an array of regional security actors and institutions that shared an interest in predictability and order in the region. But the administration remained frustrated over ASEAN's inability to address key regional security issues, such as the Korean Peninsula or Taiwan, and ASEAN's propensity to exercise too much control over the ARF's agenda and policy behaviour. As noted by then US Assistant Secretary of State for East Asian and Pacific Affairs, Stanley Roth, this frustration was compounded by the ARF's lack of institutionalised mechanisms, such as a formal secretariat, that might require individual ASEAN members to relinquish some of their own sovereign prerogatives during future regional security crises (US Department of State, 1998). It complicated any American initiative to specify precisely how bilateralism and multilateralism should relate to each other in Asia. It played into the hands of Republican presidential candidate George W. Bush, who accused the Clinton administration of policy oscillation and inconsistency.

CURRENT US POLICY CHALLENGES

George W. Bush assumed the American presidency convinced that his predecessor had lost sight of core US national interests, and was determined to resurrect them. Soon after assuming office, Bush directed the US Defense Department to prepare its Quadrennial Defense Review (QDR), shifting from a traditional 'threat-based' planning model to one highlighting the 'transformation' of US defence capabilities and force deployments. The Review characterised the requirements of this strategy:

> the nation maintains its military advantages in key areas while it develops new areas of military advantage and denies asymmetric advantages to adversaries. It entails adapting existing military capabilities to new circumstances, while experimenting with the development of new military capabilities. In short, it requires the transformation of US forces, capabilities, and institutions to extend America's asymmetric advantages well into the future. (US Department of Defense, 2001)

This posture flowed directly from the neo-conservative unipolarity strategy that was so evident when Bush's father occupied the White House during the immediate post-Cold War era. Despite its emphasis on capabilities rather than threat, the Review was prepared with new perils firmly in the minds of its authors. The 'East Asia littoral' was viewed as a 'particularly challenging area' susceptible to large-scale military competition and, because of its sheer size, devoid of the 'density of US basing and en route infrastructure' that was present in other regions. This required the United States to strengthen its traditional alliances in the region, enhance its forward maritime presence through the deployment of an additional carrier battle group in the Pacific, and also to maintain a favourable regional balance of power by dissuading potential adversaries from developing military capabilities to rival America's own. Although not mentioned specifically in the QDR, the implication of the strategy was clear when coupled with President Bush's campaign argument that China was the United States' 'strategic competitor' rather than its strategic partner. The tense Sino-American diplomatic confrontation over the Chinese air force's downing of an American spy plane off Hainan Island in late March 2001 underscored this conviction.

A Global/Regional Nexus

Two weeks before the QDR's release, America suffered the 9/11 terrorist strikes, necessitating the insertion of a hastily written forward by US Secretary of Defense Donald Rumsfeld. It argued that, while the Bush administration could hardly anticipate that specific attack, it was orienting American global strategy toward homeland defence while simultaneously preparing to neutralise peer competitors in distant global regions. Two years later, Undersecretary of Defense for Policy Douglas Feith (one of the neo-conservative instigators of the US intervention in Iraq) observed that the US wanted 'to make better use of our capabilities by thinking of our forces globally, rather than as simply regional assets'. The ideal force application, he concluded, is to focus *across* regions as well as within them, generating comprehensive responses to international terrorism, WMD proliferation and other emerging threats, sustaining stability and prosperity and promoting democracy (US Department of Defense, 2003). In this context, the neo-conservative objectives appear to differ little from the Clinton administration's liberal institutionalist approach. Arguably, the Bush administration's geopolitics has become at least as jumbled as its predecessor's, with Iraq tying down US military power so that Washington could not at present rationally contemplate fighting a second major, protracted conventional war in Asia.

In an Asian context, the key challenges confronting the Bush administration include the protracted issues of Taiwanese separatism and North Korea's nuclear ambitions, the future of Sino-Japanese relations and China's 'peaceful rise'. All of these issues have assumed global dimensions. The US and Japan, for example, have threatened to impose sanctions on European Union countries if they were to lift their arms sales embargo against China. North Korean missile targeting capabilities are projected to include American cities eventually, strengthening US, Japanese and Australian defence planners' rationale to develop missile defence technology. China has modernised its own regional missile force and is gradually moving toward deploying more sophisticated (solid fuelled and mobile) intercontinental ballistic missiles technology that could overwhelm projected missile defence capabilities (Goldstein, 2005). The interconnection between global and regional strategies is thus clearly deepening.

Initially, one might conclude that multilateralism and its correlates of confidence-building, preventive diplomacy and cooperative security are highly appropriate for bridging Asia-Pacific security issues with commensurate global security concerns. However, following 9/11, the Bush administration elected to apply a combination of US military power projection capabilities and existing regional bilateral alliance infrastructures to security issues. The 'Bush Doctrine' evolved in ways that globalised the US national security strategy. It merges American control over the global war against Al Qaeda and the Taliban with longer-term ideological objectives of eradicating global terrorism and advancing a universal peace that favours human liberty throughout the world (Bush, 2002). The US now reserves the right to move beyond mere deterrence of attacks to conduct pre-emptive attacks against terrorist enclaves or rogue states suspected of threatening the American homeland or US forces abroad. Allied support will be welcome, but is not a necessary pre-condition. The achievement of surprise through timely and decisive action is critical for the pre-emption strategy to succeed. As Secretary of Defense Rumsfeld has noted, it was not a strategy conducive to 'making war by committee' (Bush, 2002; Gurtov, 2004: 12).

Elements of the 2001 QDR transformation strategy have been updated to meet the requirements of a post-9/11 international security environment. The president announced a new Global Posture Review (GPR) in August 2004 that was designed to be the most comprehensive restructuring of America's force posture since the early days of the Cold War. Major focus was assigned to the development of more flexible, rapidly deployable US forces capable of meeting and overwhelming emerging threats in diverse regions. This reflected the administration's growing concern that too many US forces were still deployed in static basing positions, reflecting Cold War strategic requirements rather than a response to more contemporary requirements of asymmetric warfare and 'globalised threats' (US Department of State, 2003). Contrary to Rumsfeld's defence of a fundamentally unilateralist American strategy cited above, the GPR envisioned that future wars would be conducted by American-led allies and coalition partners. GPR anticipated increased force inter-operability between US and allied forces, allied facilitation of US 'footprints', access points, 'surge capabilities' and joint collaboration in force training, technology sharing and counter-insurgency operations.

In an Asia-Pacific context, the GPR has several key ramifications. One is that US strategy will be even more 'offshore' than has been the case in the first decade after the Cold War. The quantitative hallmark of US commitment in the Asia-Pacific—the forward deployment of approximately 100,000 military personnel there—has been superseded by the Bush administration's preference for force capabilities being applied in response to specific crises (International Institute for Strategic Studies, 2005). The transfer of 3000 US ground forces from traditional positions in South Korea to Iraq was illustrative. So too is an increased American preoccupation with commercial maritime security in the Malacca Straits and other critical SLOCs in the region. In early 2004, Admiral Thomas Fargo, Commander-in-Chief of the US Pacific Command, proposed a Regional Maritime Security Initiative (RMSI) for US forces to join ASEAN counterparts in counter-terrorism and anti-piracy patrolling throughout maritime Southeast Asia. Although Indonesia and Malaysia successfully resisted this initiative, both countries subsequently accepted 'practical US assistance' to these littoral states (International Institute for Strategic Studies, 2004).

A second broad implication of the GPR for US strategy in the Asia-Pacific is the shifting nature of American security commitments from predominantly deterrence-oriented guarantees to more contingency-directed scenarios. The relative value and importance of regional allies could well depend on how compliant they prove to be in realigning their own national security strategies to these changing American priorities. A cross-comparison between the US-South Korea and US-Japan alliances is instructive.

US troop strength in Korea is planned to be reduced by one third by the end of the decade and remaining US forces will be shifted to two main 'hub bases' south of the Han River to reduce their vulnerability to North Korean artillery attacks. Such relocation would also facilitate possible deployment to other regional or global contingencies. This shift in the force deployment strategy has left South Korean security officials uneasy for several reasons: (1) American forces are no longer totally dedicated to intra-peninsular missions; (2) other 'regional contingencies' could imply future operations against China, with whom South Korea is increasingly close; and (3) South Korea's self-declared 'balancing' strategy precludes it from supporting the Bush administration's hardline strategy against North Korea's suspected nuclear weapons programs (International Institute for Strategic Studies, 2005).

Japan has been far less ambivalent than South Korea in supporting the Bush administration's new Asian and international security agendas. It deployed supply ships to the Indian Ocean in support of US operations against the Taliban in Afghanistan in 2001-2002, dispatched peacekeeping troops to Iraq in early 2004 and declared its readiness to 'pursue stability' in the Taiwan Strait along with the United States. US basing operations in Japan will stay largely intact and could be used in a future contingency on the Korean Peninsula or in Taiwan. A projected command transfer of the currently home-based US Army I Corps from Washington State to Japan, and the integration of the command functions of the 13th Air Force in Guam with the 5th Air Force at Yokota Air Force Base in Japan, would bind the US to that Northeast Asian ally more closely than ever before and simultaneously increase Japan's dependence on American power. Too much interdependence, however, may be problematic for both Japan and the United States, particularly if the US concludes that it must find a longer-term *modus vivendi* with China and must work with an increasingly independent South Korea. As the International Institute of Strategic Studies has observed: 'such a prospective relationship...because of Japan's highly problematic, emotionally charged relations with China, both Koreas, and still festering differences with Russia, ought to give both Washington and Tokyo pause' (International Institute for Strategic Studies, 2005).

Where does all this leave the United States as a potential contributor to multilateral regional security politics? It is important to note that the Bush administration's pursuit of a 'Korean solution' via the Six Party Talks (involving Russia, Japan, China, the United States and the two Koreas) exemplifies *multipolar* negotiations rather than multilateral cooperation. The relevant parties are negotiating out of national interest rather than in accordance with established norms or within an institutional framework to which they collectively ascribe. Multilateral institutions remain tangential to the Bush administration's preference for strengthening the mechanisms and force assets constituting its bilateral alliance network. In part, this is because the United States is suspicious of what it views to be a growing trend of 'Asia-only' organisations emerging at the expense of 'trans-Pacific partnerships and institutions' (Revere, 2005). It also views China's approach to multilateral security politics to be diametrically opposed to the US forward force presence in the region, as underwritten by its regional alliance system (Pollpeter, 2004: 39, 97). The Bush administration has not reconciled those factions within it who argue about the meaning of growing Chinese power to

US regional and global interests: that is, is there a 'China threat' or is history witnessing 'China's peaceful rise'? Without resolving this fundamental question, the Bush administration cannot resolve another choice that inherently flows from it: 'Should alliance relations remain the centerpiece of US security policy in Asia, or should they be diminished in favour of greater accommodation of rising powers like China and India, and more active reliance on multilateral forums...that are the centerpiece of a growing interest in multilateralism in Asia?' (Sutter, 2004: 60).

CONCLUSION

After more than a decade of policy fluctuations, the United States has reached a historical crossroads in the Asia-Pacific. It must sell its vision of a trans-Pacific community to East Asia at a time when its own global profile is increasingly under fire for excessive unilateralism and a narrow and inflexible ideology. Prospects for US support of intra-regional approaches to security and institution-building are unlikely if such key regional actors as China and Malaysia continue their long-standing opposition to US wealth and strategic influence on Asian multilateral arenas. Indeed, the Bush administration's recent nomination of an avowed opponent of the United Nations to become ambassador to that body demonstrates how disinclined it would be to commit US energy and resources to building up intra-Asian institutions that would compete with Washington in shaping a new Asia-Pacific regional order. East Asian actors must become reconciled to seeking compromise and reciprocity with the world's one established superpower if they are eventually to realise an Asian 'security community'. The United States will need to be a full player in the way that community evolves.

However, the second and equally critical precondition for achieving long-term regional stability is for the Bush administration to modify its own global and Asia-Pacific security postures and to work more effectively with its East Asian counterparts. Washington must endeavour to broaden its security agendas (some would say myopic preoccupations!) beyond GWOT and WMD proliferation to engage in the critical processes of Asia-Pacific conflict reduction and to facilitate long-term, high-profile Asian sustainable development and human security projects. The tsunami crisis, for example, gave the US Navy a unique opportunity to show a different side of American power as it spearheaded regional rescue operations. President Bush's belated but welcome decision to allocate substantial US funding for tsunami reconstruction created a positive American image. President Clinton's decision to intervene against Chinese military harassment of Taiwan during that island's March 1996 presidential election also struck the right balance between restraint and assertiveness. However, overall, American regional engagement must become viewed as more enduring and less hierarchical if the US is to sustain and prevail over attempts within the region to isolate it institutionally and geopolitically.

Three initial strategies can be considered by future U.S. policy architects as a basis for a revised approach to regional order building in the Asia-Pacific commensurate with its global strategic objectives. By themselves, these approaches hardly constitute a panacea for all of the challenges discussed in this chapter. But undertaken collectively, they could illustrate an improved American policy thrust in the region.

Initially, the United States must extend a more positive outlook toward regionally indigenous multilateral politico-security dialogues and institutions. To do so, it must find ways that the ARF, and other bodies with which it is involved, can relate to impending East Asian summit policy initiatives. An example of such an approach was the Clinton administration's initial drive to find complementary purposes for the ARF and the US bilateral security network in its first term. The time appears propitious for a second George W. Bush administration to revive a modified version of the Regional Maritime Security Initiative designed to work *within* ASEAN states' maritime agendas while still incorporating basic counter-terrorism and anti-piracy imperatives. More aggressive collaboration by the Center for Disease Control with the World Health Organization and regional instrumentalities to prevent new pandemics and to address intensifying health-related environmental and energy concerns are other areas of multilateral collaboration ripe for greater American collaboration. None of these relate to alleged Chinese agendas to isolate US power in the region, but they respond to issues that directly affect Asia-Pacific citizens' quality of life and, ultimately, the United States' own prosperity and security.

A second strategy that might be pursued relates to amalgamating existing Asian security networks and infrastructures into a more cohesive regional security framework. This author has elsewhere labeled such an approach as 'convergent security' (Tow, 2001). It requires the US to gradually transform its regional alliance system from a threat-based network into one designed to cultivate strategic reassurance. The administration's record in incorporating strategic reassurance into its policy agenda is mixed. The Proliferation Security Initiative (PSI) is a positive instance in this regard; it enforces collective norms of WMD non-proliferation through low-key but widely accepted measures of international maritime patrolling. It has been less active in formalising multipolar dialogues in Northeast Asia (the Six Power Talks and bilateral China-Japan security discussions). Forming a security grouping specifically for Northeast Asia could help identify and implement interim phases of conflict reduction on the Korean Peninsula and defuse Sino-Japanese tensions or lingering Korean-Japanese differences. US participation in any such grouping would be critical to provide a buffer against intra-group tensions overwhelming cooperative dialogue.

In this sense, the Bush administration's Global Posture Review doctrine is, at best, irrelevant and perhaps even unhelpful. The administration's preferred brand of crisis response is to apply 'hard power' (e.g., military capabilities), either pre-emptively or at the preliminary stages of crises with America's own national security interests foremost in mind. The GPR also anticipates that regional allies will inevitably support and participate in US hard power projection campaigns within or beyond the Asia-Pacific region. This is the embodiment of George Bush's famous condition enunciated in the aftermath of 9/11: 'You are either with us or against us'. Such a US posture affords small latitude for US friends and allies to exercise independent and potentially highly useful conflict mediation when US power and capabilities may be less relevant or even detrimental to escalation control. It may well be that the time has come for US forward deployed force structures to be modified or reduced. That does not mean that the US should anticipate reinstalling or projecting its military power across the globe at the outset of every new contingency where it believes American national security may be threatened. The policy hazards of faulty intelligence and misplaced hubris undermined this postulate in the case of Iraq. Strategic reassurance and convergent security could introduce a sense of proportion and prudent constraint into US thinking about Asia-

Pacific security issues that appear to be absent under the administration's current strategic approach.

A third policy adjustment will be the most difficult in relation to the conservative character of the American electorate that re-elected George W. Bush in November 2004. A second Bush administration should return to the foreign policy reasoning advanced by candidate George Bush during the 2000 presidential campaign: the United States is better off as a balancer than it is as an unmitigated hegemonist. Discretionary use of power, candidate Bush noted, is particularly appropriate at a time when America's military resources are stretched to their limits by involvement in distant conflicts that appear only marginal to the national interest. Good strategy inherently embodies the principle that even the strongest power's resources are ultimately expendable and its influence tangential. America's traditional allies will remain loyal if their relations with the US embody mutual and enduring interests. Conflict avoidance with potential rivals is best ensured through addressing common interests and concerns via hard negotiation, while simultaneously holding one's own resolve. Although criticised by Bush, the Clinton-Jiang summits of 1997-1998 met such criteria. Presidents Clinton and Jiang Zemin achieved the epitome of Sino-American engagement; nothing like it has been produced by their successors. President Bush would do well to move away from demonising many of those extremist elements in the world who would oppose or attack US interests because they strongly—and erroneously—believe the United States offers no hope or inspiration for their own lives. He would also generate more credible international security policy by focusing less on what he clearly regards as an all-encompassing terrorist threat and on suppressing any potential strategic competitor. Embracing the challenge of managing contemporary insecurities with allies and competitors alike is a better way of reducing long-term American vulnerability to a complex series of international security challenges and of realising the promise of Asia-Pacific prosperity and democratisation that this administration claims to be pursuing.

REFERENCES

Anderson, Desaix (2003) 'Crisis in North Korea: The US Strategic Future in East Asia'. *Policy Forum On Line*. Nautilus Institute, PFO 03-25, 27 March, http://www.nautilus.org/fora/security/0325A_Anderson.html

Bell, Coral (2000) 'East Timor, Canberra and Washington: A Case Study in Crisis Management'. *Australian Journal of International Affairs*, 54(2): 171-176.

Bush, George H.W. (1991) 'George H.W. Bush's State of the Union Address: Envisioning One Thousand Points of Light'. 29 January, http://www.infoplease.com/ipa/A0900156.html

Bush, George W. (2001) 'Address to a Joint Session of Congress and the American People'. 20 September, http://www.whitehouse.gov/news/releases/2001/09/20010920-8.html

Bush, George W. (2002) *The National Security Strategy of the United States of America*, Washington, D.C.: The White House.

Chomsky, Noam (2000) *Rogue States: The Rule of Force in World Affairs,* London: Pluto Press.

Clinton, William (1993) Remarks by President Clinton to Students and Faculty at Waseda University, Tokyo, Japan, 7 July, http://www.mofa.go.jp/region/n-america/us/archive/1993/remarks.html

Clinton, William (1998) *A National Security Strategy for a New Century*. Washington, DC: The White House, http://clinton2.nara.gov/WH/EOP/NSC/html/documents/nssr.pdf

Cotton, James (2001) 'Against the Grain: The East Timor Intervention'. *Survival*, 43(1): 127-142.

Crispin, Shawn W., and Shim, Jae Hoon (1999) 'Buying Time'. *Far Eastern Economic Review*, 162(13): 18-20.

Dibb, Paul, Hale, David D., and Prince, Peter (1998) 'The Strategic Implications of Asia's Economic Crisis'. *Survival*, 40(2): 5-26.

Dorsch, Joern (2003) 'The Post-Cold War Development of Regionalism in East Asia'. In Fu-Kuo Liu and Philippe Regnier (eds), Regionalism in East Asia: Paradigm Shifting? London: RoutledgeCurzon: 30-51.

Eizenstadt, Stuart E. (1998) 'Asian Financial Crisis: Broader Implications'. Remarks before the House Ways and Means Committee. Washington, DC, 24 February.

Garofano, John (1999) 'Flexibility or Irrelevance? Ways Forward for the ASEAN Regional Forum'. *Contemporary Southeast Asia*, 21(1): 74-94.

Goh, Evelyn (2004) 'The ASEAN Regional Forum in United States East Asian Strategy'. *The Pacific Review*, 17(1): 47-69.

Goldstein, Lyle J. (ed.) with Andrew Erickson (2005) *China's Nuclear Force Modernization*. Naval War College Newport Papers 22. Newport, Rhode Island: Naval War College.

Green, Michael (2001) 'The United States and East Asia in the Unipolar Era'. *Journal of Strategic Studies*, 24(4): 21-46.

Gurtov, Mel (2004) 'American Crusades: Unilateralism, Past and Present'. In Gurtov, M. and Peter Van Ness (eds), *Confronting the Bush Doctrine: Critical Views from the Asia-Pacific*, London and New York: RoutledgeCurzon.

Halloran, Richard (1998) 'China's Decisive Role in the Asian Financial Crisis'. *Global Beat*. Issue Brief 24, 27 January, http://www.nyu.edu/globalbeat/pubs/ib24.html

Henning, C. Randall (2002) 'East Asian Financial Cooperation'. *Policy Analysis in International Economics* 68. Washington, DC: Institute for International Economics.

International Institute for Strategic Studies (2004) 'Piracy and Maritime Terror in Southeast Asia: Dire Straits'. *Strategic Comments*, 10(6), http://www.iiss.org/stratcomments.php

International Institute for Strategic Studies (2005) 'America's Alliances in East Asia: Purposes and Prospects'. 11(3), http://www.iiss.org/stratcomments.php

International Monetary Fund (1999) 'The IMF's Response to the Asian Financial Crisis'. *Factsheet*, http://www.imf.org/external/np/exr/facts/asia.htm

Krauthammer, Charles (1990-1991) 'The Unipolar Moment'. *Foreign Affairs: America and the World*, 70(1): 23-33.

Layne, Christopher (1993) 'The Unipolar Illusion: Why Great Powers Will Rise'. *International Security*, 17(4): 5-51.

Lim, Robyn (1998) 'The ASEAN Regional Forum: Building on Sand'. *Contemporary Southeast Asia*, 20(2): 115-136.

Mann, Jim (2001) 'Bush's N. Korea Stance Signals a Shift'. *Los Angeles Times*, 9 March, http://hpe60.ibl.co.kr/dprk/ReadBoard.asp?DBname=3andtCode=123andcFile=20010313021635andpage=1.

Pollpeter, Kevin (2004) *US-China Security Management: Assessing the Military-to-Military Relationship*, Santa Monica and Washington, DC: RAND.

Revere, Evans J.R. (2005) 'US Policy Priorities in the East Asia-Pacific'. Remarks to the Baltimore Council on Foreign Affairs. *Scoop Independent News*, 3 May, http://www.scoop.co.nz/stories/WO0505/S00128.htm

Rice, Condoleezza (2000) 'Promoting the National Interest'. *Foreign Affairs*, 79(1): 45-62.

Samore, Gary (2003) 'The North Korean Nuclear Crisis'. *Survival*, 45(1): 7-24.

Shorrock, Tim (1998) 'Asian Financial Crisis'. *Progressive Response ezine*, 3(36), http://www.fpif.org/briefs/vol3/v3n36asia_body.html

Sigal, Leon V. (1997) *Disarming Strangers: Nuclear Diplomacy with North Korea*, Princeton: Princeton University Press.

Snyder, Scott and Richard H. Solomon (1998) *Beyond the Asian Financial Crisis: Challenges and Opportunities for US Leadership*. United States Institute for Peace, Special Report 29, http://www.usip.org/pubs/special reports/early/asiafinancial.html

Sukma, Rizal (2000) 'US-Southeast Asia Relations After the Crisis: The Security Dimension'. Background Paper Prepared for The Asia Foundation's Workshop on America's Role in Asia. Bangkok, 22-24 March, http://www.asiafoundation.org/pdf/ussearelationfs_aria.pd

Sutter, Robert (2004) 'United States: Leadership Maintained Amid Continuing Challenges'. In Tellis, Ashley J. and Michael Wills (eds), *Confronting Terrorism in the Pursuit of Power: Strategic Asia 2004-2005*, Seattle and Washington, DC: National Bureau of Asian Research.

Taylor, Ian (2004) 'APEC, Globalization and 9/11'. *Critical Asian Studies*, 36(3): 463-478.

Taylor, Patrick E. (1992) 'US Strategy Plan Calls for Insuring No Rivals Develop'. *New York Times*, 8 March.

Tow, William T. (2001) *Asia-Pacific Strategic Relations: Seeking Convergent Security*, Melbourne: Cambridge University Press.

US Department of Defense (2001) *Quadrennial Defense Review Report 2001*, Washington, DC: USGPO, 30 September, http://www.defenselink.mil/pubs/qdr2001.pdf

US Department of Defense (2003) 'Transforming the US Global Defense Posture'. Address by Douglas J. Feith, Under Secretary of Defense for Policy, Center for Strategic and International Studies, Washington, DC, 3 December, http://www.defenselink.mil/policy/speech/dec_3_03.html

US Department of Defense (1998) 'The United States Security Strategy for the East-Asia Pacific Region'. Washington, D.C.: USAGPO, http://www.defenselink.mil/pubs/easr98

US Department of State (1998) 'ASEAN Regional Forum Exemplifies Multilateral Approach—Assistant Secretary Stanley Roth on Multilateral Approaches to Regional Security'. Washington D.C., Henry L. Stimson Center, 21 July, http://usembassy.state.gov/seoul/wwwh4444.html

——— (2004) 'History of the Department of State During the Clinton Presidency (1993-2001)'. Released by the Office of the Historian, Bureau of Public Affairs, http://www.state.gov/r/pa/ho/pubs/8530.htm

USIA (United States Information Agency) (1993) 'Lord Lays Out 10 Goals for US Policy in East Asia'. USIA, *Washington File*, 5 April.

Chapter 7

REDEFINING IDEOLOGY:
RUSSIA AND ASIA IN THE PUTIN ERA[1]

Felix Patrikeeff

With the collapse of Communism in 1991, Russia struggled to regain internal political and economic stability, doing so in an international environment marked by uncertainty (the Soviet Union's demise being paralleled by the rise of the United States, as best depicted in the relative imbalance between the superpowers in the Gulf crisis of 1990-91[2]). Furthermore, while political change in Russia was welcomed by the west, it was, at the same time, shadowed by the splitting away of former Soviet buffer-state republics. The latter resulted in a heightened sense of vulnerability with regard to borders in Central Asia and the Russian Far East. This reopened a recurrent debate in Russian history: was Russia a Western, Eastern or Eurasian state? Whereas in earlier periods this debate was of an essentialist nature, its modern form incorporates considerations of security. The splitting away of the Central Asian states left Russia with a highly vulnerable southern rump, exposed to the potentials of unfettered Islamic radicalism. The problems of communications and an economy in dramatic decline, in contrast, left the Eastern parts of Russia open to influences from states it had rivalries and conflicts with (China), or had gone to war against (Japan). Any weakness shown by Moscow in relation to its eastern extremities might result in the loss of effective economic control over them, encouraging its Eastern neighbours to make geopolitical inroads there, or for regional political autarchy to show itself in the Russian Far East (Blank, 1998: 28-29).

Concerns such as these were reflected in the fact that, while Russia removed a great deal of its conventional weaponry from its European borders at the end of the Cold War and the collapse of the Soviet Union, its military resources beyond the Urals remained remarkably great; remarkably because, in effect, the end of the Cold War had largely neutralised the

---

[1] My warm thanks go to Harry Shukman, St Antony's College, Oxford, who read the draft version of this paper in detail and provided a number of insights and instances of clarity to it.
[2] The Soviet Union was in a poor position to resist the logic of the US's drive to use force to remove Iraqi forces from Kuwait. A Russian expert, Alexei Vassiliev, considers that the US was able to conduct its policy there through the 'indulgence' of the Soviet Union (Kreutz, 2004: 12). Be that as it may, whether through indulgence or inability to pose credible political opposition to the US, the Soviet Union lost some $US 40 billion in revenue from the Gulf War and the subsequent sanctions against Iraq (Kreutz, 2004: 13).

Northeast Asian region with regard to a Soviet threat (Taylor and Kim, 1996: 5). Post-Soviet policy in the region was based on the foreign policy lines laid down in the late Gorbachev period, under the rubric of his foreign policy of *novoe myshlenie* (new thinking).[3] Gorbachev had, in his characteristically politically breathless fashion, opened up the Eastern Question in a multi-fronted way. In his Vladivostok Speech (July 1986) he outlined his government's plans for a rapprochement with China, addressing the three main sticking points in Sino-Soviet relations: moving troops away from their common border; giving way on the war in Cambodia; and announcing a withdrawal of Soviet troops from Afghanistan. His Kransoyarsk Speech (September 1988) took these initial, vital further steps to a neutralisation of the Eastern 'front', announcing Soviet eagerness to develop constructive relations with the Asian region; relations based on trade and peaceful, constructive coexistence rather than suspicion and Cold War enmity (Zagoria, 1989: 120, 128-129). These pronouncements were quickly followed by a series of visits to key countries in the region: China in May 1989 (unfortunately coinciding with Beijing Spring); Japan in April 1991 (a visit full of promise, but little result—much to Gorbachev's own political detriment); and an historic summit with South Korean President Roh Tae-Woo on Jeju Island, gaining $US 3 billion in financial assistance for the ailing Soviet Union, but souring further the latter's relations with North Korea (Shuja, 1998: 169-170).

It is worth dwelling on these emerging foreign policy lines. They not only represented a radical departure for Soviet foreign policy (which had prevailed from the 1950s and through to Gorbachev's rise to power), but also formed the basis of post-Soviet policy. Andrei Kozyrev and Yegeniiy Primakov, the first two Foreign Ministers under Boris Yeltsin's presidency, took *novoe myshlenie* further, and, especially with Primakov's expertise in the West Asian area, brought further clarity and substance to the Gorbachev vision.[4] Enhanced ties with Asian states were to be used to balance relations with the west. In order to achieve this, however, certain structural forms had to be in place.

By the mid-1990s, efforts had been made to settle concerns regarding the broad southern and eastern borders, with the Shanghai and Moscow talks in 1996-97, fashioning a much-needed broad security framework for the former Soviet republics of Central Asia and China (Gleason, 2001: 1091-1092). Not enough has been said of this in terms of Kozyrev's and Primakov's contributions to Russian foreign policy, but the outcome was a geopolitically imaginative way of initiating the stabilisation of an immense and complicated border, and doing so on sound multilateral foundations.[5] This was later to be built upon, with a treaty on prevention of terrorism (in 2001) and, finally (in 2002), a full charter signed by the Shanghai Cooperation Organization (the SCO being made up of Kazakhstan, the People's Republic of China, the Kyrgyz Republic, the Russian Federation, the Republic of Tajikistan and the Republic of Uzbekistan), providing the most stable conditions Russia had enjoyed on its

---

[3] For an excellent, concise analysis of the place of New Thinking in Soviet and post-Soviet Foreign Policy, see C.S. Wallander (2002).
[4] For a discussion of Primakov's and Kozyrev's role in refining New Thinking, see Wallander (2002: 119-123).
[5] There is an interesting study to be carried out on the two Foreign Ministers and their role in re-fashioning the post-Soviet approach to the outside world. Primakov especially has been singled out by a number of commentators as a political actor who, as Caspar Weinberger once summed it up: 'wherever [he] went, there seemed to be trouble' (1999). Despite this reputation, Primakov did much to stabilise some of Russia's most vulnerable relations in the East, although he did take a far more critical position with regard to the west.

southern and eastern border regions in over a century.[6] Together with rapid improvements in bilateral relations between China and Russia (based on mutually beneficial economo-strategic links and exchanges), it was apparent that Russia was re-casting its place in Inner and Northeast Asia under the Yeltsin presidency. Moreover, with China and Russia both experiencing increasingly cool relations with the United States, the logic of a more fundamental linkage between the former socialist rivals became even more compelling (Wishnick, 2001: 800).

The 'Look East' policy that Russia seemed to be shifting to was further emphasised by the difficulties the 'new' Russia was experiencing in becoming accepted as a *bona fide* Western European state (not well-off enough to lock fully into the Western European sphere, and unable to develop sound relations with NATO, which appeared to be swallowing more and more of the former Soviet empire). This was despite the fact that Yeltsin's successor, Putin, was very firmly a Europhile, having served in Dresden, East Germany, for 15 years and spent much of his professional life engaged in work associated with Europe. Moreover, he was born and educated in Leningrad (now St Petersburg), itself regarded as the most European of Russian cities (Treadaway, 1999). This in itself has not succeeded in allowing Russia the entrée it has sought into the European circle of nations. Rather, it has at times resulted in shrill ultimatums being lodged with the Europeans. In July 2001, Putin, relatively new to the presidency, advised Western Europe that NATO should be dissolved as a security organisation, or else Russia should be allowed to become a member (Baker, 2001). Despite such spectacular interventions, Russia was, and indeed is still, regarded by many in the west as 'an abnormal country, shaped by pre-Enlightenment forces' (Rosefielde, 2005: 14). Such is the ambivalence that Europe has consistently shown towards Russia, that the notion of either economic or political security flowing from the development of thoroughgoing ties between Europe and the former superpower seemed remote.[7] Overall, however, the sum of these measures, and Europe's persistence in not recognising post-Soviet Russia as a *bona fide* member of its number,[8] was to add impetus to the search for a satisfactory reshaping of internal security and a stabilisation of border relations with former, and some new, neighbouring states.

The replacement of an ailing, increasingly erratic President Yeltsin by his chosen successor, Putin, at first appeared to do little to develop Russia's role in the East. At the same time, the new president seemed to be able to achieve only modest gains in furthering Russia's fragile relations with the western bloc, and notably the United States. Russia's relations soured dramatically after George W. Bush came to power (as president-elect, Bush had already threatened to withdraw aid from Russia until Putin was able to clean up corruption and demonstrate that he had enacted far-reaching market and legal reforms [Sanger and Bruni, 2001]). Rather than becoming an increasingly confident Eurasian state in terms of its foreign policy outlook, Russia appeared to uncomfortably straddle the gap between East and

---

[6] So stable had the border relations become with China, for example, that as early as 2001, Putin was already able to assure Zhang Deguang, the new Chinese Ambassador to Russia, that 'Russia-PRC relations have entered the historically best and most fruitful period' (NAPSNet, 2001).

[7] In 2004-05 a fresh round of controversy and vigorous debate has emerged over the nature of Russia and its place as a stable state/power. The debate, triggered by a controversial article 'Putin's Decline and America's Response' (by Anders Aslund) in Carnegie Endowment Policy Brief (No. 41, 2005), can be tracked in Johnson's Russia List (http://www.cdi.org/russia/johnson/default.cfm), demonstrating that Russia's 'abnormality' is still very much a live issue.

[8] As one commentator put it: 'Russia is still tapping on the "window into Europe"' (Warren, 2002).

West, belonging clearly to neither—a debilitated role it had played out at many stages of its early and modern history (Cohen, 2001). On the eve of the overturn of the Soviet Union, the Russian nationalist writer-dissident Alexander Solzhenitsyn asked the question that had regularly appeared in the course of modern Russian history: 'What is Russia?' There were no straightforward answers. 'Who, today', Solzhenitsyn enquired, 'considers himself part of the future Russia? And where do Russians themselves see the boundaries of their land?' (Solzhenitsyn, 1991: 11). In great part, the new president's approach appeared to establish precisely the answer to this enduring question. The way in which this emerged was in great measure due to Putin's own presidential style, one that was characterised by liberal conservatives as resulting in Russia's current system of 'managed democracy' (*CDI Russia Weekly*, 2002) and the outlook that 'effective statehood' should be the answer to Russia's long search for its own 'national idea'.

Nowhere was this clearer than in Putin's inability to deal with Russia's chronic security problems in Chechnya and the Caucasus in any way but by emphasising and re-emphasising Russia's 'effective statehood' by steadily and consistently turning its vice-like grip on the region through blunt—and remarkably crude—political controls.[9] In dealing with its troublesome southwest, Russia was neither a dominant, modern western state, nor was it able to blend seamlessly into the ethnically subtle political configuration in the region itself. In this regard, Putin's inability to grasp the complex nature of Central Asian politics appeared to be matched by his clumsiness as a national leader. In the early part of his presidency Putin was unable to cast himself in the western mould (as was demonstrated so emphatically by his seemingly inept, remarkably thoughtless handling of the Kursk affair—this was more an example of a benighted, insensitive 'Asiaticism' of the old Soviet Union, than the enlightened policies of a new, western-informed democratic Russia[10]). Nor, predictably, was he entirely comfortable in dealing with East Asia at first, although he made a succession of visits to Asian states in the early part of his presidency. One of the first of these was to North Korea (in mid-2000), thereby formally resolving the problems raised by Gorbachev and the latter's opening up of relations with South Korea. In September 2000, he flew to Japan for talks with the new Prime Minister Yoshiro Mori. Early the following year, the new Russian president visited both South Korea and Hanoi (the latter, again, one senses, in order to restore some balance to a relationship dealt very heavy blows in the closing stages of the Soviet Union's existence, and its collapse) (Blagov, 2001).

The events, and the immediate aftermath, of September 11 brought with them considerable changes to this emerging, troubling picture. At a stroke, Putin—by providing the United States with sympathy, logistic support and a firm commitment to a war on terrorism—was able to shift Russia's geopolitical heartland emphatically into the western camp. As dramatically as Peter the Great (whose portrait reputedly hangs on Putin's office wall [Baev,

---

[9] The Putin formula for the Chechen problem can be summed up in the following: an uncompromising tactic of no negotiation with Chechen pro-independence groups and no international mediation (BBC News World Edition, 2004). In other words, it has been, and still is, regarded as a purely internal Russian concern, a departure from Yeltsin's more conciliatory stance on the Chechen question, and a vote-winner for Putin when he declared his hardline position on the issue. Given horrific consequences of Chechen-related terrorist action (including the carnage at the school in Beslan in September 2004), and the damage that this has done to Putin's own standing, his policy may well come to be moderated in time, but at present the hardline approach remains uncompromised.

[10] See, for example, Douglas Herbert's interesting article comparing Putin's response to the Kursk tragedy and Gorbachev's handling of the Chernobyl disaster in 1986 (2000).

2003]) did, Putin showed that Russia was committed to a western perspective in its foreign policy. Coincidentally, and perhaps conveniently, such a commitment also meant that Russia was able to apply itself with renewed confidence and vigour to its own problems with 'terrorists' (notably the Chechens), and begin building bridges at an astonishing pace with the United States (as exemplified by the exchange of visits by Putin and Bush in late 2001 and mid-2002, respectively). But did Russia abandon entirely its preoccupations with Eurasianism? And had the dramatic shifts facilitated by the Russian-American rapprochement been a sign of Russia's firm commitment to Europe and the west?

The answer is that September 11 allowed Russia to crystalise a fresh ideology-driven foreign policy, one that was not simply reflexive or accommodating itself in an *ad hoc* fashion to changing conditions. By proclaiming itself to be firmly in the western camp, and confirming itself to be a state that is implacable in the war against terrorism, Putin's Russia provided shape and a long-absent direction to its foreign policy, as well as leverage with regard to achieving short-, medium- and possibly even long-term goals. In this regard, before the shocking events in New York and Washington, it would have been difficult to imagine the ease with which Russia achieved accommodation and cooperation with its former Cold War opponent—NATO. Likewise, it is doubtful that Russia could otherwise have been trusted in continuing controversial policies of 'calming' the Caucasus, or increasing its technical and material support to Iran's nuclear energy program (Kerr, 2002). Perhaps as significantly, it was the strength of the Russo-American understanding that allowed Putin's Russia to, for a time, accept the enhanced role of the United States in the Central Asian region, where the latter built up a strong foothold in order to advance on Afghanistan and to wage its 'war on terror' at close quarters. Under different circumstances it would have been difficult to imagine Russia seeing such developments as anything but a threat to its own security. This was, after all, the location of the 'Great Game' that Russia had played out against imperial Britain in the nineteenth century, a period in which the Central Asian states became a sphere of influence and buffer for Russia. Such an attitude remained in the early Bolshevik period through to the late Soviet period (the Soviet invasion of Afghanistan is best interpreted as an attempt to maintain that sphere of influence).

The breakthrough that Putin achieved by acting so decisively and swiftly in 2001 was two years later given body in strategic-military terms through the so-called 'Ivanov Doctrine' (first enunciated by Russian Minister of Defence Sergei Ivanov in his October 2003 policy statement: 'Urgent Tasks for the Development of the Armed Forces of the Soviet Federation'). This redefined the threat posed by NATO, terrorism and small-scale conflicts (reducing the former, and emphasising the latter), and highlighted the issues impacting upon Russian military reform and modernisation (Bouldin, 2004).

Some momentum was subsequently lost in relations with the United States, due to Russia's firm opposition to the latter's intention to overturn Saddam Hussein's regime in Iraq. But in important ways the strong position adopted by Putin's government over the highly divisive Iraq question gave Russia a greater degree of credibility as a responsible European player that was able to make difficult decisions in the face of considerable pressure from the United States.[11]

---

[11] According to some commentators, Russia still needs to do a great deal more in order to fully achieve such a status. See, for example, Stephen Blank's conclusions in 'Is Russia a Democracy and Does it Matter?' (2005: 125-136).

In late August 2005, Russia took its independent stance further still, by using the SCO to engage in military exercises with China (*Pravda*, 2005), thereby asserting not only its ability to make deeper inroads in its relations with the rapidly developing Asian power (and one that finds itself at odds with the United States and Japan in political terms), but also further refining Russia's own place as a Eurasian power. The level of discomfort that has undoubtedly been felt by United States' foreign policymakers as a result of these war games and their broader strategic implications has been all the more pronounced because of the earlier setback the United States experienced with Uzbekistan (one of the member states of the SCO), when the latter requested the closure of the US's key air force base (Karshi-Khanabad, or K2) in that country. This came on the heels of a joint demand from Russia, China and four Central Asian states that the US make plain its timetable for troop withdrawal from the region (BBC, 2005).

And it is perhaps here that we see Putin's foreign policy line mature and come into its own. Russia had, throughout the Yeltsin period and into Putin's own first years of presidency, been forced to wear the yoke of its 'post-Soviet transition'. This was not something that was easily accepted by the more hardline critics: 'How can one keep telling the country during all these years that it is going through a transitional period? It is not just that nobody bothered to explain clearly where exactly the transition is directed, but rather this very tedious term itself reeks of overdue repair works' (Privalov, 1997).

Many had come to want a clean, decisive break with the past, to create a Russia 'without adjectives', 'simply Russia' or 'Russia Proper' [*prosto Rossiya*] (Pavlovsky, 2000). Putin had a good deal of sympathy for the clean break, and a shift to the notion of a Russia 'without adjectives'. Indeed, his 1999 Prime-Ministerial manifesto (titled *Russia at the Millennium*) made this clear by proposing a 'domestication' of western liberal ideology for the purposes of arriving at something of a workable synthesis for Russia. 'We can hope,' Putin's manifesto concluded, 'for the future if we can organically synthesise the universal principles of market economy and democracy with the *Russian reality*' (Putin, 1999). The window of opportunity for furthering this notion appeared only in the northern autumn of 2001. Until then, both as prime minister and subsequently as president, Putin had to balance the uncompromising views of the liberal conservatives against the (many) others of a national-patriotic persuasion, for whom 'post-Soviet transition' did mean something. Consequently, Putin set as his presidency's foreign policy priority the 'creation around Russia of a stable, secure situation and conditions allowing the Russian Federation to concentrate maximum efforts and resources on tackling the socio-economic tasks of the state' (*ITAR/TASS*, 2001a). Only by achieving that could Russia tackle the conditions of globalisation and 'find its place in the world' (*ITAR/TASS*, 2001a), thereby potentially satisfying both the liberal camp and the national-patriotic groups.

While Putin's government worked to neutralise the areas around Russia, his internal policies ensured that threats from 'outsiders' such as the Chechens were, as suggested earlier, dealt with sternly. Some might argue that it was on the back of the Chechen 'problem' that Putin was able to build up his initial appeal.[12] But this is to tell only half the story. In April 2001, Putin addressed the Federal Assembly of the Russian Federation. In his speech he observed that:

---

[12] The BBC's 2001 profile of Putin concludes that '[his] tough treatment of rebel guerrillas in Chechnya ensured his popularity with the Russian people'.

foreign policy is an indicator and substantial factor of state affairs within the country. Not only the authority of our country [in] the international arena, but also the political and economic situation within Russia depend on how intelligently and effectively we make use of our diplomatic resources. (*ITAR/TASS*, 2001c)

Here is an image of a holistic approach to the conduct of politics in the broad; it is an image, moreover, that encourages seeing Russia as a seamless unitary state, working coherently in building simultaneously and interrelatedly its internal and external image.

The furthering of priorities in his early foreign policy was to ensure that the thorny issues carried over from the late Soviet period and Yeltsin's erratic years were dealt with quickly and emphatically. Japan, India, the Koreas and Vietnam were high on the list of problems to be addressed (*ITAR/TASS*, 2000; Kuchins, 2001). In tackling the lingering areas of unease, Putin was also laying the groundwork for another, broader goal: building the potential for 'cooperation and integration in regional structures in Asia and the Pacific ... [and] giving Moscow a better balance in world relations' (United Press International, 2001). Some of the issues proved too difficult to resolve or make substantial headway on, most notably the Northern Territories/Kuril Islands issue. But even here, the engagement has been positive, insofar as it has been possible.[13]

The initiatives taken by Putin early on in his first term as president have shown themselves not to be simply a haphazard patchwork, but part of a broad tapestry of foreign policy towards the region, and one which is now beginning to pay dividends. Putin has maintained an energetic pace in ensuring that his government is engaged both bilaterally and multilaterally in the conduct of regional diplomacy: early pronouncements on the value and importance of ASEAN as a regional forum have been followed up with rounds of visits to some of the key member states of the organisation, with statements issued that very much reflect the 'ASEAN spirit' (*Pravda*, 2001). His approach has been one of that has allowed most, if not all, of the countries of the region to feel comfortable with the revised role of Russia in the region: measured, diplomatic and deft of touch, in contrast to the ponderously ideological presence of the Soviet Union, or the mercurial—and often unpredictable— presence of Yeltsin's Russia. The benefits of this have been not only the opening of channels of communication, but also of revealing growing potential. Under Putin, there has been a growing realisation that Russia's Far East can be integrated into the Asian sphere through constructive multilateralism. Indeed, before his trip to Seoul in early 2001, Putin said in an interview with South Korean MBC and KBS television stations:

most of Russia's population live in the European part [of Russia]. But it was always said in Russia that its power will grow in Siberia and the eastern territories. This is absolutely right. For this reason we want to look into the future.... We want to develop our eastern territories.... [B]alanced...policy directed into both Asia and Europe is absolutely justified for...Russia, for a Euro-Asian country. (*ITAR/TASS*, 2001c)

---

[13] A poll conducted in Russia on 20 November 2004 shows that 65 per cent of Russians are against the return of any of the islands to Japan, while only 9 per cent are for this (Xinhua News Agency, 2004a). Under such circumstances, it is difficult to see how any Russian government can make any headway on the issue. Nonetheless, Putin maintains that under the Soviet-Japanese Declaration signed in 1956, two of the islands, Habomai and Shikotan [or the Southern Kurils], would return to Japan after the signing of a peace treaty (Xinhua News Agency, 2004a). Yet, such a position remains at odds with an earlier pronouncement he made

Such engagement has also provided the necessary groundwork for moving ahead with major economic projects, most notably in providing avaricious Chinese and South Korean economies with supplies of natural gas and materials.[14] Japan, too, has been alive to the potential represented by Russia as a regional supplier of oil and gas.[15]

It is important to realise that these developments have not been in isolation. Putin's consistent application of a measured approach to the members of the international community as a whole has resulted in benefits. Time and again Russia has demonstrated this deft approach to foreign policy, incorporating a universalist perspective, while at the same time being quite clear as to what its own national interests are (and how these can be promoted through constructive engagement). Such a policy line has brought considerable gains. Rarely, if at all, do we now find Russia at loggerheads with major powers. This has allowed Russia to take quite emphatic stances on major international issues such as Iraq, but with the forthright criticism of the United States on its conduct of policy there being one that comes from a 'good international citizen' rather than from the standpoint of a self-interested potential rival.[16]

Gradually, then, Russia has been developing a sense of internal unity and outward direction, as flagged by Putin in his Prime Minisitership and early months as President. The integration of foreign and domestic policies was something that Gorbachev attempted to achieve, but with mixed success at first and, ultimately, personal disaster. Putin is far lighter of touch, but his direction seems similar.[17]

In all of this, there is no doubt a broader ideological agenda; one that was spelt out by Yeltsin in nominating Putin: to make Russia a great power again. Whereas Yeltsin's style was pugnacious, uneven and, ultimately, very heavy-handed, Putin's has been one of a 'grey bureaucrat' (Peel, 2002). In appearing this way, he has steadily—and as importantly *consistently*—assembled a place for Russia in the complex post-Cold War global architecture.

---

on the issue (indeed, one that came en route to Tokyo in September 2000): 'But who has said we are going to give up the islands?' (Vremia MN, 2000).

[14] Russia-Petroleum (which controls the Kovykta gas field in Eastern Siberia), led by BP, signed a preliminary deal on 15 November 2003 with China National Petroleum Corp (CNPC) and Kogas of the Republic of Korea to supply Siberian gas beginning in 2008. China had been working with Russia and ROK for some time on drafting the blueprint for a huge gas trunkline (to be the largest in Asia) to supply Northeastern China, the Bohai Bay region and ROK with gas. The proposed 4,800 kilometre trunk line would go from China to ROK via a sub-sea route circumventing the Democratic People's Republic of Korea. Interestingly, this gas agreement came just half a month after Mikhail Khodorkovsky, Russia's richest tycoon and founding shareholder and chief executive of YUKOS, the Russian side's initiator in the crude pipeline, was arrested. (http://english.people.com.cn/200312/07/eng20031207_129865.shtml)

[15] Russia has committed itself to building a Japanese-funded oil pipeline to Nakhodka (in place of one to China) and there are firm plans in train for oil and gas exploitation projects on the island of Sakhalin. While there has been no undertaking from the Russian side that these projects mark a softening of the Russian position on the Kurils, there is sufficient promise of positive developments there in order to allow Japan to commit itself (Rutland, 2004).

[16] In an interview with The Hindu on the eve of his annual summit talks with Indian Prime Minister Manmohan Singh, Putin urged the US to learn from its experiences in Iraq. Stressing that unilateral actions were counter-productive, he commented: 'we have repeatedly called our American partners' attention to this reality. And eventually they realized the need to reach a political settlement in Iraq using UN mechanisms. I believe that the new administration will undoubtedly bear in mind "Iraqi lessons" when determining its foreign policy'. At the same time, he commented on the 'great pleasure' it was to congratulate George W. Bush on his re-election and 'was convinced that his second term would be fruitful for bilateral ties' Xinhua News Agency (2004b).

[17] See, for example, 'Putin-Shaped Foreign Policy Meets Russia's National Interests', ITAR/TASS News Agency (2001d). As suggested by Shukman, Putin's training in Judo is put to good use in the conduct of his foreign policy: he uses the weight of the opponent in order to gain advantage (personal correspondence, August 2005).

It is one, however, that few commentators have recognised in its essential character; a point made by Mikhail Gorbachev in late 2001, when he declared of Putin's foreign policy that many of the latter's proposals had not been fully grasped in the west. 'They refer,' Gorbachev added, 'to approaches that could help establish a [legitimate] new world order, based on cooperation and balance of interests, not on confrontation typical of the past century' (*ITAR/TASS*, 2001e).

But even Gorbachev misses one important dimension: behind the new internationalist approach is an immovable will to fulfil a nationalist agenda. If we had to reach a conclusion regarding Russia's new place in the world, it would be to recognise that it seeks to become another China: using a state-driven—and controlled—boost in prosperity to gather a fresh sense of respect for itself, and a more profound understanding of what the 'new Russia' represents.

REFERENCES

Aslund, Anders (2005) 'Putin's Decline and America's Response'. Carnegie Endowment Policy Brief 41. In *Johnson's Russia List*, http://www.cdi.org/russia/johnson/default.cfm

Baev, P.K. (2003) 'Putin's Western Choice: Too Good to Be True?' *European Security*, 12(1): 1-16.

Baker, P. (2001) 'Putin: NATO should Disband or Allow Russia to Join'. *Washington Post*, 18 July.

BBC (2001) http://www.bbc.co.uk/bbcfour/documentaries/profile/putin.shtml

BBC News World Edition (2004) 'Analysis: Putin's Permanent Chechen Problem'. 1 September, http://news.bbc.co.uk/2/hi/europe/3617782.stm

——— (2005) 'US Asked to leave Uzbek Air Base' 30 July, http://news.bbc.co.uk/2/hi/asia-pacific/4731411.stm

Blagov, S. (2001) 'Putin's East Asian Adventure to court old Allies'. *Asia Times Online*, 23 February, http://www.atimes.com/c-asia/CB23Ag01.html

Blank, S.J. (1998) 'Russia's Armed Forces on the Brink', Carlisle, PA: Strategic Studies Institute Report, http://carlisle-www.army.mil/ssi/pubs/1998/brnkrefm/brnkrefm.PDF

——— (2005) 'Is Russia a Democracy and Does it Matter?' *World Affairs*, 167(3): 125-136.

Bouldin, M. (2004) 'The Ivanov Doctrine and Military Reform: Reasserting Stability in Russia'. *Journal of Slavic Military Studies*, 17:4: 619-641.

CDI Russian Weekly (2002) 'Managed Democracy....' 7(10), 13 March, http://www.cdi.org/russia/197-11.cfm

Cohen, A. (2001) 'Putin's Foreign Policy and U.S.-Russian Relations'. *The Heritage FoundationBackgrounder#1406*,18January, http://www.heritage.org/Research/RussiaandEurasia/BG1406.cfm

Gleason, G. (2001) 'Inter-State Cooperation in Central Asia: From the CIS to the Shanghai Forum'. *Europe-Asia Studies*, 53(7): 1077-1095.

Herbert, Douglas (2000) 'Submarine Drama: A No-Win Proposition for Putin?' CNN.com, 18 August, http://archives.cnn.com/2000/WORLD/europe/08/17/putin.kurskeffect/

ITAR/TASS News Agency (2000) 9 June: 1008161t4194.

——— (2001a) 26 January: 1008026t6572.

—— (2001b) 26 February: 1008057t0403.
—— (2001c) 3 April: 1008093t6489.
—— (2001d) 'Putin-Shaped Foreign Policy Meets Russia's National Interests'. 25 May: 1008145t2471.
—— (2001e) 2001 24 November: 1008327t3363.
Kerr, P. (2002) 'U.S. Irked by Potential Growth in Nuclear Aid to Iran'. *Arms Control Today*, September, http://www.iranwatch.org/privateviews/ACT/perspex-act-potentialgrowthinrussnucaid-0902.htm
Kreutz, A. (2004) 'Russia and the Arabian Peninsula'. *Journal of Military and Strategic Studies*, 7(2): 1-58.
Kuchins, A.C. (2001) 'Russia's Relations with China and India: Strategic Partnerships Yes; StrategicAlliances,No'.*Demokratizatsiya*,9(2) http://www.findarticles.com/p/articles/mi_qa3996/is_200104/ai_n8952102
Pavlovsky, G. (2000) '*Proshai Belovezhje!*' *Nezavisimaya Gazeta*, 235.
Peel, Q. (2002) 'Putin Plays a Weak Hand Well'. *Financial Times*, 18 March.
Pravda (2001) 'Vietnam, ASEAN Appreciate Russia's Role in Asia, Pacific'. 24 July, http://english.pravda.ru/world/2001/07/24/10885.html
—— (2005) 'Russian-Chinese War Games a New Level in Bilateral Relations—Russian DefenseMinistersays',25August,
http://newsfromrussia.com/world/2005/08/25/61727.html
Privalov, A. (1997) '*Inertsia Sudby*'. *Expert*, 32, August.
Putin, V. (1999) '*Rossiya na Rubezhe Tysyacheletiy*'. *Nezavisimaya Gazeta*, 230.
—— (2001) NAPSNet, 28 August, http//www.nautilus.org-archives-pub-ftp-napsnet-daily_reports-2000-08-01-August-AUG28.txt
Rosefielde, S. (2005) 'Russia: An Abnormal Country'. *The European Journal of Comparative Economics*, 2(1): 3-16.
Rutland, P. (2004) 'Russo-Japanese Relations Improving'. *Eurasia Daily Monitor* 1(57), 22 July.
Sanger, D.E. and F. Bruni (2001) 'In His First Days, Bush Plans Review of Clinton's Acts'. *New York Times*, 14 January.
Shuja, S.M. (1998) 'Moscow's Asia Policy' *Contemporary Review*, 272(1587): 169-176.
Solzhenitsyn, A. (1991) *Rebuilding Russia*, London: Harvill.
Taylor, W.J. and A. Kim (1996) 'The Koreas in the Changing Northeast Region'. In W.J. Taylor and A. Kim *et al.* (eds) *Asian Security to the Year 2000*, Carlisle, PA: Strategic Studies Institute Report, http://www.carlisle.army.mil/ssi/pdffiles/PUB86.PDF
Treadaway, C. (1999) 'The Spy Prime Minister Vladimir Putin: The Face of Russia To Come'.*Stratfor.com*,4November,
http://www.geocities.com/Pentagon/Barracks/6122/persrussian.html
UPI [United Press International] (2001) 26 January: 1008026u7046.
Vremia MN (2000) 6 September, network edition http://www.vremya.ru
Wallander, C.S. (2002) 'Lost and Found: Gorbachev's "New Thinking"'. *Washington Quarterly*, 25(1): 117-129.
Warren, Marcus (2002) 'Putin's Palace Can't Mask the Shambles that is Russia'. *The Electronic Telegraph*, 14 August, http://www.cdi.org/russia/johnson/6403-1.cfm

Weinberger, Caspar (1999) 'Historical Solutions Would Have Worked Better'. In Kim R. Holmes *et al. Who Lost Russia*, The Heritage Foundation, Heritage Lecture 629, http://www.heritage.org/Research/RussiaandEurasia/HL629.cfm

Wishnick, E. (2001) 'Russia and China: Brothers Again?' *Asian Survey*, 41(5): 797-821.

Xinhua News Agency (2004a) 25 November.

―――― (2004b) 3 December.

Zagoria, D.S. (1989) 'Soviet Policy in East Asia: A New Beginning?' *Foreign Affairs*, 68(1): 120-138.

Chapter 8

JAPAN AND A NEW INTERNATIONAL ORDER: A CASE FOR AN EAST ASIAN COMMUNITY

Eiichi Katahara[1]

Since the end of the Second World War, Japan has embraced an American-centred security order in East Asia and the Pacific. Within the security framework provided by the US-Japan alliance, Japan has sought to play an active role in the region; yet its relations with its Asian neighbours, including China, South Korea and the Southeast Asian nations, have been focused primarily on economic issues and concerns such as trade, investment and foreign aid for most of the post-war period. It was in the early 1970s that Tokyo decided to normalise its relationship with the People's Republic of China (PRC), following President Richard Nixon's about-face on America's China policy. There has been a remarkable growth in Japan-China economic relations, primarily driven by trade and Japan's official development assistance (ODA), despite the historical issues that beset the two nations. In the late 1970s Tokyo began to formulate a political diplomacy toward the Association of Southeast Asian Nations (ASEAN). When Prime Minister Fukuda announced the so-called 'Fukuda Doctrine' in August 1977, Japan's diplomatic profile in Southeast Asia was to some degree upgraded. Fukuda declared that Japan would never become a military power; that Japan would promote 'heart-to-heart' understanding with the nations of Southeast Asia; and that Japan would be an equal partner of ASEAN, while improving relations with the nations of Indochina.

It was in the 1990s that Japan began to establish 'comprehensive' relations with the countries of ASEAN, developing more diverse relations that encompassed economic, political and security cooperation, and thus broadening the spectrum of Japan's interests and involvement in the region. At the same time, Japan's proactive engagement in political and security issues in East Asia during this period meant a relative shift in Tokyo's diplomatic focus away from Washington to East Asia, although it maintained the Japan-US alliance as the lynchpin of Japan's security policy. Cases in point were Japan's Self-Defense Forces (SDF) serving as peacekeepers in Cambodia, Tokyo's pro-ASEAN diplomacy *vis-à-vis*

---

[1] The views expressed are those of the author and do not reflect the official position of the National Institute for Defense Studies, the Japan Defense Agency or the Japanese government.

Myanmar (Burma) and the SDF's involvement in peacekeeping operations in East Timor. More recently, Japan participated in disaster relief operations and reconstruction activities in the nations hit by the 26 December tsunami in the Indian Ocean. As Michael Green argues, Japan's broadening relationship with ASEAN beyond economics suggests that 'this relationship will be characterized by competition with China for strategic influence and competition with the United States for an independent identity' (Green, 2001: 167-192).

Japan has been an active participant in multilateral institutions and mechanisms for regional cooperation, including the Asia-Pacific Economic Cooperation forum (APEC), the Korean Peninsula Energy Development Organization (KEDO), the Six Party Talks on North Korea, the ASEAN Regional Forum (ARF), the Asia-Europe Meeting (ASEM), and the ASEAN+3, which now consists of the 10 ASEAN members plus Japan, China and South Korea. In December 2005, the first East Asian Summit meeting was held in Kuala Lumpur, assembling the leaders of the ASEAN+3, India, Australia and New Zealand—a significant step forward towards an East Asian Community (EAC). Japan has also been playing a role in promoting a second-track security dialogue through forums such as the Council for Security Cooperation in the Asia Pacific (CSCAP) and the Northeast Asia Cooperation Dialogue (NEACD).

On balance, however, Japan's approach toward regional security remains largely focused on its alliance with the United States, lacking a long-term and comprehensive strategic vision for the region at large. The American-centred security order in which Japan plays an important role could be sustained or strengthened in the foreseeable future. Yet questions arise as to a long-term security order in East Asia and Japan's place in it. The accelerating integration of Japan's economy into that of China and the fact that China has become Japan's biggest trading partner present profound strategic implications for Japan's role in an emerging international order, especially when the situation on the Korean Peninsula is stabilised and the Taiwan problem is resolved at some point in the future. Will the US-centred security order still be viable and desirable under these changing circumstances? Are there any credible alternatives to the US hegemonic security order in the region?

My central purpose here is to explore the prospects for an East Asian Community and the strategic implications of such a development for regional security. I will first outline the strategic environment in East Asia, focusing on the centrality of the US-centred regional order. Second, I will discuss how Tokyo has been responding to the changing strategic environment. Third, I will assess the prospects for the emergence of an East Asian Community and analyse the strategic implications of such a region-wide security community for regional security. Finally, I will conclude this chapter on a cautious, yet hopeful, note about the idea of an East Asian Community.

EAST ASIAN STRATEGIC ENVIRONMENT AND US HEGEMONY

In East Asia (defined here as the region involving the countries of both Southeast Asia and Northeast Asia), there are a plethora of territorial disputes, inter-state tensions, proliferation threats, examples of mutual distrust and intensifying arms-acquisition processes. In addition, there are the specific and well-known epicentres of potential conflict: the Korean Peninsula, the Taiwan Strait and in the South China Sea. Unlike Southeast Asia, which has shown a marked progress in strengthening regional institutions for dialogue and consultation, multilateralism is distinctively underdeveloped in Northeast Asia. The existing institutions such as KEDO, the Six Party Talks on North Korea, and the Trilateral Coordination and Oversight Group (TCOG)—the latter an arrangement between Japan, South Korea, and the United States—have proved to be insufficient, if not entirely inadequate, as effective mechanisms for political dialogue, coordination of security policies, and crisis management (Nishihara, 1999: 102-111). Indeed, North Korea's nuclear weapons program, its ballistic missile and chemical weapons capabilities, along with its unpredictable and provocative behaviour, represent a serious threat to Japan and regional security.

China's re-emergence as a central strategic player presents a challenge for its neighbours and for the Asia-Pacific region-at-large, given its potential for affecting a major shift in the balance of power of the region. Its rapid economic growth, increasing military spending and growing navy have aroused widespread concerns throughout the countries of East Asia. Yet developments in recent years suggest that China has been progressively integrated into a multi-layered system of regional and global institutions, including APEC, ARF and the World Trade Organization (WTO). In particular, China has been keen to deepen economic and political cooperation with neighbouring countries, and it is clear that China's approaches to Taiwan have become less belligerent (Morrison, 2003; Shambaugh, 2004/05).

Historical legacies, suspicions, resentments and animosities are still evident in East Asia, especially between Japan and its neighbours China and Korea, causing tensions and frictions for interstate relations between them. A case in point is Prime Minster Koizumi's visit to the Yasukuni Shrine, where several war criminals are interred among the Japanese war dead. Many Chinese and Koreans were angered and criticised Tokyo in strong terms (Morrison, 2004: 111).

A key to the peace and stability of Asia and the Pacific during the post-World War II decades and the post-Cold War period has been America's 'hegemonic strategy—one that reserves a special role for the United States as the principal guarantor of regional order' (Mastanduno, 2002: 193). Michael Mastanduno argues that US hegemony, though designed to serve its own geopolitical and economic interests, makes important contributions to regional order (Mastanduno, 2002: 181-210). First, US hegemony plays a critical role in 'keep[ing] potential power rivals at bay'. America's security guarantee obviates Japan's need to confront its potential adversaries by means of offensive military capabilities. Second, the US military presence can serve as a source of reassurance for many countries in the region, except for North Korea. Third, US hegemonic strategy plays a role in managing security crises and avoiding its escalation to broader regional conflict. Fourth, US hegemonic strategy also has an economic dimension. It seeks to liberalise the capitalist markets of East Asian countries, while integrating China into the liberal world economy. In the near term, Mastanduno contends that US hegemony remains 'the best available pathway to regional order' (Mastanduno, 2002: 181-210).

In the longer term, however, the American-centred regional order may prove to be inadequate and unsustainable. First, America's willingness and capability to be the global hegemonic power can be problematical, given the vagaries of American public opinion. To put it another way, the US-centred security order 'rests on a fragile foundation: the American political system and the parochialism of its domestic politics' (Ikenberry, 2002: 12). To expect the United States to bear the tremendous costs necessary for maintaining external security commitments may prove to be difficult in its domestic political terms on the one hand, and on the other, the likely emergence of regional centres of power, for instance, in Europe, East Asia and perhaps India, which together may compete with or displace the US-centred security order at some point in the future. Charles Kupchan advances this line of argument, suggesting that 'the United States and its main regional partners must begin to prepare for life after *Pax Americana*' (Kupchan, 2002: 69-97; Kupchan, 2003).

Second, many people in East Asia oppose, resent or worry about some prominent aspects of the Bush administration's strategic thinking or strategic culture, and this could lead to quiet alienation or a backlash against US hegemony. For example, many East Asians, including their elites, have growing misgivings over America's proclivity for unilateralism, its impulse to use military force pre-emptively if deemed necessary (as in the war in Iraq), and its intrusive and self-righteous international behaviour. Anti-American sentiment has been on the rise not just in the Muslim nations in Southeast Asia, but also in South Korea, a long-term ally of the United States.

Third, America's allies in the region would find the costs of maintaining the alliance increasingly unacceptable, given the ending of the Cold War more than a decade ago and changing international conditions, such as the rapprochement between Seoul and Pyongyang and a stable relationship between Beijing and Washington. In particular, US bases in South Korea and Japan, which represent a derogation of their respective country's sovereignty, cast a legitimate doubt on the long-term viability of the existing security arrangements.

JAPAN'S RESPONSES

Japanese security policy in the post-war period has been based on two fundamental legal documents: Japan's own constitution and the Japan-US Security Treaty. While the former was a product of the US occupation reforms, the latter stemmed from the realities of the emerging Cold War at the time. The Constitution has long been a major source of controversy in post-war Japanese politics. The fundamental problem derives from the ambiguous status of the Japanese Self-Defense Forces, Japan's *de facto* armed forces, whose existence is not provided for in the Constitution. Article 9 of the Constitution reads as follows:

> Aspiring sincerely to an international peace based on justice and order, the Japanese people forever renounce war as a sovereign right of the nation and the threat or use of force as a means of settling international disputes.
> In order to accomplish the aim of the preceding paragraph, land, sea and air forces, as well as other war potential, will never be maintained. The right of belligerency of the state will not be recognized.

Despite the ambiguous constitutionality of Japan's having armed forces, successive governments since the 1950s have interpreted Article 9 of the Constitution as not precluding the exercise of the right to self-defense. Hence, the establishment of the SDF in July 1954, which in part represented Tokyo's response to the geopolitical realities of the international situation.

Article 9 of the Constitution has had far-reaching implications for Japan's security policies. Indeed, it proved to be the source of some uniquely innovative security policies in post-war Japan. Its 'exclusively defensive defence' posture, the ban on sending military units for combat abroad, the three non-nuclear principles which prohibit Japan from possessing, manufacturing or introducing nuclear weapons into Japan, the ban on the export of arms, political constraints on defence spending, the prohibition of the execution of the right of collective self-defence, the ban on conscription and commitment to the peaceful use of space all come from the interpretation of Article 9 of the Constitution offered by successive Japanese governments. Provided the constitution remains intact, along with the significant restraints placed on Japan's security policies, there is little prospect of Japan re-emerging as a great military power.

This is further reinforced by important cultural constraints. Japan's commitment to the 'Peace Constitution' and an array of political restraints on Japan's security policies reflect the pacifist sentiment entrenched in the minds of many Japanese. As Thomas Berger puts it, Japan's post-war culture of anti-militarism is 'one of the most striking features of contemporary Japanese politics and has its roots in collective Japanese memories of the militarist takeover in the 1930s and the subsequent disastrous decision to go to war with America' (Berger, 1993: 120; 1998). One of the bitter lessons the Japanese have learned from their wartime experiences is that 'the military is a dangerous institution that must be constantly restrained and monitored lest it threaten Japan's post-war democratic order and undermine the peace and prosperity that the nation has enjoyed since 1945' (Berger, 1993: 120). During most of the post-war years, therefore, the issues of national security had been politically taboo. Under these circumstances, the SDF was rigidly contained in an intricate web of political, legal and social restraints.

It was not until the mid-1970s to the early 1980s that a national consensus on the fundamentals of Japan's security policy was able to emerge—namely the desirability of maintaining the SDF and the Japan-US security arrangements (Katahara, 2001). The Gulf crisis and war of 1990-91 proved to be a watershed in Japan's security policy, culminating in the enactment of the Law Concerning Cooperation for United Nations Peace-Keeping Operations and Other Operations ('International Peace Cooperation Law') and the Law Concerning the Dispatch of Japan Disaster Relief Teams ('Disaster Relief Law') in June 1992. These reflected Tokyo's awareness of its responsibility to contribute to international peace and stability in the evolving post-Cold War world. The International Peace Cooperation Law represented a significant expansion of the roles and missions of the SDF.

In addition to establishing the legal basis for Japan's participation in UN peacekeeping and humanitarian relief operations, in the 1990s Tokyo also adopted a series of new security policies, including the revised National Defence Program Outline (1995 NDPO) in November 1995 and the new Guidelines for Japan-US Defense Cooperation (US-Japan Guidelines) in September 1997. In the Asia-Pacific region, the realities of the post-Cold War world, including the prospect of instability on the Korean Peninsula, North Korea's military capabilities and provocative behaviour, the uncertainty of America's long-term commitment to East Asian security, and the rise of China as a great power began to loom large in the minds of Japanese policymakers (Katahara, 1996: 218-219; Morrison, 1998: 65-67). The 1995 NDPO substantially expanded the roles and missions of the SDF, to include response to large-scale disasters, terrorist attacks and 'various other situations that could seriously affect Japan's peace and security' (which could mean regional military contingencies), as well as participation in UN peacekeeping operations. The 1997 US-Japan Guidelines provide a comprehensive framework for defence policy consultation and coordination between Tokyo and Washington, both in peacetime and during contingencies that affect Japan's security.

They also emphasise the need for active peacetime security cooperation aimed at stabilising an international security environment (Morrison, 1998: 70-73). This includes promoting security dialogues in the Asia-Pacific region, participation in UN peacekeeping operations, and conducting emergency relief operations. The scope of the SDF's non-combat support operations in the case of regional contingencies was clarified and expanded to include logistic support for US combat forces, enhanced surveillance operations, minesweeping, interception of contraband on the high seas, measures to deal with refugees and non-combatant evacuation operations. The 1995 NDPO and the 1997 US-Japan Guidelines together represent Japan's response to the changing strategic environment through a combination of the SDF's expanding roles and missions and the significant strengthening of the Japan-US alliance.

Since the September 11 terrorist attacks in the United States, Tokyo strongly supported and assisted the US-led coalition in the war against terrorism. With the passage in October 2001 of the Anti-Terrorism Special Measures Law, the scope of Japan's SDF has been expanded: SDF vessels were sent to the Indian Ocean to provide supply of fuel to US and UK naval ships in the Indian Ocean; and SDF aircraft were engaged in transportation support for US forces.

The process of establishing a legal framework for mobilising the SDF in the event of a military emergency represents a further step forward toward normalisation of Japan's security posture, and a substantial adjustment to changes in the strategic environment surrounding Japan. On 6 June 2003, three defence bills related to emergency legislation were endorsed by around 90 per cent of the lawmakers in both chambers—an unprecedented development in view of the fact that emergency legislation had long been taboo in post-war Japan (Morrison, 2004: 113). The legislation included: (a) the 'bill to respond to armed attacks', which stipulates the basic principles for response to armed attacks, the respective responsibilities of the national and local governments and public organisations, and other measures required; (b) the bill to amend the SDF Law that would enable SDF personnel to seize land and other property for operations and exempt the SDF from certain peacetime legal procedures, such as those related to road traffic, medical services and constructing facilities for their use, thus allowing for effective operations in emergency situations; and (c) the bill to amend the Security Council Establishment Law so as to grant the Council greater power to deal with an emergency (Morrison, 2004: 113).

Japan's support for the US proved to be resolute in the 2003 conflict in Iraq. Indeed, Prime Minister Koizumi put the US alliance ahead of the UN, citing the security threat from North Korea as a major reason for backing Washington. In July 2003, the Japanese government passed a legislation (the Law Concerning Special Measures on Humanitarian and Reconstruction Assistance in Iraq), allowing SDF troops to be dispatched to 'non-combat zones' in Iraq for humanitarian assistance to people in Iraq, and for logistic support for US-led coalition forces (Morrison, 2004: 110). In January 2004, the SDF members began operations in Samawah in southern Iraq. About 600 Ground Self-Defense Force (GSDF) and 200 Air Self-Defense Force (ASDF) troops have been dispatched to Iraq to engage in humanitarian and reconstruction activities including medical services, water supply and transportation activities. (Japan Defense Agency, 2004a).

Another significant development in Japan's security policy was the adoption in December 2004 of the 'National Defense Program Guidelines for FY 2005 and After' (the new NDPG), which replaces the 1995 NDPO and articulates Japan's security policy objectives and new measures in response to the changing strategic environment, including new security threats such as proliferation of weapons of mass destruction and ballistic missiles, as well as that of international terrorism (Japan Defense Agency, 2004b). The new NDPG stipulates Japan's future defence capability as being 'a multi-functional, flexible, and effective force with high level of readiness, mobility, adaptability and multi-purpose capability', equipped with state-of-the art technologies and intelligence capabilities (Japan Defense Agency, 2004b: 5). While maintaining an exclusively 'defence-oriented' defence posture, the new NDPG calls for a proactive role for Japan in international peace cooperation activities (Japan Defense Agency, 2004b: 6-7). The critical importance of the Japan-US security arrangements for Japan's security and for the peace and stability of the Asia-Pacific region is emphasised, suggesting that 'Tokyo will proactively engage in strategic dialogue with the US on wide-ranging security issues' (Japan Defense Agency, 2004b: 6).

On 19 February 2005, in a meeting of the US-Japan Security Consultative Committee (SCC) held in Washington, DC, the governments of the US and Japan addressed a broad array of security issues, and formulated 'common strategic objectives' both at the regional and global levels. Among twelve common strategic objectives in the region identified are:

- supporting 'peaceful unification of the Korean Peninsula';
- seeking 'peaceful resolution of issues related to North Korea, including its nuclear programs, ballistic missile activities, illicit activities, and humanitarian issues such as the abduction of Japanese nationals by North Korea';
- developing 'a cooperative relationship with China, welcoming the country to play a responsible and constructive role regionally as well as globally';
- encouraging 'the peaceful resolution of issues concerning the Taiwan Strait through dialogue';
- encouraging 'China to improve transparency of its military affairs';
- encouraging 'Russia's constructive engagement in the Asia-Pacific region';
- promoting 'a peaceful, stable, and vibrant Southeast Asia';
- maintaining 'the security of maritime traffic.' ('Joint Statement', 2005)

Global common strategic objectives include the promotion of 'fundamental values such as human rights, democracy, and the rule of law in the international community,' consolidation of the 'US-Japan partnership in international peace activities and development assistance to promote peace, stability, and prosperity worldwide,' the promotion of the 'nonproliferation of weapons of mass destruction (WMD) and their means of delivery,' the prevention of terrorism, coordinated efforts 'to improve the effectiveness of the United Nations Security Council,' and maintaining and enhancing 'the stability of the global energy supply' ('Joint Statement', 2005). The specifics of Japan's strategic collaboration with the US, including operational cooperation in regional contingencies as well as in missile defence, remain to be seen.

The foregoing review of Japan's responses to the changing security environment confirms the gradual transformation of Japan into a normal state (Katahara, 2001). The centrality of the US-Japan alliance has been a defining characteristic of Japan's foreign and defence policy throughout the post-war years and in the post-9/11 world as well. With the US-Japan alliance intact, however, a new strategic vision has been injected into Japan's strategic thinking: a vision of East Asian regionalism in the form of an East Asian Community.

AN EAST ASIAN COMMUNITY

In January 2002 in Singapore, Prime Minister Koizumi proposed the creation of an East Asian Community with ASEAN, Japan, China, South Korea, Australia and New Zealand as its 'core members'. In his own words:

> Our goal should be the creation of a 'community that acts together and advances together.' And we should achieve this through expanding East Asia cooperation founded upon the Japan-ASEAN relationship. While recognizing our historical, cultural, ethnic and traditional diversity, I would like to see countries in the region become a group that works together in harmony. Our pasts may be varied and divergent, but our futures can be united and supportive of each other. The realization of such a group needs strategic considerations in order to produce positive consequences. (Koizumi, 2002: 4)

In this endeavour, the driving force would be the promotion of the ASEAN+3 process, the deepening of Japan's cooperation with China and South Korea, and a strengthened economic partnership in the region. Prime Minister Koizumi hastened to add that

> the role to be played by the United States is indispensable because of its contribution to regional security and the scale of its economic interdependence with the region. Japan will continue to enhance its alliance with the United States. (Koizumi, 2002: 5)

This formulation of an East Asian community by Prime Minister Koizumi, however, is long on rhetoric, but short on substance, and hence is subject to divergent interpretations. It acknowledges the 'indispensable' security role played by the United States in regional security, but it is silent on the durability of the latter as a central strategic player in the region. It is also silent on the specific security roles for major powers in the region, China, Japan and ASEAN. And it is interesting to note that what Tokyo proposed here is not a 'Pacific Community' (in line with President Clinton's formulation), not an 'Asia-Pacific Community' as an extension of APEC, but an East Asian community, which may exclude the United States as its core member. Hence, the idea of an East Asian community can be seen as a hedge against changes in US commitment to regional security.

The security dimension of the idea of an East Asian Community requires further analysis and elaboration. What follows is my tentative attempt to tease out the crucial elements of an East Asian Community. First, as in the case of an emerging ASEAN Security Community (Acharya, 2002: 146-166; 2003), an East Asian Community will require as its basic ingredients: the absence of armed conflict; the absence of an arms race; the existence of institutions for conflict prevention and resolution; and a significant degree of functional interdependence, integration and cooperation. The bottom line will be a shift from the US-centred security order to a balanced and cohesive East Asian community where East Asian states take charge of their own collective security. In light of these requirements, East Asia today is a far cry from a regional security community. As noted above, there are a wide range of trouble spots, territorial disputes, seeds of armed conflict and historical animosities that would impede progress toward a security community. Yet dynamic trends (economic, political, military and cultural) may propel East Asian states toward a regional power centre to be linked economically and strategically with other centres of power, such as the United States and Europe.

Second, stable major power relations, buttressed by norms, agreements, and multilateral institutions, would be a critical precondition for an East Asian Community. A major challenge in this regard would be the establishment of a concert system in which a shifting balance of power can be accommodated, and the responsibilities for the maintenance of peace and stability can be shared primarily by the members of an East Asian Community. The concert system would be predicated on shared strategic interests, as well as a stable balance of power. Explicit rules and agreements on how member states would act in times of crisis could be worked out in the context of a security community. It should also be necessary for the member states to renounce the use or threat of force as a means of settling intra-regional disputes. A well-established system of conference diplomacy, as exhibited in ARF and the ASEAN+3, is yet another essential element of a concert system (Katahara, 1998: 18-20). The launching of an East Asian Summit (EAS) in December 2005, built on the ASEAN+3 framework, can be seen as a significant step forward. Establishing a new permanent five-power organisation in Northeast Asia, built on the Six Party Talk on North Korea, would serve as a small building block in a larger multi-multilateral edifice (Fukuyama, 2005: 75-87).

Third, the US-Japan alliance will need to be redefined through burden-sharing by devolution or power-sharing so as to adjust the time-honoured alliance to changing strategic imperatives (Calleo, 1992; Katahara, 1996: 223-225). Burden-sharing by devolution means sharing the responsibilities for the maintenance of a stable international order. Measures for devolution would include: an enhanced self-reliance of Japan's defence force structure with limited power projection capabilities; Japan's enhanced intelligence collection and analysis capability, and strengthened intelligence cooperation between Japan and the US; and its active participation in international peacekeeping and humanitarian and disaster relief activities under the aegis of the United Nations or relevant international organisations. Strengthening strategic consultations and coordination of security policies between Japan and the United States would also be a precondition for the burden-sharing by devolution so as to meet the new security challenges of the twenty-first century.

Fourth, for an East Asian Community to serve as a hedge against the potential for Chinese hegemony, it would be desirable for the United States to remain strategically involved in regional security affairs, although most of the regional security burden would fall on the core members of the community. In this connection, a mature partnership between the United States and Japan will be critical both in regional and global terms (Institute for National Strategic Studies, 2000; Przystup, 2005), and hence a precondition for an East Asian Community.

Fifth, Russia's participation in an East Asian Community could contribute to the security of the entire region in important ways. The energy potential of Siberia and the Russian Far East remains largely underestimated in East Asia, yet in the long run, Russia could play a critical role in meeting the region's growing demands for energy resources. On the diplomatic front, co-option of Russia could yield substantial leverage *vis-à-vis* North Korea and the United States. In strategic terms, Japan's and China's closer economic and political partnership with Russia would provide its neighbours with considerable reassurance, which in turn would prevent the re-emergence of rivalries between major powers.

Finally, an East Asian Community will require not just the deepening of economic interdependence and integration, security policy coordination and consultation among the member states, but also concerted commitment to common values such as democracy, market economy and the rule of law. In this regard, East Asian countries would benefit from strengthening cultural and educational relationships among themselves and with Europe and the United States. This will lead to a wider understanding of Asian values, thus contributing to the establishment of an East Asian identity.

What would be the potential benefits to be gained from an East Asian Community? First, it would represent East Asian countries' serious preparation for life after *Pax Americana*. It could offer a hedge not only against possible changes in America's commitment to regional security, but also a hedge against the possible re-emergence of major power rivalries in the region in case the United States withdraws from the region. It should be noted here that process matters as well as outcome; in the process of establishing an East Asian Community, there would emerge a convergence of strategic values and interests among the member states.

Second, an East Asian Community, if established, would have the positive effect of relieving part of the security burden of the United States in substantial ways. By reducing its security burden in East Asia, a greater share of America's military and human resources could be devoted to the new and growing requirements for homeland defence. The focal point of America's global strategy would therefore be properly and effectively directed to the requirements for addressing new security threats emanating from international terrorism and the proliferation of weapons of mass destruction.

A third possible benefit of the proposed East Asian Community has to do with its psychological impact on the attitudes of America's allies in East Asia toward defence and regional security. Relinquishing their heavy dependence on American hegemony, East Asian policymakers would become more independent, capable and responsible in the formulation and implementation of their own security policies, so that they could take the primary initiatives for maintaining security order in their own space.

Finally, an East Asian Community, underpinned by common values such as democracy, market economy and the rule of law, would represent a powerful instrument that enhances peace and stability in the region, thus supporting the national interests of East Asian countries and contributing to the broader security interests across the globe.

CONCLUSION

A regional security community in East Asia may be a remote possibility. Given the evolving strategic environment in East Asia, and in the world at large, it is likely that a regional security order built on American hegemony will probably remain for the foreseeable future. As Brzezinski argues, the United States could bring China and Japan with it into a strategic partnership in East Asia, while enlisting Europe in global management, thereby building a world concert of great powers (Brzezinski, 2004: 107-123). As long as American global hegemony, sustained by the military omnipotence of the United States, remains a fact of life in the international system, Japan's future strategic options would continue to be predicated on the centrality of the US-Japan alliance.

Nonetheless, I would argue that Japan, together with its East Asian neighbours, should begin to think about life after *Pax Americana* now. The idea of an East Asian Community provides just one attractive option available to us. This idea, I believe, should be taken seriously, and is worth pursuing in a serious, cautious and constructive way.

REFERENCES

Acharya, Amitav (2002) *Regionalism and Multilateralism*, Singapore: Times Academic Press.
―――― (2003) 'Strengthening ASEAN as a Security Community'. *The Jakarta Post*, reprinted in *The Japan Times*, 17 June.
Berger, Thomas U. (1993) 'From Sword to Chrysanthemum: Japan's Culture of Anti-Militarism'. *International Security*, 17(4).
―――― (1998) *Culture of Antimilitarism: National Security in Germany and Japan*, Baltimore: Johns Hopkins University Press.
Brzezinski, Zbigniew (2004) *The Choice: Global Domination or Global Leadership*, New York: Basic Books.
Calleo, David P. (1992) 'Can the United States Afford the New World Order?' *SAIS Review*, 12(2).
Fukuyama, Francis (2005) 'Re-Envisioning Asia'. *Foreign Affairs*, 84(1) (January/February): 75-87.
Green, Michael J. (2001) *Japan Reluctant Realism*, New York: Palgrave.
Institute for National Strategic Studies (INSS) (2000) *INSS Special Report The United States and Japan: Advancing Toward a Mature Partnership*, Institute for National Strategic Studies, National Defense University, Washington DC, 11 October.
Ikenberry, G. John (2002) Introduction. In G. John Ikenberry (ed.), *America Unrivaled: The Future of the Balance of Power*, Ithaca: Cornell University Press.
Japan Defense Agency (2004a) *Defense of Japan 2004*, Tokyo: Inter Group.
―――― (2004b) *National Defense Program Guidelines for FY 2005 and After* http://www.jda.go.jp/e/index_.htm
Katahara, Eiichi (1996) 'Japan's Concept of Comprehensive Security in the Post-Cold War World'. In Susan Shirk and Christopher P. Twomey (eds), *Power and Prosperity: Economic and Security Linkages in Asia-Pacific*, New Brunswick: Transaction Publishers: 223-225.
―――― (1998) 'Strategic Changes in Asia-Pacific: Political, Economic and Technological Dimensions—An Asian Perspective'. In Joachim Krause and Frank Umbach (eds), 'Perspectives of Regional Security Cooperation in Asia-Pacific: Learning from Europe or Developing Indigenous Models?' *Arbeitspapiere Zur Internationaeln Politik* 100, September.
―――― (2001) 'Japan: From Containment to Normalization'. In Muthiah Alagappa (ed.), *Coercion and Governance: The Declining Political Role of the Military in Asia,* Stanford: Stanford University Press.
Koizumi, Junichiro (2002) 'Japan and Australia toward a Creative Partnership', Asia Society, Sydney, 1 May, http://www.mofa.go.jp/region/asia-paci/pmv0204/speech.html

Kupchan, Charles A. (2002) 'Hollow Hegemony or Stable Multipolarity?' In G. John Ikenberry (ed.), *America Unrivaled: The Future of the Balance of Power*, Ithaca: Cornell University Press.

—— (2003) *The End of the American Era*, New York: Alfred A. Knopf.

Mastanduno, Michael (2002) 'Incomplete Hegemony and Security Order in the Asia-Pacific'. In G. John Ikenberry (ed.), *America Unrivaled: The Future of the Balance of Power*, Ithaca: Cornell University Press.

Morrison, Charles E. (ed.) (1998) *Asia Pacific Security Outlook 1998*, Tokyo: Japan Centre for International Exchange.

—— (2003) *Asia Pacific Security Outlook 2003*, Tokyo: Japan Centre for International Exchange.

—— (2004) *Asia Pacific Security Outlook 2004*, Tokyo: Japan Centre for International Exchange.

Przystup, James J. (2005) *U.S.-Japan Relations: Progress Toward a Mature Partnership*, Institute for National Strategic Studies, Occasional Paper 2, National Defense University, June.

Nishihara, Masashi (1999) 'Hokuto ajia ni okeru anzenhosho shisutemu no shoraisei' (Prospects for a Northeast Asian Security System), *Gaiko Forum '21seiki no anzenhosho'* (International Security in the 21st Century), Tokyo: Toshishuppan.

Shambaugh, David (2004-05) 'China Engages Asia: Reshaping the Regional Order'. *International Security*, 29(3): 64-99.

US Department of State (2005) 'Joint Statement: US-Japan Security Consultative Committee', 19 February, Washington, DC.

In: Asia-Pacific and a New International Order
Editors: Purnendra Jain et al. pp. 133-144
ISBN 1-59454-986-9
© 2006 Nova Science Publishers, Inc.

Chapter 9

PEACEFUL RISE: CHINA'S 'POLICY OF ASSURANCE'

Jia Qingguo

One of the most important challenges facing China since the mid-1990s is how to address the rising foreign concerns over its increased international presence. Confronted with China's rapid economic development and growing international influence, some critics have begun to revive discussions concerning historical disorders and wars associated with the growth of great power (Bernstein & Munro, 1997; Kristof, 1993; *Economist*, 1992). Others have come up with a worrying image of a communist power, backed by virtually unlimited economic potential, challenging the western way of life (Chanda, 1996: 20).[1] Still others working on strictly technical issues have predicted the potentially disastrous impact that a modernising China would have on the world's supplies of food, energy, minerals and other resources, as well as on the globe's ecological balance (Brown, 1994).

The implication of these differing perspectives is, however, the same: if China represents a threat, they suggest, the world needs to do something about it. Subsequently, a variety of suggestions have been made to address the 'problem'. Some commentators, for example, have called for the introduction of a broad containment policy (Krauthammer, 1995). A narrower approach has also been suggested, such as the strengthening of the US-Japanese military alliance (Bernstein & Munro, 1997: 31-32). Others have advocated stricter regulations to control the international transfers of military technologies (Cox Report, 1999).[2] In addition to these geopolitical containment strategies, attention has also been drawn to the need to liberalise and democratise China. The ultimate hope is that these measures would make China's increasing stature less threatening (*Economist*, 1996: 12). Some have embraced a push for a tougher American stance on the question of Taiwan as a way of stymying China (Friedman, 1997: 31-32; *Far Eastern Economic Review*, 1992: 3). On the other hand, somewhat less confrontational approaches have included exerting greater pressure on China to spend more of its resources on environmental protection, and inducing the country to

---

[1] According Nayan Chanda of the Far Eastern Economic Review, the French military was opposed to the proposed sale of a French aircraft carrier to China for ideological reasons.
[2] See the Cox Report recommendations (Select Committee, United States House of Representatives, 1999).

adhere more closely to international standards of behaviour deemed more desirable by the critics.[3]

Confronted with such a broad array of critical perspectives, the Chinese government has realised that it must respond if it wishes to continue to exist in a peaceful international environment. Accordingly, it has gone to some lengths to alleviate international concerns over its emergence as a global power. *Inter alia*, it has worked to reassure the outside world that it harbours no sinister ambitions, working instead to reinforce perceptions that China's destiny is tied to, and compatible with, those of other countries. Moreover, China has encouraged the view that its development as a rapidly emerging international power presents not just challenges, but, more importantly, opportunities for others. However, rhetoric not being enough to provide this comprehensive reassurance, the Chinese government has introduced numerous specific measures to back up its professed position. Taken as a whole, the Chinese government's approach constitutes what I would term a 'policy of assurance'.

This paper describes and analyses China's 'policy of assurance' by first of all outlining the central features of this policy. It then seeks to explore the major factors shaping it. Finally, this paper speculates as to its future possible development. In doing so, it seeks to engender a more balanced understanding of China's foreign policy.

THE POLICY OF ASSURANCE

A policy of assurance needs to satisfy at least three requirements if it is to work. First, the party doing the assuring needs to clarify its general policy objectives. Second, the party doing the assuring must address the specific concerns and fears of the party that is to be reassured. Finally, it is important that such a process allows the latter to believe that it is not in the former's interests to betray its own commitments. This is, it can be argued, exactly what the Chinese government has been seeking to achieve in recent years.

Clarifying Policy Objectives

The Chinese government has repeatedly stressed that peace and development constitute China's most important foreign policy objectives. In his report to the Sixteenth National Representative Congress of the Chinese Communist Party, Jiang Zemin, the then Secretary General of the Chinese Communist Party (CCP) Central Committee, stated that the goal of China's foreign policy is to maintain world peace and promote common development (Jiang, 2002: 47). Jiang's successor, Hu Jintao, in his speech to the opening ceremony of the 2004 annual conference of the *Bo'ao Forum for Asia*, stated that: 'The very purpose of China's foreign policy is to maintain world peace and promote common development' (Hu, 2004a). Shortly after this, in an address to mark the fiftieth anniversary of the formulation of the Five

---

[3] An editorial of the Economist argued that the US should abandon efforts to link China's most favoured nation status with China's human rights record and arms sales behaviour and that it is more fruitful to do business with China while trying to promote change in China's human rights situation and arms sales behaviour consistently but quietly (1993: 16). In another editorial, the Economist argued that 'the best hope of getting rid of dictatorship in Beijing is the West's continued economic engagement' (1996: 12).

Principles of Peaceful Coexistence,[4] Premier Wen Jiabao also stressed the importance China attaches to peace in the conduct of its foreign relations (Wen, 2004a).

In addition to peace and development, the Chinese government has stated that it wants to see the evolution of a harmonious world that tolerates diversity and provides benefits to all countries, while maintaining full regard for national sovereignty. Indeed, according to Premier Wen Jiabao, national sovereignty is the essence of national independence, constituting the collective manifestation, and reliable protection, of national interests. He has pointed out that, despite growing interdependence between states in the age of globalisation, national sovereignty remains an important and useful international institution. No state, he observes, has the right to impose its will on other states; the practice of showing disrespect for other states' sovereignty in international relations simply will not work (Wen, 2004a).

Beyond the more mechanical aspects of national sovereignty, according to the Chinese government, the international community should also recognise, and show respect for, the reality of cultural and political diversity in the world. Diversity of civilisations in the world, according to Premier Wen, is a basic feature of human society. It is also an important driving force for world progress. The numerous differences in historical tradition, religion, culture, social system, values and levels of development, he argues, are what make the world colourful and fascinating. Countries should recognise and accept such a reality. They should show greater tolerance and respect for diversity, and, he concludes, should learn to live in peace despite the differences between and among them (Wen, 2004a).

Moreover, to the Chinese government, the international economic system needs to be reformed to benefit all countries, especially the poorer and less developed ones. A major challenge to the international community, it argues, is to provide a favourable international environment for the poorer countries to catch up with the richer ones, thereby arresting the trend of further polarisation. To meet such a challenge, the international community should strive to respect poorer countries' perspectives, allowing them to pursue development in accordance to their own needs and conditions (Wen, 2004a). At the same time, developed nations should also do as much as possible to help poorer states in their efforts to develop. As Chinese Foreign Minister Tang Jiaxuan put it, the developing countries sustain greater difficulties in the age of globalisation, and the developed states 'ought to lend them a helping hand in such areas as finance, trade, technology transfer and development aid and make good on their debt relief promises' (Tang, 2002). In the eyes of the Chinese government, helping the poorer countries to develop not only benefits the latter, but also the developed countries themselves. Thus, in Tang's words: 'Assisting the developing countries today is to invest in the common destiny of all human beings' (Tang, 2002).

China has often stated that multilateralism is the right path for coping with the world's problems. According to former Vice-Premier Qian Qichen, the international community 'should opt for multilateralism and give full play to the important role of the UN. Our world is one big family. Naturally, family affairs should be handled by all its members through consultations' (Qian, 2004). In areas of multilateral cooperation, the Chinese government believes that the United Nations has an especially important role to play. Qian has observed that the United Nations is

---

[4] Mutual respect for sovereignty and territorial integrity; mutual non-aggression; non-interference in each others' internal affairs; equality and mutual benefit; peaceful coexistence.

the core of the collective security mechanism and the best venue for multilateral interchanges.... [Therefore, it] should continue to play its important role in international affairs. Facts have proved that no major international issues can be tackled by just one or two countries or a group of countries laying down the law. (Qian, 2004)

In stressing the need for multilateral cooperation, China sees this as not only an important condition for peace, but also an important requirement for development. As Chinese Foreign Minister Tang put it in 2002:

It would not be in the interest of a sound world economy if the laws of the marketplace were given a free rein to dominate globalization. The international community needs to reform the current rules in the world economy, strengthen guidance and management of the globalization process, take account of fairness and reduce risks while seeking efficiency, and steer globalization in an 'all-win' direction of coexistence. (Tang, 2002)

Whether in a multilateral or bilateral setting, the Chinese government believes that dialogue and negotiation is the preferred approach to dealing with international problems. Chinese Premier Wen reiterated this when arguing that it was time to abandon the old Cold War mentality and develop a new way of thinking on the basis of mutual trust, mutual benefit, equality and cooperation. The international community should seek security through dialogue and stability through cooperation. It should work together to fight against terrorism, the proliferation of weapons, drug smuggling and other forms of transnational crime. It should also join hands in dealing with such global problems as AIDS and ecological degradation (Wen, 2004a).

Finally, China has reaffirmed in a number of ways the firm position that it will not seek hegemony,[5] even when it becomes a global power. In his speech at the second annual meeting of the *Bo'ao Forum*, Premier Wen Jiabao announced that the world should rest assured that a dynamic, strong and prosperous China will be dedicated to world peace and development, and will never seek to gain hegemony (Wen, 2003).

Addressing Specific Concerns

In addition to clarifying its broad foreign policy objectives, the Chinese government has also tried to address the specific concerns of the outside world, and to do so on a whole range of issues. On the question of terrorism, the Chinese government has repeatedly stated that it is opposed to any resort to terrorism as a means of attaining political goals, and has called for international cooperation in the war against terrorism. At the Opening Session of the Asia Europe Meeting (ASEM) Seminar on Anti-Terrorism on 22 September 2003, China's Assistant Foreign Minister Shen Guofang argued that: 'As a victim of terrorism, China has firmly supported and actively participated in the international campaign against terrorism while pushing for the leading role of the UN in this regard'. China, he concluded, 'has

---

[5] In the Chinese vocabulary, hegemony is translated as baquan. It means the power to manipulate and control on the basis of power capabilities. It is often understood in negative terms, as opposed to power gained by virtue and example.

earnestly implemented the relevant Security Council resolutions and acceded to most counter-terrorism conventions':

> [It] has advocated vigorous regional anti-terrorism cooperation and conducted fruitful bilateral cooperation with countries concerned.... [It] has also stepped up within our competent departments the crackdown on terrorism, including measures in legislation, aviation, finance, customs and other fields with a view to preventing terrorist incidents. (Shen, 2003)

On the question of arms control and non-proliferation, the Chinese government has repeatedly stated that it is committed to participating in any international efforts undertaken in these areas. According to Vice-Foreign Minister Zhang Yesui, the Chinese government is firmly opposed to the proliferation of weapons of mass destruction and their means of delivery, pointing out that China has already set up a complete system of laws and regulations on export control. This, he concludes,

> cover[s] various kinds of sensitive technologies and items in nuclear, biological, chemical and missile fields, employed universally-practiced export control measures including the end user/use certificate, licensing system, control list and catch-all, and introduced clear-cut punishment measures against acts in breach of the relevant laws and regulations. (Tang, 2002)

As a result of these efforts, China's non-proliferation export control practice is 'basically in line with such mechanisms as MTCR [missile technology control regime] and NSG [nuclear suppliers group] and the practice of the US' (Zhang, 2004). According to government sources, China will 'complete further improvement on its export management mechanisms for biological and chemical dual-use items' in the days to come. Moreover, it 'supports the international community in taking effective measures to prevent the dangerous trend of weaponization in outer space' (Tang, 2002).

With regard to regional security mechanisms, China has voiced its full support to efforts at institutionalising regional security cooperation. For example, it has endorsed the 10+3 Cooperation Mechanism between ASEAN and China, Japan and the Republic of Korea (South Korea). It commended the mechanism for respecting 'the diversity of national conditions and the unevenness in the level of economic development of various countries' (Zhu, 2001a). China also stressed the importance of furthering 'such principles as mutual benefit, incremental progress and stressing practical results' (Zhu, 2001a). Finally, it gave 'full consideration to the interests of all parties, the small and medium-sized countries in particular, which makes it unique among regional cooperation mechanisms in the world' (Zhu, 2001a).

On the question of human rights, the Chinese government has made clear its intention to improve its human rights situation and engage in international efforts to promote human rights on a basis of equality and mutual respect. According to Vice-Foreign Minister Wang Guangya, human beings are 'the most precious among all things on earth.... To promote their development and protect all their due rights is not only the common pursuit of mankind, but also the symbol for the evolving progress of human civilization' (Wang, 2002).

The Chinese government acknowledges that China's human rights situation is by no means perfect and, in the words of Wang, it still has 'a long way to go before human rights and fundamental freedoms are fully realized' (Wang, 2002). Accordingly, the Chinese government will be 'firmly and unswervingly' committed to such a goal. The government points out that China stands ready to strengthen dialogues and exchanges with all countries, the Office of the UN High Commissioner for Human Rights (UNHCHR) and other international organisations, but to do so on the basis of equality, mutual respect, 'a positive and open attitude, [and] with a view to learning from each other and making common progress' (Wang, 2002).

On the question of international economic relations, the Chinese government has advocated 'a global partnership geared to development' (Tang, 2002). In his speech at the General Debate of the 57th Session of the United Nations General Assembly on 13 September 2002, Chinese Foreign Minister Tang Jiaxuan observed that governments, international organisations, transnational corporations, and non-governmental groups are all 'parties to the cause of development and should work together for the implementation of the UN's millennium development goals. Between the South and the North, the aid recipient countries and international aid institutions, there should be a partnership characterized by mutual benefit, equality and cooperation' (Tang, 2002).

In response to international concerns over China's rapidly growing economic influence, Chinese authorities have argued that while China's economic development may appear as a challenge to the outside world, it also offers fresh and expanding opportunities. At the Fifth China-ASEAN Summit on 6 November 2001, Former Premier Zhu Rongji reassured Southeast Asian neighbours that China's accession to the World Trade Organization (WTO) would 'provide other countries ... with [a] better environment for investment and more business opportunities' (Zhu, 2001b). Elsewhere, Wen Jiabao argued in a similar vein by stating that 'China's growth will provide enormous business opportunities for all countries and regions of the world' (Wen, 2004b). Hu Jintao, too, has observed: 'A more prosperous China is destined to offer more business opportunities to the rest of the world', adding: 'China's WTO accession has resulted in further improvement in its investment environment' (Hu, 2004b). Indeed, Hu has promised that China would:

> keep its market open by reducing access restrictions, improving our laws and regulations on foreign investment and making more services and trade available to foreign investors,... creat[ing] new ways of attracting foreign investment, and push for greater reform in government administrative system by building a predictable and more transparent management system for sectors open to foreign investment..... [At the same time it would] protect still more effectively the intellectual property rights of overseas investors and their enterprises in China and provide a better environment and more favorable terms to both foreign investment in China and China's foreign trade and economic cooperation with the other countries. (Hu, 2004b)

Concerning the issue of environmental protection, China has stated that it attaches great importance to this, and has repeatedly expressed its determination to do more in this area in future. At the World Summit on Sustainable Development on 3 September 2002, Premier Zhu said: 'We in China will, as always, energetically participate in international environment cooperation and work with all other countries in protecting the global environment and realizing sustainable development throughout the world' (Zhu, 2002).

China also has a number of more immediate localised concerns, but ones which potentially have considerable implications for the region and, indeed, for the world as a whole. One of these is the Korean nuclear crisis. In this, the Chinese government has repeatedly stated that it is opposed to nuclearisation of the Korean Peninsula and urges for peaceful resolution of the crisis. Premier Wen has stated that China advocates a nuclear-free Peninsula and a peaceful solution of the Democratic People's Republic of Korea (DPRK) nuclear issue with diplomatic means, to maintain peace and stability of the Peninsula (Permanent Mission of the PRC to the UN, 2003).

The other relates to the problem of Taiwan and reunification. The Chinese government has made it clear that even though the Taiwan problem is a domestic issue, it will take into account other countries' concerns and interests and make greater efforts to seek a peaceful resolution. In his visit to the US, Premier Wen told President Bush that China would make the greatest efforts with utmost sincerity to achieve the peaceful reunification of the motherland (Permanent Mission of the PRC to the UN, 2003). In addition to this, Chinese leaders have made numerous comments to this effect on various occasions.

Words and Deeds

The Chinese government understands that its efforts to formulate, clarify and disseminate increasingly sophisticated policies are not enough in themselves sufficient to allay the concerns and fears of the outside world. It needs to follow these up with concrete actions. Accordingly, it has adopted a series of measures to back up its rhetoric. To begin with, China has assumed many legally binding international responsibilities by subscribing to international agreements and covenants. On the question of arms control and non-proliferation, for example, it is a party of:

- Protocol for the Prohibition of the Use in War of Asphyxiating, Poisonous or Other Gases, and of Bacteriological Methods of Warfare
- Convention on Prohibition or Restriction on the Use of Certain Conventional Weapons Which May Be Deemed to Be Excessively Injurious or to Have Indiscriminate Effects
- Antarctic Treaty
- Treaty on Principles Governing the Activities of States in the Exploration and Use of Outer Space
- Convention on the Prohibition of the Development, Production and Stockpiling of Bacteriological (Biological) and Toxin Weapons and on Their Destruction
- Treaty on the Prohibition of the Emplacement of Nuclear Weapons and Other Weapons of Mass Destruction on the Seabed and the Ocean Floor and in the Subsoil Thereof
- Treaty on the Non-Proliferation of Nuclear Weapons
- Convention on the Prohibition of the Development, Production, Stockpiling and Use of Chemical Weapons and on Their Destruction (Information Office of the State Council of the PRC, 1995).

This is also the case on other issues such as environment, human rights and trade.

Second, China has increased its levels of support for multilateral cooperation, both at regional and global levels. In recent years, it has increased markedly its financial contribution to the UN, as well as its participation in various UN peacekeeping operations.[6] It has also played an active role in regional security mechanisms, including official dialogues such as the ASEAN Regional Forum and many second-track security dialogues such as the Shanghai Cooperation Organization (SCO), Conference on Interaction and Confidence-Building Measures in Asia (CICA), Council on Security Cooperation in the Asia-Pacific Region (CSCAP), Northeast Asia Cooperation Dialogue (NEACD). It has attached much importance to playing such a role (Informational Office of the State Council of the PRC, 2002).

Third, China made significant concessions to join the World Trade Organization (WTO) and has made substantial efforts to fulfil its commitments, despite domestic political resistance to some of the dimensions of its membership of this body. It has *inter alia* repealed, revised or enacted more than a thousand laws, regulations and other administrative measures in its efforts to comply WTO requirements (United States Trade Representative, 2004: 3). It has lowered its trade tariffs, reduced thresholds for foreign investment in previously restricted sectors, and given access to foreign presence in financial, legal and other sectors that had previously been closed to foreign involvement. Furthermore, it has actively promoted the establishment of free economic areas with ASEAN countries, and free trade agreements with Australia and other countries.

Fourth, China has made significant efforts to improve security relations with its neighbours. It has concluded border agreements with a number of countries with which it shares borders, including Russia, Kazakhstan, Tajikistan, Kyrgyzstan and Vietnam. It has also stepped up negotiations over borders with India, a country with which it has had tense relations for some time. China has also advocated peaceful resolution of the disputes over maritime borders between itself and other countries in the region, such as disputes with Vietnam, the Philippines, Malaysia and Brunei over the ownership of the Spratley Islands in the South China Sea, and disputes with Japan over Diaoyu Island and the East China Sea. And it is a principal founding member of the Shanghai Cooperation Organization and has tried to work together with Russia and Kazakhstan, Tajikistan, Kyrgyzstan and Uzbekistan to promote broad spheres of cooperation between these states, such as joint efforts to fight against terrorism, separatism and extremism, as well as maintaining regional stability and promoting economic relations among member states.

Finally, China has tried to promote peaceful settlement of the Korean nuclear crisis. Ever since the recent round of tension over the alleged North Korean nuclear program escalated, the Chinese government has tried to bring the concerned parties together and push for a peaceful settlement of the problem. It conducted shuttle diplomacy between Washington, Pyongyang, Seoul, Moscow and other capitals. Furthermore, it has successively hosted a three-party dialogue and several rounds of six party talks.

---

[6] 'China's representative said his country's assessment for 2004-2006 would increase by 35.18 per cent over the last period.... Not only had China fulfilled its financial obligations to the Organization, but as a permanent member of the Security Council it had also assumed additional financial obligations towards peacekeeping' (UN Press Release GA/AB/3576, 2003).

INTERESTS, PRIORITIES AND PERCEPTIONS: AN EXPLANATION

In describing the dimensions of China's 'policy of assurance', one finds that three factors play an especially important role in shaping the latter: (1) China's interests and priorities; (2) China's growing stake in peace and prosperity of the world; and (3) evolution in China's view of its relations with the rest of the world.

China's Interests and Priorities

China's interests and priorities have made the adoption of the 'policy of assurance' not just a choice, but a necessity. As a developing country undergoing drastic social, political and economic transformations, China is confronted by numerous domestic challenges, ranging from uneven economic development, to the poor management of state-owned enterprises; from growing social inequality, to a worsening ecological environment; and from official corruption, to human rights abuses. Some of its main priorities have been, as discussed earlier, to find ways to devote both effort and resources to the business of dealing with these complex challenges. In order to succeed in these areas, and in the process transform China into a modern, humane and harmonious state, the Chinese government needs all the time, energy and resources it can muster. For these reasons alone, it badly needs the perpetuation of a peaceful, stable international environment.

However, the growing international uneasiness and fear about the rise of China represents a potential problem. If left unaddressed, this unease and fear is likely to spread, and lend itself to manipulation by forces hostile to China.[7] This could lead to an elaboration of defensive, and perhaps even the projection of aggressive, policies by foreign governments against China. The unfolding of such policy lines would tend to undermine China's international environment. To avoid this, the Chinese government must continue to do all in its power to ease the fears of the international community.

China's Political and Economic Integration with the Outside World

In the same way that China's interests and priorities have made the adoption of the 'policy of assurance' necessary, China's political and economic integration into the outside world has helped to define the ways in which it reassures the outside world. Following China's rapprochement with the United States in the early 1970s, China established diplomatic relations with most countries in the world and became an active member of most important international governmental organisations. In the process, and especially after the launching of the Open Policy in 1979, China's economic relations with the outside world have increased rapidly. The ever-deepening political and economic linkages between China and the outside world have provided China with enhanced channels via which it can express its views, defend its legitimate interests, and promote the reform of the existing international order. With time, China has also developed the expertise and experience necessary to take

---

[7] Such as the so-called 'Blue Team', a group of people inside and outside the official establishment in Washington who believe that China is a threat and the US should devote its resources to contain China (Branegan, 2001).

advantage of the opportunities afforded by its membership in a variety of international institutions. This has allowed it to defend and facilitate its interests and aspirations. The latter have included efforts to reform existing rules and formulate new rules for proper international behaviour. Growing economic relations between China and other countries have given China an ever-larger stake in international stability and prosperity. This has in great measure—and most usefully—reduced the distrust and hostility China harboured towards aspects of the international order, and has in the process provided China with an enhanced sense of identity.

All this has, in turn, done much to change the nature of China's relations with the outside world. It has enabled China to reassure the outside world. The task at hand, however, is to prevent these gains from being reversed or tarnished by growing suspicions and fears of what China might do with its enhanced place in the world.

Evolution in China's View of its Relations with the Outside World

China's changing perceptions of its relations with the outside world has, it has been argued above, enhanced the way it can reassure the outside world. As China's interactions with the rest of the world have increased, China's view of international relations has undergone three important changes: (1) from viewing international relations in ideological (that is, Marxist or communist) terms to viewing them in more conventional terms; (2) from viewing international relations as a zero-sum game to a positive-sum game; and (3) from a position of suspicion and hostility toward the international system, to one with which China identifies. These attitudinal changes have, in turn, led to China's conceptualisation of its relations with the outside world, and its redefinition of the objectives of its foreign policy in a way that is reassuring to the international community.

In sum, China's interests and priorities, China's integration with the outside world and China's changing perceptions of its relations with the outside world, have made it necessary for China to take the previously discussed measures to assure the outside world of its benign intentions, but in so doing has also helped to shape positively the way in which China engages in the sphere of international cooperation.

PROSPECTS

Will the Chinese government adhere to the 'policy of assurance' discussed in this essay? Analysis of the factors shaping this policy shows that it is likely. To begin with, at least for the foreseeable future, China will continue to face considerable—and pressing—problems at home, so the goal of maintaining a peaceful international environment is likely to remain its key foreign policy objective. Second, as China's integration with the outside world deepens, its identification with the existing international system is likely to grow stronger. This will in turn continue to shape the way it reassures the outside world of its intent and sense of responsibility. Finally, short of drastic changes in China's relations with the outside world, China is likely to continue to view these in a non-zero sum way, aligning its interests to, and advocating policies largely consistent with, those of the international community.

REFERENCES

Bernstein, Richard and Ross H. Munro (1997) 'The Coming Conflict With America'. *Foreign Affairs*, March/April.

Branegan, J. (2001) 'The Hardliners: A 'Blue Team' Blocks China'. *Time*, 16 April.

Brown, Lester (1994) 'Who Will Feed China?' *World Watch*, 7(5).

Chanda, Nayan (1996) 'No Cash-Carrier: France May Be Buckling on Chinese Arms Embargo'. *Far Eastern Economic Review*, 10 October.

Cox Report (1999) Select Committee, United States House of Representatives, *U.S. National Security and Military/Commercial Concerns with the People's Republic of China*, Chapter 11, Washington: U.S. Government Printing Office.

Economist (1992) 'The Titan Stirs: The Chinese Economy'. 28 November: 3-18.

——— (1993) 'Gripped By China'. 27 November.

——— (1996) 'Changing China'. 23 March.

Far Eastern Economic Review (1992) 'A New China'. 29 October.

Friedman, Edward (1997) 'Chinese Nationalism, Taiwan Autonomy and the Prospects of a Larger War'. *Journal of Contemporary China*, March.

Hu, Jintao (2004a) *China's Development is an Opportunity for Asia*, 27 April. http://www.chinataiwan.org/web/webportal/W5023952/A2175.html

——— (2004b) *Advancing Win-Win Cooperation for Sustainable Development: Speech by President Hu Jintao of China At the APEC CEO Summit*, 19 November, http://www.fmprc.gov.cn/eng/wjdt/zyjh/t172475.htm

Information Office of the State Council of the PRC (1995) *China: Arms Control and Disarmament*, November, http://www.china.org.cn/e-white/army/a-7.htm

——— (2002) *China's National Defense in 2002*, Beijing, December, http://www.china.org.cn/e-white/20021209/VI.htm#1

Jiang, Zemin (2002) *Quanmian jianshe xiaokang shehui: kaichuang zhongguo tese shehuizhuyi shiye xin jumian*, Beijing: Renmin Publishing House.

Krauthammer, Charles (1995) 'Why Must We Contain China?' *Times*, 31 July.

Kristof, Nicholas D. (1993) 'The Rise of China'. *Foreign Affairs*, November/December.

Permanent Mission of the PRC to the UN, *Premier Wen Jiabao Holds Talks with the US President Bush*, 10 December 2003, http://www.china-un.org/eng/xw/t56088.htm

Qian, Qichen (2004) *Multilateralism, the Way to Respond to Threats and Challenges*, Statement by H.E. Mr. Qian Qichen, Former Vice-Premier of China at the New Delhi Conference, 2 July, http://www.fmprc.gov.cn/eng/wjdt/zyjh/t142393.htm

Shen, Guofang (2003) Speech by H. E. Mr. Shen Guofang, Assistant Foreign Minister of China, at the Opening Session of ASEM Seminar on Anti-Terrorism, 22 September, http://www.fmprc.gov.cn/eng/wjdt/zyjh/t26278.htm

Tang, Jiaxuan (2002) Statement by H.E. Tang Jiaxuan, Minister of Foreign Affairs of the People's Republic of China, and Head of the Chinese Delegation, at the General Debate of the 57th Session of the United Nations General Assembly, 13 September, http://www.fmprc.gov.cn/eng/wjdt/zyjh/t25092.htm

UN Press Release GA/AB/3576 (2003) *Importance of Timely, Full Payment of UN Contributions, 'Capacity to Pay' Principle Reaffirmed, as Fifth Committee Takes Up*

Scale of Assessments, Fifty-eight General Assembly Meeting- Fifth Meeting (AM), 14 October, http://www.un.org/News/Press/docs/2003/gaab3576.doc.htm

United States Trade Representative (2004) *2004 Report to Congress on China's WTO Compliance*, http://www.cecc.gov/pages/virtualAcad/commercial/USTR.china.2004.pdf?PHPSESSID=fdbf190484029bff1b8d5fb0881d1c2db

Wang, Guangya (2002) *Make Joint Efforts Towards a Healthy Development of the Cause of Human Rights*, Statement at the 58th Session of the United Nations Commission on Human Rights, Geneva, 2 April, http://www.fmprc.gov.cn/eng/wjdt/zyjh/t25072.htm

Wen, Jiabao (2003) *Yong bu chengba de zhongguo jiang wei yazhou zhenxing zuochu xin gongxian* (*The China That Never Seeks Hegemony Will Make New Contributions to the Rise of Asia*), 2 November, http://finance.sina.com.cn/g/20031102/1129501516.shtml

────── (2004a) *Hongyang wu xiang yuanze: cujin heping fazhan* (*Uphold Five Principles and Promote Peace and Development*), 28 June, http://www.fmprc.gov.cn/chn/wjdt/zyjh/t140781.htm

────── (2004b) *Strengthening Partnership Through Increased Dialogue and Cooperation: Speech at the Fifth Asia-Europe Meeting*, 9 October, http://www.fmprc.gov.cn/eng/wjdt/zyjh/t164329.htm

Zhang, Yesui (2004) *Speech by Vice Foreign Minister Zhang Yesui at the Fifth China-US Conference on Arms Control, Disarmament and Non-Proliferation*, 20 July, http://www.fmprc.gov.cn/eng/wjdt/zyjh/t143538.htm

Zhu, Rongji (2002) 'Steadfastly Take the Road of Sustainable Development'. Speech by H.E. Mr. Zhu Rongji, Premier of the State Council of the People's Republic of China, at the World Summit on Sustainable Development, 3 September, http://www.fmprc.gov.cn/eng/wjdt/zyjh/t25091.htm

────── (2001a) *Premier Zhu Rongji Attended the 5th Leaders' Meeting between the Association of Southeast Asian Nations (ASEAN) and China, Japan and the Republic of Korea and Issued A Speech*, 5 November, http://www.fmprc.gov.cn/eng/wjdt/zyjh/t25045.htm

────── (2001b) 'Working Together to Create a New Phase of China-ASEAN Cooperation'. Address by Premier Zhu Rongji at 5th China-ASEAN Summit, 6 November, http://www.fmprc.gov.cn/eng/wjdt/zyjh/t25046.htm

In: Asia-Pacific and a New International Order
Editors: Purnendra Jain et al. pp. 145-164
ISBN 1-59454-986-9
© 2006 Nova Science Publishers, Inc.

Chapter 10

SOUTH KOREA *VIS-À-VIS* THE INTERNATIONAL DISORDER: INTERNAL SPLIT AND EXTERNAL INITIATIVES

Myongsob Kim and Yongho Kim

INTRODUCTION

The present South Korean government seems to be trying to bring North Korea out of the decades of isolation and self-imposed confinement into a peaceful and prosperous regional system, complementing at the same time some lacunae of regional relationships that have developed between Japan, the United States, Russia, China and the two Koreas since the Second World War, let alone the Korean War.

We might say that a war is not really ended until a new order is established. The Thirty Years War was followed by the Westphalian order. The chaos of Napoleonic War was sealed by the order of Vienna. World War I was followed by the order of Versailles. How about the Cold War? Even though it is over, a new international order that can seal the hostilities has not yet developed, especially in Northeast Asia.

According to Robert Cooper, 'the year 1989 marks a break in European history.... What happened in 1989 was not just the cessation of the Cold War, but also the end of the balance-of-power system in Europe' (Cooper, 2003: 3). What kind of order can we dream after the end of this system? We might dream of Pax Imperial or Pax International, but at present the term 'international disorder' seems to be more appropriate, at least in Northeast Asia. Personally, we find ourselves living in a jungle with a bewildering number of poisonous snakes that have sprung out from the blood of Medusa; terror, Weapons of Mass Destruction, the growing gap between the rich and the poor, the growing possibility of a disastrous big bang caused by China and India, immigration and minority tensions, AIDS and Mad Cow Disease, environmental degradation, no global consensus on environmental improvement, and, last but not least, a unilateral American empire in which the real concept of 'international' is becoming archaic.

It might be fair to say that the current Northeast Asian disorder is somewhere between a regional international order and a global imperial order dominated by the US, while China looms as a potential challenger. Most importantly, it is highly possible that this disorder will persist if major powers continue to be preoccupied with strong realist, conflict-oriented ideology. This speculation posits that Northeast Asia is most likely to head toward a new Cold War. Thus, the tragedy of great power politics is a major threat to the current meta-stable regional condition (Friedberg 1993/94; Mearsheimer 2001).

The pessimistic view presented in Mearsheimer's 'Back to the Future' (1990a) has been proved to be less relevant to Europe, but the Cassandra seems to have been resurrected in Northeast Asia which is 'yet to establish whether its geopolitical future will resemble the Europe of the first half of the twentieth century or the Europe of the second half of the twentieth century' (Brzezinski, 2004: 107). Northeast Asia is metastable (Brzezinski, 2004: 107) — as a physical term, metastable state means a stable state until subjected to a sudden impact that sets off a destructive chain reaction — due to a number of conditions: the absence of a Peace Treaty between North Korea and Japan since World War II; the absence of a Peace Treaty between North Korea, China and the United States after the Korean War; the North Korean violation of the inter-Korean non-nuclear declaration; China's quest for the recovery of a 'traditional' Sinocentric order; the reluctance of the Japanese to follow the German way of closing the war memory; the unresolved territorial issues between Russia and Japan; and, last but not least, the unstable relationship between China and Taiwan.

In Northeast Asia too many sources of disorder coexist with too limited a capacity for institutional governance. As Mearsheimer notes, we cannot expect China to act differently from a United States that reacts harshly when other great powers send military forces into the Western Hemisphere (Brzezinski and Mearsheimer, 2005). According the prediction of Mearsheimer, this offensive realism is then almost the same for North Korea—Better to be Hedgehog than Bambi, if great powers think that being Godzilla is better than being Bambi. There is no reason why we should expect North Korea to act differently from India, Pakistan, or even France when these states fought against Anglo-Saxon and Soviet duopoly of the atomic bomb in the early Cold War era.

As our analysis shows, Koreans, especially the younger generations, are becoming more reluctant to accept the status of a military outpost of a Cold War empire. Reflecting a very active participation of this 'people's will', the present South Korean government envisages a regional cooperation in Northeast Asia where disorder is still preponderant. To understand the present South Korean government's 'Northeast Asian Cooperation Initiative', a review of the phenomenon of the 'two South Koreas' is a *sine qua non*. According to the official website of presidential office, participatory government opened 'a new era of people's victory where principles prevail and the people's sovereignty is substantiated.... popular participation will play a pivotal role in the future operation of this government, as it did during its birth'. The Northeast Asian Cooperation initiative is an international extension of this philosophy.

This paper analyses South Korean responses to the present international situation, one that causes an internal split that might be called the phenomenon of 'two South Koreas' beyond the two Koreas. Globalisation, with its appearance of Americanisation, seems to be accelerating the internal split. The option that the present South Korean government has chosen to resolve the internal split and tensions surrounding globalisation is the initiative which will potentially lead to a peaceful and prosperous Northeast Asia.

THE INTERNAL SPLIT: EMERGING 'TWO SOUTH KOREAS'?

Security Issues as Campaign Tools

Leadership changes in post-Cold War South Korea brought about various changes, among them the politicisation of foreign and security issues previously out of bounds because of 'national security'. Leadership changes themselves have been driving forces in South Korea's reactions to the new security environment. Kim Young Sam was elected in December 1992, the first civilian president without a professional military career since President Park Chung Hee took power in 1961. Kim was followed by President Kim Dae-jung in 1997, and then President Roh Moo Hyun in 2002. Unlike their military professional predecessors, these career-politician presidents deliberately use North Korea and security issues as campaign tools.

Kim Young Sam, the conservative ruling party candidate in the 1997 election, used the question of ideology against his primary rival, Kim Dae-jung, by claiming that unification required a man of solid (non-left or non-communist) ideology (*Hankook Ilbo*, 10 December 1992: 1). His campaign strategy of contrasting his hardline North Korea policy against Kim Dae-jung's relatively flexible stance dominated the campaign. After Kim Young Sam won the election, his hardline policy proved to be nothing but a campaign strategy. Immediately after inauguration in February 1993, Kim proclaimed a thoroughly dove-like policy toward the North, appointing a liberal scholar, Han Wan-sang, as his first unification minister, and repatriating the long-term convict, Lee In-mo, to the North (*Joong-ang Ilbo*, 1 March 1993: 1, 3). This initiative ended in a 19-month-long nuclear stalemate after Pyongyang announced its withdrawal from the Nuclear Proliferation Treaty (NPT) in March 1993.

North Korea again became a hot issue in South Korea's June 1995 elections for local government and parliaments. The Kim Young Sam government used dramatic symbolism to appeal to South Korean voters. It first asked for Japan, through diplomatic channels, to abstain from providing food aid to Pyongyang ahead of South Korea (*Hankook Ilbo*, 28 May 1995: 1). It then elicited an agreement from Pyongyang on the offer of 50,000 tons of rice that was scheduled to be shipped to the North on 25 June—the 45th anniversary of the outbreak of the Korean War. At the same time, two days before the local elections, on the evening 25 of June, the ruling party's main candidates exploited the symbolic food aid by promising a regular exchange of soccer games between Seoul and Pyongyang and suggesting a blueprint to develop the relatively underdeveloped northern Kyonggi province as a base for unification (*Chosun Ilbo*, 26 June 1995: 6). Despite this, the opposition, led by Kim Dae-jung, swept to victory, winning 122 seats out of 133 in Seoul's local parliament (*Hankook Ilbo*, 29 June 1995: 35).

Ten months after the local elections, the North Korean issue emerged again in the midst of the 1996 legislative election. Seven days before the 11 April election, North Korea declared it would not respect the armistice treaty and sent roughly 250 heavily-armoured North Korean troops into the Panmunjom joint security area (*Segye Ilbo*, 10 April 1996: 2). The ruling party won the election by winning 121 seats against Kim Dae-jung's mere 66 seats. Major news agencies such as Reuter, AP, AFP and UPI were quoted to indicate that the so-called 'north wind' operated in favour of the ruling party (*Hankook Ilbo*, 12 April 1996: 11; *Seoul Shinmun*, 13 April 1996: 5; *Hankyoreh Shinmun*, 12 April 1996: 2).

Three days before the 13 April legislative election of 2000, the first official announcement of the historic inter-Korean summit was made public. This was Kim Dae-jung's government's first attempt to exploit inter-Korean relations as a campaign tool and it failed. Opposition parties criticised the decision to announce the holding of the summit three days before the legislative election by labelling it as 'an event only for the election' and by declaring that the ruling party subsumed national interests under its own political interests (*Donga Ilbo*, 11 April 2000: 5; *Hankook Ilbo*, 12 April 2000: 7). Both the *Los Angeles Times* and *New York Times* indicated the possibility that the Kim Dae-jung government made use of the inter-Korean summit to influence the outcome of the election in favour of the ruling party. The *Washington Post* found that North Korea, by agreeing to hold the summit, helped the ruling party against the opposition conservatives (*Los Angeles Times*, 11 April 2000; *New York Times*, 11 April 2000: A6; *Washington Post*, 11 April 2000: 5; *Segye Ilbo*, 13 April 2000: 10). Nevertheless, the ruling party failed to win the election, winning only 115 seats against two major opposition parties with 133 and 17 seats, respectively.

In the 2002 presidential election, issues relating to US forces in Korea emerged as the central focus of the campaign. When two soldiers were acquitted of negligent homicide charges on 20 and 22 November, roughly four weeks before the presidential election, activist groups prompted nationwide anti-American sentiment by propounding the slogan: 'Two girls dead and no one guilty'. The accident had taken place on 13 June 2002. Two 13-year-old female junior high school students were run over by a Bradley armoured vehicle moving on a narrow local road in Yangju county (north of Seoul) during a training exercise by the US 2nd Infantry Division. The case was delivered to US court martial in accordance with the Status of Forces Agreement (SOFA) that stipulates US judicial authority over an accident during official operations. Two US soldiers, the commander of the armoured vehicle and the driver were court-martialled on charges of negligent homicide. The difference in legal systems between South Korea and the United States was a factor further agitating the South Korean public. Unlike in the US, South Korean prosecutors are permitted to appeal a not-guilty verdict by asserting that the accident was avoidable if the two soldiers had not neglected their duty of care.

Right before the election, poll results demonstrated that 64.6~65.3 per cent of the voters believed anti-Americanism would make an impact on the election outcome (*Hankook Ilbo*, 16 December 2002: 4; *Munhwa Ilbo*, 12 December 2002: 4). CNN coverage also indicated the election would 'determine the path of future relations with the United States' and described Roh Moo Hyun as 'riding the wave' of anti-Americanism (CNN, 2002). In fact, during his campaign, Roh had clearly taken an anti-American posture by stating: 'no objection against anti-Americanism…. we have to speak up [about] different opinions from that of the United States' (*Kyunghyang Shinmun*, 19 May 2003: 4) and by calling for 'President Bush's apology' (*Hankook Ilbo*, 15 May 2003: 4). Thus, Roh could consolidate support from the voters in their twenties and thirties. The same logic explains why President Roh gave his first official interview to *Ohmynews*, an Internet news website, breaking the tradition of giving the first interview to one of the major newspapers.

The politicisation of security reflects, on one hand, a significant differentiation in views between the older and younger generations, and on the other, exacerbates the spread of ideological splits in society generally. In South Korea, the post-Cold War era has coincided with the increasing influence of the baby-boom generation born in the early 1960s and now reaching their 40s in the 2000s. How to earn votes from the so-called '386 generation'[1] has become the key to winning elections. In the 1992 presidential election, voters in their 20s and 30s occupied respectively 30.5 per cent and 26.7 per cent of the population; in the 1997 presidential election, 26.9 per cent and 26.7 per cent; in the 2000 legislative election, 25.0 per cent and 26.4 per cent, with 20.4 per cent in their 40s; and in the 2002 presidential election, 23.5 per cent and 25.4 per cent, with 22.1 per cent in their 40s (*Chosun Ilbo*, 21 November 1992: 2; *Chosun Ilbo*, 13 December 1997: 7; *Donga Ilbo*, 8 October 2002: 8). Thus, the younger generation, including 'the 386', occupied more than 70 per cent of the voting population in the elections held in the 2000s, hence the generation split.

IDEOLOGICAL CLEAVAGE

In today's South Korea, nothing is as controversial as the debate between conservatism and reformism. The debate seems to be the standard for drawing distinctions between young and old, haves and have-nots, newspapers and TVs, pro-American and anti-American groups, security-first and unificationists, pro-North Korea and anti-North Korea forces, and, ultimately, pro-Roh Moo Hyun and anti-Roh Moo Hyun voters.

What is new in this debate is its impact on foreign policy. Debates in the 2000s are carving an image of South Korea's foreign policy as moving in a nationalist, anti-American, anti-Japanese, pro-North Korean direction. Roh Moo Hyun was elected as South Korea's President when anti-American sentiment, fired by the deaths of the two school girls peaked. The Roh government's move toward liquidating Korea's past history under Japanese rule has also had a strong influence on foreign policy; he and his foreign policy staff have had to work hard to repair this. As part of this process, South Korean society became entangled in ideological conflict. South Korean voters' self-proclaimed ideological positions showed sharp variations during the period from January 2002 to June 2004, as Table 1 illustrates. The percentage of voters who claimed themselves as situated between progressive and conservative decreased from 49.5 to 25.0 per cent. Instead, the percentage of admitted 'progressive' voters increased from 21.4 to 32.0 per cent. Conservative voters increased from 28.5 to 43.0 per cent.

Table 1. Changes in Voters' Ideological Position

	Jan.2002	Aug.2002	Oct.2002	Jan.2003	Feb.2004	Jun.2004
Progressive	21.4	28.6	31.5	34.0	31.0	32.0
Middle	49.5	33.0	32.7	34.8	30.0	25.0
Conservative	28.5	38.4	35.8	31.3	37.0	43.0

(Polls conducted by *Joongang Ilbo*, cited in Kang, 2004: 8.)

---

[1] This term is coined from a computer processor model type known as 386. It refers to those in their thirties, who went to college in the 1980s, and were born in the 1960s. Their anti-government demonstrations in the 1980s led to the democratisation of Korea. At the same time, they are the baby boomers, so their percentage out of the whole population is larger than any other generation. Accordingly, their voting exercises a decisive influence on the outcome of elections.

The emergence of anti-Americanism is the basis of these shifts. As Table 2 demonstrates, the United States has become the Koreans' most hated country. Although the poll was conducted under the sponsorship of a progressive newspaper, *Hankyoreh*, the result illustrates an epistemological alteration of the social mood toward the United States.

Table 2. Most-Hated Country (*Hankyoreh Sinmun*, 15 May 2003: 42)

2001	2003
Japan (45.3%)	USA (19.1%)
North Korea (17.1%)	North Korea (18.8%)
USA (8.3%)	Japan (17.5%)

However, this does not mean that there exists a society-wide call for breaking-up relations with the US, nor withdrawal of US forces, as Table 3 on relations with the US indicates.

Table 3. Opinions about South Korea's Relations with the US (*Hankook Ilbo*, 9 June 2003: A12)

	2003	2002
Strengthen Alliance with USA	17.8	6.3
Maintain Favorable Relations with USA	58.5	50.1
Get Off USA-centered Diplomacy	18.2	31.8
Adequate Distance Required	4.8	10.3
DK/ No Answer	0.7	1.4

Compared with the 2002 poll when anti-Americanism peaked, in 2003 the poll reveals that 76.3 per cent preferred favourable relations with the United States. However, the same poll offers a somewhat different picture when analysed by generation. In Tables 4 and 5, we can see these remarkable divergences between generations. Table 4 shows that, while the absolute majority of those in their 50s, 60s and above favoured better relations with the United States, more than 50 per cent of those in their 20s and 30s called for at least adequate distance.

Table 4. Opinions about Relations with the United States (Unreported poll result conducted for Hankook Ilbo in 2004)

	Better relations with the USA	Adequate Distance Required	DK/ No Answer
20s	49.6	50.4	0.0
30s	43.4	55.5	1.1
40s	59.8	37.8	2.5
50s	72.5	26.0	1.5
60s and above	77.7	16.1	6.2

Table 5 shows the decreased popularity of the United States, especially amongst the younger and '386' generations. Only 16.5 per cent of those in their 20s, 15.0 per cent in their 30s, and 24.0 per cent of 40-year-olds in 2003 checked 'like' or 'like much' category when they were asked: 'How do you like the United States?'

Table 5. Percentage Answering 'Like' and 'Like Much' to the question, 'How do you like the United States?' (*Hankyoreh Sinmun*, 15 May 2003: 42)

	All	20s	30s	40s	50s
1989	36.7	28.2	30.0	44.3	54.2
2001	36.1	35.2	33.3	36.3	39.6
2003	25.4	16.5	15.0	24.0	43.4

Intermingled with this anti-Americanism is the impact of shifts in regional security. The most notable change is that South Koreans are not concerned at all about the withdrawal of US forces, as Table 6 illustrates.

Table 6. Opinions about the Impact of US Forces Reduction on the Security of South Korea (*Hankook Ilbo*, 15 June 2004: A6)

Very much concerned	Concerned	Concerned little	Not at all concerned	DK/No answer
7.6	39.7	11.6	41.0	0.2

Some 52.6 per cent of respondents answered they are either little concerned or not concerned at all about the reduction of US forces in South Korea. When we look into the generational differences, it is not difficult to see that younger generations care little about the reduction of US forces. While 58.5 per cent of those in their 50s, and 63.2 per cent of the 60s and above were concerned about reduction of US forces, 55.7 per cent of those in their 20s and 66.2 per cent of those in their 30s answered they were concerned but little or not at all.

Table 7. Opinions about the Impact of US Forces Reduction on the Security of South Korea (Unreported poll result conducted for Hankook Ilbo in 2004)

	Very Much Concerned	Concerned	Concerned little	Not at all Concerned	DK/ No Answer
20s	3.8	40.5	45.0	10.7	0
30s	5.8	28.0	48.2	18.0	0
40s	5.5	41.0	42.7	10.8	0
50s	11.8	46.7	32.2	8.5	0.7
60s and above	15.7	48.5	28.6	6.6	0.6

Table 8 shows in more detail the views of each generation on the role of US forces in South Korea. While more than 50 per cent of those above the age of 50 regard US forces in South Korea as contributing to the regional stabilisation, only 19.3 per cent of those in their 20s, 26.6 per cent of those in their 30s, and 38.0 per cent of those in their 40s gave a positive assessment. To the contrary, 77.6 per cent of those in their 20s, 68.6 per cent of those in their 30s, and 52.3 per cent of those in their 40s indicated US forces as a source of tension either in East Asia or in the Korean Peninsula. Of those in their 50s, 32.9 per cent, along with 26.9 per cent of those in their 60s and above, answered they regarded US forces as sources of tension.

Table 8. Opinions about the Role of US Forces in South Korea
(Unreported poll result conducted for Hankook Ilbo in 2004)

	Contributing to the stabilisation of the Korean Peninsula and East Asia	Defending South Korea but a source of tension in East Asia	Contributing to East Asian Stability but a source of tension in the Korean Peninsula	Barrier to Inter-Korean dialogue and source of tension in East Asia	DK/ No Answer
20s	19.3	39.4	19.8	18.4	3.1
30s	26.6	31.2	17.0	20.4	4.9
40s	38.0	21.3	17.7	13.3	9.8
50s	51.7	15.1	11.3	6.5	15.4
60s and above	50.5	11.8	7.9	7.2	22.6

The impact of the new security environment may also be found in the attitude toward North Korea's nuclear program. As Table 9 shows, 53.9 per cent of those in their 20s, 53.5 per cent of those in their 30s, 49.4 per cent of those in their 40s, and 56.2 per cent of those in their 50s do not consider North Korea's nuclear program as a serious threat. Only those in their 60s and above appear to consider it as a serious or major source of threat. Some 54.9 per cent of those in their 60s and above answered they had a negative assessment of Pyongyang's nuclear program.

Table 9. Opinions about North Korea's Nuclear Program
(Unreported poll result conducted for Hankook Ilbo in 2004)

	It poses a serious threat to the security of the Korean Peninsula	It is a major source of threat to the security of the Korean Peninsula	It may not lead to the actual development of nuclear weapons	It may not actually threaten the security of the Korean Peninsula	DK/ NoAnswer
20s	12.7	32.0	29.5	24.4	1.3
30s	8.7	35.9	29.0	24.5	1.9
40s	14.5	27.2	26.3	23.1	9.0
50s	12.9	23.0	35.6	20.6	7.8
60s and above	27.2	27.7	11.3	9.0	24.8

Table 10 shows those in their 20s and 30s believe that the United States is a more serious barrier than North Korea to the solution of the crisis. All other generations regarded North Korea as the main problem.

Table 10. Which Country is the Barrier to the Solution of North Korea's Nuclear Program?
(Unreported poll result conducted for Hankook Ilbo in 2004)

	North Korea	USA	South Korea	China	Japan	Russia	DK/No Answer
20s	32.1	44.7	0.9	7.7	5.8	3.8	5.1
30s	27.5	50.0	0.4	9.9	4.6	1.8	5.8
40s	38.7	31.4	4.2	11.3	4.0	1.9	8.5
50s	44.9	28.1	4.3	4.8	3.4	3.8	10.8
60s and over	35.4	19.4	11.9	7.1	1.6	3.7	21.0

Our discussion so far identifies a significant generational gap over attitudes to security issues. In the past, South Korea's security policy has been developed without any concern for domestic politics. However, according to Rose's theory, while international variables limit the possible scope of a country's foreign policy, they should be 'translated' by intervening domestic variants (Rose, 1998: 146–147). Quite often, the prevailing ideas and ideologies of the domestic scene determine the type and pattern of cooperation possible between nations or states (Press-Barnathan, 2000/2001: 57). Despite this, South Korea's security policies have often been the representation of ideas held by leaders, rather than those of public opinion. This neglect in eliciting domestic support for foreign policies has led to deficiencies in their implementation. In sum, the development of a satisfactory security policy in South Korea must now try to find a means of converging conflicting domestic attitudes about promoting security or cooperation (Press-Barnathan, 2000/2001: 58).

Changed Policy Perceptions of North Korea and the United States

The most notable difference in South Korea's post-Cold War security environment may be found in changed perceptions toward North Korea and the United States. South Korea now officially negates the conceptualisation of North Korea as the primary enemy. Discord between Seoul and Washington is also the product of this changed perception.

Kim Dae-jung had been a consistent promoter of reconciliation and cooperation with North Korea. One of the operating principles of his policy, 'flexible dualism', aims for increasing inter-Korean economic interdependence, calling for 'economy first, politics later' and 'give first, take later' (Moon, 1999: 39). This policy connotes a fundamental change from previous government-oriented politics-first approaches of the preceding governments. The Kim Dae-jung government then launched several inter-Korean trade projects, including Mt Kumkang tours, to provide economic assistance to North Korea. As a result, the volume of inter-Korean trade in 2000 doubled to $US 425.1 million compared with $US 221.9 million in 1998.

Kim's 'Sunshine Policy' was the application of liberalist ideas of economic interdependence or commercial liberalism. This approach posits that commercial relations constrain states from using force against one another because trade spins a web of mutual self-interest. Trade generates economic benefits; these benefits produce an anticipation that conflict would disrupt trade gains; the anticipation is likely to lower risk-acceptance and ultimately prevent a decision to go to war (Barbieri and Levy, 1999: 464). Statistical research by Oneal and Russet verified that economic interdependence is 'generally associated with a reduction in interstate violence' (Oneal and Russet, 1999: 439; Oneal and Russet, 1997: 267–294). As shown, one of the primary objectives of Kim's Sunshine Policy was to decrease the possibility of armed conflict between the two Koreas.

The Sunshine Policy may be also viewed as having its roots in democratic peace. The emphasis on increasing economic interdependence is, in the long term, related to North Korea's human rights situation. As Kim Dae-jung once put it, eliciting a feasible amelioration of North Korea's human rights conditions requires increased dialogue and foreign investment, because poverty is the most serious barrier to better human rights conditions in Pyongyang (*Yonhap News*, 27 February 2000). His emphasis on increased trade with North Korea may be thus understood as a first step towards the democratisation of North Korea. This was a sensible approach, because in East Asian countries, democracy is usually preceded by economic development. The democratisation of North Korea, according to democratic peace propositions, would diminish the possibility of an inter-Korean war.

Another major achievement of the Sunshine Policy was the realisation of the reunion of separated families. After the June 2000 inter-Korean summit, some selected groups of separated families were able to meet their parents, wives, sons, daughters and other relatives for the first time since the Korean War. The reunion (theoretically) functioned to revive the common Korean identity. During the three-year period after Kim Dae-jung's inauguration, 1,174 reunions took place. This was a dramatic rise from only 155 reunions between 1989 and 1997. In addition, the number of letters exchanged after Kim Dae-jung's inauguration totalled 3,130 (it was only 4,407 for the whole period between 1989 and 1997). Constructivists posit that increased social interaction accompanies motivational and cognitive processes in which negative identification of an adversary is gradually converted into a positive one of a friend (Chafets, Spirtas and Frankel, 1998/1999: x). Constructivists refuse to accept that national interests are determined solely by material concerns. Rather, they argue that national interests reflect national identity, a product of slow but repeated interactions. Kim Dae-jung's emphasis on the reunion of separated families was to help formulate an inter-Korean community. Implicit in the constructivist argument is that social interaction promotes something beyond cooperative behaviours. Shared values facilitate a sense of positive identification, which leads to the forming of a community. Nationwide televised scenes of reunion instigate nationalist sentiments of 'us', evolving shared values between South and North Koreans.

In this process, the growing 'us' sentiment affects a fifty-year-long conceptualisation of North Korea as the primary enemy. Debate revolving around the usage of the term 'primary enemy' started right after the June 2000 inter-Korean summit. At the National Defense Committee of South Korea's National Assembly, Kim Dae-jung's party called for a policy of ambiguity with regard to the usage of the term (*Munhwa Ilbo*, 22 June 2000: 4). Two weeks after the summit, South Korea's Ministry of Defense announced its decision to change the term 'North's puppet army' into 'North Korean army' in its publications. The decision was made to reciprocate North Korea's abstinence in using such provocative expressions as 'war-maniac' and 'foe' (*Seoul Shinmun*, 1 July 2000: 2). Nevertheless, the ministry published its *White Paper* with the concept of primary enemy intact on 4 December 2000.

The debate revolving around the idea of a primary enemy became a hot issue as North Korea filed an official request to abolish the concept. South Korea's Ministry of Defense responded by continuously postponing the publication of the *White Paper* that had been published annually since 1988. On 12 December 2000, one day before the fourth ministerial talks, North Korea registered its regret over South Korea's continued usage of the phrase (*Segye Ilbo*, 12 December 2000: 2; *Chosun Central Broadcasting*, 11 December 2000). North Korea raised the issue again on 8 February 2001, at the Panmunjom Working Level Conference for the second inter-Korean talks between defense ministers, by refusing to engage in ministerial talks if 'primary enemy' usage was not abolished (*Seoul Shinmun*, 13 February 2001: 4). Finally, at the end of 2001, with the excuse of avoiding redundant contents, the Ministry of Defense postponed the publication of the *White Paper* until May 2002 (*Hankook Ilbo*, 23 November 2001: 33). In May 2002 it was postponed indefinitely, thereby igniting another series of ideological debates. On 25 May the ministry declared it had decided to publish a document summarising the overall achievement of defense affairs under the Kim Dae-jung government. The decision was made following the concerns of diverse sources about a specific term used in the *White Paper*, signifying that the primary enemy concept was the main reason for the indefinite delay (*Chosun Ilbo*, 25 May 2002: 1; *Seoul Shinmun*, 25 May 2002: 5). President Kim Dae-jung thereby passed the political burden to his successor. Nevertheless, North Korea filed another call for omission of the concept at a working-level Panmunjom conference on 3 October 2002 (*Chosun Ilbo*, 8 October 2002: 2).

The inauguration of the Roh government was accompanied by significant changes in the usage of the primary enemy concept. Even before his inauguration, Roh, as elected president, mentioned that it would not be appropriate to use the concept outside the military, namely in politics or diplomacy (*Munhwa Ilbo*, 9 January 2003: 22). In July 2003, the Ministry of Defense developed a concept of 'core enemy' (*haeksimjokin jok*) for its own publications (*Chosun Ilbo*, 4 July 2003: 2). In November 2004 Roh's top security aides orchestrated efforts to abort the use of the concept altogether, to the extent that, on November 12, Yoon Kwang-ung, the defense minister, labelled it 'preposterous' (*Hankook Ilbo*, 17 November 2004: 2; *Chosun Ilbo*, 17 November 2004: 1; *Hankyoreh Sinmun*, 17 November 2004: 2). Five days later, Chong Dong-young, Unification Minister and chairman of National Security Council (NSC) called for a change in the primary enemy concept at the Committee of Unification, Foreign Affairs and Trade in the National Assembly. Yi Chong-sok, deputy secretary general of the NSC, declared: 'No country in the world uses the term, "primary enemy" directed toward [their] "major threat"' (*Donga Ilbo*, 18 November 2004: 5). Finally, on 18 December 2004, the Ministry of Defense announced its decision; it introduced the softened concept of 'major threat' for the *White Paper*, finally published in mid-January 2005 (*Munhwa Ilbo*, 18 December 2004: 2; *Donga Ilbo*, 18 November 2004: 5; *Kyunghyang Shinmun*, 30 October 2004: 1).

In contrast to the softened stance towards North Korea, there was noticeable discord as early as March 2000 when Kim Dae-jung visited Washington. President Bush's early realist policy sharply conflicted with Kim's Sunshine Policy, especially on questions such as whether Kim Jong-il was a credible and legitimate negotiation partner and whether it was worth tolerating North Korean brinkmanship. The inauguration of the Roh Moo-hyun government in South Korea further exacerbated Washington-Seoul friction. During his campaign, Roh made strong anti-American statements, such as having 'no objection to anti-Americanism', declaring: 'we voice different opinions from those of the United States' (*Kyunghyang Shinmun* [*Kyonghyang Daily*], 19 May 2003: 4), and calling for a presidential apology for the accident which killed the two school girls (*Hankook Ilbo*, 15 May 2003: 4). President Roh then reversed his anti-American stance when addressing the Korea Society on 13 May 2003, declaring: 'I would have been in the political prisoner's camp had the United States not helped South Korea during the Korea War' (*Hankook Ilbo*, 15 May 2003: 4). Despite this statement, immediately after his return to Seoul, Roh stated that his behaviour in Washington was a diplomatic choice, putting national interests ahead of his political faith. During his visit to Europe in November-December 2004, he again made several diplomatic statements with anti-American connotations. In Poland, he warned against possible US hardline approaches to Pyongyang's nuclear program by hawks in the US administration (*Korea Times*, 6 December 2004: 1; *Korea Times*, 7 December 2004: 1). On 6 December, he took a firmer posture, stating, 'I am willing to turn my face red with somebody if it is necessary', in the process of settling the North Korean nuclear issue (*Chosun Ilbo*, 7 December 2004: 31).

EXTERNAL INITIATIVES FOR A NORTHEAST ASIA

Northeast Asia Engaging with North Korea

The internal split is accelerated by a deep epistemological gap between the US and the present South Korean government, or at least between some of their respective advisers and policymakers. In a policy report which outlined the Northeast Asian vision (PCPP, 2003), the problem of North Korea was perceived as the key point of a new geopolitical vision that South Korea should pursue. Many policymakers of the present South Korean government agree that North Korea is not a problem that South Korea could pass to other countries. They are determined to engage with the North. This perception is rooted on the assumption that North Korea is far from collapsing, despite such predictions in 1989. Although the 1994 death of Kim Il-sung, father of the present North Korean leader, accelerated the upsurge of opinions on North Korean demise, the regime has persisted.

Why, how and whether North Korea survives in spite of the undeniable crises it has faced is a hot issue. Once again, there is a deep epistemological cleavage between the two emerging South Koreas, even though the absolute majority of South Koreans recognise the aberrations of the North Korean regime. If we compare the theory of the US neo-conservatives with that of South Korean decisionmakers of the present government, the difference is dramatic. However, the orientalism of the US neo-cons on North Korea and the occidentalism of some South Korean scholars are both preventing a more accurate calculation of North Korea's situation (Said, 1995; Buruman and Margalit, 2004).

There are several reasons why the North Korean regime has not collapsed, despite the breakdown of the Soviet Union, the death of the elder Kim and the great famine caused by endemic food shortages. First, the basis of Kim's regime was set in the era of the Japanese invasion of Korea and China. This historical experience left behind the threefold secrets of the Kim dynasty's longevity. First of all, the war against the Japanese army bequeathed to Kim's regime a sense of community and common destiny. Secondly, the record of military struggle against Japan contributed to the Kims' strong legitimacy among North Koreans. This historical record had not been recognised by the South Koreans until very recently. Many policies towards North Korea had been made on the false assumption that the elder Kim was just a bandit from Manchuria. Thirdly, the common military fight against the Japanese invasion gave birth to the so-called 'alliance with a blood pledge' (*HyolMeng*) between China and North Korea even before the Korean War, during which even a son of Mao Zedong was killed. Chinese leaders in power are not free from this historical legacy. Furthermore, as China is rising rapidly, North Korea has more of a chance to maintain itself as China's backyard as China attempts to establish its hegemony in this traditionally Sinocentric region.

The Korean War also bequeathed a threefold logic for consolidating Kim's regime. First of all, the Korean War gave a chance for the regime to eliminate Kim's political rivals led by Park Honyong (who had led a communist movement against Japanese imperialism before 1945). As the Korean War was initiated by Kim Il-sung, Kim's regime confronted a crisis at the end of the war. But Kim Il-sung transformed this crisis into an opportunity to consolidate his regime by shifting all blame to his political rivals and executing them on the charge of being US spies. Secondly, the Korean War gave the North a principal enemy, that is, the US, against which fear of the unknown drove North Korean society into a monolithic solidarity. The frequent bombardment of the US during the Korean War reinforced this collective mentality (Kim, 2001: 15). As pointed out by Selig Harrison, while the South had suffered brutal but relatively brief anguish, 'the North, by contrast, endure[d] three years of heavy US bombing in addition to the Yalu offensive on the ground' (Harrison, 2002: 8). Thirdly, the ruins left behind by the Korean War provided the rationale for the voluntary participation of people because of their desire to repair their houses and workshops. This was a good chance to use mass mobilisation for consolidating Kim's regime, which could be compared to the role of mass mobilisation in the process of European state formation as explained by Charles Tilly (Tilly, 1990).

Due to the successful mass mobilisation and the legacy of Japanese industrial facilities concentrated on the northern part of the Korean Peninsular before 1945, North Korea was wealthier than South Korea and remained so at least until the end of the 1960s. Even in 1972, Harrison Salisbury of the *New York Times* wrote, 'North Korea is the most intensively industrialised country in Asia, with the exception of Japan' (Salisbury, 1973: 199-200). The experience of economic success under Kim's regime provided a rationale for the North Korean argument that the cause of its economic failure is not internal, but external, that is, the US containment and blocks against North Korea. The more intense the US pressure on the North Korean regime, the better for North Korean propaganda.

A threefold cultural explanation is also possible. Firstly, a strong Christian influence can be found in the North Korean regime. Kim Il-sung's father became a Presbyterian elder after graduating from a school established by an American missionary. Il-sung's mother was named Bansok, which literally means 'Big Stone', like the name of the apostle Peter. Kim's maternal uncle was a pastor who became a vice-president of the North Korean regime after the liberation from Japanese rule. Secondly, the Confucian heritage also influences the regime. After the dethronement of the Korean king by the Japanese, many Koreans wanted him replaced. Syngman Rhee, the first South Korean President, interpreted his name as 'succeed' (Syng), 'lately' (man), Rhee dynasty (same family name as the last dynasty of

Korea), capitalising on the Korean collective mentality of waiting for the lost king's return. But there was a big difference. Whereas Syngman Rhee left behind an 'amenable regime' in South Korea, Kim Il-sung left behind a closed regime based on a bizarre theory of *SooRyong* (the leader and the people compose one body). From this perspective, North Korea is more a neo-Confucian kingdom than a Stalinist regime (Cumings, 1998). Kim Il-sung carried on traditions of centralised authority inherited from the Confucian-influenced Korean dynasties of the past (Harrison, 2002). Thirdly, Kim's regime is also supported by a shamanistic culture, the influence of which still lingers in even South Korean Christianity. In North Korea, in a society led on the basis of *SooRyong*, members are linked by a shared consciousness of kinship. North Korean nationalism as an 'imagined community' fits with this quasi-tribal mentality. Fourthly, the effects of *Hangul*, the Korean alphabetical system, cannot be neglected. Using *Hangul* as an efficient vehicle, Kim could diffuse his doctrines very easily and rapidly. We can compare North Korean leaders with others such as the anti-colonialist leaders who fought against France but always used the French language, and those who fought against Britain but remained proud of their British influences.

Another important factor shaping North Korean attitudes is a 'Stockholm Syndrome'. They consider themselves to be behind the times *vis-à-vis* the fierce and rapid globalisation happening around them, and, unable to face the international disorder, they tend to unite under their familiar 'affectionate' *SooRyong* (North Korean leader). In this collective mental state, the effects of small, kind acts by their familiar *SooRyong*, often using external aids, are magnified. In contrast, some rescue attempts such as the US North Korean Human Rights Act can be seen as a threat.

As there is no strong possibility of an imminent North Korean demise, the present South Korean government voluntarily takes the position of 'saloon keeper', a position different from that of sheriff (Kagan, 2003: 36-37). Changing the North Korean regime, mentioned so often by some US neo-cons, seems to be a mission that is not only impossible, but would also be fatal in the eyes of many South Korean decisionmakers. Thus, the present South Korean government wants to change the North in a piecemeal way, the historic structure of disorder among China, Japan, Russia, the United States and two Koreas and instead create a forward-looking regional system for peace and cooperation. This initiative for a peaceful and prosperous Northeast Asia is also expected to cure the domestic split over the problem of North Korea.

Northeast Asian Initiative: Globalisation from in to Out, Not Only from Out to in

The Northeast Asian Cooperation Initiative for Peace and Prosperity is the new South Korean response to the international disorder of the Post-Cold War era. The political map of the region is shaped and affected by global politics, as well as the geopolitical intentions of its members. Upon its inauguration on 25 February 2003, the Roh Moo-hyun Government of the Republic of Korea launched an ambitious initiative aimed at creating a new Northeast Asia, and the Presidential Committee on Northeast Asian Business Hub (PCNEABH) was established. The PCNEABH postponed peace in favour of prosperity on the assumption that the realisation of prosperity would automatically bring about positive effects such as peace-building.

Yet the risk of political instability could be a major obstacle to success if the South Korean government simultaneously but not sequentially pursues both peace and prosperity in Northeast Asia. By not only reorganising the previous Presidential Committee on Northeast Asian Business Hub (PCNEABH) into the Presidential Committee on Northeast Asian Cooperation Initiative (PCNEACI), but also by expanding its scope, the PCNEACI is mandated to take over the previous committee's responsibility for building business hubs. But additional tasks, such as medium-to-long-term strategic planning, peninsular and regional peace-building, as well as cooperative projects for community-building in the region, have also been added. The Initiative is now South Korean's key long-term strategy (PCNEACI, n. d.: 6-7).

This South Korean vision is summarised in Table 11.

Table 11. South Korean Vision for Northeast Asia

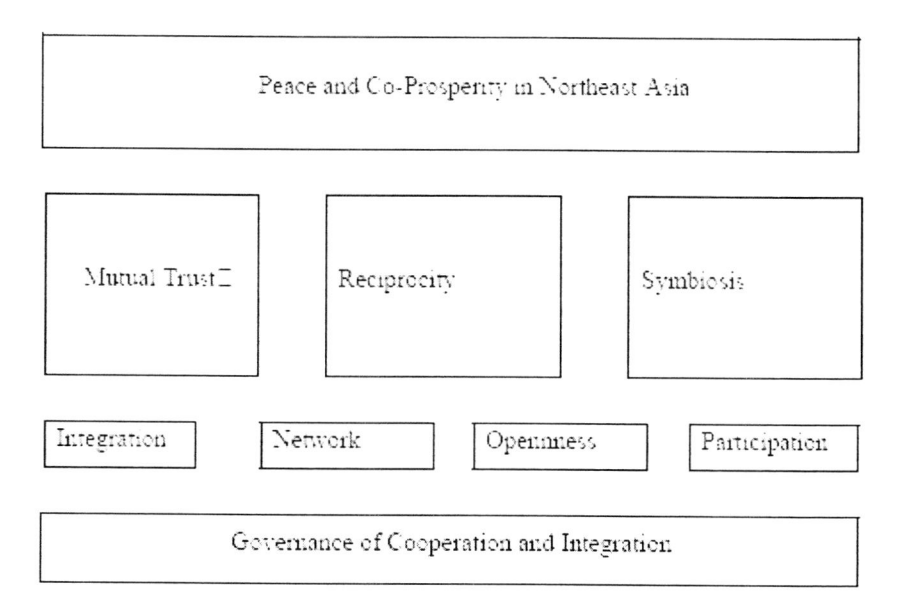

```
┌─────────────────────────────────────────────────────────┐
│         Peace and Co-Prosperity in Northeast Asia       │
└─────────────────────────────────────────────────────────┘

┌───────────────┐   ┌───────────────┐   ┌───────────────┐
│  Mutual Trust │   │  Reciprocity  │   │   Symbiosis   │
│               │   │               │   │               │
└───────────────┘   └───────────────┘   └───────────────┘

┌───────────┐  ┌───────────┐  ┌───────────┐  ┌───────────────┐
│Integration│  │  Network  │  │ Openness  │  │ Participation │
└───────────┘  └───────────┘  └───────────┘  └───────────────┘

┌─────────────────────────────────────────────────────────┐
│        Governance of Cooperation and Integration        │
└─────────────────────────────────────────────────────────┘
```

Source: PCNEACI (n.d.): 31.

With the end of the Cold War, the US has undoubtedly become the single dominant superpower, something unprecedented in history (Ikenberry, 2001: 191). It is a global empire defining in large measure the standards of international society. In East Asia, the primary institution designed by the US is the American-Japanese alliance. Another bilateral arrangement, the Republic of Korea-US alliance, is attached to this backbone alliance of former enemies. As long as no other challenger emerges to reverse the regional mechanism, the US will be central in shaping and maintaining the regional order while equipped with strong intentions of engagement. Nevertheless, at present we continue to experience international disorder.

While globalisation seems to be spreading a global imperial order, there are two opposite and emotionally charged approaches to its effects. On one hand, there exists an opinion that globalisation should be accelerated on the grounds it is beneficial. This opinion involves the belief that globalisation is an opportunity for individuals and that this opportunity exists equally for all. On the other hand, the opposing view considers globalisation to be 'unification for the dominant' (Bourdieu, 2001, cited in Brzezinski, 2004: 153). According to this opinion, globalisation 'is not an expression of the evolution' of human history, but is 'designed and created by human beings with a specific goal: to give primacy to economic—that is, corporate—values above all other values' (Cananagh et al., 2002, cited in Brzezinski, 2004: 153). Globalisation is increasing the gulf between rich and poor, under the pretext of realising human desires, and sacrificing the poor majority for the rich minority. While globalisation furthers the liberal circulation of capital, it does not guarantee the liberal circulation of labour. From this perspective, globalisation represents a threat, not an opportunity.

Both sides of the globalisation debate agree that the vital force behind globalisation is the United States and that globalisation has the appearance of Americanisation. From the pro-globalisation perspective, the United States, representing the cutting-edge of global progress, is at the centre of all discussions. At the same time, the United States is at the centre of all anti-globalisation theories, and the view is of a new global empire. Our empirical study, undertaken in 2004 and based on a nationwide survey of college students in Korea, showed that, among those Koreans capable of responding confidently to the challenges of globalisation, and who consider globalisation as an opportunity rather than a threat, the degree of trust regarding the United States is high. In contrast, among those who are not capable of responding confidently to such challenges, and who consider globalisation as a threat, the degree of trust in the United States is low. Thus, globalisation is accelerating South Korea's internal split. Thus, the present South Korean government chose the option of one peaceful and prosperous Northeast Asia as a means of resolving these differences.

Previous South Korean governments' geopolitical vision has been far wider than Northeast Asia. The Kim Young-sam government (1993-1998) proclaimed its vision of *segyewha*, which can be literally translated as 'globalisation', as its main tenet of foreign policy. The vision of the Kim Dae-jung government (1998-2003) narrowed this, limiting it to ASEAN+3 and launched the East Asia Vision Group. The present government has been criticised (even by an author of this chapter) of being even narrower in scope and too introverted in its regional orientation by setting its geographic focus solely on Northeast Asia (Kim, 2004a). This critique was to the point. However, if we take account of the propensities of recent South Korean society, we might be able to see this in another light. Without settling the immediate political, economic and socio-cultural challenges arising from domestic politics and from its more proximate region, globalisation could pose more of a threat to than an opportunity for South Korea.

At present, the North Korean nuclear issue seems to be a litmus test for all the participants shaping the future regional order. The Korean Peninsula, even though (the) Korea(s) has (have) been a relatively minor actor(s) in the regional politics, has determined the regional weather chart, mainly because of its geopolitical position. The future of East Asia, despite/because of its meta-stability, is always open to other possibilities. As in the title of Brzezinski's book, there was a 'grand failure' in the communist design for East Asia. However, can we really be sure that there was no 'failure' in the American perception of Northeast Asia in the post-Cold War era? If we can interpret the present East European tilt toward the US as a Thermidorian reaction of the historical stream, a sophisticated measure is also needed to calculate the same kind of reaction now accelerating in Northeast Asia as a result of globalisation, which appears as Americanisation, and the rise of China.

CONCLUSION

During the Cold War, and due largely to the Korean War, the world has become accustomed to two Koreas. Since the end of the Cold War, there has been a strong tendency to await a North Korean collapse and subsequent absorption by South Korea. However, instead of waiting to see some explosion in the North or see the status quo continue, the present South Korean government has chosen to engage more actively with North Korea. This engagement policy has its motivation in the long-standing desire for reunification written into the Constitution. However, our paper shows that a 'two South Koreas' phenomenon, in addition to the two Koreas, is emerging, due largely to this engagement policy and attitudes to the United States. The present South Korean government believes that it is not possible to expect economic prosperity if there is no peace on the Korean Peninsula. It believes that a more permanent peace can be achieved only through a regional approach. If this South Korean initiative is to succeed, even the domestic split is expected to attenuate, providing the basis of bipartisan support for the present government.

Needless to say, this initiative cannot succeed without significant support from the countries of Northeast Asia and the role of the US is still decisive for the success of this South Korean project. As Winston Lord, Assistant Secretary of State for East Asian and Pacific Affairs, argued in his 1993 confirmation testimony before the Senate, the US should have paid more attention to 'developing multilateral forums for security consultations while maintaining the solid foundations of alliances' (Lord, 1993). The role of US foreign policy is still a determining factor in the unsolved issue of regional governance. But there could a clash of visions. In the eyes of many Northeast Asians, the post-war US 'containment' policy that supported the Japan-centred East Asia should have been revised after the end of the Cold War. The time has come to reconsider the meaning of other regional schemes buried in historical oblivion, such as the Pacific Pact or Colombo Plan. Even today, there is nothing comparable in Northeast Asia to the web of multilateral and regional cooperative ties that bind Europe together.

Although the US has given a nod to multilateralism and cooperation among the countries in the region, there is a great deficiency in its efforts to incubate a stable East Asian regional order. This deficiency has been growing in importance since the awful tragedy of 9/11 and the War on Terror. Meanwhile, the US has become the 'strategic other' in a series of discourses on South Korean identity. This politics of identity accelerated the emergence of 'Two South Koreas', while blurring the boundaries between North and South. The blowback of the 'Americanisation via globalisation' has become one of the key phrases for explaining and understanding South Korea's increasing desire for a regional peace structure. Between the deficiency of the American multilateral initiative and the predominance of the US-centred unilateral globalisation, a strong inclination to recapture the past Sinocentric conception or Japanese Greater East Asian vision before World War II exists in Northeast Asia. A trans-Pacific effort to construct a new international order, away from the legacies of the Cold War confrontation that was maintained on the basis of an exclusive bilateral alliance system, is more urgent than ever.

REFERENCES

Barbieri, Katherine and Jack S. Levy (1999) 'Sleeping with the Enemy: The Impact of War on Trade'. *Journal of Peace Research*, 36(4).

Brzezinski, Zbigniew (1989) *The Grand Failure: The Birth and Death of Communism in the Twentieth Century*, New York: Charles Scribner's Sons.

────── (1997) *The Grand Chessboard: American Primacy and Its Geostrategic Imperatives*, New York: Basic Books.

────── (2004) *The Choice: Global Domination or Global Leadership*, New York: Basic Books.

────── and John J. Mearsheimer (2005) 'Clash of the Titans'. *Foreign Policy* (January/February).

Bull, Hedley (1977) *The Anarchial Society: A Study of Order in World Politics*, London: Macmillan.

Buruman, Ian and Avishai Margalit (2004) *Occidentalism: The West in the Eyes of Its Enemies*, New York: Penguin.

Buzan, Barry (1991) *People, States, and Fear: An Agenda for International-Security Studies in the Post-Cold War Era*, 2nd ed., Boulder, CO: Lynne Rienner.

Chafets, Glenn, Michael Spirtas Benjamin Frankel (1998/1999) 'Introduction: Tracing the Influence of Identity on Foreign Policy'. *Security Studies*, 8(2/3).

Chosun Central Broadcasting, 11 December 2000.

Chosun Ilbo, 21 November 1992; 26 June 1995; 13 December 1997; 25 May, 8 October 2002; 4 July 2003; 17 November, 7 December 2004.

CNN (2002) http://archives.cnn.com/2002/WORLD/asiapcf/east/12/18skorea.elex/index.html

Cooper, Robert (2003) *The Breaking of Nations: Order and Chaos in the Twenty-First Century*, New York: Atlantic Monthly Press.

Cumings, Bruce (1998) *Korea's Place in the Sun: A Modern History*, New York: Norton.

Donga Ilbo, 11 April 2000; 8 October 2002; 18 November 2004.

Friedberg, Aaron (1993-1994) 'Ripe for Rivalry: Prospects for Peace in a Multipolar in Asia'. *International Security*, 18(3).

Gaddis, John L. (1987) *The Long Peace*, New York: Oxford University Press.

────── (2004) *Surprise, Security, and the American Experience*, Cambridge: Harvard University Press.

Hankook Ilbo, 10 December 1992; 28 May, 29 June 1995; 12 April 1996; 12 April 2000; 23 November 2001; 16 December 2002; 15 May, 9 June, 2003; 17 November 2004.

Hankyoreh Shinmun, 12 April 1996; 15 May 2003; 17 November 2004.

Harrison, Selig S. (2002) *Korean Endgame: A Strategy for Reunification and U. S. Disengagement*, Princeton: Princeton University Press.

Huntington, Samuel P. (1996) *The Clash of Civilizations and the Remaking of World Order*, New York: Simon and Schuster.

────── (2004) *Who Are We? The Challenges To America's National Identity*, New York: Simon and Schuster.

Ikenberry, G. John (2001) 'American Power and the Empire of Capitalist Democracy'. *Review of International Studies*, 27.

────── (2001-2002) 'American Grand Strategy in the Age of Terror.' *Survival*, 43(4).

Jervis, Robert (1999) 'Realism, Neoliberalism, and Cooperation: Understanding the Debate'. *International Security*, 24(1).

Joong-ang Ilbo, 01 March 1993.

Kagan, Robert (2003) *Of Paradise and Power: America and Europe in the New World Order*, New York: Basic Books.

Kang, Won-taek (2004) 'Namnam Kaldungui Inyomjok tulsonge Taehan Kyonghumjok Punsok' (Empirical Analysis of South Korea's Ideological Conflict). Manuscript presented at the IFES seminar on 1 September.

Kim, Myongsob (2001) 'Reexamining Cold War History and the Korean Question'. *Korea Journal*, 41(2).

Kim, Myongsob (2004a). 'Why Contain into Northeast Asian Framework?' *Chosunilbo*, 12 March.

Kim, Myongsob and Jun Young Choi (2004b) 'Can We Trust America? An Empirical Analysis of Anti-Americanism in South Korea'. Paper presented at the Northeastern Political Science Association meetings, Boston.

Kim, Myongsob and Horace Jeffery Hodges (2005) 'On Huntington's Civilizational Paradigm: A Reappraisal'. *Issues and Studies*, 41(2).

Korea Times, 6 December, 7 December 2004.

Krauthammer, Charles (2004) 'In Defense of Democratic Realism'. *National Interest*, 77.

Kyunghyang Shinmun, 19 May 2003; 30 October 2004.

Lord, Winston (1993) 'Ten Goals for the Future'. *Asia-Pacific Defense Reporter* (June/July).

Los Angeles Times, 11 April 2000.

Mearsheimer, John J. (1990a) 'Back to the Future: Instability in Europe after the Cold War'. *International Security*, 15(1).

——— (1990b) 'Why We Will Soon Miss the Cold War'. *The Atlantic* (November).

——— (2001) *The Tragedy of Great Power Politics*, New York: Norton.

Moon, Chung-in (1999) 'Understanding the DJ Doctrine: The Sunshine Policy and the Korean Peninsula'. In Chung-in Moon and David I. Steinberg, *Kim Dae-jung Government and Sunshine Policy: Promises and Challenges, 39*, Seoul: Yonsei University Press.

Munhwa Ilbo, 22 June 2000; 12 December 2002; 9 January 2003; 18 December 2004.

New York Times, 11 April 2000.

Ninkovich, Frank A. (2001) *The United States and Imperialism*, Malden: Blackwell Publishing.

Oneal, John R. and Bruce M. Russet (1997) 'The Classical Liberals Were Right: Democracy, Interdependence, and Conflict, 1950-1985'. *International Studies Quarterly*, 41(1).

——— (1999) 'Assessing the Liberal Peace with Alternative Specifications: Trade Still Reduces Conflict'. *Journal of Peace Research*, 36(4).

PCNEACI (Presidential Committee on Northeast Asian Coorporation Initiative) (n.d. 2004?) *Toward a Peaceful and Prosperous Northeast Asia.* Office of the President, Republic of Korea.

PCPP (Presidential Commission on Policy Planning) (2003) 'Pyongwha wa Bonyoung ui DongBukA Sidae ShinKooSang'. 19 June.

Press-Barnathan, Galia (2000/2001) 'The Lure of Regional Security Arrangement: The United States and Regional Security Cooperation in Asia and Europe'. *Security Studies*, 10(2).

Rose, Gideon (1998) 'Neoclassical Realism and Theories of Foreign Policy'. *World Politics*, 51.

Said, Edward W. (1995) *Orientalism: Western Conceptions of the Orient*, London: Penguin.

Salisbury, Harrison (1973) *To Peking and Beyond: A Report on the New Asia*, New York: Quadrangle.

Segye Ilbo, 10 April 1996; 13 April, 12 December 2000.

Seoul Shinmun, 13 April 1996; 1 July 2000; 13 February 2001; 25 May 2002.

South Korean Presidential Office, official site http://www.president.go.kr

Tilly, Charles (1990) *Coercion, Capital, and European States, AD 990-1990*, London: Blackwell.

Washington Post, 11 April 2000.

Wendt, Alexander (1999) *Social Theory of International Politics*, Cambridge: Cambridge University Press.

Yonhap News, 27 February 2000.

In: Asia-Pacific and a New International Order
Editors: Purnendra Jain et al. pp. 165-179
ISBN 1-59454-986-9
© 2006 Nova Science Publishers, Inc.

Chapter 11

INDONESIA TRANSFORMING[1]

Malcolm Cook

The last decade has been a tumultuous one for Indonesia. It has fundamentally changed the Indonesian state and society and Indonesia's regional and international position. In 1995, Indonesia was a 'known quantity' internationally, boasting three decades of solid growth, political and policy continuity and had a well-established reputation as the leader of Southeast Asia. The chaos and concerns of the late Sukarno period and Konfrontasi seemed distant memories. Since 1997, fears for Indonesia's economic future, territorial integrity and communal harmony have resurfaced. Indonesians are still working through these challenges, while foreign governments and investors are coming to grips with what these changes mean for relations with Indonesia.

The two greatest shocks to Southeast Asia's regional order and the position of Southeast Asia in the global order since the end of the Cold War[2] have been at the centre of these changes. The 1997 Asian financial crisis hit Indonesia the hardest, with its economy still in recovery mode today. This regional crisis was the tipping point for Indonesia's political system, toppling Suharto's one party rule, and then rapidly consolidating a new democracy and a radical devolution of power. With impressive speed and smoothness, Indonesia has moved from being a unitary, authoritarian state to a vibrant and fluid democracy with newly empowered regional and municipal authorities.

The rise of global Islamist terrorism and the declaration of a Global War on Terror after the September 11 attacks in 2001 have also redefined Indonesia's regional and global position. While the threat of terrorism has little resonance locally (Rieffel (2004), the presence of Jemaah Islamiyah in Indonesia and its links to Al Qaeda have thrust Indonesia front stage in the War on Terror. Indonesia's political metamorphosis has revived the identity struggle between its Islamic majority status and its diverse multicultural make-up. The War on Terror has focused the world's attention on how this social and political struggle plays out.

---

[1] I would like to thank Purnendra Jain for inviting me to the Adelaide conference that led to this volume and to Andrew MacIntyre for his comments on my presentation at this conference.
[2] The end of the Cold War in the late 1980s, while very significant for Southeast Asia as a whole, was not such a historical watershed for maritime Southeast Asia or Indonesia. The end of the Cold War opened up Eastern Europe to democracy. The Asian financial crisis opened up Indonesia.

Since the shock of 1997, Indonesia's society and government, understandably, have been preoccupied with crisis recovery and the country's political transformation. However, this preoccupation has meant that Indonesia has not fully addressed some pressing regional and global issues. These include the shift to bilateral and regional preferential trading agreements and China's and Japan's more assertive efforts for East Asian leadership. Southeast Asia's and ASEAN's natural leader has been detained elsewhere while the parameters of Southeast and East Asian regionalism are changing.

This chapter is divided into two thematic sections and each follows a loose chronological order. It first looks at how the Asian financial crisis served as the tipping point for Indonesian democratisation and how the political system has changed. Second, it looks at the new global importance and position of Indonesia in the Global War on Terror and how this has changed Indonesia's relations with the United States, Australia and Southeast Asia. In conclusion, it looks at the new regional and global issues Indonesia has yet to respond to.

INDONESIA'S DOMESTIC TRANSFORMATION

The Asian financial crisis of 1997 took the region and the world by surprise. Suddenly an 'Asian tiger' (South Korea) and three 'tiger cubs' (Thailand, Malaysia and Indonesia) went from being paragons of development success to being devastated economies threatening the global financial system. The speed and depth of this crisis, and the fact that it hit economies with few fiscal problems and strong records of growth, enhanced the crisis' shock value and its social disorientation effects. The crisis, along with its severe short-term social costs, was a key factor in political successions in all crisis countries. It undermined coalitions between ruling elites, local business elites and foreign investors. It exposed some of the weaknesses and abuses of what previously appeared to be political and economic consensus, and opened up political systems to new actors.

All of this was true in spades for Indonesia. The crisis hit Indonesia the hardest, discrediting the ruling elite and some of its local business friends, and triggered the most comprehensive political transformation. Indonesia's track record of strong, consistent growth and poverty alleviation under Suharto provided his regime with a strong element of performance legitimacy and effective cover for the lack of political freedom and state actions favouring family members, chosen business associates and the military. The Asian financial crisis removed this cover and fused, under the rubric of *reformasi*, growing demands for more political freedom. Widespread frustration over the economic abuses, which had become especially prevalent in the late Suharto years, became a wave of popular anger against the Indonesian political order.

Indonesia's crisis pain (percentages)

	1996	1997	1998
GDP per capita growth	8.0	4.0	-13.6
Gross domestic savings/GDP	30.2	31.0	24.0
Gross dom. investment/GDP	30.8	31.6	25.0
Real wage growth	6.6	4.2	-37.8
Inflation (CPI)	7.9	6.6	20.0
Poverty incidence (approx)	16	14	21

Sources: IMF, World Bank, ILO, ADB, Bank Indonesia

The crisis triggered (it did not cause) Indonesia's democratisation and fiscal decentralisation. While Indonesia's economy is still struggling to return to a sustained growth path, these political changes have already taken on the air of permanence. Without the Asian financial crisis, it would be hard to imagine that the transition from the Suharto era would have been so bloodless and that it would have led to the flowering of a vibrant democracy.

Indonesia's sudden and rapid shift to democracy has meant that it is difficult to gain a clear picture of what kind of democracy Indonesia is and how and when the present period of democratic consolidation will end. The fact that democratisation occurred during modern Indonesia's worst social crisis deepened concerns that Indonesia's rapid 'bottom-up' political change carried many risks from internecine communal warfare to 'national disintegration' to a violent military backlash (Huxley (2002). Few believed that Indonesia's military forces would peacefully accept being forced out of a formal political role that was at the heart of their dual function (*dwi fungsi*) ethos. Yet, today the military has no formal role in politics and no reserved seats in parliament.

Indonesia's rapid democratisation after three decades of an active state campaign of depoliticisation stoked three major fears that have so far not been borne out. The deepest fear in Indonesia and for those with close ties to Indonesia was that democratisation would exacerbate Indonesia's largest unanswered political question, namely, how to marry its diverse, multi-ethnic population—Indonesia has the largest Melanesian population in the world—with the fact it is over 80 per cent Islamic. Indonesia is the world's largest Islamic country. Even though it is in economic strife, it is also a test case for the compatibility of Islam and stable, consensual democracy—a topic of renewed, vigorous debate globally—as well as for the balance between a rising Islamic political identity and inter-faith harmony. The recent global focus on Islamist terrorism has deepened the world's active interest in Indonesia's democratic success and fixated its attention on potential signs of failure.

Moderating Religious Tensions

The apprehension that Indonesia's democratisation would exacerbate the tension between Indonesia's majority Muslim population and the country's multi-cultural make-up reflects fears that history may repeat itself. From 1949 to 1962, the Indonesian state faced the Islamist *Darul Islam* revolt that spread over six provinces in the heart of the country and killed up to 65,000 people (Effendy (2003). The *Darul Islam* forces pushed for Indonesia to jettison its statist-nationalist creed for an Islamic state.[3] In Indonesia's first elections in 1955, Islamist parties won 114 of 257 seats. Indonesia's democratisation in this period, reading history backwards, was seen to exacerbate tensions between Islamists and statist-nationalists and to threaten the territorial integrity of Indonesia. The *Darul Islam* movement was particularly strong in Aceh. Suharto's New Order regime used this fear that Indonesia was unsuited for full democracy to justify its program of depoliticisation and the curtailing of independent Islamist voices.

The links between the *Darul Islam* movement and *Jemaah Islamiyah* (Bubalo and Fealy (2005), and the rise of other violent jihadist groups like *Laskar Jihad* after the fall of Suharto, deepened these fears. Yet, the two largest Islamic movements in Indonesia (and in the world) played a leading role in *reformasi*. Both the traditionalist *Nahdlatul Ulama* under Abdurrahman Wahid and the modernist *Muhammadiyah* under Amien Rais were among the main organisational pillars behind *reformasi*, working hard to mobilise their millions of followers and promoting a peaceful, liberal approach to political transformation.

Wahid (aka Gus Dur) contested the first post-Suharto elections as the head of the newly formed PKB (National Awakening Party), while Rais contested the elections as the head of the newly formed PAN (National Mandate Party). Wahid became the first indirectly elected president in the post-Suharto era. Amien Rais, who was deeply involved with Wahid's rise and premature fall from the presidency, became the speaker of the DPR (Indonesia's parliament) under Wahid's replacement, President Megawati Sukarnoputri. The leaders of the two main Islamic organisations in Indonesia used the post-Suharto political opening to turn themselves into national politicians and to form inclusive Islamic parties. Both have now faded somewhat from the national political scene, with both PKB and PAN garnering fewer votes in 2004 than they had won in 1999.

The four main Islamic parties that ran in 1999 amassed just over 30 per cent of the vote and 121 of 462 DPR seats. The two main statist-nationalist parties, the Suharto-era Golkar party and Megawati's PDI-P (Indonesian Democratic Party of Struggle), won over 55 per cent of the vote and captured 274 seats. While parties organised around Indonesia's traditional divide between status quo statist-nationalist parties and Islamic parties, the main battle was between Golkar and PDI-P, with the smaller Islamic parties being courted by both statist-nationalist giants to favour them. Megawati's vice-president, Hamzah Haz, was leader of PPP (United Development Party), the largest and least inclusive Islamic party.

---

[3] The founders of *Jemaah Islamiyah* have their roots in the *Darul Islam* movement that remained an underground movement throughout the Suharto years (Anthony Bubalo and Greg Fealy, *Joining the caravan? The Middle East, Islamism and Indonesia*. Lowy Institute Papers 05. Sydney, Lowy Institute for International Policy, 2005.

Parliamentary fortunes

Party*	% vote, 1999	Seats, 1999	% vote, 2004	Seats, 2004
Golkar (s-n)	22.44	120	21.58	128
PDI-P (s-n)	33.74	154	18.53	109
PPP (I)	10.71	39	8.15	58
Partai Demokrat	---	---	7.45	57
PKB (I)	12.61	51	10.57	52
PAN (I)	7.12	35	6.44	52
PKS (I)	1.01	6	7.34	45
PBR (I)	---	---	2.44	13
PDS (C)	---	---	2.13	12
PBB (I)	1.94	2	2.62	11
Others	10.37	55	12.75	13
Total		462		550

Source: (Cook, 2004)

The 2004 parliamentary and presidential elections saw a further mutually beneficial mingling of Islamic and statist-nationalist parties and a weakening of Indonesia's traditional parties. The 2004 elections did not provide any ammunition for the fear that democracy and Indonesia are a dangerous, combustible mix. Rather, Indonesia's new directly elected presidency and its diffuse party system are helping to overcome the Islamic/statist-nationalist divide in a peaceful, evolutionary manner (Cook (2004). Statist-nationalist parties promoted more candidates with strong Islamic political credentials, while PAN, PKB and PKS promoted non-Islamic candidates to appeal to a wider electorate and to back up their inclusivist rhetoric. Some Indonesian political analysts now even argue that Golkar has gone so far in attempting to burnish its Islamic image that it is no longer a statist-nationalist party (Badsewan (2004).

Indonesia's 2003 shift from an indirect to a direct presidential ballot to be decided by a majority vote, with runoffs if necessary, forced all major political parties to come up with nationally attractive presidential/vice-presidential tickets. The large number of parties contesting the elections (10 parties won over 2 per cent of the national vote in the 2004 parliamentary elections) meant that no party came close to winning a majority of seats. Therefore, the main parties have to seek and maintain a variety of coalition partners.

The biggest losers in Indonesia's 2004 elections were the two statist-nationalist giants, Golkar and PDI-P. PDI-P saw its share of the vote and seats plummet, while Megawati lost badly in the October presidential runoff. Megawati came second to the eventual winner, Susilo Bambang Yudhoyono, in 28 of Indonesia's 32 provinces in the October runoff election. Golkar defended its share of the parliamentary vote—concentrated in poorer rural peripheries—but its presidential candidate ex-General Wiranto did not even make it to the runoff. Golkar's and Wiranto's New Order baggage proved more decisive than Golkar's famed machine vote and electoral war chest. Golkar has taken over from PDI-P as Indonesia's largest party, but its vote has plateaued and its two main lights in 2004, Wiranto and Akbar Tandjung, are no longer around.

The two big winners in 2004 were a new statist-nationalist party, *Partai Demokrat*, unencumbered by ties to past leaders, and a new Islamist party, PKS (Peace and Justice

Party), which rose from an anti-establishment student movement born during the late Suharto era. *Partai Demokrat* was set up in 2001 and has acted as the electoral vehicle for ex-General Susilo Bambang Yudhoyono, a charismatic reformist military man previously courted by all the main parties. Yudhoyono and his party were able to present themselves as the voice of *reformasi* and capture many voters who were repelled by Golkar and PDI-P, but unwilling to vote for Islamic parties.

PKS, the only party in Indonesia truly committed to programmatic politics, presents itself as a new voice committed to reviving Indonesian Islam, cleansing society and ridding politics of corruption. PKS is strongly influenced by Muslim Brotherhood thought and did particularly well amongst the educated Islamic middle class. PKS won the most seats in Jakarta's municipal elections, also held in 2004. Both of these parties differentiated themselves from Indonesia's traditional parties and appealed to alienated voters.

The rise of new, smaller parties and the erosion—but continuing dominance—of traditional statist-nationalist parties have combined with Indonesia's new political system to dilute the statist-nationalist/Islamic divide and to work against the development of an 'Islamic bloc' of parties united under one leader. The April 2004 parliamentary elections delivered a very fractured parliament, where no party won even a large plurality of seats and no party could hope to win the presidency without seeking coalition partners.

Both Golkar and PDI-P sought during their presidential bids to soften their statist-nationalist image and to tap into the Islamic vote by selecting *Nahdlatul Ulama* luminaries as their vice-presidential running mates. Megawati's vice-presidential candidate was Hasyim Muzadi, *Nahdlatul Ulama's* chairman, while ex-General Wiranto's was Solahudin Wahid, the son of Abdurrahman Wahid. Yudhoyono and *Partai Demokrat* stuck to its statist-nationalist roots and chose Golkar's Jusuf Kalla (one of Indonesia's richest *pribumi* businessmen and a regional leader of *Nahdlatul Ulama*) as Yudhoyono's running mate in a successful effort to split the Golkar vote.

During the second runoff round of presidential elections, party coalitions coalesced around the two remaining candidates. PKS and PPP, the two major Islamic parties associated with supporting the introduction of *syariah* law also supported Yudhoyono's ticket. Golkar, under Akbar Tandjung, supported Megawati's ticket and threatened to use their parliamentary weight to quash Yudhoyono's administration after Yudhoyono's overwhelming victory in October 2004. Golkar, now under Jusuf Kalla, has shifted alliances to support President Yudhoyono, ending the threat of legislative gridlock.

Indonesia's 2004 elections proved that Indonesia's Islamic parties and leaders and its statist-nationalist parties and leaders are political animals ready to switch sides when it suits them and willing to compromise doctrinal purity for political gain. 2004 also politically divided *Nahdlatul Ulama* and put paid to their earlier announcements that they would stay outside (above) politics. The political fracturing of *Nahdlatul Ulama* and the willingness of Islamic parties to switch coalitions has undermined any slight chance these parties had of uniting to present a single Islamic political voice. Rather, individual Islamic parties have joined up with statist-nationalist parties to gain access to power, while these statist-nationalist parties have courted Islamic parties for their voting constituencies and cleaner, more devout images. With Yudhoyono and Jusuf Kalla as the early front-runners for the 2009 presidential elections, this pattern of statist-nationalist-Islamic party cooperation is likely to be repeated.

Moderating Regional Tensions

The sudden and turbulent end of the Suharto regime and the ineffectual Wahid and Megawati administrations deepened fears that Indonesia's political transformation may lead to the dismembering of Indonesia. 'National disintegration', a deep fear at the core of post-colonial Indonesia's political identity, lies behind the TNI's regional command structure. Like the Islamist threat discussed above, Suharto's New Order also used this threat to justify authoritarian rule and the central political role of the military. While the rise of groups like *Laskar Jihad* were seen by many as the harbinger of Indonesia's new diffuse political order that would encourage Islamist extremism, the rapid revival of pro-independence groups in Papua has been interpreted as a sign of national disintegration (Chauvel (2004, Sukma (2004). President Habibie's support for the ill-fated referendum in East Timor, and President Wahid's promises of a referendum in Aceh along with conciliatory gestures towards Papuan leaders, angered Indonesian nationalists. They saw that these efforts would encourage secessionist groups and open the door for foreign intervention, with East Timor held up as the case in point.

So far, Indonesia's political transformation, while undoubtedly emboldening separatist voices, has helped moderate highly charged centre-periphery relations. The single largest legislative change in post-Suharto Indonesia was the passage of two decentralisation laws in 1999 that diffused power and financial resources to regional and municipal governments. It also established a new national legislative chamber, the Regional Representatives Council (DPD), made up of regional representatives. This bill seriously diverged from Indonesia's unitary political tradition in favour of assuaging regional anger over central control of resource rents. This anger is most deeply felt in Aceh, the Riau islands and Papua, Indonesia's three most rebellious (and amongst its poorest) regions. While the decentralisation law will complicate Indonesia's fiscal system (and thus was opposed by international financial institutions) and extend corruption networks, it has provided local elites with a substantial stake in the territorial integrity of Indonesia and a larger voice in national deliberations. The decentralisation bill brings Indonesia's political order closer to Indonesia's vast archipelagic, multi-ethnic nature.

Indonesia's democratisation has not played into the hands of Indonesia's secessionist powers as many feared. Despite the fractured nature of parliament, no regional parties have made the running in the new Indonesia, and certainly none of the parties advocating regional secession or even regional autonomy. The only party that comes close to this is the Christian-based PDS party established to defend Christian interests in Maluku and surrounding areas after an upsurge in communal violence. Yet it represents an effort to defend minority rights within Indonesia, not an effort to secede from Indonesia. All the major parties are national in aspiration and the new law on political parties require all parties competing for the DPR to be national in scope. The popularity of Yudhoyono exemplifies the strength of 'Indonesia' as a popular idea. He beat Megawati by a wide margin in Indonesia's Javanese heartland and in its most restless peripheries. Indonesia's directly elected presidency favours national politics and national figures, while its fractured parliament has not been allowed to host regional separatist parties.

Here to Stay

Despite a stuttering economy, stagnant per capita income and an extended period of political and policy flux since 1998, Indonesia's democracy has held strong and shifted from a period of transition to consolidation. Most Indonesia watchers expect Yudhoyono to remain in power for his full five-year term and possibly even rule Indonesia until 2014 by winning a second term in 2009. Indonesia's shift from an indirectly to a directly elected presidential ballot in 2004 strengthened Indonesia's new democracy. In 1999, it was possible for Wahid to be chosen as president, despite his party (PKB) winning less than 13 per cent of the vote, because Golkar and other minor parties plotted against PDI-P and Megawati. Megawati was able to replace Wahid less than halfway through his term by convincing Golkar and PAN to switch sides. Indonesian voters had little say in the selection of their first two presidents, while the fear of legislative impeachment hovered over both administrations, undermining their ability to push through difficult reforms. Now voters directly elect their leader, while impeachment proceedings face a much tougher road. Indonesia's democracy is now more stable and more representative.

While the 2003 changes to Indonesia's presidential system will help political continuity going forward, there were serious fears (and some 'I told you so' voices) predicting that New Order forces and the Suharto family would prosper in 2004 on the back of a wave of popular nostalgia. Many thought that Indonesia's turbulent ride since 1997 would lead voters to wish for a return to the more predictable—and prosperous—days of the New Order regime: Indonesia's second experiment with democracy would prove as short-lived and underwhelming as its first. Two of Suharto's daugthers started new parties to take advantage of this perceived mood swing, while Golkar and ex-General Wiranto toned down Golkar's 1999 campaign drive to distance itself from Suharto and the New Order. Wiranto's presidential campaign focused on the need for Indonesia to regain its lost glory and influence, and the need for Indonesia to be led by a powerful, authoritative figure.

Yet Suharto's daughters' parties barely registered in the parliamentary elections, and none of the major parties sought their public support for the presidential campaign, despite these parties being well-funded and having nationally-known leaders. Likewise, ex-General Wiranto failed to make the second round as his close association with the late Suharto years hurt him electorally. With the rise of *Partai Demokrat* and PKS, and the transfer of power in Golkar, Indonesia's political system is leading the country's move away from the New Order period. It is not acting as the vehicle for a return to it.

In spite of having four very different presidents in six years from four different parties, Indonesia's political transformation has survived well and now looks well-entrenched. Indonesia's democratisation was triggered by an economic collapse and has been able to survive its transition period, despite unstable socio-economic times. Indonesia's new democracy has helped moderate the expression of Indonesia's main political faultlines and provided a mainstream political space for Indonesia's new Islamic and regional voices. Indonesia is a successful test case for Islam and democracy in a multi-ethnic country. Indonesia's domestic political transformation has also changed its regional and global position and attracted newfound external support.

INDONESIA'S GLOBAL SECURITY TRANSFORMATION

In the 1950s and 1960s, Indonesia was a front line country in the early days of the Cold War, with the Sukarno regime seen to be shifting towards communism in its later chaotic years, while Suharto positioned Indonesia as a staunch anti-communist regime winning favour in Washington, Tokyo and Canberra. Indonesia's own foreign policy was deeply affected by its position in this global ideological battle. Sukarno was one of the driving forces behind the Non-Aligned Movement, while the primary goal of Indonesian foreign policy has been to shelter Indonesia, and by extension Southeast Asia, from great power interference and intervention. This defensive foreign policy mandate reflected the Indonesian state's deep fears over the fragility of Indonesia's territorial integrity. It also explains Suharto's active role in the formation and development of ASEAN and Indonesia's deep pain and remaining ambivalence towards East Timorese independence and the Australian-led United Nations intervention.

The greatest global security transformation since the end of the Cold War, the declaration of an open-ended Global War on Terror, has again placed Indonesia at the forefront of global security concerns and revived Indonesian fears of great power intervention. Jemaah Islamiyah tapped into this fear by justifying bombings of western targets in Indonesia (like Bali and Jakarta's JW Marriott Hotel) by linking them to the west's, especially Australia's, role in the 'loss' of East Timor. The Global War on Terror shares many symbolic similarities with the Cold War, and Indonesia's Cold War experiences are informing its approach to its new, unwanted global security status. As with the Cold War, the Global War on Terror is increasing many countries' interest in close and harmonious ties with Indonesia (which sits on the world's most important sea lane of communication, the Malacca Straits). The War on Terror has created new areas of shared interest between the Indonesian state and states concerned with the War on Terror, especially the United States and Australia.

Under Suharto, the Cold War fused the Indonesian state's primary domestic security interest with strong popular support, defeating communist forces, and a core foreign policy interest—namely, strong, supportive relations with the United States and Japan. In contrast, the War on Terror has created new political difficulties for Indonesia's leaders who have to balance their own interests in supporting the War on Terror and popular concerns that this war is a veiled attack on Islam. Fortunately, the leaders in the War on Terror have shown themselves to be sensitive towards Jakarta's balancing act and have not pushed Indonesia (or Malaysia) to take too hard a public line on the Global War on Terror. Washington did not criticise either country for their lack of active support in the Invasion of Iraq, which Washington presented as a major offensive in the War on Terror. In Indonesia, the Invasion of Iraq was very unpopular and stoked popular recriminations that the War on Terror was an anti-Islamic exercise in American imperialism.[4]

September 11 instantly transformed Indonesia into a global symbol in the new age of terrorism. How the world's largest Muslim country traditionally committed to secular politics would react to the bombings in the United States, and what role it would play in the War on Terror, became the new focus of international attention on Indonesia and for American-Indonesian relations. President Megawati was permitted to continue with her planned trip to

---

[4] In a poll conducted in May and June 2003, 66 per cent of Indonesian respondents agreed that the United States was a greater threat to world peace than Al Qaeda Poll suggests world hostile to US. *BBC News*, 17 June 2003.

the United States soon after the bombings, despite the United States being in a state of national 'lock down.' President Megawati's condemnation of the bombings, taking place on American soil so soon after they had occurred, had great symbolic import and backed up the assertions that the War on Terror was not a War on Islam (Smith (2003). Similar condemnations of the bombings and terrorism by Nahdlatul Ulama and Muhammadiyah strengthened this image.

The September 2002 Bali bombings that killed 202 people (including 88 Australians) placed Indonesia at the centre of regional concerns about Islamist terrorism, and Indonesia became more than an important symbolic player in the War on Terror. It was now a primary victim and battlefield of the War. The 2004 bombings of the JW Marriott Hotel and outside the Australian embassy in Jakarta have reconfirmed the long-term, open-ended nature of this War and Indonesia's central position in it.

Jemaah Islamiyah was responsible for these three bombings, as well as the earlier spate of bombings of Christian churches during the Christmas period in 2000, which offered the first signs of this renewed threat in Indonesia. Jemaah Islamiyah is a mirror of this new wave of Islamist terrorism in Southeast Asia. The organisation's personnel and ideology meld together local influences from the Darul Islam movement, the muhajideen struggle and victory in Afghanistan with the global ambitions and spread of Al Qaeda. The organisation's links to Al Qaeda and other violent Islamist groups (like the Abu Sayyaf and the Moro Islamic Liberation Front in the Southern Philippines) enhance its operational capacity, affect its selection of targets and turn it into more than a local concern. This has also meant that Indonesian attempts to address Jemaah Islamiyah's local crimes have been watched very closely and frequently commented on outside Indonesia.

The Indonesian-American Thaw

Beyond focusing attention again on Southeast Asia, and Indonesia in particular, as a source of security threats, the War on Terror has deepened Washington's and Canberra's relations with Indonesia and opened up new areas of cooperation that would not have existed otherwise. For the United States, the Asian financial crisis and its political ramifications seriously strained relations with Jakarta. The IMF's tough line on Indonesia, including pushing for politically sensitive reforms not directly linked to crisis recovery, earned the ire of the Indonesian government and population. Washington's lack of financial support for the earlier Thai bail-out package and the close links between the United States Treasury and the IMF, especially over this crisis, meant that, in practice, the IMF and Washington were seen as one (Grenville (2004). The blame and animosity that Indonesia directed towards the IMF spilt over directly into relations with Washington. Indonesia has recently refused a new IMF program, despite its continuing need for concessional funding, while the front-running candidate to be Yudhoyono's finance minister after his election victory in October 2004 did not get the job due to her perceived association with the IMF.

The United States Congress also acted to downgrade military ties with Indonesia since the death of over 100 civilians in East Timor in 1991. A series of events in Indonesia, including the violence surrounding East Timorese independence and the army's involvement in the 2002 murder of two Americans in Papua, have delayed full normalisation. Since the late 1990s, United States-Indonesian relations have suffered, while the popular image of the United States in Indonesia and Indonesia's image in the United States have been battered.

Since the War on Terror began, Washington has boosted both its financial and military support for Indonesia, while Yudhoyono made it clear that one of his top foreign policy objectives was to re-establish normal military relations with the United States. American aid to Indonesia doubled from 1999 to 2004, with a growing focus on counter-terrorism and Indonesia's largely unregulated Islamic education system. Especially after the victory of Yudhoyono and Indonesia's good record of incarcerating terrorism suspects, Washington has pushed for the normalisation of military ties. In February 2005, Secretary of State Rice announced that Indonesia had fulfilled all the requirements to be restored to the list of countries able to be offered International Military Education and Training (IMET) funding. There has been a concerted effort in Washington since 2002 to re-establish full military relations. Thawing relations between Washington and Jakarta both facilitated and were bolstered by the United States' rapid deployment to help Aceh after the Boxing Day tsunami. Indonesian-American relations have been revived by the War on Terror, and they have overcome differences of opinion over Iraq.

The Indonesian-Australian Thaw

Indonesia's new position in global, and particularly regional, security has served a similar, but more comprehensive, function for Indonesian-Australian relations. The role of Australia in the independence of East Timor and long-standing Indonesian concerns over Australian interests in Papua soured bilateral relations only four years after the landmark 1995 joint security agreement. Australia became a favourite target for Indonesian nationalist politicians just as it was in Mahathir's Malaysia, while Indonesia abandoned the joint security agreement after Australia led the United Nations into East Timor in 1999. Terrorism in Indonesia, and more recently Australia's overwhelming government and public response to Aceh's tsunami devastation, have brought the two countries closer together and may lead to a more institutionalised cooperative relationship than even in the heyday of the Keating-Suharto friendship.

The Bali bombings of September 2002 acted as a catalyst for this change in the tone and direction of relations. The bombings emphasised the shared nature of the two neighbours' security threats, rather than the previous focus on threats from each other. Indonesia was the first of the ASEAN countries to sign a counter-terrorism Memorandum of Understanding (MOU) with Australia, while the Bali bombings led Jakarta to permit Australian Federal Police involvement in the case. Australia and Indonesia signed this MOU eight months before the Bali bombings. The relationship between the Federal Police and their Indonesian counterparts has blossomed into a long-term commitment of personnel and funds by the Federal Police in Indonesia. The Federal Police and AusAID in 2003 committed $A38 million for the Jakarta Centre for Law Enforcement Cooperation in Semarang, Indonesia, which now serves as a regional training centre.

The smooth and understated cooperation between the Federal Police and Indonesian police has been supported by President Megawati and President Yudhoyono and has been held up as the model for future bureaucratic cooperation. It is likely that such cooperative programs set the groundwork for Jakarta's acceptance of a major Australian role in tsunami relief, including the secondment of Australian officials to BAPPENAS, the main government agency in charge of tsunami recovery. Indonesia also accepted a joint high-level panel as the means to distribute the $A1 billion tsunami package Australia has committed, rather than demanding that it be transferred directly to the Indonesian government for disbursement.

Australia's aid program to Indonesia—Indonesia is the second largest recipient of Australian aid after Papua New Guinea—has also reflected the more intense relationship focused on counter-terrorism. As with American aid, Australian aid has been reallocated to focus more on the Islamic education system in Indonesia. The Australian government, under Foreign Affairs Minister Downer, has also funded large inter-faith meetings in Australia and Indonesia, while Canberra has allocated up to $A20 million for counter-terrorism cooperation.

As with Washington, military relations between Jakarta and Canberra have been on the mend after Australia stopped joint training exercises with Indonesia's special forces *Kopassus* in 1999 over East Timor and human rights abuses. Australia reinstituted these exercises in 2003, citing the need for closer counter-terrorism cooperation after the Bali bombings. After the election of President Yudhoyono, Australia promoted negotiating a new, more comprehensive security agreement to replace the abandoned 1995 agreement. However, reflecting the depth and endurance of bilateral security sensitivities, little progress with both countries agreeing to put this issue on the back burner. Australia and Indonesia have also agreed to begin framework discussions on a bilateral preferential trade agreement (PTA) to complement Australia's pacts with Singapore, Thailand and ongoing talks with Malaysia. These will be Indonesia's first bilateral PTA talks. Indonesia and Australia have begun to move beyond the rancour caused by East Timor, and counter-terrorism concerns are at the heart of this new rapprochement.

Regional Cooperation

Regional terrorism and Southeast Asia's place in the Global War on Terror have also acted to strengthen Southeast Asian cooperation with Indonesia again at the heart of this. The Malacca Straits is the world's single most important sea lane of communication and place littoral Southeast Asian countries at the heart of world trade. A quarter of world maritime trade uses the Straits that host over 50,000 commercial vessels a year. The Straits' high density of traffic and numerous choke points make this area an ideal target for maritime terrorism (Richardson (2004). In some areas, the sinking of one major ship could effectively block the whole Straits for days, pushing world crude oil prices up sharply and posing serious problems for East Asia's booming economies. Naturally, the Malacca Straits have become a major concern for the planners of the War on Terror.

In 2004, this growing concern over the vulnerability of the Straits led the head of the American Pacific Command, Admiral Fargo, to ponder the benefits of US patrols in the area. Echoing shared concerns over great-power intervention in Southeast Asia, Malaysia and Indonesia flatly rejected this trial and quickly agreed with Singapore on coordinated patrols of the Malacca Straits, opening up an unexpected basis for naval cooperation among these three traditionally wary neighbours. Recently, these three littoral states have agreed to increase the number of joint patrols. The plan for joint patrols with American ships was rejected, but shared concerns over the Straits and external pressure combined to foster new regional cooperation among navies traditionally seen as latent adversaries.

INDONESIA'S MISSED TRANSFORMATIONS

The traumatic events that sparked both of Indonesia's post-Cold War transformations and the fact that they happened within a short period of time have meant that Indonesian society and the Indonesian state have been preoccupied. Indonesia has not been able to comprehensively respond to other major regional transformations that, together with serious domestic policy challenges, present the country with a pressing foreign and economic policy agenda that the state is just beginning to address. Hopefully, democratic consolidation will deliver more policy continuity and fewer political diversions.

On the foreign policy front, China's initiative of an East Asian Summit to enhance (or replace) the ASEAN+3 process poses new challenges for ASEAN's relevance and unity. The ASEAN+3 process placed ASEAN and Indonesia at the centre of East Asian regional cooperation and regime building. ASEAN's centrality and its consequent agenda-setting power helped ensure that the organisation has been strengthened not weakened by wider consultations and that East Asian regionalism did not aggravate ASEAN members' long-standing fears of great power interference and control. The yet-to-be-defined East Asian Summit holds the potential to weaken the say of ASEAN as an organisation and Southeast Asia as a group of small powers, over wider East Asian regionalism. The title of the new regional effort clearly symbolise that the playing field of regional integration has moved from ASEAN and Southeast Asia to East Asia and the Northeast Asian giants. Japan's economy is roughly six times larger than Southeast Asia's combined economy. Can ASEAN find a way of maintaining its privileged position in East Asian regionalism and how will Indonesia, as the largest power in ASEAN, respond?

The apparent end to the ASEAN Free Trade Agreement (AFTA) process, in which Indonesia has been one of the laggards, has led the other major ASEAN members to shift towards bilateral PTAs either through ASEAN or by themselves. By definition, these PTAs undermine AFTA's potential benefits and, through their thicket of diverging rules of origin, AFTA's goal of strengthening Southeast Asia as a single, seamless economy. Singapore and Thailand have led this charge to PTAs beyond ASEAN, while Indonesia is the only major ASEAN economy not to come up with a clear position on bilateral PTAs. Its framework agreement discussions with Australia are its first venture into bilateral PTAs outside of ASEAN.

Recent efforts by Indonesia to deepen intra-ASEAN cooperation, such as Megawati's idea of developing an ASEAN Security Community, show that Indonesia is committed to continuing its leadership of ASEAN. Its lack of a clear position on ASEAN and bilateral PTAs, as well as the lack of movement on the ASEAN Security Community plan or the Indonesian idea for an ASEAN peacekeeping force, suggest that Indonesia will have to work harder.

On the economic policy side, the Asian crisis simultaneously exposed Indonesia's serious structural problems and highlighted China's status as the new global engine of growth. China has replaced Southeast Asia as the favoured site for emerging market foreign direct investment. Since the mid 1980s, the world has become increasingly attracted to the promise of China and worried about the problems of China overheating.

Since the Asian crisis, Indonesia has suffered a net foreign direct investment withdrawal and has not returned to its sustained high-growth path. Instead, the Indonesian GDP has failed to expand at 7 per cent per annum—the growth figure needed to absorb new labour market entrants and raise per capita income (Basri (2004). Since the Asian crisis, Indonesia's corruption perception ratings have worsened. Indonesia was recently identified as the most corrupt country in East Asia. China's corruption ratings, on the other hand, have been improving.

Indonesia's and China's export profiles have been converging since the Asian crisis, while Indonesia's competitiveness has been in decline (EAU (2003). At the same time that China's demand for raw materials is growing rapidly, Indonesia has become a net oil importer. Indonesia's structural weaknesses, aggravated by the crisis, and its inability to return to a sustained high growth trajectorywould have posed a serious problem for the Indonesian state. The simultaneous Chinese boom and its attention-diverting nature simply deepen Indonesia's economic policy challenges, while making Indonesia's economic environment more competitive.

If Indonesia does not respond effectively to the changing tides of East Asian regionalism, its leadership of Southeast Asia, and the enhanced voice this provides Indonesia in East Asia and beyond, will suffer. If Indonesia does not respond effectively to its manifold structural problems and the rise of China economically, then its future economic development and its beneficial role in democratic consolidation will also suffer. Indonesia has gone through two major transformations since 1997 smoothly, each of which has strengthened its foreign relations. The democratic transition is the most meaningful and will likely last much longer than the transformation brought about by the War on Terror. However, Indonesia will need to pull off at least two more transformations to guarantee its regional position and its economic and political future.

REFERENCES

Badsewan, Anies Rasyid. Political Islam in Indonesia: Present and future trajectory. *Asian Survey* 44 (5) 2004, pp. 669-690.

Basri, Faisal. *Political and Economic Outlook, 2004*. Puri Consulting, JW Marriott Hotel, 20 January 2004.

Bubalo, Anthony and Greg Fealy. *Joining the caravan? The Middle East, Islamism and Indonesia*. Lowy Institute Papers 05. Sydney, Lowy Institute for International Policy, 2005.

Chauvel, Richard. Australia's strategic environment: the problem of Papua. *Agenda* 11 (1) 2004, pp. 37-49.

Cook, Malcolm. *Supporting democratic Indonesia: British and European options*. Policy Briefs. London, The Foreign Policy Centre, 2004.

EAU. *China's industrial rise: East Asia's challenge*. Canberra, DFAT, 2003.

Effendy, Bahtiar. *Islam and the State in Indonesia*. Singapore, ISEAS, 2003.

Grenville, Stephen. The IMF and the Indonesian crisis. *Bulletin of Indonesian Economic Studies* 40 (1) 2004, pp. 77-94.

Huxley, Tim. *Disintergrating Indonesia? Implications for regional security*. Adelphi Papers 349. London, IISS, 2002.

Philippines branded as Asia's 2nd most corrupt place for business. *Business World*, 9 March 2005.

Poll suggests world hostile to US. *BBC News*, 17 June 2003.

Richardson, Michael. *A time bomb for global trade: Maritime-related terrorism in an age of weapons of mass destruction*. Viewpoints. Singapore, ISEAS, 2004.

Rieffel, Lex. Indonesia's quiet revolution. *Foreign Affairs* 83 (5) 2004, pp. 98-110.

Smith, Anthony L. A glass half full: Indonesia-U.S. relations in the age of terror. *Contemporary Southeast Asia* 25 (3) 2003, pp. 449-472.

Sukma, Rizal. *Security operations in Aceh: Goals, consequences, and lessons* Policy Studies 3. Washington, East-West Center, 2004.

In: Asia-Pacific and a New International Order
Editors: Purnendra Jain et al. pp. 181-194
ISBN 1-59454-986-9
© 2006 Nova Science Publishers, Inc.

Chapter 12

MALAYSIA AND THE CHANGING REGIONAL SECURITY ENVIRONMENT: RESPONSES AND OPTIONS[1]

Kamarulnizam Abdullah

INTRODUCTION

The international relations debates, after the end of the Cold War, have focused on the probable structure of the international system. Many argued that the world would be a multi-polar system whereby more actors would play and have greater stakes in the world. Nonetheless, there were also arguments that only one superpower, namely, the United States, would dominate the international political system after the collapse of the Soviet Union. What can be said is that all these analyses were centred on realist perspectives by looking at states as still the main actors. Yet at the same time, a liberal perspective seems to have gained prominence. The world is said to have entered the era of globalisation. Governments have no choice but to accept the ideas of free trade, democratisation, and good governance, that is, political transparency and accountability. In addition, there were hopes that the post-Cold War era could produce a stable international system. However, the three Gulf Wars (the Iran-Iraq confrontation in the 1980s, the Iraqi invasion of Kuwait and the 2003 US-led coalition invasion of Iraq), and the September 11 incident shattered that hope and dream. The world is still as it is, full of conflicts and wars.

The September 11 incident has given an added dimension to the regional and international systems. Although a state's political agenda is still about maintaining national interest, sovereignty and political legitimacy, threats to state survival seem to be coming in a new form. Perceived threats to national security are no longer in the form of state invasion of another state, but could also be in the form of threats emanating from non-state actors, for example, terrorist groups or international criminal organisations. Terrorism, as Castro (2004:

---

[1] I would like to express my sincere gratitude to Professor Andrew MacIntyre from the Australian National University, Canberra and Dr Arujunan Narayanan from the Universiti Kebangsaan Malaysia, Bangi, for their invaluable comments and suggestions.

195) argues, is not 'simply single and coherent entities like nation-states. Rather, they are systems with diverse elements, many of which are transnational in nature'. This is a challenge to countries in the Southeast Asian region.

The impact of the September 11 Incident on the Muslims in Southeast Asia can be analysed at two different levels. At the individual level, Muslims all over the world who do not share the sentiments propounded by radicals have to react and realign themselves. They have to rethink, not only about the fundamental teachings of Islam, but also about their place in the world community. Similarly, ordinary Muslims ask whether they have to subscribe to the calls of Muslim extremists? Do they become less Muslim if the idea of an Islamic-based state and community does not materialise? Even more confusing, Islamic scholars, that is, the *ulama*, fail to come out with convincing *fatwas* on whether they are sanctioning the radical acts propounded by extremists who use the holy Koran to justify their actions. For those who share the radical ideas, the arguments are always centred around three main precepts. Firstly, all Muslim governments are accused of being politically and socio-economically corrupted by aligning themselves with the Christian west; secondly, these corruptions are due to the failure of these Muslim governments to uphold *syariah* (Islamic law) based on the Koran; hence, thirdly, the only way to clear the impurity is to call for *Jihad Fi-Sibilant* (Holy war in the name of God), using force in order to set up an Islamic state based on what was allegedly envisaged by the prophet Muhammad.

At the state level, moderate Muslim countries, like Malaysia, tend to distance themselves from the militant ideology and are thus faced with a political dilemma. On the one hand, these Muslim countries have the upper hand in suppressing radical religious elements in their societies without having fear of being scrutinised by major powers and the western community. Some countries use the United States-led Global War Against Terrorism campaign to justify their actions against Islamic groups deemed threats to national security. Preventive laws once condemned as draconian with hidden political motives are now seen as the most effective tools to contain the spread of terrorism and religious radicalism.

Moderate Muslim countries, especially those in Southeast Asia, as Abuza (2004) has argued, were constrained by the domestic growth of the radicalisation of political Islam. Malaysia and Indonesia, for instance, have to limit their use of the political language of Islam to avoid upsetting their western allies. At the same time, they have no choice but to react to the rise of political Islamic revivalism either by suppressing it, which is politically suicidal, or by becoming more Islamic. Yet, by becoming more Islamic, these Muslim governments have given more space for radical movements to expand politically and socially. This political gamble did not produce the expected outcome, but created more problems. Still, these Muslim governments have little option but to use Islam to gain political support. Having said that, the following questions are raised: How have Muslim majority countries in the Southeast Asian region, especially Malaysia, responded to the new US-led regional order? What are the options available? Finally, how far can Malaysia support the US-led global war against terrorism?

This chapter analyses Malaysia's responses to the current changes in the regional security architecture, especially in the aftermath of the September 11 Incident. It also analyses the options and approaches open to the country in dealing with the global threat of terrorism. I argue that Malaysia's political pragmatism has been the determining factor in dealing with the new order in the Southeast Asian region. Furthermore, Malaysia's responses and options to the changing structure of the regional security environment must be understood in the context of, firstly, the dynamics of domestic political Islam; and secondly, its long and strong relations with the west, especially the United States of America.

THE DYNAMIC OF DOMESTIC POLITICAL ISLAM

Terrorism is not new to Malaysia; nor did it begin with the September 11 Incident. Malaysia experienced the threat of communist terrorism/insurgency for 43 years after the end of World War II. The threat was overcome, not solely through military action, but also through winning the hearts and minds of the people. The latter targeted the Chinese, the main supporters of the insurgency. Under British rule, psychological warfare was also used, as well as large-scale evacuations of people from areas near the communist stronghold to new military-guarded villages. Although these programs continued after independence in 1957, Chinese support to the communist insurgents failed to subside. The government then identified that the root causes of disaffection 'stemmed mainly from the isolation felt amongst the Chinese and [it] redressed the problem by offering citizenship[,] thus undercutting reasons to continue support' for the guerrillas (Noor, 2003:161).

Nonetheless, dealing with the current threat of religious militancy and terrorism poses new challenges for the government. It requires more than winning the hearts and minds of the people. It is about religion, identity and legitimacy. Questions have been raised as to whether the regime in power has the political legitimacy to label certain Muslim organisations as terrorist. The decision by the Malaysian government to outlaw an influential Muslim organisation, the Darul Arqam, was criticised as politically motivated (Abdullah, 2003b). The Malaysian government argued that the group was a threat to the national security for its serious doctrinal controversies pertaining to Islamic teachings (ibid.). Yet critics argued that the decision was a response to Arqam's challenge to the government's self-proclaimed status as the national guardian of Islam. The Arqam case and subsequent questions of political legitimacy are not peculiar to Malaysia, but have major concerns for Third World regimes in countries dealing with national security challenges (Collins, 2003: 10). Unlike the communist insurgency, the source of the current security threat is more difficult to identify. The culprits may be part of the society, and worse, might be respected community leaders. Further, the issue involves Islam, the most important religion and a source of political strength in Malaysia. Although terrorists represent a distinct minority of the population, 'their ability to cause political and economic instability' means that Malaysia has to take them seriously to ensure political stability (Abuza, 2003: 1).

Islam in Malaysia is at the centre stage of Malay politics. It has been used not only for rhetorical purposes, but also to garner grassroot political support (Abdullah, 2003b). The political rivalry between the dominant ruling party, the United Malay National Organization (UMNO), and its main rival, the Pan Islamic Party of Malaysia (PAS), over the true meaning of Islam makes the problem manifest. Furthermore, the current is also associated with the rise of the radicalisation of domestic political Islam. It reflects concern over the state's commitment to protect the social and political fabric of the Malay community in a multi-racial society and its ability to act as an effective gatekeeper maintaining societal cohesion among the three major races (Abdullah, 2003a: 223) The result has been that, since independence, the regime has responded by ensuring that there is only one official and authoritative version of Islam to be followed by all Muslims.

The UMNO-led government must also recognise that political Islam has played a dominant role in Malaysian politics. By ignoring the influential role of Islam propagated by PAS and other Islamic movements, UMNO might lose the political support of the Malay population. The formulation of domestic and foreign policies has to take into account this support base and the influential role of Islam in politics and society. In the early 1980s, for instance, the Malaysian government, under the Mahathir administration, embarked upon an Islamisation program aimed at introducing a progressive and moderate version of Islam. The purpose of the program was to ease non-Muslims' concern over the increasing call by some segments of the Malay-Muslim community to incorporate radical Islamic values into government machinery. The program, however, was viewed suspiciously by PAS. At the same time, there was also apprehension from the non-Muslim community over the Islamisation program. Yet failure to continue with Islamisation would jeopardise the government's popularity and could cost its political survival.

Over the years, however, the Islamisation program has placed the UMNO-led government in a quandary. The image of clean, moderate and progressive Islam was marred by scandals of the leadership's moral laxity, corruption and money politics. Furthermore, the 1997 Asian Financial Crisis, followed by the sacking of the then Deputy Prime Minister Anwar Ibrahim, and the subsequent rise of the *reformasi* movement placed the UMNO-led government under intense political pressure. It seemed to lose its grassroots support. During the 1999 General Elections, its popularity dipped to its lowest ever. The state of Terengganu was lost to the opposition. The election demonstrated, as Tan argues, 'the growing influence of political Islam in Malaysian politics' (2003: 89).

THE RISE OF RADICAL POLITICAL ISLAM

The protracted and usually emotional debates over the role of Islam between UMNO and PAS have had a negative impact on the development of Islam in the country. The fierce political rivalry has created dissenting elements, which have views and opinions radically different from the two influential Malay-Muslim political parties. These elements wanted to see Islam as the single most influential element of Malaysia's multi-racial society, but were frustrated by the fierce political confrontation between UMNO and PAS. They averred that the UMNO-PAS confrontation was delaying the development of Islam (Abdullah, 2003a: 224). In other words, UMNO-PAS rivalry impeded the attempts to promote Islam as an alternative political ideology. They also envisage radical transformation of Malaysian polity. For these radicals, democracy was neither an appropriate political ideology nor a solution for Malaysia. They argued that the Taliban model of Islamic political ideology should be part of Malaysian political, social and economic systems. Moreover, the multi-racial composition of Malaysian society would not hinder its implementation.

There was also another militant group, Kumpulan Mujahidin Malaysia (Mujahidin group of Malaysia) or KMM, which viewed the current UMNO-led government as too harsh towards and discriminating against Islamic movements or parties such as PAS. They averred that under the current regime, Islam plays a minimal role in politics. The UMNO-led government tends to separate religion and politics. Continued efforts by the regime to silence and undermine PAS's Islam by using 'draconian' laws, such as the Internal Security Act (ISA), Official Secret Act (OSA) and the Press and Publication Act, hamper their efforts to set up an Islamic state in Malaysia. In several instances, the UMNO-led government was threatening to arrest PAS leaders, some of whom they considered to be the party's spiritual leaders because of their radical political ideas. For UMNO, given the secular nature of Malaysian society, ideas for an Islamic state could harm the racial and religious understandings between the Malays and non-Malay communities (Abdullah, 2003a: 224). In order to contain those radical ideas that might cause instability, the government had to arrest notable leaders of the political opposition.

How then did the idea of religious radicalism gain a footing on Malaysian soil? The 1979 Iranian Revolution, the Arab-Israeli conflict over Palestine, civil wars in Bosnia and Chechnya, and the Soviet invasion of Afghanistan may partly explain the rise of global Islamic consciousness among the Malaysian Muslims. More specifically, the rise of radical Islamic ideas in Malaysia can be traced to the influence of the sizeable number of Malaysian students educated in the *madrasah* systems in Egypt, Pakistan, India and Libya. Some of these students were involved, apparently without the knowledge of the Malaysian government, in conflicts in West and Central Asia, and received military training while studying abroad. Their skills in handling weapons and explosives could be exploited by militant movements. These students were also captivated by PAS's political agenda for turning Malaysia into an Islamic state.

Furthermore, the independent *madrasah* school system in Malaysia has also been identified as a breeding ground for radicalism. The teachers, alumni of Pakistani *madrasah* schools and Indonesia's *pasentran*, became ideologues to the students. Graduates of these Malaysian *madrasahs* were sent to Pakistan or India to strengthen their networking, thus paving the way for the establishment of Kumpulan Mujahidin Malaysia (KMM) that shares PAS's political inclination towards black-and-white Islam.

The emergence of the KMM, Al-Maunah and the Malaysian branch of Jemaah Islamiyah (JI) can be seen as conduits to bring about immediate changes to the role of Islam in Malaysia. The Al-Maunah group was one of several Islamic militant movements frustrated with the political rivalry between UMNO and PAS. The KMM was initially a politically motivated Islamic movement intending to protect PAS leaders from being arrested by the government. Since the September 11 Incident, however, the movement has proven also to be part of the Al Qaeda networks in Southeast Asia.

While the KMM threat appears to be confined to Malaysia, the major challenge to Malaysian security is that posed by Al Qaeda's Southeast Asian network led by JI. Historically, JI was the offshoot of Indonesia's Darul Islam. It was established in 1993 in Malaysia when Abdullah Sungkar, the first JI leader, decided to break away from Darul Islam. He and his followers were fleeing the Suharto regime and became fugitives in Malaysia after 1985. The organisation was very active in recruiting locals through religious gatherings and classes. The group set up a *madrasah* known as Lukmanul Haqim, believed to be a key breeding ground for religious radicalism.[2] Abdullah Sungkar and the subsequent

---

[2] The *madrasah* ceased operation under the State's Religious Department Order after the government found out about its activities.

leader of JI, Abu Bakr Basyir, decided to return to Indonesia in 1999 when the Suharto regime collapsed and the *reformasi* era began.

The rise of Islamic militancy globally and regionally has given the government an opportunity not only to defeat its political enemies, but also to use preventive detention by applying the Internal Security Act (ISA) more freely. Previously critical western powers have now played down their opposition. When Mr James Kelly, the United States Assistant Secretary for East Asia and the Pacific, met Dr Mahathir Mohamad in April 2002 to personally hand over President Bush's invitation to visit Washington, the envoy neither raised the Anwar issue, nor touched on any issue on political prisoners held under the ISA (Sodhy, 2003: 367). So far, 99 members of Muslim militant groups have been detained under the ISA (*Berita Harian*, 2003). Fifty-eight of them are members of JI, eighteen from KMM and fifteen from Al-Maunah.

The September 11 Incident disadvantaged PAS. Although it made it clear that PAS did not share Al Qaeda's ideology, the involvement of its members in such groups made it difficult for PAS to be credible. Given its history of supporting radical Islamic groups, for example in the Memali[3] and Sauk[4] incidents, the party has an uphill task to convince the society of its claim. Its dismal performance in 2004 (when the PAS not only lost Terengganu state government seats to UMNO, but also barely managed to form the government in Kelantan) is a manifestation of Malaysian rejection of PAS's Islam.

The Malaysian government has taken steps to reduce, if not pre-empt, the possible expansion of Islamic radical ideas in the country. Although the *madrasah* school system and other independent Islamic schools, such as Sekolah Agama Rakyat (People's Religious School), were run independently by Islamic foundations, individuals and, to some extent, political parties, the schools also received small annual grants from the government through the state's Baitulmal (Alms Collection Agency) and the Religious Affairs Department. After realising the school system was being used to spread radical Islam and as a platform for criticising the government, the grants were withdrawn until the schools fulfilled conditions set by the government (*Utusan Malaysia*, 2003). One of these conditions was to restructure and revamp their academic curriculum to adhere to the national syllabus. The schools were not allowed to teach only religious subjects, but also had to incorporate other important sciences and vocational subjects. Since most of the teachers did not have formal training in education, they were also required to attend teaching seminars and courses organised by the Ministry of Education (*Utusan Malaysia*, 2003).

---

[3] Memali is a small village situated in the district of Baling, Kedah (at the northwestern part of peninsular Malaysia). The Memali incident occurred on 19 November 1985, when a group of people led by Ibrahim Mahmud (better known as Ibrahim Libya) refused to surrender to the police forces under ISA. Ibrahim Libya, who was a respected religious teacher and also an important PAS leader, was accused of abusing and exploiting Islam for personal and political ends (Abdullah, 2003b). He was also accused of stirring up hatred against the Malaysian government and called for armed rebellion through *jihad* against the so-called arrogant and *kafir* (infidel) government. Open clashes took place on that day which resulted in the deaths of four police personnel, Ibrahim Libya himself and fourteen of his followers.

[4] Sauk is another small village situated in the district of Hulu Perak, Perak (about 200 km north of Kuala Lumpur). The incident took place in July 2000 when a group of 29 Muslim militants known as Al-Maunah began a heist of assorted weapons from a military outpost. The clashes between the security forces and the group ended in tragedy, claiming the lives of several Al-Maunah members, a Special Branch detective and a police commando, who were shot dead in the durian orchard. The incident also became a racial issue, when the leader of the group openly admitted that they killed the security officers because they were non-Malays and non-Muslims. PAS, furthermore, claimed that the incident was purposely staged by the government to discredit the party and to justify the government's action against the group.

It short, it can be argued that the September 11 Incident and the subsequent global war against terrorism have forced Malaysia to control the use of Islamic political language for fear that it would adversely effect not only individual Muslims, but also the government itself. The excessive use of such language might give extra cause to radical Islamic groups and hamper the government's effort to contain their influence. The UMNO-led government has been able to use preventive laws such as the ISA to control the spread of domestic terrorism, although such moves were once criticised by western powers as draconian. Malaysia has made clear that it is not a terrorist haven. Yet at the same time, the post-September 11 security threats require more than just a political commitment to maintain internal order; it also requires Malaysia to be part of the international community to combat terrorism that transcends cultures and national borders. Malaysia needs not only to be willing to cooperate, but also to be seen to cooperate with the world, especially under the US-led Global War against Terrorism.

MALAYSIA AND MAJOR POWERS: THE BALANCING ACT

In the contemporary regional security environment, Malaysia has to readjust its position in order to maximise its external security. Although the threat of communism has receded, the post-September 11 environment generates a new set of challenges. Malaysia needs to have a balancing strategy to control the domestic security environment and at the same time enhance its external security capability. The ASEAN Regional Forum (ARF), as a loose consultative forum to discuss regional security issues, has been partly responsible for changing perceptions of threats and developing new opportunities.

The ARF has played its part by creating political confidence, not only among the ASEAN members, but also with major regional powers such as India, Japan and China. Nonetheless, as Singh (2004: 14) argues, the important component of ARF is that the USA provides regional security stability. Malaysia has played an instrumental role in 'patching together the ARF as a regional security regime' (Singh, 2004: 14). Malaysia's attachment to the US for security was reinforced through several formal defence agreements and links. America has also been regarded as the keeper of peace in the region and, furthermore, as having the ability to check and limit undue Chinese influence. Yet at the same time, some American behaviour and foreign policies have annoyed countries—friends and foe alike—in the region. Washington's over-emphasis on the so-called 'global values' of human rights and democracy sometimes became an irritating factor in its relations with several Southeast Asian countries, including Malaysia and Indonesia. President Bush, Jr's call for the Global War Against Terrorism through his infamous slogan, 'Either you are with us or against us', has placed countries in the region in a very difficult position. Malaysia's inability or failure to control the threat of terrorism could be interpreted by the superpower as indifference and could further damage relations between the two countries, already rocky since Al Gore's support for Malaysia's *reformasi* movement during the Kuala Lumpur Asia-Pacific Economic Cooperation (APEC) Meeting in 1998. At the same time, Malaysia also has to ensure that its involvement in diffusing terrorist threats at the regional level by cooperating closely with the United States would not seriously affect its domestic political survival. Malaysia's conception of national security in the post-September 11 period, therefore, involves pragmatic adaptation.

Dr Mahathir Mohamad, the then Prime Minister of Malaysia, was among the world leaders who openly condemned the September 11 attacks. The incident resulted in improved Malaysia-United States relations, which were at their lowest ebb after both countries exchanged heated political arguments over human rights and the Anwar saga.[5] Hence, Bush's War against Terrorism was openly accepted by the Malaysian government as a way not only to mend relations, but also to wipe out the threats of domestic religious militancy. Nonetheless, the United States attacks on Afghanistan later in 2001, followed by the unilateral attack on Iraq in March 2003 under the pretext of Sadam's failure to observe the Non-proliferation Treaty (NPT) on Weapons of Mass Destruction (WMD), again produced another diplomatic row between the two countries. Malaysia, like other countries that opposed the war, questioned the justification and the legality of the United States' use of force against Iraq without the consent of the United Nations (Ulfstein, 2003).

The Malaysian government, and Mahathir in particular, was vocal in condemning the United States' unilateral action and demanded clarification over the definitions and the root causes of terrorism. In addition, Malaysia argued that modern terrorism has been associated with western policies in Middle East, particularly the intractable conflict between Palestine and Israel. The alleged remarks against the Jews by Mahathir during the opening session of the 10th Organization of the Islamic Conference (OIC) in October 2003, and the subsequent rebuke by President George Bush, Jr, further worsened diplomatic relations.

Malaysia's critical stance against American actions may be partly due to the fact that the country is part of the OIC and the Non-Aligned Movement (NAM). As the chair of both, Malaysia needs to be proactive in trying to find solutions to the long and intractable crises involving the Muslim world, such as the Middle Eastern Crisis and regional conflicts in the Southern Philippines, Southern Thailand and Indonesia's Aceh. The chairmanship not only provides Malaysia with an opportunity to revitalise the role of the OIC and the NAM as significant and influential international organisations, but it also enables it to represent the voice of developing countries on the world stage. The position is a challenge to Malaysia, especially in the midst of the global fear of terrorism. Critics argue that the OIC in particular failed to live up to expectations, since it is still unable to unify its member countries and achieve a consensus, even when the political agenda concerns the plight of Muslims. Furthermore, members tended to react separately and within the framework of national interests, rather than utilising the OIC to voice a 'unified' opinion on international issues. In addition, the members 'have depended on other developed nations to preserve and pursue their national interests. When it comes to promoting Islamic solidarity, they pursue their own national interests in accordance with the agenda as laid down by the Western powers' (Shaikh Mohd Salleh, 2003). Another major problem is the inability of either the OIC or NAM to translate their commitments into action on several key political issues. Malaysia has been critical of this disunity, arguing that the lack of interaction among member states has

---

[5] The whole Malaysian political scenario entered into an unprecedented crisis when, on 2 September 1998, Anwar Ibrahim, the Deputy Prime Minister cum Finance Minister and the heir apparent to Malaysian leadership, was sacked by none other than his once mentor Dr Mahathir Mohamad for alleged corruption and sexual misconduct. Anwar claimed that the move to put him on trial was part of a political conspiracy by UMNO Supreme Council members. The political crisis led to relatively brief but violent *reformasi* (reformation) demonstrations, and at the same drew international sympathy for Anwar. The United States criticised the Mahathir administration over the handling of the case. During the APEC Dinner Summit in the same year, the US Vice-President, Al Gore, hailed those involved in the *reformasi* demonstrations as true political heroes for democracy. The remarks, nonetheless, irked the Mahathir administration.

prevented both organisations from becoming proactive mechanisms in solving conflict. Serious political disagreements, for instance, have long appeared in the OIC. During the 10th Annual Summit in Kuala Lumpur in 2003, discussion on terrorism failed because member states, particularly those from the Middle East, were unable to reach a consensus on the definition of terrorism. The Summit did emphasise ways to eradicate terrorism by examining and addressing the issue in a comprehensive fashion, including understanding the root causes. Yet, since the 2003 Summit, no concrete statement or resolution has been reached or announced.

Malaysia and (perhaps) other countries in Southeast Asia are not very happy with travel advice issued by the United States and other western countries. Terrorism has affected not only Malaysia's, but also ASEAN's, economy. Tourism, for instance, has been severely affected by travel bans or warnings issued by some foreign governments. Such travel bans jeopardize and threaten other related economic and social activities. Panic and fear are on the rise and this only demonstrates that terrorism has achieved its objectives. The exaggeration of terrorist threats, Limaye (2004: 81) argues, might hurt the already fragile economies of countries in the region.

Despite some occasional antagonistic political rhetoric and exchanges between Malaysia and the United States, there has been strong security and military cooperation between them. This political rhetoric is nothing new to Malaysia-US relations. In the past, political tensions focused on trade and economic issues, such as the US General Services Administration decision to release its huge rubber and tin stockpiles, the two commodities that constituted Malaysia's main export, and the protectionist campaign in 1984 by the American Soybean Association. In spite of this, Malaysia continues to enjoy the United States' annual grant of International Military Education and Training (IMET) to train Malaysian army officers. IMET programs have been carried out yearly. In addition, Foreign Military Sales (FMS)[6] continues. For the financial year 1998, the fund allocated for the IMET program in Malaysia was the highest ever, amounting to nearly $US 1 million (Defense Security Agency, 2004: 7). The progress of this program was not affected by any bilateral political friction.

The strong foundation of Malaysia-US relations can be explained by the shared perceptions of threat. During the Cold War period, Malaysia-US relations operated under the premise of the Containment Policy. Malaysia aligned itself to the west for protection and political security from the communist threat. Although relations between both countries were founded upon common interests against the communist onslaught, there was variance in the perception of the threat. The United States viewed its involvement in the Indochina War in a wider context of Cold War rivalry with the Soviet Union; Malaysia's preoccupation was the threat emanating from internal communist insurgencies led by the Communist Party of Malaya.

Despite the United States' withdrawal from the Philippines following the end of the Cold War, its strategic interests remain. Contentious issues include overlapping territorial claims in the South China Sea and problems related to the Malacca Straits. The United States still lets its presence be felt by using some regional ports and airports for non-military purposes, such as refuelling and ship maintenance. The Malaysia-US security relations are seen in the wider context of the ASEAN framework. Both countries are working for the maintenance of

---

[6] FMS credit assistance is a system that manages government-to-government military equipment sales on credit to be paid with national funds of the purchasing country.

regional security, especially in soft-security areas such as anti-narcotics, small-weapons smuggling, transnational organised crime and human trafficking (Ku, 2004: 63).

The post-September 11 period has renewed American interest in Southeast Asia, and it is not surprising that the incident has brought about heightened military and non-military cooperation and coordination with Malaysia. In turn, as a moderate Muslim-dominated and multi-racial country, Malaysia needs superpower support to contain Islamic radicalism. Both countries have to work closely to eliminate regional religious extremism. This improved relationship went in tandem with a radical change of American policy in Southeast Asia (Castro, 2004: 194). The United States needed cooperation and assistance from countries in the region to thwart Al Qaeda's Southeast Asia networking. American-Malaysian bilateral political relations were at their height when the then Malaysian Prime Minister, Mahathir, paid an official visit to the White House in May 2002, and a declaration of cooperation to combat terrorism was signed. This agreement paved the way for more mutual cooperation in counter-terrorism, in defence, banking, intelligence sharing, border control, transportation and law.

One result was that the biggest joint military exercise was conducted that year, the Cooperation Afloat and Training (CARAT) exercise between Malaysia and the United States. Ships of the American 7th Fleet intensified their plying of the Malacca Straits to provide a security umbrella from pirate and terrorist attacks. The IMET program was given higher yearly allocations. The United States believes that the program contributes 'significantly to regional stability by strengthening our [the United States'] military-to-military ties, and familiarizing the Malaysian military with US doctrines, equipment, and management techniques. For the financial year of 2004 and 2005, USD 1.2 million has been allocated for the program' (US State Department, 2004). Furthermore, despite some initial reservations from the Malaysian government, the United States was quite instrumental in the establishment of the Southeast Asia Regional Center for Counter-Terrorism based in Kuala Lumpur.

Based on the aforementioned discussion, it seems that Malaysia's security relations with the United States continue to operate under the aegis of a structure centred on the military. Yet the sophisticated but confusing networking of Al Qaeda with its sister militant group, JI, needs more than military counter measures. Unlike the counter communist insurgency measures, a two-pronged approach—military as well as non-military—has been adopted by the two countries. The non-military cooperation has also been given greater prominence. The high profile visit of FBI director, Robert Mueller, to Malaysia in March 2002 indicated, according to senior Malaysian police officer AP Paramasivem Arunasalam, a heightened cooperation in sharing intelligence information and joint law enforcement (Ku, 2004: 67). The United States also funded an anti-narcotic program for Malaysia through the International Law Enforcement Agency in Bangkok and the Baker-Mint counter-narcotic training program. In return, Malaysia amended its Anti-Money Laundering Act 2001, extending the money laundering reporting mechanism of banks. This amendment provides for measures to detect and prevent financing of terrorism, as well as the freezing, seizure and forfeiture of terrorist properties in line with Malaysia's commitment to the enforcement and implementation of the United Nations resolution to block all terrorist assets.

Nonetheless, there are challenges to this 'new' security. The Malaysian government has to ensure that the strong cooperation it enjoys with the United States won't be capitalised on by the opposition. PAS might then be able to discredit the UMNO-led government as an

American puppet. The challenge is learning how to debunk accusations that the United States 'was casting the struggle against terrorism as a struggle against Islam' (Limaye, 2004: 80). Although strongly denied by the Bush administration, tough new American visa requirements are seen as being aimed at Muslim countries. In Malaysia, the debates continue, especially on the definition of terrorism. Even Mahathir proposed on several occasions that the whole world needed a clearer idea about what constitutes terrorism. He argues that:

> we must determine who a terrorist is. This is important because people who some people describe as terrorists are regarded as noble freedom fighters by some others. More confusing still, some are condemned as terrorists one day, only to be considered respectable people another day. If we want the whole world to join in the fight against terrorists then we must ensure that a terrorist is a terrorist to all and everyone at all times. (Mahathir, 2003)

His argument was echoed in local debates, especially in influential newspapers. One article by Ashraf Abdullah in the *New Straits Times* (2001: 12) argued that: 'International law pertaining to terrorism is vague, so much so the US, the victim of today, was once the perpetrator of terrorism, at least on Afghanistan and Sudan, and let off the hook'. The article went on: 'an acceptable international definition of the term "terrorism" has to be attained. There cannot be any room for alternative interpretation in order to effectively subdue the perpetuation of terrorist activities' (Abdullah, 2001: 12).

Furthermore, Australia's increasing interest in playing a major role in the regional security architecture might not be welcomed by some in Southeast Asia, especially Malaysia. Australia's self-appointed role as deputy sheriff of the Asia-Pacific has sent mixed and confusing political signals to regional governments. Howard's doctrine of pre-emption has been regarded as a clear signal of Australian intention to interfere with neighbouring countries' internal affairs, although Canberra has made it clear that it would not intervene without the explicit authorisation of the host country and under certain strict conditions (Gorjao, 2003). Australia has also signalled that the multilateral intervention is the preferred choice under the aegis of the United Nations mandate, as being applied in East Timor and Cambodia. Yet Canberra's refusal to sign the ASEAN Treaty of Amenity and Cooperation further strengthens critics' argument that Australia does in fact have the intention to intervene in its neighbours' domestic affairs.

Malaysia's scepticism concerning the Australian plan and intentions may be partly due to troubled political relations between the two countries since the 1980s. Years of political upheaval may be fuelled largely by personal animosity between the then Malaysian Prime Minister Mahathir and successive Australian leaders. The relationship was sour for most of the 22 years of Mahathir's leadership and was at its lowest ebb after the 1986 executions of two convicted Australian drug traffickers, Kevin Barlow and Brian Chambers—a sentence the then Australian Prime Minister Bob Hawke described as 'barbaric'. Hawke's successor, Paul Keating, infuriated Mahathir by depicting him as 'recalcitrant' for his failure to attend the inaugural summit of the APEC forum in Seattle in 1993. Prior to his retirement, Mahathir also slammed the Howard government for its treatment of Aborigines and asylum seekers, and its endorsement of the Bush administration's foreign policy. He also repeatedly rejected invitations from Howard to visit Australia (*Sydney Morning Herald Online*, 2004).

Nonetheless, like Malaysia's relations with the United States, the foundation of the relations between Malaysia and Australia has not been undermined by political rhetoric.

Security cooperation continues, both in the military through the Five Power Defense Arrangements (FPDA) mechanism, and non-military aspects, such as intelligence information exchanges and anti-narcotic enforcement. Australia does acknowledge, furthermore, Malaysia's cooperation in dealing with religious terrorism in the region (Ministry of Foreign Affairs and Trade, 2004). There were intelligence exchanges between the two countries, especially after the Bali in 2002 and Jakarta's Marriott Hotel bombings in 2003.

In the post-September 11 period, Malaysia's relations with major powers such as Australia and particularly the United States seem set to improve. Although there are divergent views on some international political and security issues, Malaysia has supported the US-led Global War against Terrorism. But this support demands a balancing act between commitments, as well as actions to fight the 'threat' and the domestic imperative of expressing co-religious solidarity. This would explain the ostensibly anti-American, anti-west and anti-Semitic rhetoric expressed from time to time. The reality is, however, Malaysia has to be pragmatic and adaptable to the changing US-led regional security order.

Conclusion

In conclusion, it can be seen that Malaysia has made realistic adjustments to the changing environment of regional security. Malaysia has offered cooperation to curb the rise of terrorist and radical Islamic movements by providing information exchange and political support for other nations. The country has long encountered terrorist threats and believed that, for whatever reasons, terrorism cannot be tolerated. Yet the country needs understanding and support from major powers in dealing with these newly emerging threats. Preventative laws, such as the ISA, though contravening aspects of human rights, is the best instrument to contain the spread of Muslim terrorism. Malaysia, moreover, does not believe in a unilateral approach, as shown by its critical stance against United States' policy on Iraq. As chairman of the OIC and NAM, multilateralism is seen to be the best approach to handle international issues. Efforts to curb these threats must be jointly organised by all the countries affected. Unilateral action won't solve problems, but only exacerbate them.

Furthermore, Malaysia also consistently argues that efforts must be made, both from the western and Islamic sides, to have a continuous inter-faith dialogue, to find common ground rather than differences. At the same time, Malaysian leaders have also pointed out that there must be an effort to differentiate between the Islam practiced by the majority of Muslims in the world, and the radical Islam propounded by radical Muslim groups. Greater cooperation has been emphasised as the best way to curb the rise of local as well as terrorist and radical Muslim movements with information exchange, modernised equipment, provision of training and expertise, as well as mutual use of relevant facilities.

References

Abdullah, Ashraf (2001) 'Defining Clearly What's Terrorism'. *The New Straits Times* (Malaysia), 19 September: 12.

Abdullah, Kamarulnizam (2004) 'Islamic Militancy in Malaysia'. In *The Making of Ethnic and Religious Conflicts in Southeast Asia: Cases and Resolutions*, Yogyakarta: Center for Security and Peace Studies, Universitas Gadjah Mada.

――― (2003a) 'Islamic Militant Movements and Communal Conflict in Malaysia'. In S. Yunanto *et al.* (eds), *Militant Islamic Movements in Indonesia and Southeast Asia*, Jakarta: RIDEP Institute and Friedrich Ebert Stiftung.

――― (2003b) *The Politics of Islam in Contemporary Malaysia*, Bangi: Penerbit UKM.

Abuza, Zachary (2004) 'Regional Efforts at Responding to Terrorism in Southeast Asia'. In Mohamed Jawhar Hassan (ed.), *Asia Pacific Security: Investing in Peace*, Kuala Lumpur: ISIS Malaysia.

――― (2003) *Militant Islam in Southeast Asia: Crucible of Terror*, Boulder: Lynne Rienner Publishers.

Berita Harian (2003) Malaysia, 26 June.

Castro, Renato C.D. (2004) 'Addressing International Terrorism in Southeast Asia: A Matter of Strategic or Functional Approach'. *Contemporary Southeast Asia*, 26 (2): 193-217.

Collins, Alan (2003) *Security and Southeast Asia: Domestic, Regional, and Global Issue*, Boulder, CO: Lynne Rienner.

Defense Security Agency (2004) http:// www.dsca.osd.mil/programs/Comptroller/2002_facts /fy02_facts_book.pdf

Gorjao, Paulo (2003) 'Australia's "Regional Sheriff" Policy'. *Asian Times Online*, 6 November (accessed 4 January 2005).

Ku, Chin Wah (2004) 'US-Malaysia Relations: Rhetoric and Reality'. Masters Project Paper. School of History, Politics, and Strategic Studies, Universiti Kebangsaan Malaysia, Bangi.

Limaye, Satu (2004) 'Minding the Gaps: The Bush Administration and U.S.-Southeast Asia Relations'. *Contemporary Southeast Asia*, 26(1): 73-93.

Ministry of Foreign Affairs and Trade, Australia (2004) *White Paper on Transnational Terrorism: The Threat to Australia*.

Mohamad, Mahathir (2003) 'The Need to Identify Terrorists and Remove the Causes of Terrorism'. In Hashim Makaruddiun (ed.), *Terrorism and the Real Issues: Selected Speeches of Mahathir Mohamad*, Subang Jaya: Pelanduk Publications for The Prime Minister Department of Malaysia, Putrajaya.

Noor, Elina (2003) 'Terrorism in Malaysia: Situation and Response'. In Rohan Gunaratna (ed.), *Terrorism in Asia-Pacific: Threat and Response*, Singapore: Eastern University Press.

Shaik Mohd Salleh, Shaikh Mohd Saifuddeen (2003) 'Malaysia's Role in Revitalizing OIC'. *New Straits Times*, 26 September.

Singh, Hari (2004) 'Malaysia's National Security: Rhetoric and Substance'. *Contemporary Southeast Asia*, 26(1): 1-25.

Sodhy, Pamela (2003) 'U.S.-Malaysia Relations during the Bush Administration: The Political, Economic, and Security Aspects'. *Contemporary Southeast Asia*, 25(3): 363-386.

Sydney Morning Herald Online (2004) 11 June.

Tan, Andrew (2003) 'The Rise of Islam in Malaysia and Indonesia: An Emerging Security Challenge'. *Panorama*, 1:81-102.

Ulfstein, Geir (2003) 'Terrorism and the Use of Force'. *Security Dialogue* 34(2): 153-167.

US State Department (2004) http://www.state.gov/document/orginization/3966.pdf
Utusan Malaysia (2003) 19 March.

In: Asia-Pacific and a New International Order
Editors: Purnendra Jain et al. pp. 195-205
ISBN 1-59454-986-9
© 2006 Nova Science Publishers, Inc.

Chapter 13

THE NEW INTERNATIONAL ORDER IN THE ASIA-PACIFIC REGION: THAILAND'S RESPONSES AND OPTIONS

Chookiat Panaspornprasit

INTRODUCTION

There is no denying that the post-Cold War security challenges which confront numerous policymakers and scholars have moved beyond the decades-old traditional security paradigm. Currently, in parallel with many traditional security issues which remain unresolved in many sub-regions of Asia-Pacific, the re-emergence of multi-dimensional, non-traditional security issues is likely to pose a graver challenge than initially speculated. For instance, the 1997 financial crisis and its subsequent political, social and economic implications underscored the necessity for policymakers to focus on non-military security threats as well. Added to this are cultural, sectarian, ethnic and religious conflicts, as well as a number of multi-faceted transnational crimes (for example, cyber crimes and drug, human and small arms trafficking).

With the dawn of the twenty-first century, the international community has come under largely unforeseen pressure to deal with one of the most pressing non-traditional security issues—terrorism, especially in the aftermath of 9 September 2001 (hereafter referred to as the 9/11 attacks). Determined to highlight the importance of this threat, the Bush administration maintains a stance that, ironically, politicises this issue at the international level. In seeking as many allies as possible to fight the 'War on Terror' on a global basis, the Bush government coopted most countries of the Asia-Pacific region into the US-led global strategy. As a result, prospects for any new, viable international order in Asia-Pacific have not been bright. At the same time, some developments in the region are reconfiguring the ways in which any new international order in Asia-Pacific should be formulated. The rises of both China and India, together with the existing role of Japan, make up crucial variables for regional policymakers. On the Thai domestic front, the issue of political violence in the south, apparently linked to terrorism, also poses a grave challenge to the Thai administration's leadership.

Against the background of the changing international environment portrayed above, the question is how Thailand, under Prime Minister Thaksin Shinawatra (the business tycoon-cum-political leader), is to adopt and implement any options for responding to the dynamic of the region. The basic contention here is that a 'marriage of expediency' will probably win out.

WAR ON TERROR: SYMBOLIC ENGAGEMENT

Launched with determination and a confidence in its military superiority, the Bush administration quickly toppled Afghanistan's Taliban regime in October 2001. This was in response to the Taliban allegedly providing a safe haven for Osama bin Laden, the mastermind behind the 9/11 attacks (Morgan, 2004). The Bush administration's objectives in Afghanistan included both getting rid of the oppressive rule of the fanatical regime in Kabul, and bringing bin Laden to justice. Although the Taliban regime was toppled and a large number of bin Laden-led Al Qaeda fighters were detained indefinitely at Guantanamo Bay, the Bush administration still cannot achieve its other major objective: Bin Laden is still at large in late 2005. Thus, the Bush administration's 'War on Terror' in Afghanistan, one can argue, has not been a great success. Worse still is the increasing prominence of Jemaah Islamiyah (JI), the Al Qaeda-linked terrorist offshoot. Southeast Asian countries have been profoundly traumatised by JI's activities. Indonesia has been the most directly affected target in the region. The Bali attack in October 2002, the attack on JW Marriott hotel in Jakarta in 2003, the attack on the Australian embassy compound in Jakarta in 2004 and the second Bali bombing in October 2005 confirm the Indonesian state's consistent vulnerability to terrorist groups. Though not directly affected by the JI-planned attacks themselves, other ASEAN members, especially Malaysia, the Philippines, Singapore and Thailand, cannot feel immune from the JI terrorist operations (Tan and Ramakrishna, 2002: 142).

It is noteworthy that the Thai government has always regarded acts of international terrorism as direct threats to its own national security. Before the 9/11 attacks, the Thai National Security Council (NSC) had, in August 2001, organised a three-day workshop in Phuket on combating international terrorism (*Bangkok Post*, 29 August 2001: 4). The principal purpose was to streamline and strengthen efforts by relevant agencies in fighting terrorism. On a more practical front, the workshop was also aimed at enhancing the security training drills at the Phuket International Airport and Phuket's deep-sea port. Despite such measures, the 9/11 attacks rocked Thailand's sense of security, and tested the very foundations of the Thai-US security relationship. The issue of Islamic terrorists being globally politicised by the US administration's actions could create dilemmas for the Thai government; the government's close cooperation with the US risked antagonising Thailand's own Muslim population. Despite the fact that Thailand as a whole condemned without reservation such terrorist attacks, it nonetheless found it hard to accept the US's grand strategy for dealing with the new challenge. Thailand was not alone in this sense of unease, as the pronouncement of 'either you are with us or against us' caused a high degree of discontent amongst many of the US's close allies, both in Europe and the Asia-Pacific region (Fuller, 2001: 5).

The Thai government was taken by surprise by the 9/11 attacks, but perhaps even more so by the Bush ultimatum. The Central Islamic Committee of Thailand immediately urged

Thai leaders to refrain from permitting military bases on Thai soil to be used for any US reprisals on Afghanistan (*Bangkok Post*, 3 October 2001: 4). Prime Minister Thaksin's initial neutral position at first seemed incompatible with Bush's expectations. As in the 1991 Gulf War, the US government sought from its Thai counterpart not only general political and diplomatic support, but also direct logistical, non-combat aid (out of the U-Tapao airbase in the eastern province of Chon Buri) (Panaspornprasit, 2004: 264). However, the complications implicit in the US's Afhganistan operation compelled the Thai government to approach the matter with considerable caution. Any explicit and unequivocal Thai military support for the US military operations in Afghanistan would, the Thai government felt, trigger widespread disenchantment among the Thai Muslims. This point appeared to be reinforced by a number of the anti-war protests and demonstrations organised by the Thai Muslim communities in Thailand. These protests were non-violent, and posed no major direct threat to the stability of the Thai government; in fact, no major outbreaks of violence took place even after it was revealed (some time later) that US military personnel were given access to the U-Tapao base for purely non-combat operations during the US military campaign in Afghanistan.

In order to assure Bush that Thailand was 'with him', the Thai government made gestures of political and diplomatic support for the War on Terror. For example, the Thai Finance Ministry (together with eighteen other countries worldwide), complied with the US Treasury Department's request to order financial institutions to freeze assets allegedly linked to any terrorist groups (*Bangkok Post*, 3 October 2001: 7). Furthermore, and aided by strong US pressure to do so, the Thai government revised its immigration checks and entry visa guidelines. The latter included seriously re-evaluating the so-called 'visa privileges' policy, first implemented in 1986 to boost Thailand's tourism industry.[1]

No sooner had the major US military engagement in Afghanistan come to an end than the Bush administration planned to shift its target to one of the so-called 'axis of evil' countries: Iraq (*Bangkok Post*, 31 January 2002: 8). From March 2002, the clouds of war over Iraq grew distinctly darker as the Bush administration produced its allegations of Iraq possessing, and indeed developing, weapons of mass destruction (WMDs). It is perhaps telling of the pressure that Thailand found itself under that it was not one of the close US allies who opposed the war against Iraq.

On the diplomatic front, the White House had claimed that it could mobilise a 'coalition of the willing', comprising two groups of thirty countries, thereby demonstrating strong and explicit support for the invasion of Iraq. In addition to these, fifteen other supporters were conscripted that wanted their inclusion to remain secret. Thailand, although part of the latter group, was widely rumoured to have contributed directly to the action in Iraq. The Thai government granted permission for covert US military use of its U-Tapao military base to assist against Iraq. Thaksin preferred to keep this cooperation very low profile—a decision that caused considerable discomfort to the Bush administration. During an 'unofficial' visit to Washington in June 2003, the Thai prime minister reportedly explained his position to Bush, although Thaksin himself denied this (Morrison, 2004: 179-80). The Thai leader is said to have reassured President Bush of the appropriateness of US forward-positioning rights for its anti-terrorism campaign in Southeast Asia. As a result, Bush officially designated Thailand a 'major Non-NATO Ally' (MNNA) in December 2003 (*Bangkok Post*, 1 January 2004: 1).

---

[1] This policy legally permits citizens from 57 countries to stay in Thailand for a month without a visa; and citizens of another 96 countries are allowed to apply for a 15-day visa upon the arrival in Thailand.

Although this was regarded as only a symbolic designation, it still drew the criticism of a former foreign minister, Surin Pitsuwan, who opposed such a close alliance for security reasons (*Bangkok Post*, 13 June 2003: 4). With the post-war US-led rehabilitation and reconstruction in Iraq in operation, 448 non-combatant Thai troops were deployed in Iraq for humanitarian purposes. To date, only two Thai deaths have resulted from this involvement, and these casualties have not been enough to force a withdrawal of non-combat personnel (*Bangkok Post*, 3 December 2003: 7). Suffice it to say, the Thai government's response to the US-led War on Terror is mainly symbolic.

The threat of terrorism, especially that posed by the Al Qaeda group, remains high on the US government's security agenda. Recently, the US Central Intelligence Agency (CIA) has warned that the Al Qaeda network is fully capable of building a radioactive dirty bomb for use against the US and/or other Western nations, as well as having crude procedures for producing chemical weapons (*Bangkok Post*, 25 November 2004: 11). Even before issuing this warning, however, the Bush administration had approved two major experimental projects for the creation of advanced weaponry that ostensibly targeted the Al Qaeda threat. First, a large amount of the US's defence budget was allocated to the development of a so-called 'bunker-busting' nuclear weapon (*Bangkok Post*, 3 December 2003: 1). Second, a clandestine project was initiated at the National Biodefence Analysis and Countermeasures Centre, experimenting with bio-defence weaponry (*Bangkok Post*, 23 May 2004: 5). Against this background, there is still no confirmation of any imminent attacks by either Iran or North Korea, the two other members of the 'Axis of Evil'.

THE ROLES OF CHINA, INDIA AND JAPAN: PARTNERS OR COMPETITORS?

There has been long-standing speculation as to whether China's rise has been borne out by its increased economic and political momentum. Along with its economic liberalisation and reform campaign, the combination of China's other economic advantages has placed it in a better position to pursue its own economic growth strategy. The abundance of cheap (but increasingly skilled) labour, access to advanced technology for small- to medium-sized enterprises and the controlled deflation rate of its currency are attracting increased trade and investment-relocation. There is no denying that China's share of total global trade has expanded at a dramatic rate (Snitwongse, 2003: 38). In the last decade, it has clearly become a major trading partner with ASEAN and with Thailand in particular. Its entry to the World Trade Organization (WTO) formed a catalyst for ASEAN countries to consider forming a China-ASEAN free trade area by 2010. Moreover, Thailand is also keen to conclude its own Free Trade Agreement (FTA) with Beijing on a bilateral basis. Expectations of securing benefits from this free trade area scheme are even greater in the more developed ASEAN countries (Singapore and Thailand) than the new members of ASEAN including the so-called 'CLMV' (Cambodia, Laos, Myanmar and Vietnam). Moreover, the Chinese proposal in June 2003 of a strategic partnership with ASEAN, and its accession to the ASEAN Treaty of Amity and Cooperation (TAC), demonstrated its increased political engagement with Southeast Asian countries, a move which alarms China's main rival in the region's strategic sphere—the US.

With the rise of India, it cannot be denied that Thailand also brings to the equation a 'Look West' policy. It is imparting more significance than before to the Indian Ocean region in general and dovetailing with India's adoption of a 'Look East' policy. Thailand aims not only to maintain close political, cultural and economic relationships with India, but also advocates a peaceful solution to the Kashmir conflict. The combination of the confrontation between the two nuclear-armed arch rivals in this dispute, together with the Indo-Pakistani stand-off over long-standing religious and sectarian conflicts, plus the rise of terrorism on the subcontinent as a whole, causes major concern to countries such as Thailand who are worried about the impact of these issues on the peace, stability and order of the region in general. Significantly, the refusal of both India and Pakistan to be signatories to the Nuclear Non-Proliferation Treaty (NPT), and the missile testing conducted by both sides, led to serious doubts as to the possibility of placing the proliferation of the WMDs in South Asia under tight control.

The traditional and non-traditional security issues on the subcontinent are directly linked to the shifting configuration of power, especially in the aftermath of the 9/11 attacks. The Indian Defence Minister George Fernandes, for example, announced that India plans to buy more military hardware from the US after both sides agreed to boost cooperation on counter-terrorism initiatives (*Bangkok Post*, 10 February 2002: 4). These closer military ties appear not to be at the expense of ties with the Pakistani and Russian governments. The Bush administration and Pakistan's Musharraf government signed a new defence pact to consolidate their mutual defence needs (*Bangkok Post*, 10 February 2002: 4). As for the Indo-Russian military ties, the Indian arms procurement programme still relies heavily on its Russian suppliers. In 2002, for example, India concluded a defence deal with Russia that involved the acquisition of a Russian aircraft carrier and TU-22M supersonic bombers (*Bangkok Post*, 9 February 2002: 5).

India's bid to be a dialogue partner with ASEAN yielded fruit when it became the organisation's sectoral dialogue partner in 1993, and, three years later, a full dialogue partner. Most recently, in Vientianne, the Indian Prime Minister Manmohan Singh signed a historic partnership agreement on the ASEAN-India Partnership for Peace, Progress and Shared Prosperity Pact (*Bangkok Post*, 1 December 2004: 7). In trade relations, Thailand is India's third largest ASEAN investor, lagging behind only Malaysia and Singapore. The 2002 total of bilateral trade was $US 1,184 million, an increase of 2.6 per cent over 2001 figures. Thaksin's official visits to India in November 2001 and February 2002, together with the return visit of the former Indian Prime Minister Vajpayee in October 2003, paved the way for both countries to conclude an FTA that was intended to double the total volume of bilateral trade to $US 2 billion per year (*Bangkok Post*, 12 October 2003: 3).

In the case of Japan, leaders in Tokyo and their counterparts in Southeast Asia deem the re-evaluation of how to maintain, re-assert and perhaps even increase Japan's role in the region as timely and necessary, especially in relation to Japan's contribution to the maximisation of 'international public goods' there. This refers to the means or instruments, both tangible and non-tangible, which are utilised to enhance international peace, security, stability and mutual understanding in the international community through non-violent approaches and mechanisms.

Japan's national interests are closely linked to both the existence of some traditional security issues, and the proliferation of various non-traditional security issues in the present international system. The tension on the Korean Peninsula, the ongoing confrontation between the two nuclear rivals on the subcontinent, and the Cross-Strait relations between China and Taiwan remain vital issues (both directly or indirectly) for Japan's national strategic outlook (Haller, 1995: 118). Since 2002, the renewed North Korean crisis, when the Pyongyang government admitted that it has an active nuclear enrichment programme, and the subsequent stand-off between the neo-conservative government in Washington and North Korea's reclusive regime, have led to a major political impasse, resulting in tension for the north Pacific region. A series of the Six-Party Talks, aimed at peacefully defusing the crisis on the peninsula, has still achieved no major breakthrough. Compared with the Chinese government's role, one can argue that the Japanese role in these talks is a relatively indistinct one. Posing the same level of threat to policymakers in Japan is the tension between the Beijing government and the pro-independence ruling party in Taipei. The Chinese government's deployment of large numbers of missiles along the east coast of China has resulted—with the latter's strong resistance—in the decision of Taipei's government to procure more sophisticated weaponry from the US. For Japan, these two crises—one to its very near west and the other to its near south—pose very direct security threats.

The ongoing traditional security threats aside, Japanese and Southeast Asian national leaders expect to come up with long-term and effective solutions to the non-traditional security issues as well. For example, the horizontal and vertical networks of illegal human and drug trafficking in the Asia-Pacific region have become so transnational in their character that they have come to affect members of its societies at a number of different levels. The recent news reports on cracking down on the illegal trafficking of women into Japan have served as a further reminder of these problems. Japan and its neighbours also share a rising awareness of the significance of terrorist activities in their region. Japan's own experience of terrorism began with the Aum Cult bio-terrorism in 1995, and this has helped to establish very strong policies for pre-empting bio-terrorism in that country (*Japan Times*, 2005).

An already uncertain world becomes even more so for Japan after the spate of violent terrorist attacks in various parts of the world, especially those in the Asia-Pacific region itself. The secure sea-lanes of communication, both regionally and internationally, have formed a major lifeline for Japan's economic and financial well-being. Any unforeseen disruption to these lanes is likely to have adverse consequences not only for Japan's domestic economy, but also for its close economic ties with Southeast Asian countries, including Thailand. Under the current Thaksin government, the bilateral FTA scheme with Japan is also high on the economic agenda, and so the security dimension looms somewhat larger still in that relationship.

As mentioned earlier, it may be reasonably expected that Japan play a leading role in providing public goods in various fields in the future, and does so at both regional and broader international levels. Functional contributions by the Japanese government in these areas could ensure mutual goodwill, mutual confidence and long-term prosperity in many regions around the world. Japan's foreign direct investment (FDI) and its Overseas Development Assistance (ODA) schemes would, of course, become more effective by being shaped into forms that are more complementary to other instruments, such as Japan's cultural exchange and humanitarian assistance programmes. While such clear-cut and enhanced measures are not being adopted, Japan's currently passive foreign policy is probably running the risk of seeing Japan's status decline in the eyes of Southeast Asian states. Hence, bilateral FTA negotiations between Japan and many Southeast Asian countries, including Thailand, serve the purpose of reasserting Japan's role in the region, even if this is in response to the ongoing FTA plans pursued by both the Chinese and Indian governments.

The domestic debate in Thailand centres on whether or not the conclusion of the FTAs with the three Asian powers would really benefit its business sector. There is some concern over the possibility that only a few narrow sectors in Thailand would reap benefits from the FTAs, while Thai society as a whole would have to live with the geopolitical uncertainties deriving from them.

MULTILATERALISM AND A NEW ORDER: MYTH OR REALITY?

Apart from joining a number of multilateral cooperation frameworks like ASEAN, Thailand has become a member state of other less well-known multilateral bodies: for example, the Indian Ocean Rim Association for Regional Cooperation (IOR-ARC) and the Asian Cooperation Dialogue (ACD). Most states of the Indian Ocean region are signatories to the IOR-ARC. First launched in 1995 with seven founding-member states (Australia, India, South Africa, Kenya, Singapore, Oman and Mauritius), the prime purpose of this relatively new alliance is to enhance and uphold economic cooperation among the littoral states of the Indian Ocean region. The approach is tripartite, involving the private sector, governments and academic communities. At the Council of Ministers' meeting in March 1999, the original members reached consensus on the expansion of the organisation, with up to 19 new members being allowed for.[2]

The Thai government applied for full membership of the IOR-ARC in June 1997. Under the umbrella of the organisation, three working groups were set up in order to coordinate, facilitate and maximise opportunities for trade cooperation among the member states.[3] Unfortunately, the outbreak of the July 1997 financial crisis in the Southeast Asian region overshadowed the attractiveness of this new forum.

It is important to note that progress in building up economic cooperation under this multilateral scheme remains limited for a number of reasons. First, the leading roles of Australia and India in launching any new project always receive a lukewarm reception from other countries of the region. Second, there is a lack of well-structured coordination among the three working groups, resulting in the overlapping of various projects. Third, in the short-term, ASEAN countries Indonesia, Malaysia, Singapore and Thailand are more likely to promote trade within the ASEAN Free Trade Area (AFTA) than under IOR-ARC.[4]

Added to the existing, complicated network of multilateral frameworks in the Asia-Pacific region is Prime Minister Thaksin's initiative of the Asian Cooperation Dialogue (ACD). The fundamental objective of the ACD is to link the sub-regions of the entire Asian region. Through the ACD, the Northeast Asian countries (China, Japan and South Korea) will be closely integrated with the nine ASEAN member states (minus Myanmar), three South

---

[2] The nineteen full members of IOR-ARC are: Australia, Bangladesh, India, Indonesia, Iran, Kenya, Madagasgar, Malaysia, Mauritius, Mozambique, Oman, Seychelles, Singapore, South Africa, Sri Lanka, Tanzania, Thailand, United Arab Emirates and Yemen. The four dialogue partners are China, Egypt, Japan and the United Kingdom. (See the official documents prepared by the Division of International Economics, Department of Economic Affairs, the Ministry of Foreign Affairs, Thailand, April 2002

[3] They are Working Groups on Trade and Investment (WGTI), Indian Ocean Rim Business Forum (IORBF) and Indian Ocean Rim Academic Group (IORAG).

Asian countries (India, Pakistan and Bangladesh), and two oil-rich Persian Gulf states (Bahrain and Qatar).[5] Ideally, the ACD will be instrumental in upgrading the standard of living of the population of Asia, developing and integrating solidarity among Asian communities, and forming the basis for strategic partnerships with other parts of the world. The evolving process of this initiative emphasises the inculcation of positive thinking in areas of cooperation, and that this should be based on channels of informal and non-institutional discussion. To this end, two ministerial meetings, intended for consultative discussion, have already been convened in Thailand (in June 2002 and June 2003).

Considered by many as the 'mega-idea' for the whole Asian region, it is often argued that the ultimate motive behind this Thaksin initiative is for Thailand to take on a leading role in the region, and to allow it to further its broader geostrategic ambitions. However, this initiative brings with it many loopholes and drawbacks. First, a major (and somewhat controversial) defect of the ACD lies in the general argument that it is first and foremost meant to enhance Thailand's own modest diplomatic history, but, even more, to confirm Thaksin's political slogan of 'think anew, act anew' (Panaspornprasit, 2004: 261). Second, the framework proposed is so multi-layered that most member countries are likely to see greater benefit in consolidating the existing sub-regional cooperation in their own regions.

Putting the two multilateral schemes in the Thai political context, it is evident that the Thaksin administration pays only lip service to the IOR-ARC, especially in comparison to its attention to the ACD. For example, the former Thai Foreign Minister Surakiart Sathirathai (under the first Thaksin administration) did not attend the two IOR-ARC Council of the Ministers meetings in Muscat in 2002 and Colombo in 2004. Conversely, the same foreign minister hosted two ACD ministerial meetings in Bangkok in 2002 and 2003.

The discussion above mainly involves the changing international components that could effect the new order in Asia-Pacific confronting the Thaksin administration. In addition, Thaksin's government is now being challenged by another pressing political issue on the domestic front.

VIOLENCE IN THE SOUTH: THE RE-EMERGENCE OF TERRORISM

The security situation in southern Thailand has been a thorny long-term national issue for successive Thai governments. It is a problem that is multi-dimensional in nature, bringing to the fore historical, political, territorial, cultural and religious concerns. The separatist movement's operations, based mainly on guerrilla warfare and terrorism, have been conducted under the leadership of the Pattani United Liberation Organization (PULO), formed in 1968 and aimed at separating the southern Muslim provinces from the rest of Thailand. Although the situation was brought under some control in the 1980s through the strategy of accommodation adopted by former Prime Minister Prem Tinsulanonda, the Muslim radicals still persist in fighting for separation because of their ethno-religious differences with the Buddhist majority. As a result, only small-scale, intermittent acts of violence were reported.

---

[4] In an interview with a senior officer of the Ministry of Foreign Affairs, Thailand, 29 July 2003.
[5] See the official documents prepared by the Policy and Planning Office, the Ministry of Foreign Affairs, Thailand, 20 May 2003.

On 4 January 2004, however, the central government in Bangkok was taken by surprise by the well-planned armed attacks on the army camp in Narathiwat, the deliberate looting of 400 firearms from an army depot, and the death of four military officers (*Bangkok Post*, 5 January 2004: 1). At the same time, about twenty high schools were set ablaze. These attacks were a major blow to the reputation of the government's state-of-the-art intelligence capabilities, to the extent that the actual identity of the perpetrators still cannot be substantiated (*Bangkok Post*, 7 January 2004: 1). The lack of coordination among Thai government security agencies can be confirmed by the different explanations classing the perpetrators as local bandits, home-grown terrorists or suspected links with the JI operatives in other countries (*Bangkok Post*, 8 January 2004: 1).

Thaksin himself first vehemently denied any foreign terrorists operating on Thai territory (*Bangkok Post*, 7 January 2004: 1). Be that as it may, it is widely believed the 4 January 2004 incident flew in the face of Thaksin's official claim at the October 2003 APEC summit in Bangkok that Thailand is immune from terrorist attacks. While most of the perpetrators are still at large, the government has adopted a heavy-handed, top-down strategy for clamping down on the violence in the three southernmost provinces of Pattani, Narathiwat and Yala. To the Thai Muslim communities in these areas, the imposition of martial law and the deployment of para-military troops in the provinces do not make for a satisfactory solution to the problems there (*Bangkok Post*, 8 March 2004: 1). As a result, there emerged among the Thai Muslim populace a sense of social injustice, discrimination, alienation, frustration and mistrust. Worse still, violent and malicious attacks on civilians and public property are so commonplace that the general public has lost faith in the government's strategy and policies in the south. The disappearance since March 2004 of the Muslim human rights lawyer, Somchai Neelahphaiji, who stood firm in his defence of some Muslim suspects apprehended earlier, and the lip service of the government in probing into the case, reinforces the general perspective that respect for human rights is not on the government's agenda. This can be confirmed by two more tragic events: the April 2004 Krue Se Mosque tragedy and the October 2004 Tak Bai incidents. These events resulted in the deaths of 32 and 84 Muslims, respectively. Both tragic incidents resulted from the government's use of the armed forces in cracking down on the lightly-armed Muslims protesting against the government's strategy of handling the violence in the region.

Not only has the ongoing violence in the south of Thailand complicated the country's security agenda and planning, but also, one can argue, the overall security outlook of other ASEAN countries (such as Malaysia, Indonesia and the Philippines) as well. Some high-ranking government officials firmly believe that the current cooperation among ASEAN countries in various anti-terrorism projects could be counter-productive, if each individual country fails to put its own house in order first. In addition, the Thai government, as the argument goes, must have a real sense of urgency about regaining its people's confidence, trust and, finally, cooperation in rooting out terrorism (*Bangkok Post*, 8 February 2004: 1). The last general election, held on 6 February 2005, was expected to be a major political barometer to gauge the current Thai government's political popularity (and attitudes to its controversial policies) in the south. As the official election results showed, the ruling TRT party could secure only one constituency seat in the south, while the opposition Democrat party won 52 seats (out of its total of 70 constituency seats) there (*Bangkok Post*, 9 February 2005: 1). In order to handle the situation in the south and to 'save face' for its failure to do so thus far, the government supported the establishment of the National Reconciliation

Commission (NRC), headed by former Prime Minister Anand Panyarachun. The hope is that this commission will restore peace and stability, and lead to reconciliation in southern Thailand (*Bangkok Post*, 1 March 2005: 1). Whether this commission is successful in its mission remains to be seen.

Conclusion

During the first Thaksin administration (2001-2004), new challenges have emerged in domestic, regional and broader international arenas to test the Thaksin government. Claiming the authority stemming from being the first democratic civilian government in Thai political history to complete a four-year term, the second Thaksin administration aims to consolidate its authority in a predictable fashion. With no credible opposition (either from formal opposition parties or the civil society groups) to Thaksin's political authority in domestic politics, it is very likely that the TRT will lead the new government with more confidence, and cast into oblivion any dissenting voices. Without a clear programme or effective opposition, the government will, both domestically and internationally, continue to be reactive and launch policies of expediency.

References

Bangkok Post (2001) 29 August: 4.
―――― (2001) 'Islamic Committee Urges Neutral Stance'. 3 October: 4.
―――― (2002) 31 January: 8.
―――― (2002) 1 February: 6-7.
―――― (2002) 2 February: 8.
―――― (2002) 'Delhi to Acquire Russian Aircraft Carrier'. 9 February: 5.
―――― (2002) 'India Looks to US for Hi-Tech Arms Systems'. 10 February: 4.
―――― (2002) 20 February: 6.
―――― (2002) 27 February: 8.
―――― (2002) 17 March: 6.
―――― (2002) 13 July: 6.
―――― (2003) 13 June: 4.
―――― (2003) 'Africa Next on Agenda, Says Thaksin'. 12 October: 3.
―――― (2003) 'Bush Signs Bill for Bunker Buster Nukes'. 3 December: 1.
―――― (2003) 'Safety the Deciding Criteria in Considering Withdrawal'. 3 December: 7.
―――― (2004) 'Bush Confers Ally Status', 1 January: 1.
―――― (2004) 'Soldiers Die, School Burns', 5 January: 1.
―――― (2004) 'Deadline: 7 Days to Catch Raiders', 7 January: 1.
―――― (2004) 'Kitti: Separatists, Not Bandits', 8 January: 1.
―――― (2004) 'Open Up the Bottleneck'. (Perspective), 8 February: 1.
―――― (2004) 'Government Advised to Lift Martial Law', 8 March: 1.
―――― (2004) 'Experts Warn Against Plans on Biodefence'. 23 May: 5.
―――― (2004) 'CIA Warns of Terror Threats'. 25 November: 11.

—— (2004) 'Indian, ASEAN Leaders Sign pact for Peace, Progress, Prosperity'. 1 December: 7.
—— (2005) 'Thaksin Gets Total Control'. 9 February: 1.
—— (2005) 'Anand Heads Up Peace Panel'. 1 March: 1.
Fuller, Graham E. (2001) 'Anti-Terrorism Coalition Fatally Flawed'. *Perspectives*, 30 September: 5.
Haller, Kenneth J. (ed.) (1995) *Japanese International Responsibility and Contribution to Peace and Prosperity in the Asia-Pacific Region*, Bangkok: Japanese Studies Center, Institute of East Asian Studies, Thammasat University.
International Herald Tribune (2002) 11 March.
Japan Times (2005) 'Warning to Japan and the World'. Editorial, 27 March, http://www.japantimes.co.jp/cgi-bin/getarticle.pl5?ed20050327a1.htm
Morgan, Matthew J. (2004) 'The Origins of the New Terrorism'. *Parameters*, Spring: 29-43.
Morrison, Charles E. (ed.) (2004) *Asia-Pacific Security Outlook 2004*, Tokyo: Japan Center for International Exchange.
Panaspornprasit, Chookiat (2004) 'Thailand: Politicized Thanksinization'. *Southeast Asian Affairs 2004*, Singapore: Institute of Southeast Asian Studies.
Snitwongse, Kusuma (2003) 'New World Order in East Asia?' *Asia-Pacific Review*, 10(2).
Tan, Andrew and Ramakrishna, Kumar (eds) (2002) *The New Terrorism: Anatomy, Trends and Counter-Strategies*, Singapore: Eastern Universities Press.
Washington Post (2002) 18 March: A10.

In: Asia-Pacific and a New International Order
Editors: Purnendra Jain et al. pp. 207-225
ISBN 1-59454-986-9
© 2006 Nova Science Publishers, Inc.

Chapter 14

INDIA'S QUEST FOR STRATEGIC SPACE IN THE 'NEW' INTERNATIONAL ORDER: LOCATIONS, (RE)ORIENTATIONS AND OPPORTUNITIES

Sanjay Chaturvedi

INTRODUCTION

My key argument in this paper is that India's foreign policy today is characterised by unprecedented pragmatism as well as cautious idealism. The pragmatism is rather visible in the growing realisation that, as the twenty-first century unfolds, mediated by the hegemony of trans-national liberalism, the conventional 'commonsense' understanding of the apparently fixed geographical location of India and its 'neighbourhood' (the manner in which 'regions' as well as regional groupings tend to acquire, over a period of time, a sense of territoriality and hence an image of immutability) are due for a thorough revision. As pointed out perceptively by C. Raja Mohan, 'it is not often that a country finds itself on the verge of multiple breakthroughs on foreign policy. India is at one of those rare moments' (2005: 3).

India appears far more confident than ever before to take on the challenge posed by the complex interplay between geopolitics and geoeconomics. The normative thrust of India's foreign policy relates to a critical reassessment of the country's role in global affairs, while working towards the goal of Asian (even Afro-Asian) solidarity through inter-cultural dialogue and co-operative economic diplomacy. Of late, a serious and systematic pursuit by India of its economic-energy security, at regional as well as sub-regional levels, is a good example of how normative and pragmatic considerations are being combined in innovative policy frameworks and alliance-making.

This chapter shows how 'Asia' has been framed historically and continues to be partitioned by the dominant discourse(s) on the so-called 'New' International Order. This is followed by a discussion of how Indian leadership conceptualised 'Asia' and India's geopolitical location on the continent during the Cold War. It is against such a backdrop that the analytical focus of this chapter shifts to India's quest for energy-economic security, with special reference to India's Look East policy and its engagements with 'Mid-West' and

'Central' Asia. The concluding remarks briefly reflect on various proposals and counter proposals regarding India's strategic alliances with major Asian and non-Asian powers. Finally, it is argued that what is emerging before India, and for that matter the rest of Asia, is a novel context and conceptualisation for foreign policy and diplomacy, namely 'Oceanic Asia'. Here lies both a challenge and the opportunity for those who would like to see Asia/Asians as mapmakers in their own right—with considerable autonomy in global geopolitics—rather than as passive takers of the maps of a new hegemony.

THE 'NEW' INTERNATIONAL ORDER: GEOPOLITICS VERSUS GEOECONOMICS?

Often assumed to be innocent, the geography of the world is not a product of nature, but an outcome of the histories of struggle between competing authorities over the power to organise, occupy and administer space (Mamadouoth, 1998: 246). As Neumann puts it: 'Geography, including geopolitics, is a matter of social construction' (1997: 148). Whereas the term geoeconomics, popularised by Edward Luttwak (1990), implies that 'old fashioned' geopolitics has been displaced by the new phenomenon of geoeconomics, with disposable capital becoming more important than firepower, civilian innovation more significant than military-technical advancement, and market penetration a greater mark of power than the possession of garrisons and bases.

After the end of the East-West Cold War, there have been several calls for a New International Order. However, it is forgotten at times that the earliest version of the new international order was proposed by the non-governmental South Commission, chaired by Julius Nyerere and consisting of leading Third World economists, government planners, religious leaders and others. As pointed out by Noam Chomsky: 'reviewing the miserable state of the traditional Western domains, the Commission called for a "new world order" that will respond to the "south's plea for justice, equity and justice, and democracy in the global society" though its analysis offers little basis for hope' (1994: 4). However, what emerged instead was a (re)appropriation of the phrase 'New World Order' by George Bush as a rhetorical cover for his war in the Gulf.

What is 'new' about the US-centric New World Order discourse? Where does Asia, or for that matter the Asia-Pacific region, figure in the proposed neo-liberal geopolitical version of the post-Cold War world order? While seeking an answer to these questions, it might be useful to bear in mind the following perceptive comment:

> there is a conventional picture of the new era we are entering and the promise it holds. It was formulated clearly by National Security Adviser Anthony Lake when he announced the Clinton Doctrine in September 1993: 'throughout the Cold War, we contained a global threat to market democracies: now we should seek to enlarge their reach'. The 'new world' opening before us presents immense opportunities to move forward, to 'consolidate the victory of democracy and open markets', he expanded a year later(cited in Chomsky, 1996: 94).

'ASIA' IN GLOBAL GEOPOLITICAL ORDERS: THE OLD AND THE NEW

To begin with, western imperialism defined Asia in ways to suit its own interests. Geopolitics as a discursive field helped structure a view of Asia that underlined the Continent's difference from, and inferiority to, the west, thereby legitimising a pursuit of mastering space and cultural domination (Chaturvedi, 2002). Once classical geopolitics was extended to the Cold War period, Asia was re-imagined as a 'Rimland' which had to be controlled and strategically deployed for the purposes of western containment of the Eurasian 'Heartland' power: the Soviet Union (Dodds, 2003).

The Asian space was subjected to yet another round of mapping during the 1970s, as a general economic boom spread over Asia's rimland nations. What now emerged was the notion of a larger geopolitical entity, namely, the Pacific Basin. Thus, corporate globalisation and the 'new' regionalisms can also be seen as discursive structures assimilating Asia, or certain chosen segments of it, into a new imperial order. The manner in which 'Asia Pacific' has been discursively carved out of Asia in recent times by the west demonstrates that the US strategy of preponderance now reflects the credo of economic interdependency. The underlying logic can also be used to justify US intervention virtually anywhere on the globe (Peters, 1999).

After the economic crisis of 1997, East Asia, after having been integrated into the global economy all these years, seems to have acquired a sudden and unprecedented 'uncertainty' in western geopolitical imaginations (Hitchcock, 1998). As early as 1997 some analysts (Hale, 1997: 44) predicted that the sheer pace of socio-economic transformation in this region might eventually rip apart the political framework inherited from the colonial and Cold War eras.

The post-Cold War geopolitics continues to construct Asia in ways that fit into the grand strategies of neo-conservative intellectuals of statecraft in the west. According to Weinbaum (1996-97: 1) a new strategic region called 'Three Asias'—encompassing large portions of South, West and Central Asia—is in the process of emerging. A number of issue areas of strategic importance to the United States are converging here. From the standpoint of American security and non-proliferation interests, for example, this region comprises two emergent nuclear weapon states (NWS) (India and Pakistan), one acknowledged NWS (Kazakhstan), and at least one incipient NWS (Iran). It is in this region that the American discourse concerning human rights and democratisation is filtered through western fears about the contagion of a radical, politicised brand of Islam. The western political economies remain somewhat organically linked to the energy resources as well as the markets of this region. And last, but not least, this region is held responsible for the world's second largest supply of heroin.

The emergence of landlocked Central Asia and its resource endowment in the mainstream US geopolitical thinking has an important bearing on the Indian Ocean region and India's location within it. Throughout the Cold War, Central Asia had been viewed by the western powers as a marginal concern, situated firmly within the Soviet sphere of influence, on a remote edge of the Pacific Command's main areas of responsibility, namely, China, Japan and the Korean Peninsula. The same region, stretching from the Ural Mountains to China's western border, has now become an object of the so-called 'New Great Game' due to vast reserves of oil and natural gas thought to lie under and around the Caspian Sea.

In October 1999, the US Department of Defense reassigned senior command authority over American forces in Central Asia from the Pacific Command to the Central Command. This was an important indication that a significant shift in American geopolitical thinking was underway (Klare, 2003). Since the responsibility for 'securing' the Persian Gulf region has now been reassigned to the Central Command, it implies that this area is now under the close scrutiny of those responsible for protecting the flow of energy supplies to the United States and its allies against the backdrop of intensified competition over access to critical materials (Klare, 2003). The United States also depends on the Indian Ocean for the movement of about 50 different strategic materials, including magnesium, cobalt, titanium, tin, nickel, tungsten, iron, lead, copper (Berlin, 2002: 28). The National Security Council observed in the White House's 1999 annual report on US security policy: 'the United States will continue to have a vital interest in ensuring access to foreign oil supplies'. Therefore, the report concluded, 'we must continue to be mindful of the need for regional stability and security in key producing areas to ensure our access to, and the free flow of, these resources' (quoted in Klare, 2001: 62).

No sub-region of the Indian Ocean looms as large in these geopolitical calculations as the 'Middle East', which in a recent study has also been termed the 'Eurasian Energy Heartland' (Singh, 2002: 288). The geostrategic significance of the Middle East has been further reinforced on the wider canvas of what Zbigniew Brzezinski (1997) terms 'The Eurasian Balkans' on the post-Cold War 'Grand Chess Board'. As succinctly pointed out by Francois Debrix(2003: 180): 'during the Cold War and afterwards, Eurasia plays a similar role for Brzezinski. Eurasia must be controlled by the United States because, when all is said and done, Eurasia is 'our' geographical buffer. Eurasia as a buffer allows the United States to remain unique and superior in its own sphere of influence (which, after the Cold War, seems to span the entire surface of [the] globe)' More recently, a new term, 'Greater Middle East', has entered the arena of competing geopolitical imaginings (see Harkavy, 2001: 37) of 'New' Heartlands.

The analysis so far has revealed a trend emanating from the post-Cold War global geopolitical order conceived by the one and only superpower and its allies. As perceptively pointed out by Gulshan Dietl (2004), energy security, unlike other aspects of non-traditional security, has always been very closely related to military security. More often than not, it is the hegemonic consumer-states, seeking to maintain an uninterrupted supply of energy at an affordable price, who threaten and use military force. With energy-military security nexus peaking, we are likely to witness the conflict between the multilateral quests of both state and non-state actors for energy security and the 'securitisation' of energy flows by the hegemonic power(s).

INDIA'S QUEST FOR AN ASIAN ENERGY SECURITY GRID: CHALLENGES AND OPPORTUNITIES

By the first half of the twenty-first century, India is likely to be among the top four consumers of energy, just behind the US, China and Japan, and ahead of countries like France and the UK (Dadwal, 2002; Singh, 2001). In Asia, India is ranked after China as the emerging oil and gas market (Muni and Pant, 2005; Mahalingam, 2004). Natural gas is best suited to provide India with the *clean* energy the country needs for ecologically sustainable development during the first half of the twenty-first century and beyond. At the current rate of production, India's proven reserves of natural gas are likely to last for about 25 years, and Pakistan's about 36 years (Siddiqi, 2003).

According to *The Hydro Carbon Vision 2025* document, brought out by the government of India in 1999, in absolute terms the demand for crude oil and petroleum products was expected to grow to 112 million tons in 2002, 190 million tons in 2012 and 364 million tons in 2025 (Shaw, 2005). As against this trajectory of growing demand, production has been stagnating at 33 million tons per year. Indian oil reserves might run out by 2012 even if only 30 per cent of the demand is met through domestic production (Shaw, 2005). The document underlines the urgent necessity to augment domestic production and prescribes a regime of deregulation, seeking active participation of the private sector, both Indian and foreign. It sounds a note of caution that the Indian economy will increasingly rely on oil and gas imports, and will be vulnerable to fluctuations in international energy patterns. The trend to make secure energy flows, especially in and around the Gulf, are of critical concern to India for the following reasons.

Whereas the global reach of India's sourcing to meet the growing demand for petroleum crude and products is fairly diverse (as many as 30 different countries are its suppliers), 5 countries (Nigeria, Saudi Arabia, UAE, Kuwait and Iran) account for more than 75 per cent of India's total imports (Muni and Pant, 2005: 21). Saudi Arabia, UAE, Kuwait, Qatar and Bahrain combined supply more than 50 per cent of India's needs. If the Persian Gulf is taken as the critical resource-supplying region (by also including Iran and Iraq), then this region would account for about 60 per cent of India's imports. It is to state the obvious, therefore, that India has no other option but to look in as many directions as possible and evolve a multi-pronged policy to address diverse risks on the crucial front of energy-economic security (Muni and Pant, 2005: 21).

The multi-dimensional challenge of energy security before India demands a multilateral economic diplomacy; this, in turn, questions the tilt of India's foreign policy establishment in favour of bilateralism. According to Mani Shankar Aiyar, India's Minister for Petroleum and Natural Gas: 'Unless everybody is as enlightened in his politics as he is demonstrating in his economics, we are not going to reach our goals as quickly as we need to' (Aiyar, 2005). The point made by Aiyar hints at the tension, bordering on contradiction, between geoeconomics and geopolitics in India's quest for a new strategic space. As the sections to follow demonstrate, this challenge is reflected in both India's 'Look East' and 'Look West' policies.

INDIA'S LOOK EAST POLICY: EXTENDING THE NEIGHBOURHOOD

As pointed out earlier, the Cold War-induced geographies of mutual suspicion and confrontation proved instrumental in undermining the prospects of international cooperation throughout Asia. Even though not directly implicated in the Cold War geostrategic containment of the 'Evil Empire', India's foreign policy establishment chose to ignore China and Myanmar, despite a very obvious geophysical proximity (Singh, 1998: 48-49; Nanda, 2003: 7). However, geographical proximity does not automatically translate itself into geopolitical propinquity. As Jawaharlal Nehru once noted astutely:

...India is curiously situated from the geographical view as well as many other points of view. It belongs to Southeast Asia; it also belongs to West Asia. It just depends on which way you look at it, because it happens to be the centre of all these... All international routes or routes around the world have almost inevitably to pass over India. Again when you look at it from other points of view like trade and commerce, or when you think in terms of defence, India becomes the pivotal centre of South, Southeast and Western Asia. (quoted in Nanda, 2003: 12)

What is fairly obvious in Nehru's worldview is the alleged 'Centrality' of India in Asia. We might also recall in passing that the idea of an eastern federation (Deshingkar, 1999; Tan Chung, 1998) formed the core of India's Asia policy under Nehru. Even before independence, in March 1947, India convened the Asian relations conference, 'where almost any country that was perceived as constituting India's extended neighbourhood was invited. This included Tibet and Central Asia, though their independent status was under serious dispute' (Muni and Pant, 2005: 6). India also played an important role in building the Asian Relations Organization and in convening the first and the last Afro-Asian Conference in Bandung, Indonesia. However, India's initiatives for building a cooperative Asian neighbourhood failed to materialise, largely due to intervention by the Cold War ideological geopolitics.

Nehru was quite firm in his belief that the independence of a country fundamentally consists of an independent foreign policy. Consequently, he could not hide his anger over India being 'contained' within a Cold War sub-regional grouping based on ideological and strategic parameters (namely, 'South Asia'), with the help of western allies and Pakistan. He is reported to have remarked in 1953: 'What do the Americans think they are doing? Do they think they can encircle India in Pakistan, in Nepal, in the rest of Asia somehow?' (quoted in Muni and Pant, 2005: 8). India's interaction with west-inspired, anti-communist 'Southeast Asia' during the Cold War was more noticeable in bilateral relations with individual countries than with the association as an organisation (Ghoshal, 2002).

The following excerpt, from a speech delivered by Jaswant Singh, the then External Affairs Minister of India, in Singapore, June 2000, nicely sums up the rationale behind India's Look East policy in general, and India-ASEAN relations in particular. He said:

India and ASEAN face a complex, post-Cold War environment... We search for definitions and certainties in a period that is itself struggling to find answers. The influencing factors will be the reform process in Russia; concomitant political and economic changes in China; Japan's rediscovery of a more assertive political role; the ongoing tussle between unilateralism and cooperative multilateralism in the US and the challenge and opportunity of a European economic and politico-military integration...Our participation in the ARF (ASEAN Regional Forum) reflects India's increasing engagement, both in politico-security and economic spheres contributing to the building of greater trust, confidence and stability in the region. (quoted in Mattoo, 2001: 105-106)

The attraction of engaging with the fast-growing economies of South East Asia, as well as the growing disillusionment with the slow pace of economic reforms within the country, can be described as the two key catalysts behind India's Look East policy. This also explains to some extent why, in the early and mid-1990s, when regional economic cooperation was in vogue, India, faced with the unpleasant prospects of being left out of all the regional groups emerging in Asia, decided to pursue membership of ASEAN with firm resolve (Naidu, 2004).

The reorientation of India's foreign policy was facilitated by the fact that, around the same time, ASEAN too, surfeit with capital and exportable goods and technology, was searching for new markets. Many ASEAN heads of state had pronounced their intention of making their countries members of the 'rich man's club' by 2020 (Ram, 2000: 27). Such a vision, in order to become a reality, needed a pragmatic foreign policy and pro-active engagements with China and India. ASEAN thus found it prudent to launch a 'Look West' policy of its own, primarily focusing on India (Sreekumar, 2004). The early 1990s were therefore a favorable time for India to vigorously launch and pursue a policy of intensifying, deepening and expanding overall relations with the countries of South East Asia (Ibid.).

Yet another factor that prompted India to look towards the East is the apparent failure of the South Asian Association for Regional Cooperation (SAARC), which came into existence in December 1985. The central objective was to initiate regional cooperation amidst mistrust and conflict, in the hope that the process itself would generate a dynamism of its own, facilitating confidence-building and conflict resolution. However, the hopes generated by the launch of SAARC have gradually been belied. South Asia is yet to develop genuine stakeholders in a peace constituency; the persistent tension between India and Pakistan has virtually crippled the organisation and its various attempts to initiate and sustain regional dialogues, and consultations have proved futile over the years (McPherson, 2002: 252). On the other hand, ASEAN beckons as a success story in terms of centripetal cooperative endeavours overcoming centrifugal forces of all kinds and at various levels (Sabur, 2003: 85-86).

India's reassessment of its neighbours and neighbourhood is also caused by the growing dissatisfaction of a nuclear power aspiring to permanent membership of the UN Security Council with a limited and limiting value of the 'South Asian' framework for situating security concerns. During his Singapore lecture, mentioned above, Jaswant Singh is reported to have observed:

> India's parameters of security concerns clearly extended beyond confines of the convenient albeit questionable geographical definition of South Asia. South Asia was always a dubious framework for situating the Indian security paradigm. Given its size, geographical location, trade links and the EEZ [Exclusive Economic Zone] India's security environment and therefore potential concerns range from the Persian Gulf to the Straits of Malacca in the West, South and East, Central Asia in the North West, China in the North East and South East Asia (quoted in Mattoo, 2001: 105).

During much of the Cold War period, ASEAN's perception of India was based on the international systemic environment and the prevailing balance of power. At the same time, India's neglect of the region was not seen in a positive light. After the Cold War, a shift in ASEAN's perceptions of India became discernible, as the latter was invited to become a member of the ARF. India's relations with the US and China are also an enduring concern and as such are likely to influence the ways in which the region perceives India and its South Asian neighbours. The geopolitical and strategic dynamics between India and Pakistan also have a bearing on the ways in which ASEAN perceives the overall strengths and weaknesses of India as an actor with regional and global aspirations.

When all is said and done, however, the ASEAN-India dialogue relations have grown rapidly from a Sectoral Dialogue Partnership in 1992 to a Full Dialogue Partnership in 1995, and subsequently to a Summit-level interaction, with the First ASEAN-India Summit being held in November 2002. The mere fact that all of this took place in a decade seemingly reflects the confidence both ASEAN and India have developed in the dialogue partnership, which is underlined by expanding and intensifying dialogue and cooperation in many other sectors (Suryanarayan, 2002).

One important domain of this dialogue relates to the political relationship, and its related security issues. India has been an active member of the ARF since July 1996. It views the ARF as valuable in promoting stable relationships between the major powers, and as a useful complement to the bilateral alliances and dialogues which are at the heart of the region's security architecture. ASEAN and India have committed themselves to jointly contribute to the promotion of peace, stability and development in the Asia-Pacific region and the world, and respond positively to the challenges of a dynamic regional and international environment.

There has been noticeable progress in trade and investment, science and technology, tourism and human resource development. The total trade between India and ASEAN increased substantially from about $US 2.5 billion in 1993-94 to the $US 6 billion mark in 1997-98. Whereas India-ASEAN trade in 2003-04 was about $US 13.25 billion (over 5 times the 1993-94 trade figure of $US 2.5 billion), India's exports to ASEAN were $US 5.8 billion while imports about $US 7.4 billion in this period (see Confederation of Indian Industry (CII): Internet Source accessed on 7 September 2005). Compared to other regional groupings, ASEAN is the fifth most important market in the world in terms of Indian exports and fourth in terms of imports.

India's economic relationship with ASEAN encompasses an active investment component. Increasingly, ASEAN businesses are undertaking FDI in India in crucial infrastructural sectors, such as roads and highways (Mattoo, 2001: 104-114). However, two-way trade and investment between ASEAN and India still remain low, although both sides are of the view that opportunities for collaboration are yet to be fully tapped.

India's Look East policy has now entered Phase-II. According to the former External Affairs Minister Yashwant Sinha:

> Phase-I was focused primarily on the ASEAN countries and on trade and investment linkages. Phase-II is characterized by an expanding definition of 'East' extending from Australia to China and East Asia with ASEAN as its core. Phase-II marks a shift in focus from exclusively economic issues to economic and security issues, including joint efforts to protect sea lanes, coordination on counter terrorism etc. On the economic side, Phase-II is also characterized by arrangements for FTAs and establishing of institutional economic linkages between the countries of the region and India. (quoted in Gupta, Chaturvedi and Joshi, 2004 211)

ASEAN has also welcomed India's willingness to develop a network of relations with ASEAN through other means of sub-regional cooperation frameworks, as this would complement the larger goal of enhancing ASEAN-India ties (Rao, 2003a). In this regard, ASEAN has encouraged India's active participation in the so-called Mekong-Ganga Cooperation (MGC). At the 33rd ASEAN Post-Ministerial Conference held in Bangkok in July 2000, the Indian delegation suggested that the entire region from India to the Mekong Basin be included in the initiative, a measure accepted by Foreign Ministers of five ASEAN countries (Thailand, Mayanmar, Laos, Cambodia and Vietnam) sharing the Mekong Basin. The key objectives of the MGC, formally launched on 10 November 2000, are to develop closer relations and better understanding among the six countries, thereby enhancing friendship, solidarity and cooperation. The two river systems have immense potential, and multi-purpose projects could benefit the respective states.

Also, ASEAN is watching with keen interest (especially in view of the centrality of China in India-ASEAN relations) the evolution of the Kunming Initiative. China organised a Track II conference for this sub-regional grouping in 1999 in Kunming itself (the capital of Yunnan Province in China's southwest[1]). Representatives of four adjoining countries (China, India, Bangladesh and Myanmar) participated. They arrived at a broad consensus on the need for regional cooperation among the four countries and their sub-regions, and the conference decided to establish a Forum for Regional Economic Cooperation. This regional move could be a challenging one in political terms, as, for the first time ever, it locks India and China into a single forum.

ASEAN has also responded quite warmly to the five-member sub-regional grouping of Bangladesh, India, Myanmar, Sri Lanka and Thailand–Economic Cooperation (BIMST-EC), which was formed in June 1997 for promoting cooperation in matters such as the exploitation of maritime resources, communications, shipbuilding, weather forecasting and combating sea piracy and terrorism, besides sustaining the trading contacts (Upreti, 2001). BIMST-EC (also known as Group-5) is 'poised to move from mere promises to actual delivery of economic benefits to the people of the region', as well as to pursue 'business opportunities' and develop 'linkages in the region' (Reddy, 2003). Each of the member states has assumed the responsibility of focusing on the identified areas of cooperation, such as transport and communications and tourism (India), energy (Myanmar), trade and investment (Bangladesh), technology (Sri Lanka) and fisheries (Thailand) (Murthy, 2000; 2002).

A recently proposed cooperative framework of a 'Bay of Bengal Community' (BOBCOM), with the inclusion of Malaysia, Singapore and Indonesia in BIMSTEC, deserves a special mention here: 'The underlying idea is not to replace SAARC or ASEAN but to have an additional organization, which will bring together India and its southern and eastern neighbors' (Surayanarayan, 2000: 60). Within such a framework, the littoral states of Southern Asia could cooperate with one another in areas such as exploitation of living and non-living maritime resources, development of maritime communications, shipbuilding, weather forecasting, prevention of pollution, combating maritime terrorism and energy security. Whether BOBCOM would be able to initiate and sustain cooperation in the above mentioned areas, and thereby eventually turn the 'extended' neighbourhood into an 'immediate' neighbourhood, remains to be seen.

A major step forward for India in its quest for energy security is the tri-nation agreement signed in Myanmar between India, Myanmar and Bangladesh on 12-13 January 2005 (*The Tribune*, Chandigarh, 15 January 2005). This gas pipeline project is based on mutual recognition of the necessity for enhanced regional cooperation in the energy and infrastructural development sector for the common benefit of the southern Asian nations. The understanding would enable commercial trans-shipment of gas from gas fields which have an estimated reserve of 5-6 Tcf located in the massive Arkan block off the coast of Myanmar. Myanmar earns approximately $US 400 million every year from neighbouring Thailand, through its annual gas sales from its Yadana and Yetagun fields in the south. Opening the

---

[1] Mineral-rich Yunnan has emerged as the industrial hub in China's South West. Yunnan also assumes a key role as China and ASEAN seriously consider the Kunming–Singapore railway line (Rao, 2003b).

market to the west (India) would significantly increase earnings from gas, which is already Myanmar's number one foreign exchange earner (Kumar, 2005).

By giving its consent to the laying of a gas transit pipeline, Bangladesh may well have taken the political and diplomatic initiative, whereby the resolution of the issues of commercial land transit to Nepal, sharing of water resources between Bangladesh, Nepal and India, and making up Bangladesh's deficit of power by importing surplus power from India and Nepal, can all be achieved. Various details are yet to be worked out through commercial agreements, while the route of the pipeline would be arrived at through mutual agreement, paying particular attention to ensuring adequate access, maximum security and optimal economic utilisation (Parthasarthy, 2001). In the opinion of some strategic affairs experts, 'for the first time India has begun to integrate its energy policy with foreign policy by consciously promoting oil diplomacy geared towards seizing energy-related opportunities overseas. What it is not doing is to blend its energy policy with defence policy' (Chellaney, 2005).

The US-led war on 'global terrorism' has posed a series of difficult questions for India. As a civilisational polity, complete with the world's second-largest Muslim population, India simply cannot afford to internalise the 'clash of civilisations' thesis first propounded by Samuel P. Huntington (1993). India cannot turn a blind eye to the fact that internal divisive forces, dictated and driven by parochial religious and communal considerations, are already adversely affecting India's relations with its neighbouring countries, especially the Muslim countries. As pointed out by J.N. Dixit:

> the geo-strategic fact is that from Egypt and Turkey in the north and to the Philippines in the south-east, and to the countries of the Gulf in between, India's neighborhood contains a large number of Muslim societies. To look at these societies through the prism of narrow communalism would be detrimental to India's national interests (2003: 516).

Nor can India afford to accept at face value the neo-conservative discourse of 'Rogue States', or, for that matter, let it come in the way of its economic diplomacy.

According to A.N. Ram (2003), a distinguished Indian diplomat who had played a key role in drafting India's 'Look East' policy, India's bilateral relations with the ASEAN countries have yet to evolve into a meaningful partnership in which both sides have a vital stake. After the Asian financial crisis, ASEAN trade with, and investments in, India have stagnated. ASEAN also appears somewhat disillusioned with 'India's daunting procedures, requirements and an unresponsive bureaucracy' (Ram, 2003).

The long-term success of India's Look East policy also calls for institutional reforms at various levels. For example, there appears to be a problem with the decision making structure in India's Ministry of External Affairs (MEA), with regard to a newly-'discovered' Southeast Asia. India-ASEAN relations are being approached and analysed at three different levels within the MEA. Whereas Dialogue Partnership issues are being dealt with by the Economic Division, ARF-related activities are handled under the Disarmament Division. Other bilateral aspects are said to be the responsibility of the South Division. Consequently, it becomes an enormously difficult task for these divisions to take unanimous decisions, and then implement them. In the absence of any formal mechanism being available (except the central cabinet in New Delhi), the coordination among various ministries and departments (External Affairs, Commerce and Industry, Defence, Human Resource Development) also leaves much to be desired (Naidu, 2003).

INDIA LOOKS WEST: THE NEW GREAT GAME?

The kind of enthusiastic attention that India's Look East policy continues to receive has at times overshadowed a series of Indian initiatives *vis-à-vis* Afghanistan and Central Asia. Described by some analysts as a *de facto* Look West policy (Muni and Raja Mohan, 2004), the challenge before these initiatives has acquired a new level of complexity due to the events of 11 September and the subsequent launch of the American war on terrorism. While hoping that 11 September has facilitated a better understanding of India's concerns against terrorism in the United States and international community, India, with its very large Muslim population, has been cautious with regard to the 'western' discourses on terrorism in general, and the 'clash of civilisations' thesis in particular.

It is precisely in the context of 'globalisation from above' that the long-standing image (and, indeed, the reality) of many segments of Central Asia as suppliers of natural resources and markets is currently being reinforced (Bayarkhuu, 2004). Central Asia is being re-imagined as a geo-economic space awaiting development. While the intellectuals of statecraft are trying to figure out the 'new' Central Asia in all kinds of geo-economic ('Scramble for Resources'), geostrategic ('New Great Game') and 'civilisational' ('Clash of Civilisations') equations, the five landlocked republics of Kazakhstan, Turkmenistan, Uzbekistan, Tajikistan and Kyrgyzstan are coping simultaneously with an array of formidable tasks, including state-building, seeking and consolidating political legitimacy, national integration and nation-building, and accommodating pressures for political participation and social-economic justice (Dawisha and Parrott, 1997). These states are also handicapped by the lack of experience in self-government and international cooperation, communication networks, trained indigenous administrative and technical elites, and also beset by ethno-linguistic tensions both within and across the geographical region (Sievers, 2003).

The emergence of landlocked Central Asia in the international strategic context, and the discovery of substantial quantities of strategic minerals (as mentioned earlier), has discursively transformed the centrality of Central Asia in terms of resource geopolitics. India, amongst the first countries to establish diplomatic ties with these republics,[2] would not only like to see these states retain their moderate religious outlook and moorings, but also acquire and sustain a meaningful political and economic presence in the region. India and the five Central Asian republics are now well-connected by air, and greater connectivity by land and sea is being actively sought through the trilateral agreement, and the North-South corridor (Dadwal, 2002). The geopolitical and economic objectives of India in Central Asia are graphically captured in the following lines of a speech given by Yashwant Sinha in Tashkent:

> Our co-operation with Central Asia includes cultural, economic, defence and security considerations. For us Central Asia is our *'immediate and strategic neighborhood'*...Indian companies are interested in setting up refineries and new pipelines...I am convinced that Central Asia, with its oil, gas, gold, silver and other mineral wealth and water resources, can become a new silk road of prosperity once again. But we need peace and stability for full economic progress. Unfortunately both India and Central Asia have become victims of terror for a long time...for us in the region, the concern is even greater because the epicenter of terror lies in our common neighborhood...If our neighborhood is peaceful and stable, if the

only interference from outside is one of economic inputs, then Central Asia can once again be a bridge between the East and West...We are civilizational partners, we want our ancient links to have contemporary colour (reproduced in Gupta, Chaturvedi and Joshi, 2004: 228-229).

The references above to defence and security considerations have also reinforced certain apparent speculations that India has been trying to develop its military bases in the region, including a military base in Tajikistan. Against the backdrop of what appears to be a scramble for setting up military bases in Central Asia, on the one hand, and, on the other hand, growing security and defence interaction between India and Central Asian countries, both India and Tajikistan have denied that it is a 'base for India' (Raja Mohan, 2003a). Be that as it may, many analysts would argue that 'the competition with Pakistan for influence in Afghanistan and Central Asia is a reality', but, at the same time, 'while making all possible efforts to skirt around Pakistan, New Delhi must also look at the prospects for neutralizing or co-opting Islamabad in its search for access and expanded presence in Afghanistan and Central Asia' (Muni and Raja Mohan, 2004: 327).

LOOKING AHEAD: TOWARDS NEW 'STRATEGIC' ALLIANCES?

At the beginning of the twenty-first century, foreign policy establishments all over the world are in the process of re-orienting themselves, seeking new roles and alliances to meet the challenge of a globalising international geopolitical economy. India, as this chapter has shown, is no exception to a trend that is likely to become more pronounced in the decades ahead. Such a trend has also opened up the prospects of India entering into certain 'strategic' alliances with major powers within, and outside, Asia.

India and the USA as Natural Allies?

One frequently heard viewpoint on the India-US 'strategic' partnership, especially in the wake of the visit to India in March 2005 by US Secretary of State Condoleezza Rice, is that what is opening before India is a 'window of opportunity' (Subrahmanyam, 2005), provided the policymakers to shun the proclivity of running from one extreme to another. While on one hand it has been argued that,

> an uncritical alliance with the United States could significantly affect India's credibility as an independent power; the search, on the other hand, for a countervailing alliance to the United States could send India on a fool's errand. With particular reference to Asia, following the US lead and direction in the east could shrink India's strategic space in relation to China and parts of the ASEAN, and in the northwest, it may constrain India's cooperation with Russia, Iran and a number of other Islamic countries and Persian Gulf countries (Muni and Raja Mohan, 2004: 318).

---

[2] After Tajikistan opened its mission in Delhi in October 2003, all Central Asian countries are currently represented in India.

What made the headlines in the Indian media coverage of the visit of the US Secretary of State was the news that Dr Rice had made it very clear to India that the Bush administration is rather uncomfortable at the prospect of a $US 4 billion gas pipeline bridging the economies of Iran and India. Moreover, she is reported to have proposed that the US would be happy to provide superior technologies and even nuclear power, one of the most expensive energy alternatives, to India (Barman, 2005). In case India opts to 'jump on the bandwagon' with the United States by abandoning the Iran-Pakistan-India pipeline project, it might not be possible for India to escape altogether the geopolitical trappings of the US-sponsored 'New International Order', as outlined earlier. However, the message conveyed so far to the United States is that India not only enjoys cordial relations with Iran, but also that the proposed pipeline via Pakistan is a part of India's brave new geopolitical imagination of an Asia-centric design of an energy security grid (a grander scheme of pan-Asian corridors and pipelines criss-crossing from Myanmar, Bangladesh in the east, and Turkmenistan and Central Asia in the northwest) that could eventually feed into China's vast industrial belts in the south and south-west.

One thought-provoking comment on India-US relations from the standpoint of a new non-alignment has come from Pratap Bhanu Mehta (2005), who argues that the time has come to go beyond the Cold War connotation of the term 'non-alignment'. According to him, 'it is precisely in the current moment that the core aspirations of "non-alignment" need to be reiterated to give India's foreign policy a new cogency. While there is every reason for India to pursue an intense economic and political dialogue with the US, India has to be wary that this dialogue does not, slowly and unwittingly, lock India into the embrace of the US' (Mehta, 2005). According to him, India should not give up on the normative dimension of what is apparently a pragmatic imperative (that it is in its interests to cultivate and nurture such relationships with Iran as it deems fit). After all, 'America's opposition to the pipeline from Iran is not cogent politics or economics: it is simply an assertion of hegemony' (Mehta, 2005).

Geopolitics of 'Asian' Alliances?

Ever since former Russian Prime Minister Yevgeny Primakov proposed a new Big Three Alliance (consisting of Russia, China and India) to counterbalance an increasingly hyperactive US (Bhattacharya, 2004), a great many Indians have reacted enthusiastically to the concept, including the former Indian Prime Minister, Atal Behari Vajpayee. According to V.P. Dutt (1999), it needs to be clarified at the very outset that the proposal for an India-China-Russia alliance carries no military, or even 'strategic' (in the correct sense of the word) overtones, although the word 'strategic' has been loosely applied in recent times. According to Dutt, what Primakov meant was far removed from the concept of a military alliance, in which none of the countries involved was interested. He was building a case for closer dialogue and interaction between the three countries on important issues in the international arena, so that one or two countries did not become hegemonic. Furthermore, he was also pleading for greater geopolitical space for all the three major powers of Asia. The idea proceeded from the assumption that US dominance in the world order would be total, unless there were some countervailing pressures that could be applied to moderate this dominance.

In Moscow's view, such pressure could only be generated through a more coordinated interaction between China, Russia and India (Dutt, 1999).

It has been argued by another perceptive analyst, that, while this surely is a possibility worth examining, a number of factors and forces are likely to work both for and against the idea of an Asian *Directoires* of these three great powers (Sahni, 2004). The first set of factors relates to economic growth rates, competitiveness and cooperation. Varun Sahni raises a series of issues, which, in his view, have a direct bearing on the prospects for such a coalition:

> Three questions, in particular, are germane in this context: Is China going to remain the only rising power, or would the Russian decline eventually be reversed, or would India start catching up? Would Russia and India be forced to 'balance against' a rising China? Would greater economic interaction and the inevitable competition that will follow, lead to instability, or would it lead to the discovery of a larger set of mutual interests? (Sahni, 2004: 258-59).

Some of the other geopolitical issues that might further complicate the formation of a Big Three Alliance include unresolved border conflicts. The differentials, in terms of demographic growth, might also cause unregulated population movements, both within and across sovereign borders. Finally, there is the crucial question of socio-economic cleavages and regional imbalances in these large states, which potentially undermines the cohesive and territorial integrity of these states. Whereas, according to Dutt:

> [when] all [is] said and done, the logic of the world situation should push them [China, India and Russia] towards greater cooperation. The Chinese themselves have been talking a great deal about a multi-polar world and warning against one superpower hegemony. If they mean what they say, and are serious about it, then they must also contribute to the evolving of greater multiplicity in the world. What could be more effective in promoting multi-polarity than more intensive Indian-Chinese-Russian consultations and cooperation in international relations? (Dutt, 1999).

According to Varun Sahni (2004: 260-261), neither opposing axes and balance of power,[3] nor the *Directoire* of Great Powers are likely to ensure a sustainable security architecture for Asia. These arrangements, according to him, are not going to serve India's best interests in Asia. Instead, he would prefer to see the construction of a regional security arrangement in Asia, as an alternate means of containing China, maintaining stability in Asia and minimising the role of the US on the Asian continent—some kind of 'Asian Helsinki process with "baskets" of issues, 'some pertaining to inter-state relations, others to matters *within* sovereign boundaries' (Sahni, 2004: 260-261).

It would be worthwhile, it could be argued, to add the issue of 'energy security' to this basket as a matter of priority. Economic/energy interdependencies among the Asian nations could provide one of the critical foundations for supporting and sustaining a cooperative security architecture which is truly Asian, although not necessarily inward-looking. It could be added that such a cooperation need not (in fact, *cannot*) be continent-centric. In such a

---

[3] Washington-New Delhi-Jakarta-Hanoi-Tokyo axis to contain China or, alternately, Tehran-New Delhi-Kuala Lumpur-Beijing axis aimed against the West.

scheme of things, the continental pipelines and the sea-lanes of communication would complement rather than negate each other.

CONCLUSION

A 'new' mapping of India and its neighbourhood is under way; this process might bring about not only a shift in India's image of itself *vis-à-vis* the rest of the world, but also represent a critical rethinking of the conventional categorisation and compartmentalisation of the global geopolitical space. There are also positive indications that India's foreign policy now is far more willing to engage seriously with maritime issues. The much overdue process of decolonising the geographical imaginations inherited from the Cold War can neither be arrested nor reversed. A series of internal/domestic, regional and global forces are at work behind a seriously felt political urge among India's political elite to reorient India in terms of hitherto ignored directions.

A systematic analysis of an issue-area which straddles national boundaries, such as energy security, reveals beyond doubt that boundaries between various segments of partitioned Asia (for example, between 'Asia-Pacific' and the rest of Asia, on the one hand, and between the Indian Ocean and the Pacific Ocean on the other) are, in fact, already blurred and porous. The Indian Ocean region, washing the shores of the Southeast Asian countries, is fast emerging as the fulcrum of the twenty-first century global geopolitics (Rumley and Chaturvedi, 2004; Berlin, 2004; Chaturvedi, 2003). As discussed at length by Sam Bateman (2004: 13), the Indian Ocean represents some peculiarly complex problems for maritime security management, including the matter of how to ensure freedom of navigation. Despite their common stake in the freedom of navigation, and for that matter ocean management generally, earlier attempts at building cooperation in the Indian Ocean region have not been resounding successes, and the level of existing cooperation is not as high as elsewhere in the world. India has considerable capability and experience to share with the countries of Oceanic Asia in peacekeeping, anti-piracy and search and rescue operations. Useful partnerships can also be forged to meet the challenge of the transport of illegal arms, drugs and fissile material through the Indian Ocean.

What is slowly, but surely, emerging as the new context of India's foreign policy is a pattern of dynamic strategic spaces that defy fixed boundaries, something that could be termed 'Oceanic Asia'. This notion is based on the assumption that there is a steadily growing mismatch between traditional categorisations/visualisations of Asia, and the transformations induced or facilitated by various facets of globalisation. It is by acknowledging such a fact that the countries of Asia will be in a position to bring the historical mobility of Asia out of the shadows, and exploit emerging opportunities for cooperative endeavours.

REFERENCES

Aiyar, Mani Shankar (2005) 'Excerpts from the Address by Mani Shankar Aiyar, Honorable Minister for Petroleum and Natural Gas on 16th of March at the Observer Research Foundation'. *ORF Energy News Monitor*, 1(38): 3-4.

Barman, A. (2005) 'Pipe Dream: Rice Attempts to Derail India's Oil Diplomacy'. *The Times of India*, New Delhi, 2 April.

Bateman, S. (2004) 'Freedom of Navigation and Indian Ocean Security: A Geopolitical Analysis'. In D. Rumley and S. Chaturvedi (eds), *Geopolitical Orientations, Regionalism and Security in the Indian Ocean*, New Delhi: South Asian Publishers.

Bayarkhuu, D. (2004) 'Geopolitics of the New Central Asia' *World Affairs: The Journal of International Issues*, 8(1): 58-83.

Berlin, D. (2002) 'Indian Ocean Redux: Arms, Bases and Re-Emergence of Strategic Rivalry'. *Journal of Indian Ocean Studies*, 10(1): 26-45.

Berlin, D.L. (2004) 'The "Great Base Race" in the Indian Ocean Littoral: Conflict Prevention or Stimulation'. *Contemporary South Asia*, 13(3): 239-255.

Bhattacharya, A. (2004) 'The Fallacy in the Russian-India-China Triangle'. *Strategic Analysis*, 28(2): 358-363.

Bracken, P. (1999) *Fire in the East: The Rise of Asian Military Power and the Second Nuclear Age*, New York: HarperCollins.

Brzezinski, Z. (1997) *The Grand Chessboard: American Primacy and Its Geostrategic Imperatives*, New York: Basic Books.

Chaturvedi, S. (2002) 'Can there be Asian Geopolitics?' In Ranabir Samaddar (ed.), *Interpreting Space, Territory and the State: New Readings in International Relations*, Hyderabad: Orient Longman.

———— (2003) 'Re-Visioning the Indian Ocean Rim: An Indian Perspective'. *What Next? Key Issues for Corporate Decision Makers*, Fremantle: Future Directions International, December: 4-5.

Chellaney, B. (2005) 'Great Game on Energy'. *The Economic Times*, New Delhi, 18 March.

Chomsky, N. (1994) *World Orders, Old and New*, London: Pluto Press.

———— (1996) *Powers and Prospects: Reflections on Human Nature and the Social Order*, New Delhi: Madhyam Books

Confederation of Indian Industry (CII) (1992) "Enhancing India-ASEAN Trade", http://www.ciionline.org/common/92/default.asp?Page=ASEAN%20Countries.htm

Dawisha, K. and B. Parrott (1997) *Conflict, Cleavage, and Change in Central Asia and the Caucasus*, Cambridge: Cambridge University Press.

Dadwal, S.R. (2002) *Rethinking Energy Security in India*, New Delhi: Knowledge World.

Debrix, F. (2003) 'Tabloid Realism and the Revival of American Security Culture'. *Geopolitics*, 8(3): 151-190.

Deshingkar, G. (1999) 'The Construction of Asia in India'. *Asian Studies Review*, 23(2): 173-188.

Devare, S.T. (2002) 'ASEAN-India: On the Threshold of a New Era in Partnership'. *The Hindu*, Delhi, 12 November.

Dietl, G. (2004) 'New Threats to Oil and Gas in West Asia: Issue in India's Security'. *Strategic Analysis*, 28(3): 373-389.

Dixit, J.N. (2003) *India's Foreign Policy: 1947-2003*, New Delhi: Picus Books.

Dodds, K. (2003) 'Cold War Geopolitics'. In J. Agnew, K. Mitchell and G. Toal (eds), *A Companion to Political Geography*, Oxford: Blackwell: 204-218.

Dutt, V.P. (1999) 'India, China, Russia Syndrome'. *The Tribune*, Chandigarh, 17 April.

Ghoshal, B. (2002) 'India's Relations with ASEAN: The Historical Setting'. *World Focus*, September: 3-6.

Gupta, A., M. Chaturvedi and A. Joshi (2004) *Security and Diplomacy: Essential Documents*, New Delhi: Manas Publications (published in collaboration with National Security Council Secretariat).

Hale, D. (1997) 'Is Asia's High Growth Era Over'. *The National Interest*, 47: 44-57.

Harkavy, R. (2001) 'Strategic Geography and the Greater Middle East'. *Naval War College Review*, 54(4): 37-53.

Huntington, S. (1993) 'The Clash of Civilizations'. *Foreign Affairs*, 72: 22-49.

Hitchcock, D.I. (1998) 'Internal Problems in East Asia'. *The Washington Quarterly*, 21(2): 121-134.

Katzenstein, P.J. and T. Shiraishi (eds) (1997) *Network Power: Japan and Asia*, Ithaca: Cornell University Press.

Klare, M. (2001) *Resource Wars: The New Landscape of Global Conflict*, New York: Metropolitan/Owl Book.

────── (2003) 'New Geopolitics'. *Monthly Review*, 55(33).

Kumar, A. (2005) 'India-Myanmar Gas Pipeline Through Bangladesh: Pipe Dream?' 7 September, http://www.saag.org//%5Cpapers13%5Cpaper1216.html

Lieven, A. (2002) 'The Secret Policemen's Ball: The United States, Russia and the International Order after 11 September'. *International Affairs*, 78(2): 245-59.

Ludden, D. (2003) 'Maps in the Mind and the Mobility of Asia'. *Journal of Asian Studies*, 62(4). AAS Presidential Address: www.aasianst.org/catalog/jas.htm

Luttwak, E.N. (1990) 'From Geopolitics to Geo-economics, Logic of Conflict, Grammar of Commerce'. *The National Interest*, 20: 17-24.

Mahalingam, S. (2004) 'Energy and Security in a Changing World'. *Strategic Analysis*, 28(2): 249-271.

Mamadouoth, V.D. (1998) 'Geopolitics in the Nineties: One Flag, Many Meanings'. *Geojournal*, 46: 237-256.

Mattoo, A. and F. Grare (eds) (2003) *Beyond the Rhetoric: The Economics of India's Look East Policy*, New Delhi: Manohar: 115-128.

Mattoo, A. (2001) 'ASEAN in India's Foreign Policy'. In A. Mattoo and F. Grare (eds) *India and ASEAN: The Politics of India's Look East Policy*, New Delhi: Manohar: 91-118.

McMpherson, K. (2002) 'SAARC and the Indian Ocean'. *South Asian Survey*, 9(2): 251-261.

Mehta, Pratap B. (2005) 'A New Non-Alignment? India Must Talk to the US Without Getting Locked into Its Embrace'. *The Indian Express*, Chandigarh, 23 March.

Muni, S.D. and G. Pant (2005) *India's Energy Security: Prospects for Cooperation with Extended Neighborhood*, New Delhi: Rupa and Company.

Muni, S.D. and C. Raja Mohan (2004) 'Emerging Asia: India's Options'. *International Studies*, 41(3): 313-334.

Murthy, P. (2000) 'BIMST-EC: Making Positive Moves'. *Strategic Analysis*, 24(4): 833-836.

────── (2002) 'India ASEAN Relations Towards a Dynamic Partnership'. *Indian Ocean Digest*, 17(2): 53-57.

Nanda, P. (2003) *Rediscovering Asia: Evolution of India's Look-East Policy*. New Delhi: Lancer.

Naidu, G.V.C. (2003) 'India and Southeast Asia: An Analysis of the Look East Policy'. Paper Presented at the conference on *India-ASEAN: Post Summit Perspectives,* held by the Centre for the Indian Ocean Studies, Osmania University, Hyderabad, 3-5 July.

—— (2004) 'Whither the Look East Policy: India and Southeast Asia'. *Strategic Analysis,* 28(2): 331-346.

Neumann, I.B. (1997) 'The Geopolitics of Delineating "Russia" and "Europe": The Creation of the "Other" in European and Russian Tradition'. In O. Tunander, P. Baev and V.I. Einagel (eds), *Geopolitics in Post-Wall Europe: Security, Territory and Identity,* London: Sage, 147-173.

Nehru, Jawaharlal (1941) *The Unity of India: Collected Writings, 1937-40,* London. Lindsay Drummond.

Palmer, N.D. (1991) *The New Regionalism in Asia and the Pacific,* Lexington: Heath.

Parthasarthy, G. (2001) 'Some Policy Options for India'. In J. Singh (ed.), *Oil and Gas in India's Security,* New Delhi: Knowledge World: 107-115.

Peters, S. (1999) 'The "West" Against the "Rest": Geopolitics After the End of the Cold War'. *Geopolitics*, 4(3): 29-46.

Raja Mohan, C. (2003a) 'India's Pamir Knot'. *The Hindu,* New Delhi, 10 November.

—— (2003b) *Crossing the Rubicon: The Shaping of India's New Foreign Policy,* New Delhi: Viking.

—— (2005) 'India's Diplomatic Spring'. *The Indian Express,* Chandigarh, 22 March.

Ram, A.N. (2000) 'Historical Perspectives'. *Seminar* (New Delhi), 487 March: 25-31.

Ram, A. N. (2003) 'India's Look East Policy—A Perspective'. Paper Presented at the conference on *India-ASEAN: Post Summit Perspectives,* organised by the Centre of the Indian Ocean Studies, Osmania University, Hyderabad from 3-5 July.

Rao, P.V. (2003a) 'India and Regional Co-operation: Multiple Strategies in an Elusive Region'. In P.V. Rao (ed.), *India and Indian Ocean: In the Twilight of Millennium,* New Delhi: South Asian Publishers: 122-151.

—— (2003b) 'Regional Cooperation in ASEAN: Sino-Indian Strategies'. Paper presented at the conference on *India-ASEAN: Post Summit Perspectives,* organised by the Centre of Indian Ocean Studies, Osmania University, Hyderabad, 3-5 July.

Ravenhill, J. (1995) 'Competing Logic of Regionalism in the Asia-Pacific'. *Journal of European Integration,* 28(2-3): 179-199.

Reddy, Y.Y. (2003) 'Mekong-Ganga Cooperation: A Milestone in India Southeast Asia Partnership'. Paper presented at the conference on *India-ASEAN: Post Summit Perspectives,* organised by the Center of Indian Ocean Studies, Osmania University, Hyderabad, 3-5 July.

Rumley, D. (1999) 'Geopolitical Change and the Asia-Pacific: The Future of New Regionalism'. *Geopolitics*, 4(1): 83-97.

Rumley, D. and S. Chaturvedi (eds) (2004) *Geopolitical Orientations, Regionalism and Security in the Indian Ocean,* New Delhi: South Asian Publishers.

Sabur, A.K.M.A. (2003) 'Management of Intra-Group Conflicts in SAARC: The Relevance of ASEAN Experiences'. *South Asian Survey,* 10(1): 85-99.

Sahni, V. (2004) 'From Security in Asia to Asian Security'. *International Studies*, 41(3): 245-262.

Shaw, D. (2005) *Securing India's Energy Needs: The Regional Dimension*, The Centre for Strategic and International Studies, www.csis.org/saprog/0505_shaw.pdf.\

Sievers, E.W. (2003) *The Post-Soviet Decline of Central Asia: Sustainable Development and Comprehensive Capital*, London and New York: Routledge Curzon.

Siddiqi, T.A. (2003) *Enhancing Clear Energy Supply for Development, A Natural Gas Pipeline for India and Pakistan*, Honolulu, Global Environment and Energy, BALUSA for Peace Inc.

Singh, C.P. (1998) Towards a New Equilibrium: India, the Asia-Pacific and Global Geopolitical Change'. In D. Rumley, T. Chiba, A. Takagi and Y. Fukushima (eds), *Global Geopolitical Change and the Asia-Pacific: A Regional Perspective*, Aldershot: Ashgate: 260-282.

Singh, J. (2001) *Oil and Gas in India's Security*, New Delhi: Knowledge World.

Singh, K.R. (2002) 'Geo-Strategy of Commercial Energy'. *International Studies*, 39(3): 259-288.

Sreekumar, S.S. (2004) 'India and ASEAN: Geopolitical Concerns'. *World Affairs: The Journal of International Issues*, 8(1): 100-106.

Subrahmanyam, K. (2005) 'The American Offer: India Should Make Use of the Opportunity'. *The Tribune* (Chandigarh), 31 March: 10.

Suryanarayan,V. (2000) 'Prospects for a Bay of Bengal Community'. *Seminar* (New Delhi), 487 March: 58-61.

────── (2002) 'Plea for a New Regional Organization'. *South Asian Survey*, 9(2): 263-273.

Tan Chung, A. (1998) 'Nehru's dreams of an Eastern Federation'. In S. Mansingh (ed.), *Nehru's Foreign Policy, Fifty Years On*, New Delhi: Publication Info.

Upreti, B.C. (2001) 'Sub-Regional Cooperation in the Indian Ocean: Emerging Trends and Prospects in the Specific Context of BIMST-EC'. In P.V. Rao (ed.), *Regional Co-operation in Indian Ocean: Trends and Perspectives*, New Delhi: South Asian Publishers: 232-245.

Weinbaum, M.G. (1996-97) 'The Three Asias: Security, Economic, and Cultural Linkages Across Central, West, and South Asia'. *Swords and Ploughshares*, 10: 1-2.

Chapter 15

PAKISTAN AND THE BUSH DOCTRINE: CONSENSUAL FOREIGN POLICY?[*]

Samina Yasmeen

The War on Terror initiated by the United States after the terrorist attacks of 11 September 2001 has secured Pakistan a centre-stage position in global politics. Previous portrayals as a pariah and failing state have given way to Pakistan being identified by much of the world as a major partner in the war directed against terrorists. Pakistan's actions are presented as examples of good international citizenship, albeit with guarded references to the problems it is facing by virtue of its strategic location. Any objective analysis of Pakistan's role, however, needs to move beyond such agenda-driven identifications to a careful consideration of the opinions and attitudes present in one of the largest Muslim states in the Asia-Pacific region. Questions need to be asked about whether a consensus exists in Pakistan on the close official identification with the United States in the latter's War on Terrorism and the post-invasion occupation of Iraq. It is equally necessary to explore the possible implications of an absence of such a consensus for regional stability. This chapter attempts to do so with reference to Pakistan's response to the Bush Doctrine that was formally enunciated in September 2002.

This chapter argues that the history of Pakistan's relations with the United States provides the backdrop against which its foreign policy in the new millennium can be assessed. Past shifts from being treated as a chosen ally by the United States to being assailed or ignored, have resulted in the emergence of several key groups that hold differing views on American reliability as a major ally. The plurality of views among both the decisionmaking circles and the civil society reflect the way the Pakistani government and civil society have responded to and interacted with the main aspects of the Bush Doctrine. While President Musharraf's regime has opted for a selective and issue-specific support for this Doctrine, its detractors have raised questions about its long- and short-term implications and costs for Pakistan. Such divisions, this chapter argues, reveal a disjuncture between the governmental policies and the preferences among some societal groups on foreign policy issues. This, in

---

[*] I wish to thank Professor William Tow and the anonymous referee for suggestions and feedback.

turn, creates an anomalous situation where, while being a US ally determined to counter terrorism, Pakistan will also remain an agent of Islamic militancy. Washington will need to deal with the situation creatively to ensure that the relative balance remains in favour of those supporting its War on Terror. This argument is developed in three parts. The first part outlines the main elements of the Bush Doctrine and the context in which differing opinions about it have surfaced within Pakistan. The second part assesses the arguments and positions taken by the Doctrine's Pakistani supporters and detractors. The last part analyses the implications of the absence of consensus in Pakistan on the Bush Doctrine's impact on regional stability, as well as considering the appropriate course of action for Washington.

THE BUSH DOCTRINE AND PAKISTAN: THE HISTORICAL CONTEXT

The origins of the Bush Doctrine are generally traced back to the neo-conservatives (neo-cons) who had served in the administration of George Bush Senior at the turn of the 1990s.[1] Opposed to the manner in which the Clinton administration dealt with the North Korean nuclear policies and the developments in Kosovo, these neo-cons advocated a policy that differed from that being practised by the US government. Their ideas were gradually articulated by the George Bush administration after it came to power in 2001. On 9 January 2002, the Bush administration released the *Nuclear Posture Review* (*NPR*) (Department of Defense, 2002) that presented a new US strategic military doctrine. While acknowledging the improvement of relations with Russia, the *NPR* raised the spectre of the spread of weapons of mass destruction (WMD) among rogue states (Department of Defense, 2002: 7). To counter these and other emerging threats, the Department of Defense argued for 'the creation of a new triad, consisting of offensive strike systems (both nuclear and conventional), defenses (both active and passive), and a revitalized defense infrastructure' (Speed and May, 2005: 38-39). President Bush echoed these ideas during a Graduation speech at Westpoint on 1 June 2002. He maintained that deterrence and containment could not be applied against 'shadowy terrorist networks with no nation or citizens to defend' or 'unbalanced dictators with weapons of mass destruction'. Instead, he argued that US 'security will require all Americans to be forward-looking and resolute, to be ready for pre-emptive action when necessary to defend our liberty and to defend our lives' (Bush, 2002: 1-2). Two months later, in September 2002, the US government released the *National Security Strategy of the United States* (*NSS*) (US Government, 2002). Together, these reports and speeches encapsulate the main features of what has come to be identified as the Bush Doctrine.

Drawing upon the experiences and views current since the early 1990s, the Doctrine consists of four inter-related yet sometimes contradictory elements that guide Washington's foreign policy in an era of American primacy (Jervis, 2003: 365-384). Echoing the twin theses of Fukuyama's 'end of history' and the belief that democracies do not go to war, the Bush Doctrine views the foreign policy orientation of a country as being linked to the nature of the regime in power (Jervis, 2003: 365). It claims that the 'great struggles of the twentieth

---

[1] It is important to point out that some analysts argue that the initial ideas for the Bush Doctrine were contained in the internal Defense Planning Guidance written by the then Under Secretary of Defense, Paul Wolfowitz in 1992. Wikipedia Encyclopedia, http://en.wikipedia.org/wiki/Bush_doctrine#Roots_of_the_Bush_Doctrine, accessed 13 September 2005.

century between liberty and totalitarianism ended with a decisive victory for the forces of freedom—and a single sustainable model for national success: freedom, democracy, and free enterprise' (*NSS*, 2002: 3). Such a view leads the Bush administration to claim that the future prosperity of nations in the twenty-first century is closely tied to their shared 'commitment to protecting basic human rights and guaranteeing political and economic freedom' (*NSS*, 2002: 3). Such views underpin the US argument that the Middle East needs to follow the path to democratisation.

These neo-liberal notions coexist with a realist acceptance of American pre-eminence in the contemporary international system (Speed and May, 2005: 38-49). While claiming that American pre-eminence is not viewed as a route to domination, the Bush Doctrine does not exclude the US right to an active foreign policy. On the contrary, it stresses the US right and responsibility to be aware of, and counter, emerging and potential threats with the aim of ensuring global peace. The War on Terror and the policy of preventing the spread of WMD are identified as two such threats (*NSS*, 2002: 11-19). But the process of identifying and countering these and other threats is considered to be dynamic and continuous. The Bush Doctrine acknowledges the role of multilateralism as an approach to dealing with these threats, but stresses its right to engage in preventive and unilateral actions to deal with perceived threats. Such a pro-active foreign policy is based upon an assumption of the irrelevance of deterrence as a viable policy option for the United States. The *Nuclear Posture Review* (2002) deems the multiple potential opponents, sources of conflict and unprecedented challenges to render deterrence 'inappropriate' for the new century. Instead, the United States is to acquire a combination of defensive and offensive capabilities to deal with an array of potential threats (*NPR*, 2002: 7). Effectively, the Bush Doctrine combines a neo-liberal agenda with a realist approach which justifies and argues for unilateral, preventive (and even pre-emptive) actions by the United States if the need to counter a perceived threat will not result in a concerted international response. The assertion of US primacy lies at the heart of the Bush Doctrine (Jervis, 2003: 376-383).

The juxtaposition of neo-liberal ideas with neo-realist approaches within this doctrine account for some of its inherent problems. The belief in the supreme value of democracy suggests the need for active US intervention on the side of foreign civil society groups arguing for universal human rights, including freedom from authoritarianism. At the same time, the identification of terrorism as a major contemporary threat requires that Washington support some non-democratic regimes to secure their cooperation in countering terrorism. Similarly, as the invasion of Iraq has exemplified, the need to counter a perceived threat of WMD can lead Washington into setting aside, even if temporarily, the right of peoples to choose their own system of governance.

Despite these inherent contradictions, the Bush Doctrine provides the broad context in which states and societies deal with the United States, and shape their own respective foreign policies. Pakistan is no exception, especially as it has been specifically identified in the *National Security Strategy*. The document acknowledges that the bilateral US-Pakistan relations have been bolstered by Pakistan's choice to join the war against terror. It also identifies India as having the potential to become a 'great democratic power of the twenty-first century' (*NSS*, 2002: 10). But the *NSS* 2002 also requires both Pakistan and India to resolve their disputes, including 'concrete steps that can help defuse military confrontation [between the two South Asian states]' (*NSS*, 2002: 10). As such, the *NSS* assigns both a global and a regional role to Pakistan; it is an important player in the War on Terrorism, but is also expected to follow the US suggestions for negotiating with its erstwhile adversary, India.

The questions arise as to how Pakistan has responded to these suggestions and what are the implications for regional stability of these responses. The answers are closely linked to two dimensions: the chequered history of Pakistan's relationship with the United States, and the differing sets of views in Pakistan on how to deal with Washington. Soon after gaining independence in August 1947, Pakistan was drawn into a close alliance with the United States. While Washington was motivated by a need to secure Pakistan's help in containing communism, Pakistan's sole concern was containing a perceived threat from India. It viewed its membership of the US-backed alliance system during the 1950s as a vehicle for securing patronage from a strong extra-regional superpower (Kux, 2001: 17-85). The limits to this patronage, however, became apparent during the late 1950s, when growing tensions between China and India, as well as the Sino-Soviet dispute, altered the American approach to India. Within Pakistan, the US assistance to India in the aftermath of the Sino-Indian border war (1962) heralded an era of reassessment and disillusionment with Washington. With a sense of betrayal, the Pakistani government moved to establish close links with Beijing in 1963. By the late 1960s, this Sino-Pakistan *entente* enabled the Nixon administration to open channels of communication with Beijing, which ultimately resulted in the improvement of relations between the US and China. Subsequently, both major countries sided with Pakistan in the 1971 Indo-Pakistan war (Yasmeen, 1986: 325-327). Following the dismemberment of the country and the emergence of Bangladesh in December 1971, however, the United States opted for a policy of disengagement from South Asia. While occasionally expressing its concern at, for example, Indian nuclear tests and Pakistan's efforts to acquire nuclear capability, Washington avoided getting mired in the Indo-Pakistani disputes (Kux, 2001: 215-245).

The Soviet invasion of Afghanistan in December 1979 altered the trend: guided by a need to roll the Soviets back, the US government again embarked upon a process of securing Pakistan's cooperation. During the Reagan administration, Pakistan became a major recipient of American assistance in return for opening up its territory as a route to weapon supplies for *mujahideen* operating against the Soviet presence in Afghanistan. The Zia regime also provided training of *mujahideen* from Afghanistan, Pakistan, the Middle East and elsewhere. The *madrasahs* became the centres of such training in *Jihad* with active collaboration between the Inter-Service Intelligence (ISI) of Pakistan and the American Central Intelligence Agency (CIA). These considerations prevented Washington from countering Pakistan's moves to acquire nuclear weapons to balance the nuclear capability India displayed through its 'Peaceful Nuclear Explosion' of 1974. Soon after the Soviet agreement to withdraw from Afghanistan in the late 1980s, however, Washington shifted its stance: America expressed its inability to certify that Pakistan did not have a nuclear capability, and the Bush Senior administration ceased providing assistance to Pakistan in October 1990.

Coinciding with the break-up of the Soviet Union, and the Gulf War (1990-91), the US disengagement contributed to the emergence of relatively distinct views within Pakistan on how to deal with Washington. Guided by a sense of betrayal, orthodox groups in the government favoured the notion of self-reliance and distance from the United States. In terms of Pakistan's relations with India, they discounted the probability of Washington's support for Islamabad. These sceptics, therefore, favoured acquiring a nuclear capability. Islamists in the

Pakistani government and civil society articulated similar views.[2] Having gained ground in Pakistan during the 1980s, the Islamist groups presented a vision of gaining strategic depth by establishing Pakistani influence in Afghanistan, as well as structuring Islamabad's foreign relations along religious lines. For these groups in this context, the *Jihad* in Kashmir occupied a special place.

The views held by orthodox and Islamic groups were contested by the moderates in Pakistan who discounted the notion of the reliability of states in world politics. Adopting a realist approach, they argued for policies that would secure Washington's support for Islamabad. Cooperation, rather than confrontation or isolation, was their favoured option. The US policy towards South Asia for a major part of the 1990s, however, continued to tilt the balance away from the moderates in favour of orthodox and Islamist groups in Pakistan. For instance, Washington reacted negatively to the Indian and Pakistani nuclear tests in May 1998. Within Pakistan, the US reaction was viewed as treating both India and Pakistan equally. But the Kargil Crisis (1999) drew the Clinton administration into a mediatory role in which Washington took a pro-Indian stance. Although the choice was guided by the circumstances in which the Pakistani military had unilaterally undermined the status quo, Washington's support was perceived by both the Islamists and orthodox groups as vindicating their suspicions concerning 'American designs'. During the subsequent months, the Clinton administration's South Asia policy further reinforced the views that the US strategic interests in the region had caused it to move away from being a mediator to one where it openly favoured India over Pakistan. In March 2000, for instance, President Clinton spent less than twenty-four hours in Pakistan after having spent five days in India. That Clinton spent a significant part of this time openly chastising the Pakistani government reinforced the views held by orthodox and Islamic groups concerning a 'US bias in favour of India' (Personal Communications, 2000).

The terrorist attacks on the United States in September 2001 changed the dynamics of US-Pakistan relations. Having ignored and criticised Pakistan's military regime led by President Musharraf, the United States secured his cooperation in its campaign against Al Qaeda in Afghanistan. Pakistan, in return, secured American support at a stage in its history when it was increasingly being identified as a failing or failed state. The sudden change, however, did not reduce the prevalence of Pakistani views critical of American policies. The debates on the need, advisability and long-term implications of a close relationship with Washington continued as Pakistan became a Major Non-NATO Ally (MNNA) of the United States. These debates provided the context for Pakistan's response to the Bush Doctrine.

PAKISTAN AND THE BUSH DOCTRINE: THE DEBATES

Although the Bush Doctrine was formally articulated in September 2002, its main pillars were evident soon after the terrorist attacks on the United States. The need to secure Pakistan's active and declared participation in the War on Terror resulted in a change in Washington's attitude towards the South Asian state. Not only were the sanctions imposed on

---

[2] The term 'Islamists' refers to the groups within Pakistani decisionmaking circles and civil society who view the domestic and international context through the prism of their Islamic identity. They differ among themselves on the degree of emphasis on Islam, but all insist upon its significance.

Pakistan after the nuclear tests of 1998 lifted, but it also became a major recipient of American aid. However, the terrorist attacks on the Indian Parliament in December 2001 pushed the two South Asian states into a year-long period of heightened tension.

The United States adopted a balanced approach towards the two countries. It acknowledged the threat posed to Indian security by Islamic militants based in Pakistan and, in January 2002, secured President Musharraf's agreement to ban these. At the same time, it counselled and put pressure on New Delhi to lower the level of tension and initiate a process of negotiations with Pakistan. Moderate factions in Pakistan welcomed the shift in Washington's South Asia policy. However, resentment against perceived American unreliability did not diminish. Instead, it provided the backdrop against which various groups interpreted the significance of the Bush Doctrine. This was reflected in the emergence of two distinct strands of opinion: those who criticised the Doctrine, and others who viewed it as opening greater space for Pakistan to operate in an era of American primacy. The differences were articulated in terms of the global significance of the doctrine, its regional implications and direct effects on Pakistan. These views have continued to influence the debate on Pakistan's America policy and, by extension, its role in regional and global developments.

Before discussing these views, it is important to note that they are articulated mostly by a relatively small group of retired government officials, academics and members of think tanks financed by the Pakistani government. The impact of these ideas, however, is more pronounced than the number of analysts involved would suggest. It stems from the fact that, while elites in Pakistan (and India) provide the academic language for understanding strategic issues, their ideas are widely circulated by the media. Often translated into local languages, these ideas are picked up by those who may not be familiar with the language of strategy. Such transmission carries the risk of mutation of the original ideas into simplified notions of politico-strategic developments. These ideas, in turn, form part of the folk mythologies about local and international politics. They also become significant in determining the responses of groups in civil society to developments within and outside Pakistan.

The critics of the Bush Doctrine highlight its negative implications for global, regional and national security. At the global level, they argue that the doctrine had been evolving since the end of the Gulf War in 1991, and was an expression of American tendencies (Bhatty, 2003). They argue that the preference for pre-emption enshrined in the doctrine opens doors to subjective assessments of global and regional situations. Such subjectivity is identified as being 'pregnant with alarming implication for the security of the smaller states and the stability of the world order' (Shahi, 2002: 3). They argue that the vague notions of 'failing states' and 'rogue states' could enable the US to make a pre-emptive strike against 'any government or state that [is] seen as hostile to the US' (Mazari, 2004: 20). The notion of pre-emption is also criticised in terms of its contravention of international law, particularly 'Article 51 of the Charter of the United Nations which recognises the right of individual and collective defence in the specific case of an armed attack by an aggressor state' (Shahi, 2002: 3). Significantly, these critics view the Doctrine through the prism of a struggle between Islam and the west. They argue that the doctrine is directed primarily against Muslim states (Kiyani, 2005). The War on Terrorism, they maintain, has been religion-specific; it ignores certain kinds of terrorism while focusing on Muslim countries. That four of the seven states identified in terms of WMD in the *Nuclear Posture Review* (2002) were Muslim is also presented as the anti-Muslim bias in the doctrine (Shahi, 2002: 3). Interestingly, they do not discuss the remaining three states in the list that are non-Muslim.

At the regional level, the Bush Doctrine is seen as providing India with a blueprint for action in South Asia, especially with reference to the Kashmir issue and nuclear deterrence between India and Pakistan. They argue that in an era of counter-terrorism, India has successfully refused to accept that Kashmiris are engaged in a struggle for independence. Instead, they argue, events since 11 September 2001 have been used by New Delhi to cast Kashmiris into the role of terrorists. In the long term, they argue, such a portrayal of developments in Kashmir can be misused by New Delhi to resort to pre-emptive strikes against Pakistan if and when it chooses to do so. This, in turn, is seen as undermining the chances of Pakistan helping Muslim Kashmiris realise their goal of freedom.

On the nuclear issue, the critics of the doctrine do not question the assumption that deterrence has lost its relevance in global politics. Instead, they focus on the impact of this idea for countries like Pakistan. But the discussion remains rather vague on this aspect of the doctrine. For instance, they point out that it would directly impact upon Pakistan, which has opted for 'minimum nuclear deterrence' and has 'exercised nuclear restraint' (Mazari, 2004: 21), but do not elaborate.

Most of the criticism of the Bush Doctrine, however, has been linked to its perceived implications for Pakistan as a Muslim state. The critics from within the government and civil society argue that the US presence in Afghanistan and the Middle East forms part of a grand strategy that aims to neutralise 'strong' Muslim states (Quraishi, 2003: 7-8). Pakistan, with its nuclear capability and large Muslim population, it is argued, is a natural target for the United States. The process of targeting Pakistan is seen as being 'gradual' in nature. According to this perspective, Washington has secured Pakistan's participation in the War on Terrorism. But the logic of confusing freedom struggle with terrorism, which lies at the heart of the Bush Doctrine, enables the US also to side with New Delhi against Pakistan. By building a strategic partnership with India, it is slowly reducing the options for Pakistan to find a 'fair' resolution of the Kashmir issue. This process is viewed as occurring in tandem with American moves against other major Muslim states: the US invasion of Iraq and its declared opposition to Iran acquiring a nuclear weapon capability are presented as the evidence of this anti-Muslim bias in the Bush Doctrine (Malik, 2004: 182-204).

It is important to note that these critics expect the Bush Doctrine also to eventually provide a basis for the US to put pressure upon Pakistan to relinquish its nuclear capability. They argue that Washington has already started pushing Pakistan into signing the Nuclear Non-Proliferation Treaty as a non-nuclear state in the NPT Review Conference of 2005. Without naming them, these analysts also argue that top US officials have been asking Islamabad 'not to conduct nuclear test, to end the production of fissile material for nuclear weapons, and to tighten the export controls' (Irshad, 2004: 36). There is also a suspicion that the Pakistani government might have already allowed the US to 'acquire partial control [of its nuclear weapons] and mark them down' (Irshad, 2004: 36).

The fear that the Doctrine would deny Pakistan its nuclear status has been reflected in the references to the allegation that surfaced in early 2004 that the architect of Pakistan's nuclear program, Dr A.Q. Khan, had shared nuclear technology with Iran, Libya and North Korea. The critics argue that Iran's relations with Pakistan were not close enough to justify such allegations. Libya is also portrayed as a friendly Muslim state that had supported Pakistan's nuclear status and, therefore, could not have implicated Dr Khan. The allegations, it is argued, are a part of the process of putting extra pressure on Pakistan to roll back its nuclear program (Malik, 2004: 130-150). Interestingly, the critical discourse surrounding the revelations of Dr

Khan's role in nuclear proliferation portrays him as a hero who has willingly shouldered the blame to avert a negative US reaction within the framework of the Bush Doctrine. The Pakistani government, in contrast, is presented as a weak accomplice unwilling to take a stand against US pressure on the nuclear issue (Malik, 2004: 232-241). This weakness, these critics argue, has also been apparent in Islamabad's policy of appeasing the US and acting like a pawn in the latter's moves in the regions bordering Pakistan. The campaign by the Pakistan military against Al Qaeda remnants in South Waziristan is presented as a case in point (*Dawn*, 21 March 2004). The policy of cooperating with the Bush administration, it is argued, would not avert the danger of US retribution in future: Islamabad would come under additional pressure from Washington to give up its nuclear capability and drastically alter its stand on the Kashmir issue. Failure to comply with this demand would attract US retribution along lines similar to that experienced by Iraq. Effectively, therefore, the critics expect the Bush Doctrine to pave the way for America targeting Pakistan as well.[3]

The critical voices also include some liberal analysts and political leaders who focus on the inherent contradictions between different elements of the Bush Doctrine. Sometimes this criticism is articulated clearly, as in the case of speeches by a renowned parliamentarian and former Interior Minister, Aitzaz Ahsen. In other cases, it finds expression in criticism of the policies pursued by the Musharraf regime, such as in the reports published by the International Crisis Group (ICG). The need to counter terrorism, these 'liberals' argue, has prompted Washington to align itself with a military dictator, General Pervez Musharraf. In the process, the US has strengthened his position *vis-à-vis* those demanding the reintroduction of democracy in Pakistan. Interestingly, such a view presents the Pakistani government as the manipulator that provides lip service to the introduction of democracy in the country. The US administration is urged to fully appreciate the ability of the Pakistani government to exploit the inherent contradictions of the Bush Doctrine (ICG, 2002).

The supporters of the Bush Doctrine in the academic and strategic community in Pakistan contest these negative analyses. Instead, they present a more positive assessment of the doctrine. While not denying the threats to international stability inherent in the notions of unilateralism and pre-emption, they focus on the American agenda of democratisation. They distinguish between assumptions of 'instant' and 'gradual' democratisation of Muslim states (Rais, 2002: 46-56). Instead of accepting the notion that the US-Pakistan alliance militates against democratic movement in the country, they suggest that Washington has embarked upon a process of gradual democratisation of Pakistan. The economic assistance extended as a result of participation in the War on Terrorism is part of creating the conditions that would make this transition possible. Hence, President Pervez Musharraf is seen as a benevolent dictator who is guided in his alliance with Washington by the need to introduce enlightened moderation in the country and introduce 'real' democracy in which liberal voices could also be heard. The US cooperation with the military regime, in other words, is seen as part of the historical evolution of democracy in Pakistan, and not as a reflection of an inherent contradiction in the ideals of democracy and the War on Terror.

A small minority of supporters of the Bush Doctrine also identify the indirect benefits to Pakistan: the doctrine's opposition to WMD is seen as introducing an element of realism in Pakistan's defence and foreign policy. Having invested in nuclear capability at the expense of improving economic conditions, they argue, Pakistan is forced to reassess its relationship

---

[3] This assessment is based on personal discussions with analysts in Pakistan in January 2004.

with India and the relevance of nuclear capability in 'countering' the Indian threat. The long-term implications of such a reassessment are that it is considered to be beneficial for Pakistan as well as the whole of South Asia (Personal Communications, January 2004).

PAKISTANI GOVERNMENT AND THE BUSH DOCTRINE

The differing views on the Bush Doctrine in Pakistan raise a number of questions: How significant are these views in determining the context in which the Musharraf regime participates in the War on Terror? How do these views affect Islamabad's responses to issues considered important by Washington? What is the long-term impact of this plurality of views on Pakistan's alliance with the United States?

Answers to these questions are linked to the manner in which ideas and information are treated in Pakistan by decisionmakers and civil society. This, in turn, is determined by the hierarchical system and income inequalities in the country that restrict access to appropriate educational opportunities by its poor. The elite, in such a system, appropriate the right to present ideas to the wider population due to their access to relatively better educational and economic opportunities. While a lot of discussion on strategic issues is conducted in English newspapers published in Pakistan, some of these ideas are translated into Urdu and other local languages for the general public. This opens up the possibility of multiple interpretations of the ideas circulated by ordinary citizens. It also creates the space in which those subscribing to Islamic ideas can mobilise support among the majority of the masses that have an emotional attachment to the notion of their Islamic identity. This does not exclude the possibility of some in civil society supporting moderate policies. But the presence of an 'Islamic lobby' limits the ability of the state to pursue its foreign and domestic policies: the state pursues its own agenda but also constantly responds to the concerns of the wider society and to detractors within decisionmaking circles.

The Musharraf regime has, therefore, adopted mixed attitudes towards the manifestations of the Bush Doctrine. Guided by the need to retain support from the Bush administration, Islamabad has presented itself as an active participant in the War on Terror. The Pakistani government makes frequent declarations of commitment to countering terrorism. During the UN General Assembly session in September 2005, for instance, Pakistan's Foreign Minister, Kasuri stated:

> Terrorism is a global menace and requires a collective response. Pakistan has been a major target of terrorism. We are in the forefront of the international war against terrorism. At home, my government has instituted a number of short and long-term measures to eliminate terrorism and extremism. These include banning extremist organizations and detention of extremists, crackdown against hate material, halting the misuse of religious institutions, registration and reform of madrasahs and fighting illiteracy and poverty. (UN Mission-Pakistan, 2005)

These declarations are supported by Islamabad's active cooperation with the Federal Bureau of Investigations (FBI) within Pakistan. Its troops patrol the Pakistan-Afghan border to prevent infiltration by Al Qaeda members (Rizvi, 2005). This has enabled Pakistani authorities to catch at least 700 Al Qaeda operatives within Pakistan during the last four years—which is used to highlight Pakistan's role in counter-terrorism. For instance, while speaking at an international conference on global terrorism in Pakistan on 30 August 2005, President Musharraf said:

> And may I say we fought this battle [against terrorism] in the cities of Pakistan where about 700 terrorists, al Qaeda members, have been caught, eliminated, deported. Wealth of information that we got from them, ha[s] been shared with many countries of the world which led to arrests of terrorists, extremists, in those countries. That is Pakistan's contribution to fight against terrorism. That is Pakistan's contribution to helping other countries, specially the Europeans and the United States, to address the issues of extremism and terrorism in their countries. (Musharraf, 2005b)

Supporting the US preference for a 'peaceful South Asia', the Pakistani government has also embarked upon a process of rapprochement with India. It has visibly shelved its previous policy of identifying the Kashmir issue as the core dispute that needs to be resolved prior to India and Pakistan improving relations. Instead, President Musharraf has been willing to negotiate a host of issues with India while floating flexible ideas on the resolution of the Kashmir issue (*Dawn*, 2004b). In April 2005, Pakistan also agreed to initiate a bus service between the Indian and Pakistani sides of Kashmir. Meanwhile, it has also actively engaged in discussing confidence building measures with India in the nuclear field, as well as promoting people-to-people diplomacy.

At another level, however, the need to balance opposing views within Pakistan has prompted the government to take decisions to assuage the concerns of domestic critics. This dual approach has been apparent in the pronouncements by the Musharraf government on the relevance of pre-emption and deterrence in South Asia, particularly with reference to Pakistan. In September 2002, for instance, speaking at a Peace and Security in South Asia Conference, President Musharraf categorically declared:

> This doctrine of pre-emption...can apply between unequal opponents or equal adversaries. In the case of unequal adversaries the world reaction could only be diplomatic condemnation. In the case of equal opponents, the application of pre-emption will lead to war. It will be extremely dangerous. It will be more dangerous in case the opponents, being equal, also have nuclear potential. *Let there be no doubt that this doctrine does not apply in [the] Indo-Pak context at all*, at least in the foreseeable future. (Musharraf, 2002: 7-8)

Such pronouncements have been combined with statements that deterrence remains relevant in South Asia. That Islamabad is unwilling to deny itself the ability to maintain a deterrent relationship with India has been expressed in the government's assertion of sovereignty over its nuclear program. President Musharraf has made numerous statements insisting that the Pakistani government would not compromise its nuclear capability. This assertion of sovereignty extends to the way in which the Pakistani government has dealt with the allegations against Dr A.Q. Khan. While being openly critical of his actions (Musharraf, 2005a), Islamabad has refused to let the scientist be interrogated by the US and/or the International Atomic Energy Agency. This is despite the fact that American analysts have expressed concern about the possibility of the presence of 'one or two derivatives of A.Q. Khan' in Pakistan (Hassan, 2005).

The Pakistani government's assertion of sovereignty also finds expression in its operations along the Pakistan-Afghan border. It has opposed incursions by US forces into Pakistani territory in hot pursuit of terrorists. At the same time, careful to retain its credentials as an active anti-terror state, it has launched an independent operation in South Waziristan against members of Al Qaeda. As earlier mentioned, these operations have been criticised by critics of Pakistan's US policy who accuse the government of playing an American game in the tribal regions. But the Musharraf regime counters the criticism by claiming that the Pakistani military is operating independently in the region. It is an indirect message to suggest that the government has drawn clear lines between sovereignty and cooperation with Washington. At the international seminar on global terrorism held in Islamabad in August 2005, for instance, President Musharraf stated:

> We entered this area (Federally Administered Tribal Area) with the whole army. In all the seven tribal agencies, and we dared to launch operations there. In one of the agencies South Waziristan agency we have captured, seized all the valleys in South Waziristan agency where they had established sanctuaries. These sanctuaries were their command bases, logistic bases, their propaganda bases, their communication bases. So we in effect, have broken the back of al-Qaeda in Pakistan. (2005b)

This dual approach of supporting the Bush Doctrine has also been apparent in Islamabad's response to the US invasion of Iraq. Even prior to the invasion, it was keen to emphasise the helplessness of weaker states in conflicts involving unequal adversaries. However, as the invasion became imminent, and mindful of negative public reaction, the Pakistani government stressed its preference for multilateralism over unilateralism (*Dawn*, 2003). As a member of the Security Council, it came under pressure from Washington to support the second resolution, suggesting that Iraq had failed to take the 'final opportunity afforded to it' through Resolution 1441 of 2002. Senior US officials also visited Pakistan to secure its support. Instead of caving in, Islamabad adopted a mixed approach: it stated that war was not a good option but did not categorically condemn the impending invasion. It suggested that weapons inspectors be given more time to establish the presence or absence of WMD in Iraq. At the same time, it insisted that all UN resolutions be respected, thus diluting the criticism (Alam, 2003).

The Pakistani government's response to the US request for troops in Iraq also demonstrated its dual approach. In June 2003, after a meeting with President Bush at Camp David, President Musharraf stated that 'in principle' Pakistan could send troops to Iraq if some 'conditions' could be met (*Daily Times*, 2004). This was followed by a formal request from the US Chairman Joint Chief of Staff, General Myers, in July 2003. Initially, some sections in the Pakistani government responded favourably as a means of securing US goodwill (*Dawn*, 2003b). However, concerns about a domestic backlash changed the preference. Prime Minister Jamali refused to commit troops without taking the Parliament into confidence. At the same time, however, Islamabad left the option open for such a commitment in future. During his trip to the US, for instance, Jamali said that Pakistan might send troops if the Organization of Islamic Conference (OIC) or the Gulf Cooperation Council (GCC) became active in Iraq. That Pakistan did not wish to totally alienate the US became apparent as it agreed to its ambassador in Washington, Jehangir Qazi, taking up the position of the UN envoy in Iraq (*Acorn*, 2004).

The mixture of accommodation and restraint in Pakistan's Iraq policy has persisted. It has maintained a diplomatic presence in Iraq. But following the kidnapping of a staff member (who was later released) and assassination attempts on Pakistan's ambassador, Islamabad has decided to relocate its ambassador to Jordan. At the same time, in line with American suggestions, it has not withdrawn diplomatic presence altogether. The Pakistan Embassy in Iraq continues to operate (*Dawn*, 2005b).

Effectively, the Pakistani government has been keen to show that, while declaring its opposition to unilateralism, it is prepared to accept American presence and policies around South Asia. It is also prepared to accept the limits of multilateralism, provided the US continues to support Pakistan within the context of the Bush Doctrine. This attitude differs from that adopted by the critics of the Doctrine who are concerned at the negative implications for Pakistan's security and the Muslim world in general. The contrast raises a question: how do these differences impact upon regional and global stability?

DIFFERING VIEWS: IMPLICATIONS FOR STABILITY

The presence of different assessments and views of regional and global scenarios, as well as the debates on relating to super powers, is not a new phenomenon in Pakistan. However, the different opinions on the Bush Doctrine in the current international environment point to possibilities that would affect regional and global trends. These are directly connected to the significant role Pakistan has assumed as a 'key strategic ally' of the United States in the War on Terrorism, as well as its willingness to reduce the level of tension *vis-à-vis* India. The presence of alternative views provides the context in which those disaffected with US policies and Islamic militants can devise and plan their strategies.

In the South Asian context, this dynamic can impede the current process of normalisation of relations between India and Pakistan. As President Musharraf has continued to explore and suggest ideas on normalizing relations with New Delhi, detractors of the Bush Doctrine have started equating the process with compromising Pakistan's sovereignty. Approaching the situation against the backdrop of the US-Indian relationship, these critics have argued that Pakistan is being urged to demonstrate flexibility on the Kashmir issue without any reciprocal compromises by India. The Doctrine is perceived as clearing the space for New Delhi to dominate the region and realise its own expansionist goals. Such a perception in sections of the strategic community in Pakistan contributes to a cynicism towards the process of rapprochement with India. More significantly, it enables Islamic militants to pursue their plans to 'liberate Kashmir' with or without help from the Pakistani government. With a history of support from sections within the Pakistani government, these militants retain the option of undermining the rapprochement by engaging in sporadic terrorist activities in the Indian part of Kashmir. Given the presence of anti-rapprochement elements in India, the activities of Islamic militants can impact upon the confidence-building measures being undertaken by Islamabad.

The presence of alternative views on the Bush Doctrine also has implications for Pakistan's role in countering terrorism. Having agreed to cooperate with Washington, and by extension with Afghanistan, Pakistan has become a major player in the War on Terrorism in South-West Asia. But the participation has had some unintended consequences. As the United

States initiated its attacks on Afghanistan in October 2001, a number of Taliban and Al Qaeda members infiltrated the porous border into Pakistan. According to Pakistani officials, at least 1,800 Al Qaeda and 3,000 Taliban had crossed the borders in 2001 (Amnesty International, 2002). The Pakistani government has cooperated with the FBI in tracking down these terrorists and has handed them over to the US authorities. While such cooperation has prompted Amnesty International to criticise Islamabad for ignoring its own laws in supporting Washington's War on Terrorism (Amnesty International, 2005), the actions have also attracted attention from Islamic elements within Pakistan. The Islamists have provided sanctuaries to Taliban and members of Al Qaeda in major towns and cities in Pakistan. Some of these infiltrators have also been living in the border towns and Federally Administered Tribal Areas (FATA).

The presence of infiltrators directly affects developments in Afghanistan. Supported by those critical of American presence in the region, these elements have been regrouping and posing a threat to Afghanistan's government. This, in turn, has been causing resentment in the Afghan Government, which argues that Pakistan has not been reining in the infiltrators. Washington has mediated the tension between Kabul and Islamabad, but, if it cannot be contained, the resultant enmity could undermine counter-terrorism operations in the region.

More significantly, the assumption among some critics of the Bush Doctrine that it is targeted against Muslims has led some militant groups to devise strategies to counter this perceived threat. By building cooperation across national boundaries, they have established links with some Muslim immigrants living in USA, UK, Australia and other liberal democracies. The London bombings of 7 July 2005 brought into the limelight the international implications of such transnational linkages. Despite the Pakistani government's willingness to clamp down, its ability to fully contain these elements remains limited. This, in turn, means that while the Pakistani government will continue to participate in the War on Terrorism and follow some of the ideas contained in the Bush Doctrine, alternative views within the country on the meaning and implications of the doctrine would also create contradictory trends undermining the emerging cooperation between Pakistan and the United States. Despite being identified as a key strategic ally, Pakistan would remain as much a cause of militancy as an agent for containing it.

This mixed picture raises questions about the durability of the US-Pakistan alliance. Despite these concerns, however, it is important that Washington continues to support Pakistan economically and politically. Such a support is necessary for two reasons. It will strengthen those who have actively participated in countering terrorism, as well as other elements of the Bush Doctrine. But the support is also necessary to ensure that the balance of power remains in favour of moderates in Pakistan. A questioning of the viability of Pakistan as a strategic ally would weaken forces of moderation and, at the same time, empower those who have argued for more inward and even adventurous approaches to Pakistan's domestic and foreign policy. The long-term costs of this empowerment will be high, not just for Pakistan, but also for regional and global stability.

REFERENCES

Acorn (2004) 'Pakistan's Qazi is UN's New Iraq Envoy'. 13 July, http://www.paifamily.com/opinion/archives/000967.html

Alam, Absar (2003) 'US Mounts Pressure for Pakistan Vote'. *The Nation*, 28 February.

Amnesty International (2002) 'Pakistan: Transfer to US Custody without Human Rights Guarantees'.

───── (2005) *Pakistan/USA: Further Information On: Incommunicado Detention/Fear of 'Disappearance'/Fear of Torture or Ill Treatment/Fear of Forcible Transfer*, Amnesty International, 23 September, http://web.amnesty.org/library/Index/ENGASA330182005?openandof=ENG-PAK

Bhatty, Maqbool (2003) 'The US and Islamic World'. *Dawn*, 15 December.

Bush, George W. (2002) 'President Delivers Graduation Speech at West Point'. United States Military Academy, West Point, New York, http://www.whitehouse.gov/news/releases/2002/06/20020601-3.html

Daily Times (2004) 'Is There a Connection between Qazi's Appointment and Sending Troops to Iraq?' Editorial, 13 July: 3.

Dawn (2003a) 16 February.

───── (2003b) 'Troops May Be Sent to Iraq under UN'. 26 June.

───── (2004a) 'Peace Activists Hold Rally against Wana Operation'. 21 March.

───── (2004b) 'Musharraf Calls for Debate on Kashmir Options: Status Quo No Solution'. 26 October.

───── (2005a) 'Pakistan's Envoy Attacked in Iraq'. 6 July.

───── (2005b) 'Embassy in Iraq to Remain Open'. 8 July.

Department of Defense (2002) *Nuclear Posture Review [Excerpts]*, http://www.globalsecurity.org/wmd/library/policy/dod/npr.htm

Hassan, Khalid (2005) 'CIA Frustrated by Lack of Access to Qadeer'. *Daily Times*, 6 February: 1-2.

International Crisis Group (ICG) (2002) 'Pakistan: Transition to Democracy?' *Asia Report*. Islamabad: International Crisis Group: 1-49.

Irshad, Muhammad (2004) 'US Won't Accept Pakistan, India as N-States'. *Defence Journal*, 8(1): 36-37.

Jervis, Robert (2003) 'Understanding the Bush Doctrine'. *Political Science Quarterly*, 118(3): 365-88.

Kasuri, Khurshid M (2005) *Statement by H.E. Mr. Khurshid M. Kasuri, Foreign Minister of Pakistan in the General Debate of the Sixtieth Session of the UN General Assembly (21 September 2005)*, http://www.un.int/pakistan/00home051905

Kiyani, Ghulam Ullah (2005) 'Bush Ka State of the Union Khitab [Bush's State of the Union Address]'. *Ausaf*, 6 February.

Kux, Dennis (2001) *The United States and Pakistan, 1947-2000: Disenchanted Allies*, Washington DC: Woodrow Wilson Centre Press.

Malik, Zahid (2004) *Muhsan-E-Pakistan Ki De-Briefing (Debriefing of Pakistan's Benefactor)*. Volume 3. Islamabad: Hurmat.

Mazari, Shireen M (2004) 'Rethinking the National Security of Pakistan'. *Changing Global and Geo-Strategic Environment: Implications for Pakistan*, Islamabad: National Defence College, 13-26.

Musharraf, General Pervez (2002) 'Inaugural Address'. Presented at the Peace and Security in South Asia Conference, Islamabad.

────── (2005a) *Pakistan, Challenges, Responses and Opportunities, Speech by President Musharraf to the Asia Society.* Asia Society, 16 June, http://www.asiasociety.org.au/speeches/speeches_current/s40_musharraf.htm

────── (2005b) *President's Address at an International Seminar on Global Terrorism* Government of Pakistan, http://www.presidentofpakistan.gov.pk/SearchSummaryResults.aspx?Keywords=terrorism

Quraishi, Qayyum (2003) 'Talwarain Neeaam Sey Bahir a Gae-Een [Swords are out]'. *Shahdat*, May: 7-9.

Rais, Rasul Baksh (2002) 'Pakistan and the United States: Shaping a New Partnership'. Paper presented at the Peace and Security in South Asia Conference, Islamabad.

Rizvi, Hasan Askari (2005) 'Counter-Terrorism and Domestic Politics'. *Daily Times*, 16 May.

Shahi, Agha (2002) 'Welcome Address'. Presented at the Peace and Security in South Asia Conference, Islamabad, 19-20 September.

Speed, Roger and Michael May (2005) 'Dangerous Doctrine'. *Bulletin of the Atomic Scientists*, 61(2): 38-49.

US Government (2002) *The National Security Strategy of the United States of America*, Washington, DC: White House: 1-33

Yasmeen, Samina (1986) 'Chinese Policy Towards Pakistan: 1969-1979'. PhD, University of Tasmania.

In: Asia-Pacific and a New International Order
Editors: Purnendra Jain et al. pp. 243-248
ISBN 1-59454-986-9
© 2006 Nova Science Publishers, Inc.

Chapter 16

THE MIDDLE EAST: AN OVERVIEW

Andrew Vincent

INTRODUCTION

The subject of a 'new international order' for the twenty-first century is of significance to us all, and although the theme of this book has been the Asia-Pacific region, the Middle East remains of central importance to the question of international order on a global level. Historically, it is in the Middle East that the best laid plans of great powers and other players have come unstuck, and this is a tendency that may well continue. On the other hand, the Middle East is also the testing ground for neo-conservative ideas concerning aggressive democratisation that are flowing out of Washington under the Bush administration. If successful in Iraq and the Middle East in general, these ideas could herald a process which will ultimately affect the whole of the developing world, including the Asia-Pacific region. In view of this important and indeed central role that has been assigned to the Middle East, the following discussion will present two conflicting scenarios for the Middle East over the next few years: an optimistic scenario, followed by a more pessimistic one.

There is plenty of evidence to support both of these broad-ranging scenarios and, interestingly, they are not necessarily mutually exclusive. Indeed, they may both be occurring simultaneously, and not even in different parts of the region. But before exploring the implications of the two scenarios, it is important to flesh out some of the deep-seated problems faced by today's Middle East. Few could deny that for many years now, the Middle East has been one of the world's real 'problem areas'. This fact is most simply reflected by the amount of column inches (or minutes) devoted to this tumultuous region in the mass media, a degree of media coverage out of all proportion to the geographical size or population density of the Middle East.

It is a truism to say that the Middle East is an area where change is long overdue, and where there is a great deal of popular discontent and, indeed, a yearning for change. President Bush has pointed to this, and Osama bin Laden and the Al Qaeda network are just one manifestation of the discontent, for it takes on a host of other forms as well. The Middle East is also an area where small disputes can quickly escalate into major conflagrations drawing in outside players.

THE MIDDLE EAST IN THE TWENTY-FIRST CENTURY

Economically, with a few notable exceptions, the Middle East is steadily slipping behind the rest of the world according to a number of different economic and social indicators. In the early 1950s, for example, the average Egyptian enjoyed a higher standard of living than the average Malaysian. Now, however, the Middle East region is closer to sub-Saharan Africa in its economic performance than it is to the Asia-Pacific region, for example, and the average Egyptian is very poor indeed, and getting poorer.

This lack of economic performance has been paralleled by a failure to develop human resources in the areas of education and training, and particularly in the involvement of women. This is one of the major World Bank indicators of Development, or, in the case of the Middle East, the lack of it.

Politically, the region continues to be dominated by dinosaur-like authoritarian and undemocratic regimes and governments. These are by and large weak regimes, which protect their power jealously, and are often more frightened of their own people than they are of any external threat. Indeed, change is long overdue right across the region. Some changes appear to be occurring, as death from old age claims more and more of the region's rulers; however, they are increasingly followed by their sons, who change little. This is happening not just in the monarchies, such as Jordan and Morocco, but in the republics as well, such as Syria and, quite possibly, in Egypt and Libya in the not too distant future. Even Saddam Hussein was grooming his two late sons to succeed him.

The lack of change and the weakness of governments have led to a proliferation of censorship and information control, secret police forces and the accompanying human rights abuses that seem to march hand in hand with the whole concept of a national security state. The idea of a loyal opposition is alien to most countries in the Middle East, and damning reports abound from watchdog organisations like Amnesty International and Human Rights Watch about human rights abuses and the suppression of freedoms.

In 2002, the United Nations Development Program released its annual Human Development Report, which for the first time included a report on the Arab States, covering a total of 22 countries. With a population of over 280 million and stretching from Morocco to the Gulf, the Arab states contain 5 per cent of the world's population. The report catalogued widening inequality, unemployment, illiteracy and health problems, and drew particular attention to the problems in Iraq, which had not yet been 'liberated'.

With change long overdue right across the region, voices calling for reform can be heard from democrats and liberals, as well as from more orthodox Muslims and conservatives. People like Osama bin Laden, who blame the West for propping up these undemocratic governments in order to exploit the region's oil wealth and protect Israel, are not alone in their calls for change. However, their rather simplistic black-and-white solutions receive a ready audience across the Middle East, as levels of popular dissatisfaction are high.

THE OPTIMISTIC SCENARIO

In the aftermath of the September 11 terrorist attacks on New York and Washington, President Bush has followed a vigorous pre-emptive foreign policy aimed at removing potential threats to the US through 'regime change'. At the same time, this new policy, the 'Bush Doctrine', has been aimed at democratising and liberalising the Middle East, where many (but not all) of those threats seem to lie.

Even before the war against terrorism began, the Middle East was slowly coming to terms with globalisation and global information flows through the Internet, and through controversial satellite television stations such as Al Jazeera. Economically, countries like Jordan, Tunisia and Turkey were also trying to respond to the demands of globalisation and were often regarded as the direction for the future; however, their steps were taking were slow and faltering.

But since 11 September 2001, US policies have led to the overthrow of two of the most recalcitrant regimes in the region, in Afghanistan and Iraq, while a more subtle form of regime change has also been affected among the Palestinians and the Libyans. Earlier this year, in what was praised as a well-run and fair election, the Palestinians elected Mahmoud Abbas, a new, more moderate leader to replace the late Yasser Arafat. There have also been successful elections held in Afghanistan, and most importantly in Iraq, where, despite a boycott by sections of the Sunni community, a new more representative government has been installed.

Recent events in Lebanon, the so-called 'Cedar Revolution', have seen the withdrawal of Syrian forces after almost 30 years of occupation. As a result Lebanon is now poised to hold its first free elections since the beginning of the civil war in the 1970s. The holding of free elections is, of course, a major prerequisite of democracy and should be followed by increased foreign investment and development, opening the country to the positive forces of globalisation.

Even governments that have been sponsors of terrorism for decades, such as that of Libya's Colonel Ghaddafi, have seen the light and sent out peace feelers to the world community. At the same time, pressure is mounting on friends of the US, like Egypt and Saudi Arabia, to reform as well, despite resistance from the Saudi ruling family, which has strong links with the American elite.

According to this optimistic view, the war against terrorism is quite literally 'draining the swamp' of the Middle East of the kind of fundamentalist terrorism which has held the region back for so long and which has always been an even greater threat to local stability than it is to Western interests.

These developments are opening up the Middle East to President Bush's frequently articulated vision of a democratic, market-economy based region, at peace with its neighbours and the rest of the world. Moreover, it is a region that has finally become an active participant in the world economy, and is consequently enjoying the benefits of globalisation. Iraq is the major test case here, for a democratic Iraq will provide an inspiration to other countries in the region to adopt democracy, attract foreign investment and enjoy the benefits of globalisation.

So, despite temporary setbacks (and there are indeed many of them in Iraq), a process has begun which will benefit the whole Middle East region, and which is ultimately unstoppable. Already, countries such as Qatar, Oman and the UAE are reaping the benefits of globalisation. The signs of increasing openness in Egypt (which is liberalising the electoral process), Saudi Arabia (which is holding municipal elections) and Kuwait (which has broken with tradition by giving women the vote) are all indications of a groundswell of reform that is beginning to sweep the region. So, too, are the high profile World Economic Forum summits being held to discuss democratisation and globalisation. Beginning in Sea Island, Georgia, there have been a series of these summits both in the region and abroad, culminating in meetings at the Dead Sea in May, addressed by the US First Lady Laura Bush, who was on a Middle East tour trying to stem the rising tide of anti-Americanism.

On another level, the massive western aid following the Boxing Day Tsunami, much of which is flowing to Muslim Indonesia, is another indication of the kind of western, and indeed US, generosity and care that is extended to the Muslim world. This aid will go a long way toward getting the world's largest Muslim country back on its feet.

This is the optimistic view of the current developments in the troubled Middle East. I am sure that President Bush and his advisors would agree with most of the points elaborated here. So, too, would John Howard and Alexander Downer. But what of the other side of the argument, the darker, more pessimistic view? How do Arab nationalists, Muslim militants and leftists in general see what is happening in the region, and is their view, the pessimistic scenario, really so incompatible with the optimistic news coming out of Washington?

THE PESSIMISTIC SCENARIO

According to the darker view, the Middle East is now more in thrall to the one remaining superpower than ever before. Furthermore, that superpower has begun practising a new and much more aggressive form of imperialism that is more reminiscent of old style, gunboat diplomacy than the intricate web of international state-based relations operating since 1945.

The pessimists would argue that, despite all the rhetoric about freedom and democracy, US interests are in fact much more narrowly focused than ever before. They would go on to point out that, under the Bush administration, US foreign policy has been hijacked by a blinkered group of zealots, the much discussed 'neo-conservatives', whose main interest is the security of Israel and the emasculation of any Arab opposition to Israel's policies. By using the tragedy of 11 September 2001, this group has pushed through a radical agenda: despite all the claims about it being a war on terrorism, it is in fact no more than a new crusade against Islam. In unguarded moments, President Bush himself has even called the war against terrorism a Crusade!

This new crusade, or 'clash of civilisations' in the words of Samuel Huntington, is demonstrated by the ethnic profiling of Muslims and the anti-Islamic rhetoric which is permeating not just the US, but western societies in general. A new intolerance has emerged which, seemingly incidentally, is also placing our post-Enlightenment western values of liberalism, tolerance and multiculturalism under enormous strain.

For the War on Terrorism does not seem to include traditional, non-Islamic terrorist organisations like the IRA, ETA or the Red Brigade. It is focused solely on Islam and Islamic groups, and it involves the demonisation of Islam and the massive abuse of Muslims. Whether this abuse occurs in Abu Graib Prison, Bagram air force base in Afghanistan or Guantanamo Bay, the end result is just the same. Muslims are being abused and even tortured simply because they are Muslims. The profiling occurring at airports has become notorious, and even in the Netherlands, traditionally one of the most tolerant and welcoming of European countries, there is a new intolerance following the assassination of the filmmaker Theo van Gogh. It is also occurring right here in Australia.

According to the pessimists, justice is further away from the Palestinians than ever before. Many believe that the Israelis quite possibly murdered Yasser Arafat, their long time leader who, despite all his failings, stood up for Palestinian interests and refused to cave in to US and Israeli pressure at Camp David. A more compliant leader in the form of the hapless Mahmoud Abbas, whose real task is to provide security for the Israelis as a kind of Quisling-like collaborator and to persuade his people to accept the Israeli occupation of their land forever, has now replaced him.

The invasion of Iraq was an illegal war of aggression against a weak and disarmed country carried out not to democratise the Middle East, but to secure Israel from the one remaining Arab country which matched its anti-Zionist rhetoric with a limited number of deeds. But the invasion has gone badly wrong and the US is already beginning to seek an exit strategy. The hapless Prime Minister Ja'afari is another Mahmoud Abbas, or Hamid Karzai of Afghanistan, and will be hung out to dry just as they have been. Even Saudi Arabia seems to be on the brink of collapse, with a gathering insurgency, which, if left unchecked, could ultimately destabilise the whole of the Gulf region.

At the same time, Seymour Hersch tells us in the *New Yorker* that plans are already underway for military attacks on Iran, another member of President Bush's 'axis of evil'. Quite possibly Syria is a target as well, for it too is accused of sponsoring terrorism and aiding the Iraqi resistance, despite its recent withdrawal from Lebanon, as required by the Security Council. The new US Secretary of State has claimed that Syria is 'out of step' with the democratic advances in the region. These new foreign adventures may well be undertaken, at least in part, to distract attention from the Iraq disaster, which seems to grow worse on a daily basis.

The pessimistic view would suggest that, far from 'draining the Middle Eastern swamp' of terrorists, current US policies are strengthening the terrorists in a multitude of different ways, and creating thousands of recruits for Al Qaeda and similar organisations right across the region. Indeed, across the whole Middle East, levels of anti-Americanism and anti-westernism have risen to hitherto unprecedented levels: US embassies in the Muslim world are more than ever like Crusader castles. At the same time, there is a proliferation of State Department travel advisories warning Americans of the dangers of travelling in the region.

Conclusion

This is a very brief summary of the more pessimistic view of the Middle East and its prospects in the new millennium. Which of the scenarios is correct? There is no easy answer, especially as both may, and probably do, contain elements of the truth, and they may be operating in tandem. But if the history of the Middle East is anything to go by, in the longer term the pessimistic view is more likely to prevail than the optimistic one. Perhaps it is best to equivocate, for, as Carl Brown said many years ago in his important theoretical book on the

International Politics and the Middle East, in that troubled region nothing is ever as bad as it seems, or as good as it seems.

It does appear that there are disasters waiting to happen, such as an attack on Iran in order to control its weapons of mass destruction and possibly bring about regime change, or an attack on Syria for similar reasons. And there are disasters already happening, such as the ongoing tragedy of Iraq and the plight of the Palestinians. But these disasters have to be balanced against the more positive developments in the Gulf region, the reconstruction of war-torn Lebanon with its open elections, and other indications of democratic reform in the region.

Here, credit must be given to US policies, brash and misguided as they may have been, which might have provided the impetus to set the Middle Eastern dominoes in motion. But it would be a cruel irony indeed for Washington if the new Iraq were to be dominated by militant Shi'ites, Lebanon were to provide a parliamentary stage for an expanded Hezbollah, and Afghanistan were to slip back under the control of the drug lords. It would be similarly galling if the new political actors and parties, which are being encouraged to emerge in countries as diverse as Egypt, Saudi Arabia, Jordan and the Gulf Emirates, were virulently anti-American. Surveys indicate that opinion in the region has hardened against the United States, and, if the newly emerging democratic forces are truly representative, that is exactly what will happen.

But one thing seems certain: deep-seated structural change cannot be imposed from outside. It has to come from within. And because of this, the new, aggressive foreign policy agenda of the American neo-conservatives is doomed to result in ever-greater levels of anti-Americanism. With four more years of the Bush administration, and Condaleezza Rice as the new Secretary of State replacing the more moderate Colin Powell, we are, in all probability, in for a very rough ride.

REFERENCES

Brown, L. Carl (1984) *International Politics and the Middle East*, Princeton: Princeton University Press.

Hersch, Seymour (2005) *New Yorker*, 24-31 January.

Chapter 17

IRAN'S SECURITY PERSPECTIVES AND THE GREATER MIDDLE EAST INITIATIVE

Hossein Seifzadeh

INTRODUCTION

Generally positive in their feelings towards Iran as a political entity, Iranians are united in their desire to remove perceived existential threats from their security environment. Nonetheless, due to both their different readings of the situation and the existence of a wide range of tastes, interests and values embodied in the conflicting security priorities, they are also sharply divided. The primary consequence of these differences has manifested itself in the forms and the kinds of political institutions they are looking for: Islamism, secularist nationalism and pluralism. Traditional Islamists, fundamentalists and moderate Islamists respectively, want either the revival of a 'canonically illegitimate secularist state'—similar to the pre-revolutionary political regime—a totalitarian or 'democratic' theocracy /or a 'religious democracy.' The first two deem Iran as a transient 'homeland' for Muslims. The various nationalists (with modernist or militant secularist tendencies) wish to replace the present 'Islamic theocracy' with a nation-state (Melli) that allows human sovereignty. The pluralists, composed of democratic-patriotic Iranians, believe in both cultural diversity and democratisation. They want a political regime that provides secular institutions for realising human sovereignty and a party that can be Islamic but confine itself to the enactment of secular legislation without contradicting Islamic precepts.

While Iranians have remained an integrated socio-politico-cultural grouping over the last 26 centuries, they have proved unable to reach a compromise deal regarding their differential security concerns in the modern era. As a result, Iranians are confronted with conflicting ideas about their domestic and foreign security concerns. The fundamentalists and militant secularists are primarily concerned with the security of their favourite regimes. The nationalists are concerned with the security of Iran as a political entity. The pluralists, in turn, wish to overcome these mutually exclusive approaches. For them, the preservation of both democratic politics and the accommodation of diverse religious and secularist cultures are important and the regime should safeguard (but not enforce) the superior position of the moral community.

In the early days of May 2005, the brinkmanship between Iran and the US and the three European Union states (EU-3)—France, Germany and Great Britain—over the Iranian government's plan to develop its nuclear program reached a crisis point. The US warned the EU-3 that it had only until late summer 2005 to convince Iran to terminate its uranium enrichment program. Otherwise, the US would go ahead unilaterally to stop Iran's nuclear technology project. Iran rejected this ultimatum altogether. As a result, US officials are determined to build up a combination of direct and indirect international pressure while simultaneously calling upon the ostracised opponents of the Islamic Republic, itself a sizeable portion of society, to escalate their pressure also. These macro-micro-level pressures have exacerbated Iran's security predicament, either arising from regime's concern over its own security or otherwise. Not only has the Islamic Republic been increasingly estranged by from the international community, it is also estranged from a sizeable portion of Iran's population. As a result of these factors, Iran and Iranians have recently started to feel increasingly insecure and marginalised. It is plausible to hypothesize that Iran in near future will have a non-declared security administration, filled with both intelligence and military officers. Of course, the security predicament for both Iran in general and different segments of the society has increasingly become a function of both their spatial context (either domestic, global life-worlds or both) and also their conflicting 'mindsets'.

In a bid to portray Iran's security predicament, I will first discuss Iran's general security agenda. In the second section, I will focus on the security environment as shaped by the US Initiative for Greater Middle East. The third section will discuss the two complementary perspectives of Iranian factions (fundamentalists, pragmatists, and pluralist camp), unfolding in terms either assertive radicalism on the part of the former, cooperation and dialogue on the part of the latter two groups. In the final section, the pluralist views and various security scenarios will be discussed.

IRAN'S GENERAL SECURITY PREDICAMENT: A LITERATURE REVIEW

Due to first economic and then democratic reforms since 1989, there appear to be major ebbs and flows in Iran's security priorities. Unlike 16 years (1989-2005) of increasing commitment to moderation and the prevalence of civic demands reconciled through civic means, it appears that once again since mid-2005, the political inclination of a majority of Iranians is moving towards a residual struggle between militant fundamentalism and extremist secularism. Ethnic frenzy in the form of inter-ethnic violence has also been on the rise (*News Media*, 2005). Moderate nationalists and pluralists are struggling, hard pressed to contain this shift.

Islamic Republic and Iran's Military Security

From the macro-military standpoint, Iran's security seems at the risk from both the US and Israel. According to a report prepared by the American Neo-conservative 'Committee on

Present Danger', titled 'Iran, a New Approach', it is suggested that the change in Iran can be engineered through a coup (cited by Abrahamian in *Gulf 2000*, 2005). Secretary of State Condoleezza Rice, on her first overseas mission to Europe on 3 February 2005, held that, 'the goal of the administration is to have a regime in Iran that is responsive to concerns that we have about Iran's policies, which are about 180 degrees antithetical to our interests at this point'. She thinks this can be achieved by assisting Iranians with a chance to 'change their own future'. In a subsequent news conference, Rice maintained: 'We share the desire of European governments to secure Iran's adherence to its obligations through peaceful and diplomatic means'. Moreover, 'Today's announcement demonstrates that we are prepared to take practical steps to support European efforts to this end' (Rice, 2005).

Other analysts used to predict that Israel might consider a surgical blitzkrieg against Iran. Yet others anticipated that the US might opt for a selective attack against Iran's nuclear or military sites, which might weaken the regime and/or provoke popular uprisings as well. Both the Israel and the US are eager to weaken the military and other technological infrastructures allegedly supporting the Islamic Republic's 'anti-status quo' approach to either regional or global politics. In the process, it became increasingly evident that this approach might prove self-defeating, due to Islamic Republic's standing in the region. Kaveh Afrasiabi, a then visiting professor at Tehran University, refutes the feasibility of Israeli attacks, despite common Israeli fears of Iranian threats to Israel's very existence (Afrasiabi, 2005b).

Angered by procrastination in negotiations with the EU-3, on 28 April 2005—a day before the Strategic Committee was supposed to convene over Iran's nuclear technology—Kharrazi warned Europeans that Iran could not wait long for a favourable understanding. The Committee was unable to reach a final decision on 29 April. European officials emphasised that negotiations with Iran might take years. On 29 April 2005 itself, the Bush administration emphasised that the US would not let Iran start its uranium enrichment program. In response, Rafsanjani—Iran's influential but pragmatic chair of the Expediency Council—reiterated that Iran would 'wait rather solemnly and patiently to build confidence in Europeans that its uranium enrichment will never be diverted to military purposes' (Iran's 7PM news, IRIB, April 29, 2005). Yet Iran and the EU-3 failed to reach an agreement and Rowhani, the then Secretary of Supreme Council for National Security of Iran, announced that Isphahan's enrichment activities would start soon (*Quds* and *Donyaye Eqtesad*, May 1,2005).

Against these controversial disagreements between Iran and the EU-3, *Quds Daily* reported a document allegedly disclosed by Al-Menar, whereby Presidents Bush and Sharon reached a memorandum of understanding for an Israeli blitzkrieg against Iran's nuclear facilities. As a pre-cautionary measure, the Lebanese Hezbollah would be dissolved to prevent a retaliatory Hezbollah strike deep into the Israeli territory (*Quds Daily*, 2005d: 2). The demilitarisation of Hezbollah then became a new source of American-Iranian tension. *Voice of America* reported on the Israeli interest in Iran's file ultimately going to the UN Security Council for punitive measures. Japan's prime minister also stated that the global community would not tolerate an Iran with nuclear weapons (VOA, 2005a).

Nader Entessar, a US academician believes Iran is already besieged as a result of military sales to countries surrounding Iran. This, he maintains,

> has caused strategic imbalance between these countries with Iran.... [and] the treaties between Kuwait...Bahrain, Qatar, and Oman...altogether creates political insecurity for Iran. In addition much of the military equipment amassed there...is appropriate for both massive

invasion and surprise attacks. It is quite natural that these give Iran a sense of being besieged (*Quds Daily*, 2005d: 12).

Entessari concludes by quoting Richard Pearl's statement: 'After this [Iraq] it is your [Iran's] turn' (*Quds Daily*, 2005d: 12).

Seyed Rasoul Mousavi, Director of Strategic and Security Studies at Iran's Political and International Studies Institute (affiliated with the foreign ministry), deems the military threats from Persian Gulf countries against Iran to be almost nil. On the contrary, he is worried about the unnecessary engagements of Iran in the micro-level security predicaments plaguing Persian Gulf countries:

> Iran's participation in Persian Gulf security arrangements will increase Iran's security. Nonetheless, security of the Persian Gulf is not equal to Iran's national security in its entirety....Persian Gulf is only a part of the larger security environment of Iran. Iran's engagement in Persian Gulf security arrangements might involve in micro-conflicts of this sub-region. This will damage Iran's credibility. (Mousavi, *Hamshahri-Diplomatic*, 41, 26 February 2005: 2)

Ebrahim Mottaghi, Chairperson of the Department of Political Science, emphasises the impact of the Bush administration's Greater Middle East Initiative on the micro-level security of Persian Gulf countries. He believes this Initiative has caused 'strategic ambiguity' in these countries, and now 'all countries and political units are worried about their future security' (Motaghi, *Hamshahri-Diplomatic*, 41, 26 February 2005). For Mottaghi, security will be increased: 'The more regional actors play effective roles in arranging regional security, the more the instability will decline and the more stable will the region become' (Mottaghi, 2005: 4). Mottaghi maintains that Persian Gulf countries must explore their shared security interests. In addition, cultural input is also important, and a new regional identity will play a constructive role. Finally, he supplements his idealist approach with Entessari's realism: a prerequisite for closer relations with the Persian Gulf countries lies in a military balance of power (Mottaghi, 2005: 4)).

Ethno-Religious Cleavages

Iran consists of various ethno-religious groups. These cultural minorities are living mainly in the provinces adjacent to similar ethno-religious groups across the other side of national borders. For example, Armenians live in the northwest of Iran next to the neighbouring Republic of Armenia. Azeris share similar references on either side of the border. The Iranian Turkmen as an ethnic group live in the north-eastern area of Iran, neighbouring Turkmenistan. Baluch Iranians share the same ethnic identity with Baluchs in Pakistan. Arabs live in both south and southwest Iran. Kurdish minorities live across Iran, Iraq and Turkey. Thanks to Iran's all-inclusive history, the modern nation-state was generally immune from ethnic revolution when foreign belligerent states are not involved. Russia and England, for example, were behind the territorial disintegration of Iran in the nineteenth century, which left Iran with occasional ethno-religious revolts. Yet, in early April 2005, Iran experienced one of its recurring Arab revolts. Then Iranian Minister of Defence, himself an

Arab from Khuzistan, Amir Shamkhani, reported the detaining of 310 people, and the Attorney General of Ahvaz reports the arrests of 344 individuals and 4 deaths (*Quds Daily*, 2005e: 2). Hassan Rowhani declared that these 'Recent events in Khuzestan emerged in the aftermath of a counterfeit letter'and that the Al-Jezirah satellite network from Qatar contributed to ethnic rioting in late April 2005. However, Rowhani admitted that: 'some unfulfilled legitimate demands might have been exploited to provoke the riot—not inherently related to the treason of a person or group. They simply must be fulfilled' (*Quds Daily*, 2005e). Then Minister of Interior, Mousavi Lari, also claimed that: 'counter-revolutionary forces living beyond the borders have used the satellite networks to provoke ethnic groups in Iran' (*Quds Daily*, 2005e).

Iran's Economic Predicament

Iran's economic security has been endangered by various shortcomings. A passing review of the literature demonstrates that Iran suffers from a number of problems.

Brain Drain
Iran's 'brain drain' worries many scholars and officials, and much has been written on its long-term impact. Short-term impacts are increasingly being investigated. An official of Iran's Ministry of Science and Technology has warned against the long-term impacts of the brain drain on Iranian IQs. Sa'eed Pour Zand reports that Iran's export of educated minds in the aftermath of the Islamic Revolution of 1979 has cost it $US 38 billion by 2000 (1379/2000). Another report numbers Iran's intellectual émigrés up to 1,955,000. From this multitude of intellectual émigrés, 53.5 per cent have been PhDs, 17.4 per cent university professors and 36.1 per cent professional practitioners ('Iran's brain drain', 2002). Hassan Voghoufi also explored the impact of emigrated intellectuals on Iran's security in his book (Voghoufi, 2001).

Financial Mismanagement, Poverty and Bureaucratic Corruption
Mismanagement of financial resources is another security problem. Reports of the mismanagement of Iran's financial resources include unnecessary foreign trips by government officials. Accordingly, 'the crowded official trips of Iranians have caused cold receptions on the part of host countries' (*Quds Daily*, 2005d: 8). Ali-Rabi'ee also decried government corruption, satirically calling his recent book *Zandeh bad fesad* (*Viva Corruption*) (1380/2001), and Mohsen Armin also discusses this problem in depth in his *Fesade mali dar hakemiyat/Financial Corruption in the Government* (1380/2001).

In spite of Iran's rich mineral deposits, including hydro-carbonic ores, its GNP ranks it 58 amongst more than 200 countries (Khoda Bakhshi and Hosseini Nejad, 1383/2004: 6). Mazaheri, Iran's former Minister of Treasury and Economics, 'has already warned against the poverty of employees and plundering of Iran's Foreign Currency Deposit Fund' in the *Quds Daily* declaring: 'in the course of purchasing 50 cement factories by FCDF, financial misuse has been very widespread' (*Quds Daily*, 2005d: 8).

According to Habibie, there are nine different factors contributing to Iran's bureaucratic corruption. These range from the collapse of value systems, low income, the lack of effective supervision, nepotism and the opportunities by officials to create bureaucratic obstacles as tools to force clients to pay to overcome them (1375/1996: 67). He offers four complementary approaches to check and control such corruption. Ironically, all focus on supervisory mechanisms in the administration, parliament, judiciary, NGOs (including parties supported by democratic elections) and professional ones (Habibi, 1375/1996: 118).

Absence of Foreign Investment

Iran also lacks sufficient foreign investment. Professor Taghavi deems the failure of the Islamic Republic to attract foreign capital as a source of long-term insecurity because the population is young and also suffers high rates of unemployment that could be alleviated through such investment (Taghavi, 1378/1999). Despite most legal issues having already been removed by the 'illegal legislation' of the Expedience Council's economic reform acts (according to Professor Dadban's interview, 20 April 2005), Iran was unable to meet its financial needs from the international money market (Hadi Zenouz, 1379/2000: Introduction).

Iran's Political Predicament

In the aftermath of their silencing of the non-fundamentalist forces at all levels, Iran's cultural fundamentalists used their muscle to legalise their exclusive control over Iran's political structure. Thanks to the privileged position granted them by the founder of the Islamic Republic, Imami Kashani, this exclusivist approach is constitutionally legal (Kashani, 1363/1984).

Because of their guaranteed non-elected position, supported by their vigilante militia, the cultural fundamentalists were able both to filter non-fundamentalist candidates and hence generated public frustration with their victory in the minority-elected Assembly. Once elected, the fundamentalist Fourth Assembly legalised their arbitrary provisions as 'electoral law'. Reformists have subsequently also failed to convince the non-elected and elected fundamentalists to acquiesce to rising popular pressure for democratic reform. As a result, Iran is once again at a political crossroad and might well experience civil war, riots or another round of repressive government. Moreover, the fundamentalists are working hard to crush even their mildest opponents. According to Vice-President Abtahi's web report, one webblogger claimed before the Board of Constitutional Investigators that while in prison:

> theback of his head was hit to the bench-seat. As a result of the push, my nose—barely recuperating from recent surgery—started bleeding. Later on, it was revealed to me by my physician that it is smashed. [He also claims to attend others] in solitary cells for months.... During interrogations, they were accused of outdated allegations incriminating them in unlawful extra-marital sex. They (webloggers) were ordered to reveal the names of their 'alleged' boy- and girlfriends in written form: the extent to which they had sexual relations, the number of times raped.... More notoriously, a list of six reformists have been given to a female, while directing her to incriminate them for engaging in illegitimate sexual intercourse. In a bid to induce them into making this self-incrimination, they used the frustrated individuals as witnesses to give testimony of their own sexual experiences with them. (1383/2004)

Observing these developments in Iran from Australia, Shahram Akbarzadeh observes:

President Khatami's attempt to wrest power from the conservatives through constitutional means have failed.... The reformist constituency appeared to have snubbed the parliamentary election, resulting in a low turnout at polling stations: 50.5 per cent (as a contrast to nearly 70 per cent in the previous election for the Parliament). This casts a long shadow on the regime's legitimacy. Iranian politics appears set to enter a new phase of tension and instability, a trend that is likely to be confirmed in the 2005 presidential election. (2005: 7-12.)

Iran's Social Predicament

Due to the imperatives of the current transitional stage, and the vigorous resistance of fundamentalists to the modernisation of the social structure and democratisation of political culture on one hand, and globalisation on the other, Iran's security has also been threatened by some social problems. The growth of ghettos and deepening poverty seem to be the main causes of many crimes and social diseases, such as prostitution and drug addiction.

A review of Iranian newspapers demonstrates an incredible rise in crimes such as serial killing with religious motivations (for example, the 'Meshed' killings of prostitutes, Kernan's killing of 'unfavourable individuals', homicide and robbery), committed mainly by ghetto-dwellers or marginalised social groups. Various academic and government organisations have sponsored research into these issues (see Seyed Mohesen, 1371/1993). The impact of ghetto-dwelling has also been investigated by the Ministry of Hygiene and Medicine, and the findings of various research projects have already been published by the University of Rehabilitation (1380/2001).

Likewise, prostitution is another social disease, one now so prevalent it has tarnished Iran's national prestige in neighbouring countries such as the Gulf States and Turkey. Drug use is yet another security problem. Iran's taskforce responsible for fighting drug addiction denies the highe estimates that the number of addicts exceeds 4 million, but acknowleges 1.5 million. However, about 270 tonnes of drugs were confiscated in 2004 alone (*Sobhe Eqtesad*, 2005c: 31). The problem is that drug addiction combined with bureaucratic corruption increases Iran's vulnerability (Farjad, 1377/1998).

Civilisational Decadence

Some scholars deem that Iran's security predicament arises from the lack of an intellectual reappraisal, one which has resulted in the irrelevance of contemporary Iranian philosophy. Mousa Ghani-nejad (*Tajaddod Talabi va Toseeh dar Irane Mo'asser*, 1378/1998), Dariush Ashouri (*Ma Va Moderniyat/* Us and Modernity, 1377/1998) and Seyed Javad Tabataba'ee (*Dibacheei bar Nazariyeh Enhetat Iran/* A preface to Iran's Decadence, 1380/2001) are all attempting differentially to explain Iran's decadence. According to these writers, this irrelevance has been imposed on Iran by the Arab and steppe invasions and Iran's autocratic rulers. Some, like Tabataba'ee, have proposed a philosophical revitalisation using current traditional and classical thought (1373/1984: 207-277) to create a modern philosophical approach (1382/2003: Chapter 5). However, like the Postivist or Frankfurt Schools, he ignores the important role of science in salvaging Iran from chronic decadence. Hossein Seifzadeh's *Modernite va Nazariate Jadid-e Elme Syast (Modernity and New*

Theories of Political Science) contrasts Iranians' traditional mindset with that of classical, modern and post-modern thought, and criticises the attempts to ignore cultural diversity, which have resulted in the application of culturally irrelevant theories for salvaging Iran (Seifzadeh, 1379/2000). More specifically, Seifzadeh refers to Iran's security predicament in research done for the Center for Strategic Studies. He argues that Iran's security policies are neither responsive to the State's security needs, nor responsive to Iranians' need for individual security (Seifzadeh, 1382/2003).

Ayatollah Khomenei, Iran's Supreme Leader, however, deems modernity itself to be a root cause of problems for the Islamic world:

> As of today, when Muslims reflect on their destiny, they find modernity has offered the Islamic world nothing but more dependence, corruption, enfeebled nations and the feeble Islamic governments. Modernity was unable to transform Muslims into scientists and initiators, but made them dependent…. Currently, liberalism is perplexed. (cited in Seifzadeh, 1382/2003: 5)

THE GREATER MIDDLE EAST INITIATIVE AND IRAN'S *AD HOC* SECURITY PREDICAMENT

As mentioned above, Iran has become the next target of the US-European Initiative for the Greater Middle East. Yet, the 'democratisation' of Iran is only a means of facilitating US security interests in the region. The US is seeking a pro-American government that responds to short-term US security interests, rather than to Iran's own security predicament. Should this scenario materialise, Iran's foreign and domestic conditions will be at odds with each other. Most Iranians—save the militant secularists—are in search of some kind of change, although this spans a broad spectrum from the minimalist approach of fundamentalists, to the maximalists in favour of linking Iran's democratisation with a communicative-virtual state. This approach assumes both the domestic and international environments are interlinked, and that Iran can facilitate improving global security. In the meantime, Iran should stress the diversity of its native culture. However, this vision is in contrast with the US security package, the main objective of which is the democratisation of Iran. The American Iran Policy Committee (IPC) also supports precluding Iran's further acquisition of nuclear technology. Its analysis is very explicit: 'the pace of nuclear weapons development might leave Washington with what the Committee believes is the least desirable option of waging military strikes against Iran' (Seifzadeh, 1382/2003: 4).

Iran and the EU-3 have reached an impasse regarding Iran's determination to master the fuel cycle and the EU-3 is committed to preventing Iran from having the capacity to develop nuclear weapons (*Voice of America*, 2005b). In spite of Iran's preparedness to give guarantees to avoid violation of Non-Proliferations Treaty (NPT) commitments, Europeans argue they cannot trust that Iran would not later opt for a break-out capability. For its part, Iran mistrusts the intentions of the EU-3 and the US, due to its own failure to predict US intentions in the Algiers Accord of 19 January 1981, which proved so costly to Iran. It is now evident that Iran's aspiration to be treated as any other NPT-non-nuclear weapon-state (such as Japan and South Korea) is incompatible with current US policy. Moreover, Iranian rhetoric on Israel directly feeds hardline positions in both Europe and the US, just as the US-Europe rhetoric on regime change feeds Iranian hardliners.

In fact, the greatest threat to Iran is the rules of 'the game'. Not only does a military strike threaten even the 'soft' attempts to 'divide' Iranians in the hope of consequent favourable 'rule', it also has the potential for unpredictable adverse outcomes. This zero-sum game might generate a severe backlash in the form of repulsive fundamentalism or fascist chauvinism against 'others', starting with Arabs.

The negative potential reflects the fact that Iran is a complex and dynamic society that poses a puzzle for policymakers. Misunderstanding and mutual mistrust between Iran and the West play key roles. The Islamic Republic can sell its nuclear technology programme as a legitimate one to Iranians, yet there is disagreement between Western 3+1 powers and some other countries regarding the necessity for Iran to have civilian nuclear technology at all. Salehi—Iran's previous diplomat to the International Atomic Energy Agency (IAEA)—also confirms President Khatami's emphasis on Iran's benign intentions. Nonetheless, he believes the Iranian nuclear issue is politically charged. According to Salehi,

> It is not possible to verify intentions. Up to present, we have not heard about verifying intentions as a pretext for international treatment of political actors. Relations are defined in terms of conventions and agreements. Iran is already a member of NPT and voluntarily cooperate with the stipulations of the Annexed Documents in which Iran is not still a member. These are enough clues to Iran's intentions for developing its indigenous nuclear technology. (2004)

The result is that there are fears that a 'political trap' is being set for Iran:

> Our officials seem to be intelligent enough to avoid being entangled in this pre-set trap. They are determined to abuse their hegemonic status against us.... We are not obedient slaves to others and therefore others (John Edwards is implied here) are not in the position to tell us what to do. Nonetheless it is imperative and we are obliged to initiate the removal of misunderstandings upon our nuclear activities. We are entitled to take advantage of peaceful nuclear technology and do not let us others to decide for us. (Khatami, 2004)

The non-fundamentalist officials of the Islamic republic do their best to avoid a US attack on Iran or having Iran's case referred to the UN. In contrast, Iranian fundamentalists neither disregard nor even dislike the idea of an Israeli blitzkrieg against Iran's nuclear facilities. Any attack would reinforce their position and power.

In respect to human rights violations, leaders of the Islamic Republic do not intend to carry out superstructural reforms. They think any infrastructural institutional reform will cost them their power to permanently supervise Iran's politics. The West's pressure on Iran for change must therefore be in accordance with pluralism rather than the zero-sum game of 'divide and rule'. Fundamentalists need both new intellectual paradigms and institutional reform to cope with any democratic reform. Global support is needed to allow this 'democratic delivery'. Czarinan operations might be counter-productive. Of course, it might prove to be a short-term means to make Iranian opposition groups ally with the West against the Islamic Republic. Promotion of human rights have undoubtedly proved an effective tool in winning American and European domestic support for US-EU pressure on the Islamic Republic. Ambassador Mark Palmer justifies US pro-human rights policy as a requirement for US security (Palmer, 2003: 2), and promoting this cause will undermine what the Americans see as sponsorship of terrorism and 'terrorists', such as Hezbollah in Lebanon (Palmer, 2003: 236-239).

IRAN'S SECURITY

An Official Perspective

Unlike the nationalist positions of a few leaders, such as Prime Minister Mossadeq who was toppled by a US coup in 1953, almost all other Iranian politicians place the interests of their favourite regime or factions before the national interest at both macro and micro levels. Others either favoured various democratic, authoritarian, populist or totalitarian regimes or institutions such as an Ummah (community of believers), ethnicity or class. Their favourite ideal institutions are Islamic Ummah or the Iranian state as a monolithic system. Post-revolutionary reformists have always supported Iranians' security interests. Inadvertently, they ignored fundamentalists' primordial and military concerns and pragmatists' technocratic security for the internal security of the regime.

Analysts believe Rafsanjani has tacitly promised the West a compromise deal, both to secure Iran's right to uranium enrichment and the West's confidence (Khonsari, 2005). As a result, or by coincidence, the EU-3's spokesman announced that negotiations would be postponed until June 2005, near Iran's presidential election.

Fundamentalist officials view Iranian security in military terms. Some believe that a US invasion and/or an Israeli blitzkrieg on Iranian nuclear facilities might produce favourable pro-regime nationalism, and talk openly of 'retaliation', while the possible use of unconventional tactics (but not unconventional weapons) is not ruled out. The *Iran News* articulates the Iranian approach in terms of retaliating against any Israeli attacks. Kammal Kharrazi stressed that this 'war of words' between Israel and Iran has escalated due to the former's wrong assessment of Iranian intentions. Accordingly, Israelis misinterpret Iran's insistence on an independent nuclear technology as signifying Iran's actual intent to acquire nuclear weapons. On the contrary, Kammal Kharrazi also emphasises 'our legitimate right to have nuclear technology for peaceful purposes' (Kharrazi, 2004: 1). The Foreign Ministry's spokesman, Asefi, has the same vigorous tone regarding 'recent comments by US officials', declaring:

> With reliance on enormous popular support, diplomatic capacity and *full* [my emphasis] military capability, the Islamic republic of Iran will firmly respond to any unwise measure or plan.... We see such moves as a psychological campaign and political pressure (avoiding) Europe to peacefully settle some disagreements through diplomacy and talks, but to disrupt the Iran-EU—EU nuclear talks by pretending they are unsuccessful... We recommend the new American Foreign Minister avoid repeating past mistakes by reviewing America's wrong and successful policies of unilateralism and oppressions. (2005: 1, 15)

A Strategic Perspective

Due to changes in its domestic, regional and global security environment, this scholar argues the security predicament of Iran has turned for the worse. The rise in terrorism and fundamentalism and the western focus on the 'Greater Middle East' has transformed the geopolitics of the region. The 'heartland' has apparently moved from Eastern Europe to the Middle East. As a result, Iran's strategic role has changed from pre-Cold War cooperation in containing the previous heartland, to a new bastion to contain the troubled 'heartland' of the Middle East. Secondly, separates it from other neighbouring troubled regions, such as the Caspian Basin and Southern Asia in Pakistan. In this latter capacity, Iran can play a subsidiary buffer-zone role, or even act as a bridge between various anti-status quo players in the region. That is, it can play a constructive or destructive role in keeping various politicised primordial groups along its borders from joining forces. Finally, it can also play a constructive role in bridging the petro-plus-markets basin of the Caspian and the Persian Gulf on one hand, and the countries of the north on the other.

Iran can play either a constructive or destructive role. On one hand, the modern sectors of society would like to cooperate with the West to develop Iran. In fact, they see that the United States' and Iran's national interests are generally complementary. Of course, this cooperation must be based on new realities rather than a patron-client basis. On the other, the fundamentalists are prepared to use their popular support in the region to withstand western globalism. Iranian fundamentalists found a vast audience amongst the masses in the Islamic world. In the case of attacks on Iran, fundamentalists will provoke 'anti-West' and 'anti-Israel' emotions. The Middle East has long been receptive to divergent radical ideologies due to frustrated aspirations arising from the failure to withstand Israel's hegemonic status, the failure to convince the US to stop supporting Israel and to implement successful domestic reform.

Moreover, the domestic politics of Iran has added to the strategic importance of Iran. Iranians are leading the intellectual campaign for democracy in their nation. In real terms, though, the democratisation is lagging behind that in Turkey. The gap between the ideal and the practical political levels has given rise to security concerns for all actors involved in Iranian politics. Balance of power, rather than civic political processes, defines the rules of the game. Iran can now be called a 'liberated polity'; the government cannot use excessive repressive measures too frequently or too broadly against its opponents. At the same time, Iranians are unable to force the government to abide by democratic principles. Thanks to the decline of fundamentalism in Iran, and the great leaps forward in reform, Iran can influence Indian relations with Pakistan, with Turkey on behalf of Europe and Israel, as well as on behalf of the US attempts to contain fundamentalist terrorism. This potential gives Iran a unique strategic position, and Iran's decisionmakers face tough times as a result.

Notwithstanding Iran's increased strategic importance, Bush has convinced the EU-3 that Iran is an emerging threat. The 'US Policy Options for Iran', prepared by the IPC on 10 February 2005, declares Iran a threat to 'US interests and Ideals'. The report prefers supporting the Mujaheddin's militia force striking against the Islamic Republic with US support.

The list of threats enumerated by the IPC begins with Iran's nuclear technology and ends with its 'Denial of basic human rights to its own populations'. The Committee stresses the potential for a third alternative ('carrot or stick' options): to keep open diplomatic and military options, while providing a central role for the Iranian opposition to facilitate regime change. The IPC holds that:

> The [Islamic Republic]...regime is not likely to be turned from its threatening behavior by policies that mainly emphasise negotiations. IPC believes that the credible threat of economic and military 'sticks' in conjunction with diplomatic 'carrots' has a better chance of achieving change in official Iranian behavior or regime change than either alone.... Without the active participation of Iranians, moreover, regime change is unlikely to succeed. (IPC, 2005: 1-4)

The IPC stance is supported by Pollack from the Brookings Institution when he concluded that those who advocate a policy of regime change by pressing for a popular revolution illustrate a valuable kernel of truth (2005: 67, 78).

Consequently, it appears the US and Europe have reached a consensus about how to approach Iran. The Islamic Republic has to modify its hitherto anti-status quo strategy, and instead commit itself to substituting a favourable strategy contributing to the status quo. That is, Iran must pursue its national interests in promoting its status within the limits of the present international system and order. Both 'stick and carrot' measures will be used to streamline Iran, ensuring it abides with the imperatives of the emergent hegemonic global system and order led by the US. The US has started to use some 'carrots' in addition to its hitherto 'sticks' approach, and Europeans have also compromised their 'carrots' with some 'sticks'. Thus, for all the different pressure groups in the US, the democratisation of Iran is only an instrument for facilitating US security interests in the region.

The West's new approach seems to have forced the fundamentalists to acknowledge the substance of the West's strategy towards Iran: it looks as though it is imperative that they transform themselves. Recently, the official position of the Islamic Republic demonstrates the incumbent fundamentalists have got the message. Apparently, they have noticed the converging security interests of both sides of the Atlantic and their determination to uphold it.

This recent similarity in language used by both Europe and the US implies a paradigm change in western security approaches towards Iran. In the past, tough US claims played into the hands of fundamentalists and contributed to their hegemonic position in Iranian politics. However, fundamentalism can no longer be tolerated by the West. It might contribute to terrorism and the acquiring of WMDs, both of which are detrimental to the emerging world order, the international system in general and the integrity of the entire west in particular. Nonetheless, fundamentalists do not deem themselves to be helpless. Thanks to the lingering instability in Iraq and Afghanistan, and due to falling trust in US sincerity about supporting democratic reform in Iran, scepticism is on the rise in respect to the outcomes of future developments in Iran. Middle East officials and a majority of intellectuals and dissident political activists are afraid of the impact of this new strategy, though for divergent reasons. Incumbent officials are basically concerned about their future role in the Middle East.

In the meantime, the continued bloodshed in Iraq has supported the fundamentalists' cause. The US seems to them to have a great deal more work to do in Iraq before it could engage itself in yet another conflict with other states such as Iran and Syria. If the US proves unable to turn Iraq into a pluralist democracy, anti-Americanism will capture Arab capitals. It will certainly add to the self-confidence of fundamentalist faction in the Islamic Republic.

Fundamentalists' self-confidence will exacerbate domestic cleavages amongst the incumbent fundamentalists and their militant opposition. Iran will turn turbulent, with ambiguous consequences. Some US analysts contribute to this rising self-confidence. In *Quds Daily*, Henry Kissinger is quoted as being in favour of a 'secure' 'independent' Iran: 'US does not have any interest in destabilizing Iran... [in spite of the fact that the nuclear technology of Iran] is a horrendous threat....But Iran has enormous hydro-carbonic resources and large population, and I think it is a serious case to consider', (*Quds Daily*, 2005f: 19). Further:

> Iran getting the bomb could be the best thing that's ever happened to the Middle East peace process.... Look at it from their [Iranians'] perspective.... Our offer should be both simple and bold. I would send James Baker, our last good secretary of state, to Tehran as your special envoy with the following message: You can have the bomb, and we'll take you off the Axis of Evil list, plus we'll re-establish diplomatic ties and open up trade. But in exchange, not only will you bail us out on Iraq first and foremost by ending your support for insurgency, you'll also cut off your sponsorship of Hezbollah and other anti-Israeli terrorist groups, help us bully Syria out of Lebanon, finally recognize Israel, and join us in guaranteeing the deal on a permanent Palestinian state. You want to be recognized as the regional player of note. We're prepared to do that. But that's the price tag. Pay it now or get ready to rumble.

This 'misleading' advice had lured some ex-patriot Iranians like Maziar Behrooz (ironically teaching at San Francisco State University in the US) to write:

> What is left out of all these talks about attacking Iran is the IRI's response; do these people really think the medium range missiles Iran has is for parades commemorating the victory of 1979 revolution? My suggestion to the IRI: perhaps it should go nuke ASAP as 'Rome' has gone mad; Emperor Nero refuses to listen to reason and has convinced himself (or has been convinced by others) of his own self righteousness. There is no cure in sight for this madness and the world should brace for impact! (Gulf, 2005)

This quotation does not mean this author has a tendency to favour undemocratic processes in Iran. On the contrary, the most important message of this chapter warns against any the delay in the democratisation of Iran. *Prime facie*, Iran's democratisation looks to have become a dilemma in itself. A deeper analysis of the issue demonstrates that monolithic approaches have proved ineffective in Iran. As the model of Janis and Mann (in Seifzadeh, 2000: 45-70) demonstrates, there are often alternative options and uncultivated means available.

In Iran's zero-sum games, Iranian fundamentalists and militant oppositions engage in politics in regional or international forums to invigorate their standing in Iranian domestic politics. We all know progress in the Middle East is now arrested by fundamentalists' zeal for violent change. They will not hesitate to use their forces in the region. Yet these primordial games have to be avoided. The impact of the security obsessions of hawkish Israelis will be detrimental to regional security. The latter would like to see the Middle East divided and Arab-non-Arab or Shiite-Sunni conflicts are welcomed. Prior to the 1979 Islamic Revolution, Shiite Iran used to play both games. The Islamic Revolution has transformed this equation. The Iraqi-imposed war, the bilateral relations with Turkey and the Republic of Azerbaijan, the cooperation with Qatar and other Arab countries, were unable to undo the emergent equation. It is believed the retreat from Lebanon and Iraqi elections can strengthen a revival in the Shiite-Sunni rift once again. Iran is too passionately concerned about avoiding this. The emotional aspects of the Arab-Israeli conflict now overwhelm the majority of Iranian Islamists. A just resolution of the Arab-Israeli conflict will compel the Islamists to develop a new agenda.

Against this unfavourable scenario, the region could see a favourable one through a variable, positive game. Israel could represent US interests in the region. Turkey's integration into Europe could allow it to become the front window to Europe, and Iran can then play the role of independent and benign rimland actor, containing fundamentalism. A neutral Iran could play the role Switzerland did in Europe during previous global orders. This desire for order is the basic shared interest that establishes indirect linkages between the regional and international security. Of course, the democratisation of Iran can play a major facilitating role. There is certainly common ground linking the security interests of a democratic Iran with those of the West.

The militant Iranian opposition is in favour of any democratic change in Iran. It admires President Bush's commitment to 'the Greater Middle East' and sees it as an influential factor facilitating progress. Accordingly, these events would have two favourable impacts on Iran's democratic reform, both to demoralise the fundamentalists and to boost the morale of all opposition groups. These changes undermine the Islamic Republic and its allies, and will ultimately result in its collapse.

The pluralists, too, including moderate Islamists and secularists, would like the global community to play at most a mediating role. Accordingly, Iran's national security cannot be reduced to a zero-sum game in favour of either alliance with regional (in the case of fundamentalists) or global (in the case of opposition groups) power. On the contrary, Iran has the potential to compromise both. Moreover, due to rich mineral and human resources and its strategic status, the pluralists believe any efficient administration in Iran could compromise Iran's unified national interests with that of diverse partisan interests of the nation. This positive approach will be more effective and constructive. More specifically, Amir-Ahmadi argues that the Bush administrations' threats to attack or impose sanctions:

> ... would inflict significant costs on Iran and the Iranian people, [but] they would not end the regime or halt its enrichment activities. On the contrary, they will further militarize the regime, strengthen its resolve to build a nuclear bomb, destroy what is left of the reform movement, and produce an anti-American backlash among a generally US-friendly population. The only realistic option is to use the opportunity that has developed to engage Iran toward normalisation of relations. (2005)

Based upon Amir-Ahmadi's reading, it is reasonable to conclude both fundamentalists and the militant opposition are in fact united in subordinating Iran's security to their factional security concerns. For the pluralists, partisan politics must give way to pluralist politics, where national security assumes precedence.

Due to the prevalence of factionalism, each of the rival groups is prepared to trade a part of national security in a bid to buy off its own parochial security. Hence, the solutions suggested by militants, the pluralists argue, do not address Iran's general security predicament. Whereas fundamentalists close their eyes to the vast areas of shared security interests between the western global powers and Iran's regional security, the militant opposition groups blind themselves to the differential security interests Iran has *vis-a-vis* the security concerns of Israel and global powers in the Middle East. Instead, pluralists welcome an integrated approach recognising both the common and differential security concerns of Iran (Seifzadeh, 2003).

Along with opposition groups, Iranian pluralists welcome democratic reforms in Iran as an inevitable necessity. Nonetheless, they believe that democratic reform engineered by outside powers would in the longer term betray the far-reaching security interests of Iranians and global powers alike. Moreover, they argue the Middle East has diverse, rather than particular, security predicaments. These are partially in harmony and yet on other occasions contradict the security interests of global powers in the Middle East. According to them, the Middle East is the new troubled 'heartland' of the world. Hence, they welcome the attention paid to its security. In the meantime, they deem this attention has provided Iran with both new challenges and opportunities. On the positive side, Iran's infrastructural change will make it the ideal candidate for contributing to the democratisation of the 'Greater Middle East'. On the debit side, the ongoing hostilities and struggle between the region's fundamentalists, with Israel edging its asymmetrical nuclear power over all other major Middle East players combined, are also matters for deep concern. In fact, the prevalence of conflicting values and interests provides pluralists with some room for pessimism. In fact, pluralists are partially frustrated by the inability of all Iranians to strike a successful compromise amongst these divergent security concerns. These factors are perceived as highly susceptible to contributing to security issues, such as terrorism and WMD proliferation.

CONCLUSION

Iran's complexities pose a puzzle for policymakers. Misunderstanding and mutual mistrust of the West play a confusing role in Iran's security dilemma. Unfortunately, both Iran's fundamentalists and neo-conservative hawks in the US have recently engaged in intense brinkmanship. On one hand, Iran made nuclear technology a national symbol of pride, contributing to halting the regime's plummeting legitimacy. On the other hand, American neo-conservatives have sold the Islamic Republic as a 'horrible' threat to a security-obsessed American public. In early May 2005, it seems both sides have ridden on a no-return one-way road towards rising brinkmanship. Of course, this brinkmanship does not necessarily mean hot war. Whereas Western3+1 and some other powers are allegedly suspicious of a break-out capability and hence are doubtful of the necessity for Iran to have civilian nuclear technology at all, the Islamic Republic pledged to maintain uranium enrichment as a national right. As a result, it seems Iran and the EU-3 have reached an impasse.

It is now evident that Iran's aspiration to be treated like any other NPT-non-nuclear-weapon states (such as Japan and South Korea) is incompatible with current US policy. Moreover, Iranian rhetoric on Israel directly feeds hard-line positions in both Europe and the US, just as the US-Europe rhetoric on regime change feed Iranian fundamentalist hardliners. Hence, the final conclusion of this chapter is that Iran and the US plus EU-3 have embarked on a new course of relations, whose end result is uncertain.

Notwithstanding this gloomy finding, the prescription of this chapter is rather constructive. This scholar presumes any zero-sum solution will have a detrimental impact on Iran's security, and adverse impacts on regional and global security. Nonetheless, the Islamic Republic has already learned, as a result of sustained external pressures, to sketch its global interactions according to a variable-sum game. Israel is an exception to the rule. Unfortunately, fundamentalists in the Islamic Republic have little desire to soothe their hatred of Israel, settle disagreements with the US and democratise Iran. They are intellectually against pluralism and the variable-sum game, yet these changes are crucial for Iran's security.

REFERENCES

Abhari (2005) *Quds Daily*, 18 January.
Abtahi, Vice-President Mohammad Ali (1383/ 2004) web report, Saturday 7 Dey/28 December
Afrasiabi, Kaveh (2005a) 'Reforming the UN the Bush Way'. *Asian Times*, 9 March, Front Page.
—— (2005b) 'The Myth of an Israeli Strike on Iran'. *Asian Times* online, www.Asiatimes.online, 7 April.
Alizadeh (2005) *Quds Daily*, 18 January.
Akbarzadeh, Shahram (2005) 'Where is the Islamic Republic of Iran Heading?' *The Australian Journal of International Affairs*, 59(1): 7-12.
Amir-Ahmadi, Houchang (2005) American-Iranian Cooperation Update, 17 March.
Armin, Mohsen (1380/2001) *Fesade mali dar hakemiyat*/Financial Corruption in the Government, Qom: Khneh Kherad/The House of Wisdom.
Asefi, Hamid (MFA Spokesman) (2004) Cited by Khorassan, 16 February.
—— (2005) *Iran News*, 20 January.
Ashouri, Dariush (1376/1998) *Ma Va Moderniyat*/Us and Modernity, Tehran: Serat Publishers.
Behrooz, Maziar (2005) *Gulf 2000*, 21 January: 23.
Bush, President (2005) Inaugural Address, 20 January.
—— State Of Union Address, 2 February.
Committee on Present Danger (2004) 'Iran, a New Approach', December. Cited by Yrvand Abrahamian, *Gulf 2000*, 29 April 2005.
Erly, Adam (2005) *Voice of America*, 21 April, 8.30 PM, Iran time.
Esquire (2005) February.
Farjad, Mohammad Hossein (1377/1998) *Barresi Masa'el-e Ejtema'ee Iran*/A survey of Social Predicaments in Iran: Bureaucratic Corruption, Drug Addiction and Divorce, Tehran: Assatir.
Ghani-nejad, Mousa (1378/1998) *Tajaddod Talabi va Toseeh dar Irane Mo'asser*/Modernity and Development in Contemporary Iran, Tehran: Markaz Publishers.
Habibie, Nader (1375/1996) *Fesad-e edari: avamel-e mo'asser va ravesh-hay-e mobareze*/Bureaucratic Corruption: The Intervening Factors and Methods to Fight Against It, Tehran: Vatheqi.
Habibie, Seyed Mohsen (1371/1993) *gozaresh-e Pazhouheshi degargounihaye roustahaye mojaver dar shahrhaye bozorg va dar nezame eskane keshvar: motale'e moredi-e Eslam-shahr*/A Report of the Research on Transformation of the Villages Adjacent Metropolitan Areas in the Residential Paradigm in the Country: Eslam-shahr Case Study, Tehran: University of Tehran,

Hadi Zenouz, Behrouz (1379/2000) *Sarmaye gozari Khareji dar Iran*/Foreign Investments in Iran, Tehran: Nashr pazhouhesh-e Farzan.

'Iran's Brain Drain: Causes and Trends' (2002) RFE/RL. Iran Report, # 7515, January.

Iran Daily (2005) 9 March.

Iran News (2005) 20 March.

Iran Policy Committee (2005) 'US Policy Options for Iran'. 10 February.

Kashani, Imami (1363/1984) Letter to Ministry of Interior, 5 Farvardin/26 March.

Khatami, Mohammad (2004) *Asr Eghtesad*, 1 September.

―― (2005) *Iran News*, 13 January.

Kharrazi, Kamal (2004) *Iran News*, 25 August.

―― (2005) *Iran News*, 20 January.

Khoda Bakhshi, Leila and Maryam Hosseini Nejad (1383) 'Baraye defa'e foghara', 'In defense of the poor'. Majalleh farhang va pazhouhesh, *Journal of Culture and Research*, 174 (8 Dey): 6.

Khonsari, Mehrdad (2005) 'News and the Views'. *Voice of America*, 30 April.

Kouhkan (2005) *Iran News*, 13 January.

Meibodi (2005a) 25 March, 2 PM, Iranian time.

―― (2005b) The News, Radio Israel, Farsi Service, 27 March.

Mottaghi, Ebrahim (2005) *Hamshahri-Diplomatic*, 41, 26 February.

Mousavi, Seyed Rasoul (2005) *Hamshahri-Diplomatic*, 41, 26 February.

News Media, Mid-April 2005.

New York Times, 12 March 2005

Palmer, Mark (2003) *Breaking the Real Axis of Evil: How to Oust the World's Last Dictators by 2025*, Lanham and Oxford: Rowman and Littlefield.

Pour Zand, Sa'eed (1379/2000) 'Brain Drainage'. *Iran's Daily*, 1581.

Pollack, Kenneth M. (No date) 'Tackling Iran'. *The Road Ahead: Middle East Policy in the Bush Administration's Second Term*, N/P, Saban Center for Middle East Policy at the Brookings Institution: 67-81.

Quds Daily (2005a) 23 January.

―― (2005b) 10 March.

―― (2005c) 20 April.

―― (2005d) 21 April.

―― (2005e) 3 May.

Rabi'ee, AliZandeh bad fesad/Viva Corruption, Tehran: Ministry of Culture and Islamic Guidance, 1380/2001).

Rafi'ee, Ehsan, 'Baresi 2 didgah dar bareh mobareze ba mavadde mokhadder bar amniayate mell'i/Classwork Research for MA the National Security of Iran, Tehran: Tehran University, First Semester, 2004-5.

Rafsanjani (2004) *Hamshahri*, 7 August.

―― (2005) 7 PM News, IRIB, Iran, 29 April.

Reza Reza'ee, Hamid (2005) *Sobhe Eqtesad*, 6 January.

Rice, Condoleezza (2005) *New York Times*, 12 March.

Rowhani (2005) *Quds Daily* and *Donyaye Eqtesad*, 1 May.

Salehi, Ali Akbar (2004) 'Iran's Nuclear Issue'. Presented at the Center for Scientific Research and Middle East Strategic Studies, Tehran, Iran, 31 December.

Sarvari, Davoud (2004-2005) *Rouspi-gari va asib-paziriye prestige melli*/Prostitution and Its Devastating Impacts on National Prestige. An MA Research thesis submitted for the Seminar on Iran's National Security, Faculty of Law and Political Science, Tehran University, First Semester.

Seifzadeh, Hossein, (1378/1999) *Ossul Ravabet Bein-al-melal*/Introduction to International Relations, Tehran: Mizan.

——— (1379/2000) *Modernite va Nazariate Jadid-e Elme Syast*/Modernity and New Theories of Political Science, Tehran: Dadgostar.

——— (1382/2003) *Tarhe tahqiqatiye char-choube mafhoumi strategy-pardazi dar syaste khareji Iran*/The Conceptual Framework for Formulating Strategy Foreign Policy in Iran: A Scientific Research. Tehran: markaze motale'ate strategic/Center for Strategic Studies.

Sobhe Eqtesad (2005a) 6 January: 16.

——— (2005b) 1 May.

——— (2005c) 3 May.

Tabataba'ee, Seyed (1373/1984) *Javad zaval-e Andishe*/Decadence of Political Thought in Iran, Tehran: Kavir.

——— (1382/2003) *Dibache'ee bar Nazarieh enhetat dar Iran*/A Preface to the Theory on Decadence of Iran, Tehran: Negah Mo'asser.

Taghavi, Mehdi, (1378/1999) 'Iran's Negligible Share of Foreign Investment', *Akhbar Eqtesadi*, 12 Mehr /October.

Takeyh, Ray (2003) 'Iran at a Crossroad'. *The Middle East Journal*, 57:1: 42-57.

Voghofi, Hassan (1380/2001) *The Emigration of Intellectuals: farar-e maghzha: bar-resi-ye-Mohajerate Nokhbegan az Zavaya-ye gounagon*/A Survey of the Elite's Emigration from Various Aspects, Tehran: Entesharate Zohd.

Voice of America (2005a) 'News and Views'. 21 April, 8.30 PM, Iran time.

——— (2205b) 'News and Views'. 29 April, 8.30 PM, Iran time.

In: Asia-Pacific and a New International Order
Editors: Purnendra Jain et al. pp. 267-283
ISBN 1-59454-986-9
© 2006 Nova Science Publishers, Inc.

Chapter 18

BACK TO THE FUTURE: A 'COLONIAL' AUSTRALIA IN THE 21ST CENTURY?

John Bruni

AUSTRALIA AND THE WORLD

Australia is the largest South Pacific power but one of the smallest western powers in terms of its actual military and diplomatic strength. Euphemistically called a 'middle power', Australia prides itself on being able to 'punch above its weight' in international fora. Much of the country's reputed strength is said to come from the special relationship it shares with the United States, the world's leading military and economic power. Australian politicians and policymakers are generally held in high regard within Washington. Australia's strong strategic, economic and cultural ties to the United States have bound Canberra's decisionmakers extremely close to prevailing American international policy and outcomes. This is considered by many within Australia's political elite to be a critical element of the country's continuing stability, prosperity and security (Brown, 1989: 121).

It is because of this special relationship that Australia shares with the United States that other countries which do not enjoy such good relations with Washington, are encouraged to use Australia as a back channel to the US (Downer, 1999). This gives Australia a unique niche capability that can value add to American diplomatic initiatives, especially when dealing with such states as the People's Republic of China (PRC), the Democratic People's Republic of Korea (DPRK) and Iran. As a result, Australia's foreign relations are largely premised on making the country an indispensable player in preserving US power globally, and more specifically, in the Asia-Pacific region. Indeed, in this light Australia can be viewed as an agent of order—one that touts a very conservative line, especially in matters concerning the maintenance of American strategic primacy. This posture is largely held by both of Australia's major political parties. Quite possibly, Australia feels itself unable or unwilling to live in a world where the United States is not the cornerstone of contemporary international relations. Hypothetically, were such a time to eventuate, Australia's role as handmaiden to the US in a non-Anglo dominated international or regional order might not carry the same advantages as it does today. Also, such a scenario would threaten all that Australia's geopolitical certainty has been built on over the past half-century. Arguably, fear of this scenario eventuating is what drives Canberra's conservative, generally bipartisan, pro-American foreign policy agenda (Renouf, 1979). This, of course, does not mean that Canberra excludes all that is non-American in origin. Australia has made great strides toward linking itself to the economies of Asia. However, Australia is a liminal country, caught betwixt and between its Anglo/European heritage and its desire to tap into the wealth that today's Asian economies represent (Higgott and Nossal, 1997: 1-9). It is caught between its desire to act in support of American geostrategic objectives, while finding it hard to empathise with regional countries that see Australia as no more than an extension of US power in the Southwest Pacific—regional countries that do not share America's worldview in its entirety. Australia's diplomatic balancing act between pleasing the overwhelming strategic power of the US and placating the significant trading power of the Asian economies makes for an uncomfortable mix. For in the pursuit to please one power, namely the US, Canberra's political elite runs the risk of offending the political elites in many important Asia-Pacific capitals.

This paper will explore how Australia has adapted to unfolding strategic and international relations in the Asia-Pacific since 9/11.

PARADIGM SHIFT

If the Hawke–Keating governments were dominated by such issues as international and regional multilateralism, integrating Australia with Asia, UN peacekeeping missions, Aboriginal reconciliation and republicanism, since 1996 the Howard government spent most of its time repudiating much of the Hawke-Keating political legacy. It redirected Australian foreign policy away from multilateral institutions such as Asia Pacific Economic Cooperation (APEC), back towards building strong bilateral networks as evidenced by the current government's development of bilateral free trade agreements: Australia-Singapore (2003); Australia-Thailand (2003); Australia-US (2004); and others currently being considered with Japan, China, Malaysia and the Association of Southeast Asian Nations (ASEAN). It moved away from Keating's ambition to integrate Australia with Asia, especially after the 1997 Asian economic collapse. It re-emphasised what was already a constant feature in Australian foreign policy considerations—the Australia-US relationship. It de-emphasised UN peacekeeping missions, replacing them with a more robust peace enforcement role, as witnessed during Australia's involvement with East Timor in 1999. With the exception of the Australia, New Zealand and US (ANZUS) Treaty, by 2000 Australia's broader foreign and strategic policy positions were far removed from what Hawke and Keating had set in train at the declaratory level. The relatively insular Defence of Australia doctrine under Hawke was diluted by Keating to include active participation in post-Cold War UN peacekeeping and a Regional Engagement policy; but by 2000 these concepts were swept aside by Howard. When the *Bulletin* magazine interviewed John Howard in September 1999 on the state of Australia's defences, journalist Fred Brenchley misquoted him by suggesting that Australia would be the regional 'Deputy Sheriff' to the United States. Unfortunately for the Prime Minister, this tag stuck and many regional capitals baulked at the idea. Salim Said, an Indonesian political analyst, captured the prevailing regional mood when he stated:

> Howard is like a 19th-century European standing on a beach and thinking he will have to watch out for the little brown uncivilised neighbours that lie to the north. (Sheridan, 1999: 2)

Many scholars and commentators within Australia and abroad argued that the rise of political maverick Pauline Hanson, with her homespun philosophies on Asian immigration and multiculturalism (and Howard's apparent subtle alignment with her ideas), contributed to Australia's tarnished regional reputation. However, Hugh White contends that other less prosaic forces were also at play. He maintains that Australia's regional engagement was slowing down largely as a consequence of Asia still refusing to accept the country as a formalised member of the region, in spite of the inroads made by former Prime Minister Keating (White, 2003: 2). White argues that Australian policymakers were disappointed by this apparent 'wasted effort', and, coupled with the Asian economic collapse and the poor performance of the Japanese economy, the Asian region was no longer considered the miracle onto which Australia should hitch its star (White, 2003: 2).

The election of George W. Bush to the presidency of the US in November 2000 gave Howard the chance he needed to overtly realign Australia's foreign and strategic policies with Washington's. This of course was nothing new. Even during Keating's most adamant 'pro-Asia period' there was no talk of reneging the country's security ties to the US in favour of adopting similar ties to any Asian nation (Henderson, 2004). Indeed, the Hawke/Keating relationship with the US was characterised by its attempt to understand the limits of American engagement with the Asia-Pacific, and make the case for its continuing relevance to the region as a strategic stabiliser, especially following the end of the Cold War (Firth, 1999: 35-40). While Howard enjoyed reasonable relations with the Clinton administration, President Clinton and Prime Minister Howard were not ideological compatriots (White, 2003: 2-3). Howard never forgot the lukewarm support Clinton gave him during the East Timor crisis of 1999, when the burden of intervention fell on Canberra and included the possible risk of war with Indonesia. The election of Bush, however, gave Howard hope that the new administration in Washington would be more ideologically similar to his own conservative worldview. As it turned out, Howard could not want for a better US President (White, 2003: 3-4). Bush was not only conservative, but he also shared an interest in rekindling closer ties to traditional 'Anglo' US security partners—the UK and Australia.

'AUSTRALIA AS DEPUTY SHERIFF'—THE WAR ON TERROR

The first three months of the new Bush administration were reasonably uncontroversial until the EP-3 Spy Plane Incident of April 2001. The emergency landing of the American surveillance plane on Hainan Island following its collision with an intercepting Chinese fighter led to a renewed period of Sino-American tension. The death of the Chinese pilot during this incident, as well as the EP-3's internment (and the aircraft's crew) by Chinese authorities, signified the worst downturn of Sino-American relations since the 1995-96 Chinese ballistic missile tests off Taiwan. While deft diplomacy on both sides of the Pacific saw this crisis pass, policymakers in Canberra were faced with the prospect that, should war eventuate between the US and the PRC, Australia, as a close American security partner, might be called upon to deploy its forces in support of those of the United States. Such a prospect was an uncomfortable one, since Australia had expended much effort over the preceding years courting the favour of Beijing as a trading partner.

But by August 2001, the security situation began to change. Publicly, China was put on the back burner. Now the immediate threat to national security came from refugees and people smugglers (DIMIA, 2003) and reached a crescendo over Australia's handling of the Tampa incident when a Norwegian container ship picked up over 400 asylum seekers from a stranded Indonesian fishing boat and sought their disembarkation on Australian territory. With a federal election scheduled for November, the Tampa issue focused the Howard government's attention. Howard's muscular posturing against the asylum seekers proved popular with the Australian electorate. But then the following month, while Howard was in Washington celebrating the fiftieth anniversary of the signing of the ANZUS Treaty, Al Qaeda terrorists attacked the World Trade Centre and the Pentagon with four hijacked aircraft, killing some 3,500 people. Three days later, Howard, as a measure of his country's support for the US in their fight against terrorism, invoked the ANZUS Treaty for the first time since the treaty's inception (White, 2003: 3). Upon his return to Australia, Howard continued his tough line against asylum seekers. While only inferring this sentiment, during his election campaign much was made of the fact that most of the asylum seekers came from Muslim countries—especially Afghanistan, Iraq and Iran, states known for actively supporting terrorism. The external threat of Al Qaeda was blended into the alleged Fifth Column 'internal threat' posed by asylum seekers (Taylor, 2003). On 7 October President Bush ordered the commencement of Operation Enduring Freedom; ten days later Howard deployed 1,550 Australian Defence Force (ADF) personnel to Afghanistan to help dethrone the Taliban regime that had aided and abetted Al Qaeda's terrorist offensive against the US. As a result of this confluence of events, Howard won the 2001 election. But regionally, Muslim Southeast Asia was becoming wary of the rabid and shrill way western countries were treating Muslim people and the religion of Islam.

Immediately following the 9/11 attacks, the west, but more particularly America and its closest allies, were on guard for when and where the next catastrophic terrorist attack would happen. On 12 October 2002, 88 Australians were killed in Bali, along with 114 others. This attack was the initiative of Al Qaeda's Southeast Asian ally, Jemmah Islamiyah (JI). Unlike the United States, which had the luxury of being able to use military force to oust the Taliban regime from power, Australia had no such options to use against Indonesia. The Indonesian government was not complicit in supporting JI in its attack on the Kuta nightclub, and furthermore, Australian military and federal policing authorities could not take unilateral action against JI without the cooperation of the Indonesian government. While the Sukarnoputri government was very cool toward Canberra because of its involvement in the liberation of East Timor from Indonesian rule, Jakarta, sensing that an unrestrained JI terrorist campaign would be as much of a threat to Indonesia as to Australia, acquiesced to cooperate with Australia in tracking down and prosecuting the Bali bombers. The Bali bombing focused Australia's security priorities on the stability of the Indonesian government and that government's ability to reign in JI. However, complicating events was the Bush administration's renewed focus on Iraq and that country's alleged possession of Weapons of Mass Destruction (WMD), which according to Washington, fell within the ambit of the broader War on Terror being waged against Osama bin Laden and his international terrorist network (Hersh, 2004: 163-201).

The Howard government's open support for the Bush administration's theories on the complicity of Iraq in the 9/11 event and the country's apparent violations of UN Security Council Resolutions banning Baghdad's acquisition and stockpiling of WMDs, rapidly saw the central focus of the War on Terror shift from Afghanistan and Pakistan to Iraq. For Australia this meant that while Southeast Asian-based Muslim terrorism was still considered a priority, in order to assist in fighting the War on Terror the way the White House interpreted it, it was a given that its forces would eventually be called upon to back Bush's international coalition against Saddam Hussein.

America's lead-up to war against Iraq in 2002 deeply divided the international community. Many in the Muslim world who tacitly backed Washington's war against the Taliban and Al Qaeda, could see no connection between Saddam Hussein and Osama bin Laden. The manner in which Muslims were treated around the world following the 9/11 event led to a heightened sense of victimisation and many Muslims saw America's war against Iraq as further evidence of a Bush-led anti-Muslim crusade (Ali, 2003).

Led by Malaysian Prime Minister Mahathir Mohamad and quietly backed by segments of Indonesia's anti-Australian nationalist clique, the old rhetorical phrase 'Deputy Sheriff' came back to haunt the Australian Prime Minister. Making the situation worse was Howard's own reaction to these taunts and criticisms. Rather than dismissing these claims, he played up to them. In December 2002, his public proclamation of a military policy of pre-emptive strikes against any regional threat to Australia inflamed negative opinion throughout Southeast Asia. Malaysia, Thailand, the Philippines and Indonesia all saw Howard's comments as a potential threat to their collective sovereignties—Indonesia being especially sensitive, given Australia's role in separating East Timor from the archipelagic state (Baker, 1999; Viviani, 2000). At a news conference repudiating Howard's pre-emptive strike doctrine, Malaysian Foreign Minister Sayed Hamid Albar was quoted as saying: 'I think Australia must think they are a big power. They are talking the language of a big power anyway' (Xinhua News Agency, 2002).

When Howard formally acceded to become a member of Bush's Coalition of the Willing in February 2003, the only Asian 'friend' he had was Japanese Prime Minister Koizumi. Japan is largely 'American-centric' in its international outlook. While the country's post-war Peace Constitution forbids Tokyo to deploy its military forces in situations short of direct attack on Japanese territory, Japan, since the end of World War II, served as an indispensable base for American military operations throughout Northeast Asia. Also, Prime Minister Koizumi's political agenda is to see Japan as less of an economic power and more of a 'normal' power, and the prevailing international climate indicated opportunities for him to extend Japan's role in this capacity. Japan, like Australia, served as a loyal and important American ally in the Western Pacific and the country has begun to make inroads toward deploying Japanese Self Defense Force (JSDF) non-combat personnel to act in support of American anti-terrorist operations.

The other great Asian power, China, while generally supportive of American efforts, and by extension Australian efforts to fight Muslim terrorists immediately following 9/11, was no supporter of the war on Iraq. It was believed that war would disrupt access to Iraqi oil supplies where the PRC had received lucrative drilling concessions under Saddam Hussein, thereby possibly threatening the continued growth of China's economy (Renner, 2003; Gertz, 2004).

Australia and Asia Since the Fall of Saddam

For most of 2003-04, the continuing Iraqi insurgency since the fall of Saddam had frozen in place the sometimes hostile but often cool relationship between Australia and most of Southeast Asia. However, September 2004 saw another paradigm shift in Australia's relationship with at least one key regional country—Indonesia.

The alleged JI bombing of the Australian Embassy in Jakarta redoubled Australian-Indonesian cooperative efforts at fighting Indonesia-based terrorist groups. The excellent working relationship between the Australian Federal Police and Indonesian internal security continued and matured in spite of the frosty relations between the Howard and Sukarnoputri governments (Cotan, 2005). By 20 September 2004, however, Sukarnoputri was defeated in Indonesia's second presidential run-off by her rival, Susilo Bambang Yudhoyono. Yudhoyono assumed office on the promise to crack down on JI terrorists and their supporters; defeat Acehnese and West Papuan separatists; and improve the country's strained relationship with the west, particularly Australia. This development was welcomed by Canberra since it signalled that a friendly Indonesia could help Australia carve out a better position for itself in regional forums especially in relation to ASEAN and the proposed 2005 East Asia Summit (the East Asia Summit wasseen as a potential precursor to the development of a new regional trading bloc, exclusively comprising East Asian countries). Australia's relationship with Indonesia reached another milestone following the tragic Asian Tsunami (28 December 2004) which devastated Indonesia's troubled province of Aceh and other parts of South/Southeast Asia. Howard quickly announced the delivery of a massive aid package to Jakarta and dispatched elements of the ADF to help in the delivery of humanitarian assistance to survivors. Yudhoyono, in a very public display, demonstrated his appreciation for Australia's commitment to the rehabilitation of Aceh by warmly embracing Howard during his visit to Jakarta in early January 2005.

In another sign of Howard's gradual acceptance as a serious player in Asia, Malaysian Prime Minister Abdullah Badawi, who succeeded Mahathir in October 2003, visited Australia. This was the first time a Malaysian Prime Minister had visited Australia in over 20 years. However, there was a sting in the tail for Australia in this visit. While Badawi is not as caustic in his criticism of Australia as his predecessor, he is still cautious in his acceptance of Australia as a formal member of any Asian multilateral agreement. Badawi's main problem with Australia was its refusal to sign the Treaty of Amity and Cooperation (TAC) that had been signed by all the members of the ASEAN group of countries. The countries that had signed the TAC, or indicated a willingness to sign, were: China, Japan, India, Russia, South Korea and Pakistan (Kevin, 2004). This treaty asks of its members to abide by ASEAN's central tenet of non-interference in each other's internal affairs and to repudiate military pre-emption—something that Howard was loathe to do, since he believed this would unnecessarily limit Australia's foreign policy options, especially when dealing with the threat of regional-based terrorism (Howard, 2004). For some Southeast Asian countries, most notably Malaysia and the Philippines, Australia's signature to the TAC was considered a prerequisite for Australia's entry to the East Asia Summit (HarakahDaily.Net, 2005). Howard knew he could count on the support of Japan and Indonesia to lobby for Australia's inclusion in the summit. A seat at the East Asia Summit would position Australia well in its pursuit of other cooperative regional ventures, especially its possible inclusion within a new, formalised regional economic bloc. This important foreign policy issue and its ultimate outcome will determine whether Australia remains a nominal player in Asia or becomes a more significant, accepted partner in the region. With New Zealand as a TAC signatory from 13 April 2005, added pressure was placed on Howard to demonstrate his flexibility on this matter. Howard finally acceded to signing the TAC in July 2005, with the Treaty tabled in parliament on 9 August, its official ratification took place on December 2005, prior to the East Asian Summit in Kuala Lumpur onthe fourteenth of that month.

THE SOUTH PACIFIC

Australia's role in the South Pacific has been one fraught with difficulties. As a British dominion, albeit largely self-governing from the latter part of the nineteenth to the mid twentieth century, Australia is considered both an extension of British colonialism and culture by its South Pacific neighbours. During the late 1800s to mid-1900s Australia was not averse to racially caricaturing its neighbours, whether they were of Asian, Melanesian or Polynesian origin. 'White Australia' was all about protecting the fledgling, demographically diminutive and scattered European (predominantly British) settlements from the infiltration and 'corruption' of exotic cultures, or worse, their total annihilation through invasion or interbreeding (*Illustrated History of Australia*, 1979). While the Melanesian and Polynesian communities of the South Pacific were no major threat to Australia, the importation of Kanaka (Melanesian) labour into Queensland during the nineteenth century to work the colony's sugar and cotton plantations, was at the time thought to threaten to dilute the colony's British 'racial purity' (Jupp, 1988: 722-727).

Most of the South Pacific islands were under some form of colonial administration (predominantly British or French) until the 1950s. During that decade, the global phenomenon of decolonisation was liberating many people from former colonial bondage, but unlike many other areas of the world that were experiencing this phenomenon, the South Pacific suffered from a number of major handicaps. The nation-states of the South Pacific were geographically and demographically small. As European colonies, collectively, they were the least developed colonial real estate in the world. They had the least infrastructure and education, and consequently possessed the least knowledge of modern nationalism and how this quintessentially European political concept could serve them once their colonial masters set them free.

The South Pacific has undergone a number of major transformations over the past 100 years. It was a plaything of European colonial powers, a battleground against Japanese expansionism and militarism during World War II, an American strategic 'lake' during the Cold War against the Soviet Union, as well as a testing ground for American and French nuclear weapons. In and of itself, the South Pacific has at various times been coveted for its maritime resources and its strategic usefulness, but as a region, the South Pacific has always been considered somewhat of a backwater in international relations. The region is deemed important only when large powers duel among themselves, but it has never been considered important as a centre of international prominence based on its own political and social strengths. Consequently, the region has been and remains of marginal interest, continuously overshadowed by larger economies, more pressing international political disputes and strategic contests. South Pacific island-states are distant from each other and separated from key global markets and centres of trade by thousands of nautical miles; with relatively small populations, largely subsistence economies and poor infrastructure, they are dependent on the region's two major powers, Australia and New Zealand, to provide aid, trade, education and investment opportunities (AusAID, 2002). Indeed, Australia in particular regards the South Pacific as its 'backyard' (Mercer, 2003). The international community looks to Australia to ensure that the South Pacific remains a benign zone free from significant great power competition, internal political instability, civil turmoil and ethnic unrest. Arguably, Australia's greatest contribution to ensure that the South Pacific remains 'pacific' in nature as well as in name, is military intervention. Australian military forces can be deployed quickly to trouble spots within the South Pacific. This can have an almost instant effect on local crises. But with this comes the temptation to view the South Pacific as no more than an area of potentially costly and perhaps even open-ended military engagements—an 'arc of instability' (O'Keefe, 2003: 517-539). While military force can shock and awe local combatants into a short-term ceasefire, long-term solutions to ethnic conflict, and conflict over land and resources, demand political resolutions. Therein lies the problem for Australia. As a peacekeeper, just by using military wherewithal to resolve a local dispute, Australia can ignore or sidestep the complex tribal interactions that constitute most politics in the South Pacific region. Tribal politics is complex for a variety of reasons, but especially because there is no single 'type' from which Australian policymakers can draw inferences and impose their determinations. Indeed, many subtle local variations on tribal lore exist throughout the Melanesian, Micronesian and Polynesian islands. But since Australia considers itself a power with global rather than solely regional interests, it is questionable whether enough resources are, or have ever been, put into an extensive anthropological understanding of these nuances. As Australia is the South Pacific's native hegemon, Australian policymakers given the responsibility of maintaining the country's interests in the South Pacific need more than a cursory understanding of regional dynamics. But extra-regional events—such as the War on Terror, Iraq, the Middle East Peace Process, global trade and the demands and expectations of the ANZUS Treaty—each in their own way divert Australia's attention away from South Pacific affairs.

HOWARD'S INTERVENTIONIST STREAK

Interestingly, it has been under the Howard government that the South Pacific re-emerged as a foreign policy priority. During the Hawke/Keating years, Foreign Minister Gareth Evans' main concern was to keep the South Pacific from being subverted or tempted by Soviet interests or economic offers (Albinski, 1990). Australia's national *and* regional interests were served by ensuring that the South Pacific remained an area of undisputed western strategic dominance. This meant that US military aircraft, warships and submarines could traverse the length and breadth of the Pacific without the shadowing of South Pacific-based Soviet aircraft and vessels. While in hindsight there was little to fear from such a challenge emerging, Cold War considerations underwrote most security-related concerns, even during the era of Perestroika and Glasnost under Soviet reformer Mikhail Gorbachev. Furthermore, there were developments during the latter part of the Cold War that demonstrated the region's potential vulnerability to Soviet penetration: New Zealand Prime Minister David Lange's ban on the visitation of nuclear armed or powered US Navy ships (1984); ongoing political instability in Papua New Guinea (especially post-1984); and the attempted Libyan intervention in Vanuatu and New Caledonia (mid to late 1980s) (Hegarty, 1990: 424-425). Though technically non-aligned, during the 1980s Libya was strengthening its ties to the USSR, especially in terms of acquiring Soviet weapons *and* pursuing intelligence cooperation, as stated by St. John (1987) and El Warfally (1988). Further to these strategic feints were the attempts by the USSR to gain fishing agreements with Kiribati and Vanuatu during the mid 1980s. Each of these Soviet or 'Soviet proxy' attempts to infiltrate the South Pacific were low risk, high gain operations. Had they succeeded, Moscow would have gained a significant diplomatic or economic coup in an area considered exclusively an American strategic domain. But Russian policymakers were not about to strongly contest American power in this region, so the likelihood of the South Pacific becoming a new cockpit of superpower conflict remained low. During this period, Australia was also actively supporting many South Pacific states with levels of aid that could not be matched by the Soviets, who had their own dire economic circumstances in the mid to late 1980s to solve. Superimposed onto this Cold War dynamic during the late 1980s were other more localised and yet disturbing conflicts, such as the 1987 Fiji coups and the growing separatist insurgency on Bougainville (1989-98).

Nonetheless, with the end of the Cold War in 1991 and the collapse of the USSR the following year, the key security driver that formed much of Australia's South Pacific policy no longer existed. With the exception of Papua New Guinea, the largest of the South Pacific states, the region was relegated to a more marginalised position within Australian foreign policy considerations (Caritas Australia, 2003: 1).

However, by the time John Howard became prime minister, international events changed rapidly. Like most western countries, Australia too struggled to come to terms with the post-Cold War environment. Prior to 1996, most policy analysts and political leaders placed much of their faith in the concept of an Asia-Pacific Century emerging, where the major economies of East Asia would transform continental and Pacific Asia into an economic hub to rival and perhaps even surpass the United States and the European Union (EU). This was a faith that Howard did not share. He believed that Australia could and should divest its main focus away from Asia by linking Australia's economy to the traditional markets of Europe, while simultaneously reinvigorating the country's economic and strategic relationship with the United States, relations that were allegedly allowed to whither under the Keating prime ministership (Henderson, 2005). Howard's belief was reinforced by the catastrophe of the Asian Economic Meltdown of 1997.

BOUGAINVILLE

During this time Australia's main concern in the South Pacific revolved around the increasingly bloody and intractable Bougainville separatist crisis in Papua New Guinea (PNG). The main problem the secessionists posed for both PNG and Australia was that, had they succeeded in withdrawing from PNG, they would have set a precedent for other tribal groups desiring independence. This possibility could have destroyed Papua New Guinea, complicated already strained relations between Indonesia and Australia and certainly complicated Australia's strategic neighbourhood considerably. The Chan government's clumsy attempt at bringing the separatist crisis to an end by hiring South African-based mercenaries in 1997 (the Sandline Affair) not only brought down that government, but also signalled that Australia should be more proactive in the activities of its fragile northern neighbour. As a result, the Howard government redoubled its diplomatic efforts to bring the separatist crisis to an end. In 1998, a ceasefire (brokered by Canberra) was struck between the Bougainville Revolutionary Army and Papua New Guinea Defence Force (PNGDF). This finally brought an end to the fighting. A Truce Monitoring Group was deployed to maintain the ceasefire, which was followed by a multinational Peace Monitoring Group. The peace agreement between Bougainville and PNG (signed in Arawa in 2001) saw Port Moresby grant significant autonomy to Bougainville, and a pledge to allow Bougainville to reconsider its status within PNG after a 10-15 year period (Bougainville Peace Agreement, 2001).

East Timor

Almost a year after the resolution of the Bougainville crisis, another major incident erupted on Australia's doorstep—East Timor. This long-simmering problem had been the *bête noire* of Indonesian-Australian relations since the Portuguese colony's annexation by Indonesia in 1975. Australia was not in a position to thwart the Indonesian invasion of the colony at that time because it was involved with its own painful withdrawal from Vietnam, and intervening in Indonesia's actions may have sparked a major war. As a result, Australia made an uneasy peace with the Suharto government by giving it *de jure* recognition of Indonesia's sovereignty over East Timor. This in spite of the fact that many East Timorese continued to resist integration with Indonesia through guerrilla action. The guerrilla war by pro-independence FRETELIN fighters against the Indonesian Army (TNI) was one of the most vicious counter-insurgency campaigns in recent times; but for the most part, except for some international condemnation usually prompted by the Portuguese government, the Catholic Church and human rights groups, no international organisation or group of states made any serious attempt to force Jakarta from this territory. Australia's position was made all the more difficult since it shared a deep connexion to the people of East Timor for their help in fighting the Japanese during World War II. Australia also stood as a 'champion' of international human rights, and understood that its security was intimately tied to the stability of the Indonesian state.

In 1997, the Asian Economic Meltdown hit Indonesia hard. No longer considered an emerging Asian Tiger economy, political instability wracked the archipelago, opening new opportunities and posing new challenges. Suharto had promised so much in terms of economic development, but his inability to reign in Indonesian debt and institute economic reforms spelt the end of his 32 years of dictatorship in 1998. His successor, the mercurial President B.J. Habibie, tried to show the world his 'democratic' and 'reformist' impulses, but in doing so demonstrated to the Indonesian political elite and public his indecisiveness and weakness. In January 1999, Habibie indicated his willingness to allow the long-suffering East Timorese to vote on their future status—either autonomy within Indonesia or independence. The referendum, conducted under UN auspices in August 1999, quickly spiralled out of control. While the poll indicated that 78 per cent of East Timorese were in favour of independence, pro-integrationist militias began a violent rampage (in which the Indonesian military and police were complicit by their inaction to check this violence). Some 1,500 pro-independence East Timorese were said to have been killed by pro-integrationist militias aided and abetted by the TNI. Another 300,000 were forcibly removed to West Timor. Pressure from the international community forced Habibie into accepting a peacekeeping force led by Australia. The subsequent deployment of Australian Defence Force personnel was the largest of its type since Vietnam. For many Indonesians it was a provocative action and Australian-Indonesian relations plummeted.

In both the Bougainville and East Timor instances, South Pacific leaders viewed the Australian interventions positively (in the case of Bougainville, Australia's intervention ended a debilitating conflict and stabilised the island. In the case of East Timor, Australia's intervention liberated an Islander population from oppressive Indonesian rule). These interventions showed sensitivity to South Pacific concerns and Australia's willingness to shoulder the burden of regional security and stability. Importantly, these Australian interventions demonstrated that the South Pacific would not be left on the margins.

PACIFIC SOLUTION

In the prelude to the September 11 attacks on the United States, Australia was caught up in a new kind of security crisis—refugees. From 1999 onwards, Australian immigration authorities noted a marked increase in illegal immigration. Refugees, primarily from Afghanistan and Iraq, were entering Australia by boat, many of them on false or no documentation. This crisis reached a flashpoint with the Tampa incident of August 2001. As this was an election year, Prime Minister Howard made much political capital by playing on the vulnerabilities of 'border security'. Immediately after September 11, Howard's message became all the more vitriolic as illegal immigrants (many from Muslim backgrounds) came to be seen as a potential security threat. Yet, although the number of entries were growing, they were nowhere near the tens of thousands who enter EU countries or the US annually. Nonetheless, Howard mobilised a 'whole of government approach' to tackle this issue in order to deter illegal immigrants from reaching Australia. As part of this strategy, the Howard government came up with the 'Pacific Solution' (Maclellan, 2002: 12-13). This plan was for illegal immigrants to be processed offshore so that it would be harder for them to claim legitimate refugee status in Australia. The Pacific Solution entailed giving extra financial inducements to South Pacific governments who accepted Australian detention/processing centres. Since many island-state economies were barely functional, the assumption was that the Pacific Solution would not be a major diplomatic problem. Australian detention/processing centres were accepted and built on Manus Island in PNG and in Nauru. Void of western comforts, their isolation and inhospitable tropical surrounds stood as a testimony of Howard's tough message. But as international condemnation by human rights groups and the UN became more vocal in 2002, Australian 'financial inducements' did not make up for the fact that the South Pacific gained the reputation of being a dumping ground for refugees, a convenient Australian 'black hole' where Canberra could bury its problems. In 2002 President Rene Harris of Nauru publicly began to voice his own unease at hosting these 'temporary facilities' when he declared that Australia was motivated by self-interest and had no real regard in promoting the dignity and development of Pacific states (Maclellan, 2002: 12).

In 2004, the last detainee on Manus Island, Aladdin Sisalem, was released and allowed to settle in Australia. However, in spite of its 'offending' presence, the Australian detention facility in Nauru has remained part of Australia's Pacific Solution (as at 2005), holding some 32 asylum seekers.

THE SOLOMON ISLANDS

In July 2003, Australia led a multinational intervention force into the Solomon Islands, ostensibly to end the spiral of ethnic conflict between the local Malaitan and Guadacanalese islanders. This ambitious intervention saw the deployment of some 2,000 soldiers and police personnel who were given the task of imposing a peace settlement on the conflicting militias and to disarm the combatants. The operation was largely successful; however, it came at the cost of supporting the Solomon Islander government led by Prime Minister Sir Allan Kemakeza who, prior to the deployment of the Regional Assistance Mission to Solomon Islands (RAMSI), was considered part of the broader political problem due to his known links to corruption. However, in order to gain the cooperation of Honiara for the RAMSI intervention, the Australian government largely overlooked Kemakeza's allegedly 'suspect' political background. From being part of the problem of the Solomon Islands, Kemakeza was transformed into part of the solution. This short-term 'accommodation', however, may have long-term political implications. For example, while the Australian government might indeed be aware of the problems of poor governance among the island-states of the South Pacific, the contemporary governing elites and their supporters remain important collaborative partners for any peacekeeping venture to be considered successful. Kemakeza's 'invitation' to the Australian-led military intervention was a necessary prerequisite to gain the regional and international legitimacy needed to deploy the RAMSI force (it is standard international practice for peacekeepers to be invited into a country by the host government). No Australian government would risk unilateral intervention in a civil war, no matter how potentially destabilising, without that government's explicit permission—even that of a 'corrupt' government. However, the obvious down side to this is that it reinforces the view that the region's contemporary political systems and their leaders cannot easily be brought to account for their alleged misdeeds, since it will never be known whether they might prove to be useful partners in stemming the tide of ethnic conflict or other forms of civil unrest. This is a mutually reinforcing cycle. But dealing with corrupt governments in this way only serves to legitimise them, doing nothing to encourage any modification of their political behaviour.

PAPUAN INTERVENTION

In Papua New Guinea in early 2004, the Howard government began to implement a far-reaching aid package (the Enhanced Cooperation Program [ECP]) directly aimed at restructuring the nature and character of this South Pacific country. By tying aid to the PNG government's cooperation, Australian public service personnel were installed in critically important bureaucratic positions. This was done in the hope of improving the ability of national authorities to service their communities, stem corruption in Port Moresby political circles and improve the overall efficiency and effectiveness of PNG's entire governing structure (Downer, 2004). While this may indeed be seen as a bold political experiment, PNG and other South Pacific critics contend that this form of intervention smacks of neo-colonialism. Problems with the ECP came to the surface in May 2005 when PNG Prime Minister Michael Somare, himself a critic of the terms and conditions of the ECP's brief, encouraged a PNG Supreme Court challenge to an Australian condition—namely that Australian Federal Police (AFP) personnel deployed to PNG as part of the aid package would be immune from prosecution under PNG law. This legal challenge threw the ECP into disarray, the aid package now being subject to a redraft taking PNG issues of sovereignty into account—ironically all this taking place during the thirtieth year since PNG's independence from Australia. At the time of writing (August 2005), elements of the ECP seem to have been salvaged. Thirty AFP personnel have returned to PNG to advise Port Moresby on anti-corruption issues and Canberra hopes that the remainder of the aid package can soon be implemented in its entirety.

Although the intent of the ECP initiative remains to assist and improve South Pacific governance, if such intrusive aid packages become templates for future Australian aid delivery into the South Pacific it leaves the question open as to when Australian public servants can actually leave South Pacific countries to their own devices. Using PNG as an example, if bad governance is an endemic part of post-colonial PNG, at what stage will Australia know when to disengage and let indigenous personnel take over? Hypothetically, if a worst case forecast is in a generation's time, can Australia, after 25 years of direct administrative support, withdraw from the country with confidence in PNG's governing institutions? Furthermore, what kind of precedent will this set for the South Pacific? Will it become a prelude to an 'insidious Australianisation' of selected South Pacific bureaucracies, and how will this be different from former colonial administrations, except perhaps in style?

THE SOUTH PACIFIC: FUTURE TENSE

During the term of the Howard government, the South Pacific has increasingly been perceived as important to Australia's broader security brief. The implementation of good governance is seen as a major milestone to reduce poverty, tribal/ethnic secessionism, political corruption and improvement in law and order. All this is ultimately viewed as a 'pre-emptive strike' against potentially worse scenarios that could include the collapse of South Pacific states, leading to interminable instability and potentially an even greater investment of Australian military and financial capital. However, this reshaping of unstable South Pacific states does come at a cost. As the region's hegemonic power and due to its own colonial past, Australia's initiatives, no matter how they are perceived in Canberra and sold to the Australian public, may not resonate the same way among South Pacific governments and communities, all of whom are keenly aware of and sensitive to their asymmetric relationship with Australia. Indeed, from a South Pacific perspective, it is easy to portray Australia as an overtly interfering neighbour guided solely by its own base political and strategic motives.

However, while 'benign neglect' guided much of Canberra's policy in relation to the South Pacific between the 1950s and 1980s, leaving the region to develop its contemporary post-colonial political and social character, returning to this policy is not considered a viable option by the Howard government. Indeed, it is widely believed that a return to 'benign neglect' would do no more than compound what, from Canberra's perspective, are unsustainable and undesirable regional outcomes. Combined with the Howard government's sensitivity to Australia's perceived vulnerability to Muslim-based radical terrorist organisations, a proliferation of 'broken-back states' in the South Pacific could form new terrorist sanctuaries from where Australian regional interests could be attacked (Fry, 2002).

The contemporary South Pacific forms part of what some Australian policymakers and strategic thinkers consider to be an 'arc of instability'. As such, it is difficult to view the region as anything other than an area for potential intervention—usually, but not exclusively, military intervention. Both Australia and the South Pacific are locked together in a problematic relationship, one that seems to encourage stereotypical views of each other: Australia as the region's self-interested 'big brother'; the South Pacific states as a collection of small, politically inconsequential and troublesome atolls and islands. Whether this relationship can evolve into something more remains to be seen.

In August 2003, the Howard government flagged the prospect of forming a 'Pacific Union' which would transform the otherwise disconnected Oceanic states into a European Union style framework (Commonwealth of Australia, Senate Foreign Affairs, Defence and Trade Committee, 2003). This proposal was circulated at the Pacific Islands Forum in Auckland, New Zealand (August 2003). It suggested that South Pacific states adopt the Australian dollar and that key governmental institutions be amalgamated to form the architecture of a supranational regional body. Furthermore, it proposed that a regional-based unit be set up to fight transnational crime and deter the establishment of terrorist cells and havens. There might have been an indisputable logic behind this proposal, since the states of the South Pacific have till now been unable to administer their aid budgets effectively. However, any such organisation would be almost completely dominated by Canberra. Curiously, after this concept was flagged, little was made of it in the public discourse on Australia's Pacific relations, suggesting high levels of dissatisfaction with the proposal. There is, however, some evidence that indicates that the Howard government has not entirely given up on the Pacific Union concept.

The South Pacific is changing. No longer is it simply the idyllic tourist destination where nothing much happens. As the largest power in the region, Australia has a duty to itself and to the wider international community to ensure the South Pacific's stability in the face of potential economic and state break down. Ultimately, how this is constituted will determine the shape and direction of future policy options and responses to crises.

REFERENCES

Albinski, H.S. (1990) 'The Superpowers in the Pacific'. In D. Ball and C. Downes (eds), *Security and Defence: Pacific and Global Perspectives*, Sydney: Allen and Unwin.

Ali, T. (2003) *The Clash of Fundamentalisms: Crusades, Jihads and Modernity*, London and New York: Verso.

AusAID (Australian Government) (2002) *Papua New Guinea and the South Pacific: Fragile Development Settings*, September, http://www.ausaid.gov.au/hottopics/pacific/settings.cfm

Baker, R.W. (1999) 'Indonesia-Australia: Relations Moving from Bad to Worse'. *Pacific Forum CSIS Comparative Connections: An E-Journal on East Asian Bilateral Relations*, 3rd Quarter 1(2), http://www.csis.org/pacfor/cc/993Qindo_aus.html

Bali Ministerial Conference on People Smuggling (2002) *Trafficking in Persons and Related Transnational Crime*, Co-Chair's Statement, 26-28 February, http://www.dfat.gov.au/illegal_immigration/cochair.html

Ball, D. and C. Downes (eds) (1990) *Security and Defence: Pacific and Global Perspectives*, Sydney: Allen and Unwin.

Brown, G. (1989) *Breaking the American Alliance: An Independent National Security Policy for Australia*, Canberra Papers on Strategy and Defence No. 54, Strategic and Defence Studies Centre, Australian National University, Canberra.

Bougainville Peace Agreement (2001) 30 August.

Burgess, M. (2004) 'Pacific Nations Push EU-Style Union'. Aljazeera.Net, 17 May, http://english.aljazeera.net/NR/exeres/2FE18E79-D1C0-4CA0-956D-C22024379829.htm

Caritas Australia (2003) *Policy Brief—Solomon Islands Intervention*, July.

Commonwealth of Australia (2003) *Advancing the National Interest*. Department of Foreign Affairs and Trade White Paper, National Capital Printing.

——— (2003) Senate Foreign Affairs, Defence and Trade Committee, *A Pacific Engaged: Australia's Relations with Papua New Guinea and the Island States of the Southwest Pacific*, 12 August, http://www.aph.gov.au/Senate/committee/fadt_ctte/completed_inquiries/2002-04/png/report/index.htm

——— (2003) *Proof Committee Hansard SENATE, Foreign Affairs, Defence and Trade References Committee*, Reference: Australia's Foreign Policy and Trade Strategy, 21 August.

Cotan, I. (2005) Indonesian Ambassador to Australia, *Address to the Royal United Services Institute of South Australia*, Keswick Barracks, 2 May.

Department of Immigration, Multiculturalism and Indigenous Affairs (DIMIA) (2003) *Fact Sheet 73: People Smuggling*, Revised 13 June, http://www.immi.gov.au/facts/73smuggling.htm

Downer, A. (1999) Presentation to the Australia-China Business Council, *Australia and China—Partners for Progress*, November.

El Warfally, M.G. (1988) *Imagery and Ideology in US Policy Toward Libya, 1969-1982*, Pittsburgh, PA: University of Pittsburgh Press.

Firth, S. (1999) *Australia in International Politics: An Introduction to Australian Foreign Policy*, St Leonards, NSW: Allen and Unwin.

Forbes, M. (2003) 'Howard Push for Pacific Union'. *The Age*, 18 August, http://www.theage.com.au/articles/2003/08/17/1061059717704.html

Fry, G. (2002) *South Pacific Security Environment After the 9.11 Terrorism*, Public Symposium on Asian Security Environment After the 9.11 Terrorism, 18 December, Tokyo, http://www.rieti.go.jp/en/events/02121801/pdf/Fry.pdf

Gertz, B. (2004) 'Saddam Bribed China with Oil Deals CIA Finds'. *Washington Times*, 12 October, http://www.washtimes.com/national/20041011-115320-2205r.htm

HarakahDaily.Net (2005) 'Malaysia, Australia Talk Trade but Fail to Bridge Key Security Differences', 7 April, http://harakahdaily.net/article.php?sid=12591

Hegarty, D. (1990) 'The South Pacific and Papua New Guinea'. In D. Ball and C. Downes (eds), *Security and Defence: Pacific and Global Perspectives*, St Leonards, NSW: Allen and Unwin.

Henderson, G. (2004) 'Regional Neighbours—It's a Case of Neither Foe Nor Exclusive Friend'. *Sydney Morning Herald*, 27 April, http://smh.com.au/articles/2004/04/26/1082831499712.html?from=storyrhs

—— (2005) 'Howard, Keating and Asia'. *The Age*, 5 April, http://www.theage.com.au/text/articles/2005/04/04/1112489416022.html

Hersh, S.M. (2004) *Chain of Command: The Road from 9/11 to Abu Ghraib*, London: Penguin Allen Lane.

Higgot, R.A. and K.R. Nossal (1997) 'The International Politics of Liminality: Relocating Australia in the Asia Pacific'. *Australian Journal of Political Science*, 32(2).

Howard, J. (2004) 'Howard Chases Free Trade at ASEAN Summit'. Transcript of television interview with Tony Jones, *Lateline*, ABC, 30 November, http://www.abc.net.au/lateline/content/2004/s1255092.htm

Illustrated History of Australia (1979) Sydney and New York: Ure Smith.

Jupp, J. (ed.) (1988) *The Australian People: An Encyclopaedia of the Nation, Its People and Their Origins*, North Ryde, NSW: Angus and Robertson.

Kevin, T. (2004) 'Asian Leaders Press Australia on Security Pact'. Transcript, *World View*, SBS Radio, 30 November, Project SafeCom Inc., http://www.safecom.org.au/2004/12/tony-kevin-howard-in-vientiane-another.htm

Maclellan N. (2002) *Submission to Senate Inquiry on Australia's Relationship with Papua New Guinea and Other Pacific Island Countries*, July.

Downer, A. (2004) 'First Australians Deployed in Australia PNG Enhanced Cooperation'. Media release from Minister for Foreign Affairs, Australia, 12 February, http://www.foreignminister.gov.au/releases/2004/fa022_04.html

Mercer, P. (2003) 'Australia's New Taste for Intervention'. *BBC News* World Edition, 15 August, http://news.bbc.co.uk/2/hi/asia-pacific/3154033.stm

O'Keefe, M. (2003) 'Enduring Tensions in the 2000 Defence White Paper'. *Australian Journal of Politics and History*, 49(4).

Quilici, F. (1972) *Primitive Societies*, London and New York: Collins.

Renner, M. (2003) 'The New Oil Order: Washington's War on Iraq is the Lynchpin to Controlling Persian Gulf Oil'. *Foreign Policy in Focus*, Corpwatch, 14 February, http://www.corpwatch.org/article.php?id=5529

Renouf, A. (1979) *The Frightened Country*, Melbourne: Macmillan.

Scott, E. (1928) 'Chapter 30'. *A Short History of Australia (1868-1939)*. Nalanda Digital Library at National Institute of Technology, Calcutta, India, http://www.nalanda.nitc.ac.in/resources/english/etext-project/history/aust_hist/chapter30.html

Sheridan, G. (1999) 'PM's Doctrine Under Siege'. *The Australian*, 25 September, http://squawk.ca/lbo-talk/9909/1660.html

St. John, R.B. (1987) *Qaddafi's World Design: Libyan Foreign Policy 1969-87*, London: Saqi Books.

Taylor, S. (2003) *Australia's Response to Asylum Seekers in the Age of Terrorism*, Project SafeCom Inc., http://www.safecom.org.au/asylum-terrorism.htm

Urwin, G. (2004) 'Preventing Conflict in the Pacific: What Role of the Pacific Islands Forum'. Paper at Securing A Peaceful Pacific: Preventing and Resolving Conflict Conference at School of Political Science and Communication, University of Canterbury, New Zealand, 15 October, http://www.forumsec.org.fj/news/2004/October/Oct_08.htm

Verrier, J.R. (2003) 'Australia's Self-Image as a Regional and International Security Actor: Some Implications of the Iraq War'. *Australian Journal of International Affairs*, 57(3).

Viviani N. (2000) *Australia-Indonesia Relations After the East Timor Upheaval*. Japan Policy Research Institute (JPRI) Working Paper No. 64, January, University of San Francisco.

Wainwright, E. (2003) 'Responding to State Failure: The Case of Australia and the Solomon Islands'. *Australian Journal of International Affairs*, 57(3).

White, H.J. (2003) 'Mr Howard Goes to Washington: The US and Australia in the Age of Terror. *Pacific Forum CSIS Comparative Connections: An E-Journal on East Asian Bilateral Relations*, 5(2), http://www.csis.org/pacfor/cc/0302Qoa.html

WP News (2004) 'Fiji PM Opposes Pacific Union'. *Melanesian News*, 30 March, http://www.westpapuanews.com/articles/publish/article_1606.shtml

Xinhua News Agency (2003) 'Howard Outrages South-East Asian Nations'. *People's Daily Online*, http://english.people.com.cn/200212/03/print20021203_107860.html

INDEX

A

academics, 54, 55, 71, 77, 232
accelerator, 17
acceptance, 57, 154, 175, 229, 272
access, 14, 48, 61, 91, 93, 101, 138, 140, 170, 197, 198, 210, 216, 218, 235, 271
accommodation, viii, 103, 113, 202, 238, 249, 278
accountability, 32, 94
accuracy, 54
achievement, 101, 154, 155
activism, 41, 42, 43
adaptability, 127
adaptation, 187
addiction, 255
adjustment, 47, 105, 126
adoption, 126, 141, 199
affect, 40, 41, 42, 51, 104, 125, 174, 187, 200, 218, 235, 238, 243
Afghanistan, vii, 50, 65, 73, 81, 82, 83, 84, 86, 88, 102, 110, 113, 174, 185, 188, 191, 196, 197, 217, 218, 230, 231, 233, 238, 239, 245, 246, 247, 248, 260, 270, 271, 277
Africa, 72, 79, 83, 201, 204
age, 34, 135, 152, 173, 179
agenda-setting, vii, 177
agent, 228, 239, 267
aggression, 61, 135, 247
aging, 57
aging population, 57
AIDS, 136, 145
Al Qaeda, 35, 78, 86, 101, 165, 173, 174, 185, 186, 190, 196, 198, 231, 234, 235, 237, 239, 243, 247, 270, 271
alienation, xii, 92, 124, 203
alternative, 5, 56, 62, 66, 74, 184, 191, 238, 239, 259, 261
alternatives, 42, 66, 122, 219
ambiguity, 154, 252
ambivalence, 111, 173
ambivalent, 102
anger, 83, 166, 171, 212
animals, 170
annihilation, 273
anxiety, 42, 46
Arab countries, 261
argument, 75, 76, 78, 100, 124, 154, 157, 191, 202, 203, 207, 228, 229, 246
armed conflict, 128, 154
armed forces, 124, 203
Armenia, 252
Armenians, 252
arms control, 92, 137, 139
arrest, 81, 185
ASEAN, 4, 6, 7, 8, 9, 12, 18, 46, 50, 91, 93, 96, 97, 98, 99, 101, 104, 106, 107, 115, 118, 121, 122, 128, 129, 131, 137, 138, 140, 144, 160, 166, 173, 175, 177, 187, 189, 191, 196, 198, 199, 201, 203, 205, 212, 213, 214, 215, 216, 218, 222, 223, 224, 225, 268, 272, 282
Asia, i, iii, vii, viii, ix, xi, xii, xiii, 1, 3, 4, 5, 6, 7, 8, 9, 10, 11, 12, 13, 14, 15, 16, 17, 20, 24, 28, 29, 31, 32, 33, 34, 35, 36, 39, 40, 41, 42, 44, 45, 46, 47, 48, 49, 50, 51, 52, 53, 54, 57, 63, 66, 68, 71, 74, 75, 77, 78, 79, 82, 84, 91, 92, 93, 95, 96, 97, 99, 100, 101, 102, 103, 104, 105, 106, 107, 109, 115, 116, 117, 118, 121, 122, 123, 125, 127, 128, 129, 130, 131, 132, 134, 136, 140, 143, 144, 146, 157, 158, 160, 161, 162, 163, 164, 165, 177, 178, 179, 187, 190, 191, 193, 195, 196, 200, 201, 202, 205, 207, 208, 209, 210, 211, 212, 213, 214, 215, 217, 218, 219, 220, 221, 222, 223, 224, 225, 227, 231, 236, 238, 240, 241, 243, 244, 259, 267, 268, 269, 272, 275, 282
Asia Pacific Economic Cooperation, vii, 93, 268
Asian countries, 17, 20, 30, 130, 176, 200, 218, 272
Asian crisis, 177, 178
Asian values, 96, 99, 130
aspiration, 171, 256, 263
assassination, 238, 247

assault, 8
assertiveness, 103
assessment, 14, 29, 33, 43, 46, 54, 65, 92, 140, 152, 234, 258
assets, 48, 100, 102, 190, 197
association, 172, 174, 212
Association of Southeast Asian Nations, 4, 91, 121, 144, 268
assumptions, 9, 71, 72, 74, 96, 234
asylum, 191, 270, 278, 282
asymmetry, 49
atrocities, 77, 98
attachment, 187, 235
attacks, vii, 14, 36, 75, 83, 101, 102, 125, 126, 165, 188, 190, 195, 196, 198, 199, 200, 203, 227, 231, 239, 245, 247, 251, 252, 258, 259, 270, 277
attention, 4, 9, 40, 46, 47, 48, 49, 50, 53, 116, 133, 161, 165, 167, 173, 174, 178, 202, 216, 217, 239, 244, 247, 263, 270, 274
attitudes, 5, 50, 51, 80, 130, 153, 158, 161, 203, 227, 235
Attorney General, 253
attractiveness, 54, 64, 201
Australasia, 5
Australia, viii, xi, xii, xiii, xiv, 5, 10, 11, 33, 45, 46, 47, 48, 49, 51, 58, 65, 122, 128, 131, 140, 166, 173, 175, 176, 177, 178, 191, 192, 193, 201, 214, 239, 247, 254, 267, 268, 269, 270, 271, 272, 273, 274, 275, 276, 277, 278, 279, 280, 281, 282, 283
authoritarianism, 34, 64, 229
authority, 3, 55, 115, 148, 158, 204, 210
autonomy, 84, 171, 208, 276
availability, 41
avoidance, 105
awareness, 63, 75, 125, 200
Azerbaijan, 261

B

baby boomers, 149
backlash, 77, 81, 95, 97, 124, 167, 237, 257, 262
baggage, 169
Bahrain, 202, 211, 251
bail, 174, 261
Balkans, 210
Bangladesh, 24, 26, 27, 35, 73, 74, 88, 201, 202, 215, 216, 219, 223, 230
banking, 4, 62, 190
banks, 95, 190
bargaining, 95
behavior, 260
Beijing, 49, 58, 60, 61, 67, 97, 110, 124, 134, 143, 198, 200, 220, 230, 270

benign, vii, 5, 9, 84, 142, 257, 262, 274, 280
bias, 231, 232, 233
bilateralism, 51, 97, 99, 211
binding, 139
birth, viii, 157
BIS, 12
black hole, 277
blame, 72, 74, 157, 174, 234, 244
bleeding, 254
blocks, 157
blogger, 254
blood, 49, 145, 157
bloodshed, 260
body, 7, 77, 103, 107, 113, 140, 158, 280
border control, 190
border security, 277
Boris Yeltsin, 110
Bosnia, 98, 185
brain, 253
brain drain, 253
breakdown, 40, 41, 156
breeding, 81, 84, 185
Britain, 113, 158
bureaucracy, 216
Burma, 6, 61, 122

C

Cambodia, 6, 18, 20, 25, 27, 58, 110, 121, 191, 198, 214
Camp David, 237, 247
campaigns, 104, 276
Canada, viii, xi
candidates, 147, 169, 170, 254
capital controls, 96
capitalism, 28, 66, 75
cardiac arrest, 79
carrier, 48, 100, 133, 199
Caspian Sea, 209
cast, vii, 112, 124, 204, 233
catalyst, 96, 175, 198
Catholic Church, 276
Caucasus, 112, 113, 222
Central Asia, xi, 83, 92, 109, 110, 112, 113, 114, 117, 185, 209, 210, 212, 213, 217, 218, 219, 222, 225
certificate, 137
changing environment, 9, 192
channels, 115, 141, 147, 202, 230
chaos, 145, 165
Chiang Mai Initiative, 96
children, 58, 73

Index

China, vii, viii, xii, 4, 5, 6, 7, 9, 10, 12, 14, 15, 17, 20, 22, 24, 26, 32, 33, 35, 36, 40, 42, 43, 45, 46, 47, 48, 49, 51, 53, 54, 56, 57, 58, 59, 60, 61, 62, 63, 66, 67, 68, 69, 91, 93, 96, 97, 99, 100, 102, 103, 104, 106, 107, 109, 110, 111, 114, 116, 117, 118, 119, 121, 122, 123, 125, 127, 128, 129, 130, 132, 133, 134, 135, 136, 137, 138, 139, 140, 141, 142, 143, 144, 145, 146, 153, 156, 158, 160, 166, 177, 178, 187, 189, 195, 198, 200, 201, 209, 210, 211, 212, 213, 214, 215, 218, 219, 220, 222, 223, 230, 267, 268, 270, 271, 272, 281
Christian Right, 79
CIA, 82, 198, 204, 230, 240, 281
circulation, 160
citizenship, 183, 227
civil liberties, 22, 24, 25, 26, 28, 34, 35
civil rights, 64
civil society, 84, 204, 227, 229, 231, 232, 233, 235
civil war, 83, 185, 245, 254, 278
classes, 185
clean energy, 211
cleavage, 156
cleavages, 220, 260
clients, 254
closed economy, 17
closure, 18, 114
cobalt, 210
coercion, 61, 94
cognitive process, 154
coherence, 8
cohesion, 183
cold war, 97
Cold War, vii, viii, 3, 5, 9, 12, 14, 16, 28, 29, 30, 31, 32, 36, 44, 52, 64, 75, 82, 89, 91, 92, 99, 101, 106, 109, 113, 116, 123, 124, 125, 131, 136, 145, 146, 147, 148, 153, 158, 159, 160, 161, 162, 163, 165, 173, 177, 181, 189, 195, 207, 208, 209, 210, 211, 212, 213, 219, 221, 223, 224, 259, 268, 269, 273, 274, 275
collaboration, 101, 104, 127, 214, 223, 230
college students, 160
collusion, 97
colonial rule, 80
coma, 79
commitment, 41, 48, 50, 60, 61, 101, 112, 125, 128, 130, 175, 183, 187, 190, 229, 235, 237, 250, 262, 272
communication, 99, 115, 173, 176, 200, 217, 221, 230, 237
communism, 16, 28, 173, 187, 230
Communist Party, xii, 33, 58, 134, 189
community, viii, 8, 42, 43, 73, 83, 93, 94, 98, 103, 116, 122, 127, 128, 129, 130, 135, 136, 137, 141, 142, 154, 157, 158, 159, 182, 183, 184, 187, 195, 199, 217, 234, 238, 245, 250, 251, 258, 262, 271, 274, 277, 280
compatibility, 167
competition, 47, 81, 100, 122, 210, 218, 220
competitiveness, 178, 220
competitor, 7, 47, 92, 100, 105
complement, 176, 214, 221
complexity, 7, 217
complications, 197
components, 46, 97, 202
composition, 184
conception, 63, 161, 187
concrete, 139, 189, 229
conduct, 11, 101, 109, 115, 116, 135, 233
confidence, 34, 113, 196, 200, 212, 214, 236, 251, 258, 279
configuration, 112, 199
confinement, 145
conflict, 15, 40, 72, 75, 103, 104, 122, 123, 126, 128, 146, 149, 154, 185, 188, 189, 199, 210, 213, 229, 260, 262, 274, 275, 277, 278
conflict prevention, 128
conflict resolution, 213
conformity, 60
confrontation, 4, 28, 100, 117, 161, 181, 184, 199, 211, 229, 231
Confucius, 63
connectivity, 217
consciousness, 158, 185
consensus, 41, 44, 60, 125, 145, 166, 188, 201, 215, 227, 228, 260
consent, 71, 188, 216
consolidation, 127, 172
conspiracy, 188
constitution, 33, 57, 58, 73, 124, 125
construction, 94, 220
consulting, xii, 79
consumer goods, 56
consumer markets, 56, 58
consumers, 210
consumption, 9
content analysis, 75
context, 6, 8, 10, 14, 41, 43, 47, 50, 51, 60, 63, 73, 75, 76, 78, 79, 81, 84, 94, 100, 101, 129, 182, 189, 202, 208, 217, 220, 221, 228, 229, 231, 235, 236, 238, 250
contingency, 5, 48, 102, 104
continuity, 14, 36, 165, 172, 177
control, 40, 42, 58, 60, 63, 80, 81, 95, 99, 101, 104, 109, 133, 136, 137, 171, 177, 187, 199, 202, 233, 244, 248, 254, 276
convergence, 130

conviction, 100
coping, 10, 135, 217
copper, 210
corporations, 95
correlation, xii, 75, 81, 84
corruption, 22, 24, 28, 35, 62, 111, 141, 170, 171, 178, 184, 188, 253, 255, 256, 273, 278, 279
costs, 77, 123, 124, 227, 239, 262
cotton, 273
Council of Ministers, 201
counterbalance, 219
coverage, 4, 148, 219, 243
covering, 72, 244
crack, 272
creativity, 60
credentials, 6, 237
credibility, 98, 113, 218, 252
credit, 189, 248
crime, 93, 136, 280
criminals, 33, 123
crisis management, 123
critical analysis, 77
criticism, 98, 116, 198, 233, 234, 237, 272
cronyism, 16
crude oil, 176, 211
Cuba, 61
culture, 44, 55, 56, 58, 59, 60, 61, 62, 63, 64, 65, 66, 72, 74, 75, 76, 79, 91, 124, 125, 135, 158, 255, 256, 273
currency, 6, 7, 16, 95, 96, 198
current account, 7
current account balance, 7
curriculum, 65, 186

D

damage, 112, 187, 252
danger, 39, 74, 79, 81, 234
death, 72, 78, 156, 174, 203, 244, 269
debt, 45, 95, 135, 276
decentralisation, 167, 171
decision making, 216
decisions, 34, 49, 79, 113, 216, 236
defense, 124, 155, 228, 265
deficit, 216
definition, 9, 189, 191, 213, 214
deflation, 198
degradation, 136
delivery, 41, 78, 127, 137, 215, 257, 272, 279
demand, 76, 77, 178, 211, 234, 274
democracy, 15, 16, 33, 34, 55, 56, 61, 64, 75, 78, 92, 100, 112, 114, 127, 130, 154, 165, 167, 168, 169, 172, 184, 187, 188, 208, 229, 234, 245, 246, 249, 259, 260
democratic consolidation, 167, 177, 178
democratic elections, 64, 254
Democratic Party, 33, 168
democratisation, xii, 8, 28, 34, 43, 75, 80, 84, 99, 105, 149, 154, 166, 167, 171, 172, 181, 209, 229, 234, 243, 246, 249, 255, 256, 259, 260, 261, 262, 263
democrats, 244
demographic change, 76
Denmark, 62, 64
density, 100, 176
Department of Defense, xii, 39, 46, 52, 93, 99, 100, 107, 210, 228, 240
deposits, 253
deregulation, 96, 211
derivatives, 236
desire, 46, 47, 59, 60, 63, 83, 157, 161, 249, 251, 262, 264, 268
destruction, 27, 73, 228
detention, 186, 235, 277, 278
deterrence, 51, 97, 101, 228, 229, 233, 236
developed countries, 135
developed nations, 135, 188
development assistance, 121, 127
deviation, 72
devolution, 129, 165
differentiation, 148
direct measure, 22
disaster, 57, 112, 116, 122, 129, 247
disaster relief, 57, 122, 129
disbursement, 176
discomfort, 8, 41, 114, 197
discourse, 207, 208, 209, 216, 233, 280
discrimination, 203
dislocation, 33
disorder, 145, 146, 158, 159
disposition, 34
dissatisfaction, 213, 244, 280
disseminate, 65, 139
distribution, 56, 65, 92
divergence, 46, 47
diversity, 13, 44, 135, 137, 249, 256
domain, 81, 214, 275
domestic economy, 200
dominance, 63, 66, 76, 170, 219, 274
draft, 109
dream, 145
drug addict, 255
drug addiction, 255
drug trafficking, 200
drugs, 40, 41, 45, 221, 255

dualism, 153
dual-use items, 137
dumping, 277
duopoly, 146
durability, 128, 239

E

earnings, 216
East Asia, xiii, 11, 12, 16, 17, 20, 22, 24, 26, 29, 33, 36, 44, 45, 46, 47, 48, 50, 52, 58, 61, 63, 93, 96, 97, 98, 99, 100, 103, 104, 105, 106, 107, 112, 117, 119, 121, 122, 123, 124, 125, 127, 128, 129, 130, 152, 154, 159, 160, 161, 166, 176, 177, 178, 186, 205, 209, 212, 213, 214, 223, 272, 275, 281, 283
East Germany, 111
Eastern Europe, 56, 165, 259
eating, 59
economic assistance, 153, 234
economic boom, 209
economic change, 3, 212
economic crisis, vii, 6, 95, 96, 209
economic development, 3, 4, 6, 8, 10, 13, 14, 61, 133, 137, 138, 141, 154, 178, 276
economic globalisation, 14, 15, 19, 36
economic growth, 3, 4, 6, 9, 11, 15, 20, 35, 53, 95, 123, 198, 220
economic growth rate, 220
economic ideology, 9
economic institutions, 15, 16
economic integration, 4, 17, 97, 141
economic performance, 244
economic policy, 97, 177, 178
economic systems, 16, 184
economic transformation, 141, 209
economics, xii, 33, 122, 211, 219, 223
egalitarianism, 55
Egypt, 8, 72, 185, 201, 216, 244, 245, 246, 248
elaboration, 7, 11, 76, 141
election, 35, 57, 64, 79, 103, 116, 147, 148, 149, 169, 174, 176, 184, 203, 245, 255, 258, 269, 270, 277
embargo, 100
emergence, 4, 10, 41, 75, 84, 93, 122, 123, 124, 129, 130, 134, 150, 161, 185, 195, 209, 217, 227, 230, 232
emotions, 259
employees, 253
empowerment, 239
encouragement, 83
endurance, 176
energy supply, 127

England, 252
entrepreneurs, 60
environment, vii, viii, 10, 14, 35, 36, 39, 41, 43, 48, 50, 91, 101, 109, 122, 126, 127, 130, 134, 135, 138, 139, 141, 142, 147, 152, 153, 178, 182, 187, 196, 212, 213, 214, 238, 249, 250, 252, 259, 275
environmental degradation, 92, 145
environmental protection, 133, 138
EP-3, 269
equality, 61, 135, 136, 137, 138
equating, 55, 238
equipment, 49, 189, 190, 192, 251
equities, 45
equity, 208
erosion, 170
ETA, 246
ethics, 63
ethnic culture, 79
ethnic groups, 253
ethnicity, 258
EU, 20, 35, 250, 251, 256, 257, 258, 259, 263, 275, 277, 281
euphoria, 94
Eurasia, 118, 210
Euro, 115
Europe, 5, 11, 44, 48, 50, 58, 77, 78, 84, 92, 111, 113, 115, 117, 122, 124, 129, 130, 131, 136, 144, 145, 146, 156, 161, 163, 196, 224, 251, 257, 258, 259, 260, 262, 263, 275
European Union, 50, 53, 100, 250, 275, 280
evacuation, 126
evidence, 3, 20, 28, 30, 47, 53, 59, 63, 71, 73, 77, 98, 233, 243, 271, 280
evil, 63, 197, 247
evolution, 43, 58, 62, 97, 135, 141, 160, 215, 234
exaggeration, 189
exchange rate, 96
exclusion, 62
excuse, 155
execution, 125
exercise, 60, 96, 99, 104, 124, 148, 173, 190
expectation, 14, 28
expenditures, 29, 30, 31
expertise, 65, 110, 141
experts, 58, 216
exploitation, 116, 215
exports, 53, 54, 59, 62, 63, 66, 94, 214
exposure, 95
expression, 56, 160, 172, 232, 234, 237

F

fabric, 183

failure, 14, 57, 64, 72, 81, 82, 96, 157, 160, 167, 182, 184, 187, 188, 191, 203, 213, 244, 254, 256, 259
fairness, 136
faith, 71, 72, 75, 167, 176, 192, 203, 275
family, ix, 60, 135, 157, 166, 172, 245
family members, 166
famine, 94, 156
fear, 58, 62, 82, 141, 157, 167, 168, 169, 171, 172, 173, 182, 187, 188, 189, 233, 268, 274
feedback, ix
feelings, 95, 249
feet, 246
Fiji, 275, 283
films, 65
finance, 96, 174
financial capital, 279
financial crisis, 15, 24, 44, 92, 93, 95, 96, 97, 98, 165, 166, 167, 174, 195, 201, 216
financial institutions, 171, 197
financial resources, 171, 253
financial support, ix, 95, 174
financial system, 95, 97, 166
financing, 96, 190
firearms, 203
firms, 56, 62, 65
fisheries, 215
fishing, 270, 275
flexibility, 48, 238, 273
flooding, 94
fluctuations, 81, 103, 211
fluid, 165
focusing, 44, 92, 105, 122, 174, 213, 215, 232
food, 57, 74, 94, 133, 147, 156
forecasting, 215
foreign aid, 56, 57, 121
foreign direct investment, 178, 200
foreign exchange, 216
foreign investment, 138, 140, 154, 245, 254
foreign policy, xii, xiv, 3, 7, 33, 42, 46, 55, 76, 82, 84, 93, 105, 110, 111, 113, 114, 115, 116, 117, 134, 136, 142, 149, 153, 160, 161, 173, 175, 177, 191, 200, 207, 208, 211, 212, 213, 216, 218, 219, 221, 227, 228, 229, 234, 239, 245, 246, 248, 268, 272, 274, 275
fragility, 173
France, 59, 143, 146, 158, 210, 250
franchise, 15
free trade, 33, 140, 181, 198, 268
free trade area, 198
freedom, 34, 55, 56, 61, 78, 82, 84, 166, 191, 221, 229, 233, 246
freezing, 190
friction, 156, 189

friends, 45, 46, 47, 49, 99, 104, 166, 187, 245
friendship, 175, 215
frustration, 99, 166, 203, 254
fuel, 94, 126, 256
funding, viii, 83, 103, 174, 175

G

GDP, 29, 30, 53, 69, 167, 178
GDP per capita, 167
gender, xii
general election, 34, 203
generation, 33, 35, 148, 149, 150, 152, 279
genes, 72
geography, 13, 64, 72, 208
Georgia, 246
Germany, 63, 131, 250
gestures, 171, 197
girls, 148, 149, 156
global economy, 4, 28, 209
global forces, 221
global management, 130
global markets, 274
global trade, 17, 179, 198, 274
globalization, 136
GNP, 29, 253
goals, 9, 41, 46, 60, 211
God, 182
gold, 217
goods and services, 16
governance, xiii, 16, 81, 146, 161, 181, 229, 278, 279
government, xii, 16, 22, 24, 28, 29, 33, 34, 39, 50, 51, 54, 57, 60, 63, 74, 81, 82, 83, 113, 114, 115, 126, 134, 135, 136, 137, 138, 139, 140, 141, 142, 145, 146, 147, 148, 149, 153, 155, 156, 158, 159, 160, 161, 174, 175, 176, 183, 184, 185, 186, 187, 188, 189, 190, 191, 195, 196, 197, 199, 200, 201, 202, 203, 204, 208, 211, 217, 227, 228, 230, 231, 232, 233, 234, 235, 236, 237, 238, 239, 245, 253, 255, 256, 259, 268, 270, 274, 276, 277, 278, 280
graduate students, 60
grants, 186
grassroots, 5, 10, 184
gravity, 3
Great Britain, 250
Great Leap Forward, 62
grouping, 104, 212, 215, 249
groups, xiv, 61, 75, 76, 77, 79, 80, 81, 112, 114, 138, 148, 149, 154, 168, 171, 174, 181, 182, 186, 187, 192, 196, 197, 201, 204, 212, 227, 229, 230, 231, 232, 239, 246, 250, 252, 257, 259, 261, 262, 263, 272, 275, 276, 277

growth, 3, 5, 6, 9, 20, 35, 53, 54, 56, 62, 76, 121, 133, 138, 165, 166, 167, 177, 178, 182, 220, 255, 271
guidance, 58, 136
guidelines, 197
guilty, 148
Guinea, 176, 275, 278, 281, 282

H

hands, 5, 46, 73, 99, 136, 171, 260
harassment, 103
harm, 61, 128, 165, 167, 185, 263
harmony, 128, 165, 167, 263
hate, 72, 235
hazards, 96, 104
health, 40, 104, 244
health problems, 244
heavy oil, 94
height, 3, 4, 190
helplessness, 237
hemisphere, 71
heroin, 209
high school, 203
highways, 214
hiring, 276
homicide, xiii, 148, 255
Honduras, 77
Hong Kong, xiii, 3, 6, 10, 17, 52
host, 65, 171, 176, 191, 236, 243, 253, 278
host societies, 65
hostility, 94, 142
hub, 97, 102, 215, 275
human development, xiii
Human Development Report, 244
human resource development, 214
human resources, 130, 244, 262
human rights, 24, 55, 61, 73, 134, 137, 139, 141, 154, 176, 187, 188, 203, 209, 229, 244, 257, 259, 276, 277
human security, 92, 103
humanitarian intervention, 98
husband, 79

I

ideas, xii, 3, 55, 58, 59, 60, 61, 63, 64, 65, 66, 80, 153, 154, 181, 182, 185, 186, 228, 229, 232, 235, 236, 238, 239, 243, 249, 269
identification, 55, 142, 154, 227, 229
identity, 9, 11, 73, 76, 122, 130, 142, 154, 161, 165, 167, 171, 183, 203, 231, 235, 252
identity politics, 76

ideology, 5, 61, 62, 71, 74, 76, 78, 79, 84, 103, 113, 114, 146, 147, 174, 182, 184, 186
idiosyncratic, 30
illiteracy, 235, 244
imagination, 3, 219
imbalances, 220
IMF, 15, 20, 36, 95, 96, 98, 106, 167, 174, 179
immigrants, 239, 277
immigration, 72, 145, 197, 269, 277, 281
impeachment, 172
imperialism, 157, 173, 209, 246
implementation, 71, 79, 84, 95, 130, 138, 153, 184, 190, 279
imports, 211, 214
incentives, 81
incidence, 167
inclusion, 13, 57, 197, 215, 272
income, 62, 235, 253
incompatibility, 75
indecisiveness, 276
independence, 34, 42, 44, 61, 64, 80, 112, 135, 171, 173, 174, 175, 183, 184, 200, 212, 230, 233, 275, 276, 279
India, vii, viii, xi, xiii, 9, 12, 13, 19, 20, 24, 26, 28, 34, 40, 42, 43, 45, 47, 50, 53, 54, 63, 64, 65, 66, 68, 82, 103, 115, 118, 122, 124, 140, 145, 146, 185, 187, 195, 198, 199, 201, 202, 204, 207, 209, 210, 211, 212, 213, 214, 215, 216, 217, 218, 219, 220, 221, 222, 223, 224, 225, 229, 230, 231, 232, 233, 235, 236, 238, 240, 272, 282
Indians, 64, 65, 219
indication, 29, 35, 49, 84, 210, 246
indicators, 13, 17, 244
indices, 53
indigenous, 42, 91, 104, 217, 257, 279
individualism, 64
Indonesia, vii, xi, 4, 6, 18, 24, 26, 27, 28, 30, 34, 35, 41, 46, 49, 73, 75, 80, 81, 85, 86, 87, 88, 95, 96, 98, 101, 165, 166, 167, 168, 169, 170, 171, 172, 173, 174, 175, 176, 177, 178, 179, 182, 185, 187, 188, 193, 196, 201, 203, 212, 215, 246, 269, 270, 271, 272, 275, 276, 281, 283
industry, 65, 197
inequality, 141, 244
inferences, 274
inferiority, 209
influence, 7, 10, 14, 17, 35, 43, 53, 54, 55, 59, 60, 64, 65, 66, 81, 83, 84, 91, 92, 93, 97, 103, 105, 113, 122, 133, 138, 148, 149, 157, 172, 184, 185, 187, 209, 210, 213, 218, 231, 232, 259
information exchange, 192
information technology, 65
infrastructure, 35, 100, 228, 273, 274

innovation, 208
input, ix, 252
insecurity, 36, 251, 254
insertion, 100
insight, 82
inspectors, 237
inspiration, 64, 105, 245
instability, 35, 125, 183, 185, 220, 252, 255, 260, 274, 279, 280
institutional reforms, 216
institutionalisation, 92
institutions, vii, viii, xi, 16, 33, 34, 44, 46, 50, 55, 58, 61, 81, 93, 99, 102, 103, 104, 122, 123, 128, 129, 138, 142, 235, 249, 258, 268, 279, 280
instruments, 199, 200
integration, 28, 44, 45, 65, 76, 92, 102, 115, 116, 122, 128, 129, 142, 177, 212, 217, 262, 276
integrity, 61, 135, 165, 168, 171, 173, 220, 260
intellectual property, 138
intellectual property rights, 138
intelligence, 48, 71, 82, 104, 127, 129, 190, 192, 203, 250, 275
intent, 142, 258, 279
intentions, 142, 158, 159, 191, 256, 257, 258
interaction, xiv, 46, 154, 188, 212, 214, 218, 219, 220
interactions, 43, 84, 142, 264, 274
interdependence, 13, 44, 92, 102, 128, 129, 135, 153, 154
interest, ix, xiii, 7, 42, 55, 71, 82, 93, 96, 99, 102, 105, 136, 154, 167, 173, 181, 190, 191, 210, 215, 246, 251, 258, 261, 262, 269, 273
interest rates, 96
international law, 232
International Monetary Fund, 20, 36, 95, 96, 106
international relations, vii, xi, 47, 49, 135, 142, 181, 220, 267, 268, 273
international standards, 134
international terrorism, 71, 127, 130, 196
international trade, 17, 66
internationalism, 93, 97
interoperability, 48
interpretation, 78, 83, 125, 191
intervention, 91, 98, 100, 171, 173, 176, 191, 209, 212, 229, 269, 274, 275, 277, 278, 279, 280
interview, 6, 82, 115, 116, 148, 202, 254, 282
investment, 7, 50, 121, 138, 214, 215, 254, 274, 279
investors, 8, 9, 96, 138, 165, 166
Iran, xiii, 72, 86, 113, 118, 181, 198, 201, 209, 211, 218, 219, 233, 247, 248, 249, 250, 251, 252, 253, 254, 255, 256, 257, 258, 259, 260, 261, 262, 263, 264, 265, 266, 267, 270

Iraq, vii, 33, 49, 50, 55, 77, 84, 92, 100, 101, 102, 104, 109, 113, 116, 124, 126, 173, 175, 181, 188, 192, 197, 211, 227, 229, 233, 234, 237, 238, 240, 243, 244, 245, 247, 248, 252, 260, 261, 270, 271, 274, 277, 282, 283
Iraq War, 283
iron, 73, 210
Islam, 10, 11, 64, 71, 72, 73, 75, 76, 78, 79, 80, 81, 84, 85, 86, 87, 88, 167, 168, 172, 174, 178, 182, 183, 184, 185, 186, 192, 193, 232, 246
Islamic law, 71, 73, 83, 182
Islamic movements, 168, 184, 192
Islamic world, 77, 79, 256, 259
isolation, 44, 116, 145, 183, 231, 277
Israel, 188, 244, 246, 247, 250, 251, 256, 258, 259, 261, 262, 263, 264, 265

J

Japan, vii, viii, xi, xii, 3, 4, 5, 7, 10, 17, 22, 26, 29, 33, 35, 36, 40, 41, 42, 45, 46, 47, 48, 49, 51, 53, 54, 56, 57, 58, 59, 60, 63, 64, 65, 66, 67, 68, 69, 91, 93, 96, 97, 100, 102, 104, 106, 109, 110, 112, 114, 115, 116, 121, 122, 123, 124, 125, 126, 127, 128, 129, 130, 131, 132, 137, 140, 144, 145, 146, 147, 150, 153, 157, 158, 161, 166, 173, 177, 187, 195, 198, 199, 200, 201, 205, 209, 210, 212, 223, 251, 256, 263, 268, 271, 272, 283
Japanese schools, 57
jihad, 83, 186
jobs, 35
joint demand, 114
Jordan, 238, 244, 245, 248
judges, 79
judicial branch, 79
junior high school, 148
justice, 78, 124, 217, 247
justification, 93, 188

K

Kazakhstan, 110, 140, 209, 217
kidnapping, 238
knowledge, 61, 62, 80, 83, 185, 273
Korea, 4, 12, 29, 46, 47, 49, 54, 57, 58, 67, 93, 94, 95, 102, 106, 112, 116, 123, 127, 137, 139, 144, 146, 147, 148, 149, 152, 153, 154, 155, 156, 157, 158, 159, 160, 161, 162, 163, 200, 267
Kosovo, 98, 228
Kuwait, 91, 109, 181, 211, 246, 251
Kyrgyzstan, 140, 217

L

labour, 160, 178, 198, 273
labour market, 178
land, 80, 112, 124, 126, 216, 217, 247, 274
landscapes, 35
language, 57, 64, 80, 158, 182, 187, 232, 260, 271
Laos, 5, 6, 18, 25, 27, 30, 198, 214
large-scale disasters, 125
Latin America, viii, 77
law enforcement, 40, 190
laws, 136, 137, 138, 140, 171, 182, 185, 187, 192, 239
lead, 9, 43, 45, 58, 63, 66, 94, 124, 130, 141, 146, 152, 171, 172, 175, 204, 210, 218, 220, 229, 236, 271
leadership, 8, 29, 33, 34, 61, 81, 82, 92, 94, 96, 166, 177, 178, 184, 188, 191, 195, 202, 207
leadership style, 29
learning, 57, 62, 64, 138, 191
Lebanon, 245, 247, 248, 258, 261
Lee Kuan Yew, 34
legality, 188
legislation, 49, 126, 137, 249, 254
lending, 84
lens, 15
liberalisation, 20, 28, 29, 31, 34, 35, 75, 95, 198
liberalism, 15, 16, 34, 75, 78, 154, 207, 246, 256
liberation, 74, 157, 270
lifetime, 72
likelihood, 6, 7, 77, 275
limitation, 54
linkage, 111
links, 9, 45, 46, 111, 165, 168, 174, 187, 203, 213, 218, 230, 239, 245, 278
listening, 55, 56
loans, 74, 95
local government, 126, 147
location, 48, 113, 207, 209, 213, 227
logistics, 49
long run, 129
longevity, 157
love, 78
low risk, 275
loyalty, 63

M

machinery, 184
macroeconomic stabilisation, 96
magnesium, 210
magnet, 9

Malaysia, xi, 4, 6, 11, 18, 26, 33, 35, 41, 45, 49, 80, 81, 86, 87, 88, 96, 97, 101, 103, 140, 166, 173, 175, 176, 181, 182, 183, 184, 185, 186, 187, 188, 189, 190, 191, 192, 193, 194, 196, 199, 201, 203, 215, 268, 271, 272, 282
management, 10, 19, 35, 43, 51, 58, 136, 137, 138, 141, 190, 221
manipulation, 63, 141
manufacturing, 7, 10, 125
mapping, 209, 221
market, 15, 16, 42, 56, 59, 65, 66, 72, 96, 99, 111, 114, 130, 138, 177, 208, 210, 214, 216, 245, 254
market economy, 16, 66, 114, 130
market penetration, 208
marketing, 56
marketisation, 15, 33, 35
markets, 15, 35, 61, 62, 66, 76, 96, 123, 209, 213, 217, 259, 275
marriage, 196
mass, 56, 74, 157, 228, 243
mass media, 243
matrix, 7, 13
Mauritius, 201
measurement, 29
measures, 50, 53, 61, 94, 95, 96, 104, 111, 126, 133, 134, 137, 139, 140, 142, 190, 196, 200, 235, 236, 238, 251, 259, 260
media, xi, 71, 79, 219, 232, 243
mediation, 42, 60, 104, 112
membership, 11, 140, 142, 201, 212, 213, 230
memory, 146
men, 74, 83
mental state, 158
mentor, 33, 188
metamorphosis, 165
middle class, 35
Middle East, viii, xiv, 10, 47, 48, 72, 76, 77, 79, 84, 86, 87, 88, 168, 178, 188, 210, 223, 229, 230, 233, 243, 244, 245, 246, 247, 248, 249, 250, 252, 256, 259, 260, 261, 262, 263, 265, 266, 274
migrants, 65
military, 5, 10, 15, 30, 32, 33, 34, 35, 40, 42, 46, 47, 48, 49, 50, 53, 54, 55, 57, 60, 72, 76, 77, 81, 82, 83, 91, 92, 93, 98, 99, 100, 101, 103, 104, 105, 109, 113, 114, 121, 123, 124, 125, 126, 127, 128, 130, 133, 146, 147, 155, 157, 166, 167, 170, 171, 174, 175, 176, 183, 185, 186, 189, 190, 192, 195, 196, 197, 199, 203, 208, 210, 212, 218, 219, 228, 229, 231, 234, 237, 247, 250, 251, 252, 256, 257, 258, 260, 267, 270, 271, 272, 274, 277, 278, 279, 280
military aid, 82
military dictatorship, 81

military spending, 30, 32, 123
militias, 277, 278
Ministry of Education, 186
minorities, 10, 44, 73, 80, 81, 252
minority, 73, 145, 160, 171, 183, 234, 254
missions, 48, 77, 102, 125, 268
mobile phone, 74
mobility, 127, 221
mode, 99, 165
models, 97
moderates, 231, 239
modernisation, 42, 76, 84, 113, 255
modernity, 60, 66, 76, 256
momentum, 3, 9, 113, 198
money, 184, 190, 254
money laundering, 190
Mongolia, 4
mood, 150, 172, 268
morale, 262
morality, 53
Morocco, 244
Moscow, 109, 110, 115, 118, 140, 220, 275
motion, 248
motivation, 161
motives, 75, 182
movement, 16, 17, 19, 24, 64, 74, 83, 98, 157, 168, 170, 174, 177, 184, 185, 187, 202, 210, 234, 262
multiculturalism, 10, 246, 269
multi-ethnic, 167, 171, 172
multilateralism, 48, 50, 93, 94, 97, 98, 99, 101, 103, 115, 123, 135, 161, 192, 212, 229, 237, 238, 268
multinational companies, 65
multiple interpretations, 235
murder, 78, 174
music, 55, 56, 65, 66
Muslim extremists, 182
Muslim states, 10, 84, 227, 232, 233, 234
Muslims, xiv, 72, 73, 78, 79, 80, 81, 84, 86, 182, 184, 185, 186, 187, 188, 192, 197, 203, 239, 244, 246, 249, 256, 271
mutation, 232
mutual respect, 61, 137, 138
Myanmar, 18, 25, 27, 30, 122, 198, 201, 211, 215, 219, 223

N

narcotic, 190, 192
narcotics, 190
national identity, 154
national income, 32
national interests, 45, 61, 99, 116, 130, 135, 148, 154, 156, 188, 199, 216, 259, 260, 262

national security, xi, 29, 92, 93, 95, 98, 101, 102, 104, 125, 147, 181, 182, 183, 187, 196, 232, 244, 252, 262, 270
National Security Council, 46, 47, 155, 196, 210, 223
nationalism, viii, 7, 42, 96, 158, 249, 258, 273
nation-building, viii, 80, 84, 217
NATO, xi, 111, 113, 117, 197, 231
natural gas, 116, 209, 211
natural resources, 217
Nauru, 277, 278
needs, 11, 42, 45, 51, 54, 113, 128, 133, 134, 135, 136, 139, 141, 187, 188, 190, 192, 199, 211, 219, 227, 229, 236, 254
negative consequences, 77
neglect, 153, 213
negotiating, 102, 176, 230
negotiation, 105, 112, 136, 155
Nepal, 19, 26, 27, 30, 35, 81, 212, 216
nervousness, 6
Netherlands, 247
network, 5, 8, 33, 93, 98, 102, 104, 118, 185, 198, 201, 214, 243, 253, 270
networking, 185, 190
New Zealand, viii, 122, 128, 268, 273, 274, 275, 280, 283
newspapers, 148, 149, 191, 235, 255
next generation, 34
NGOs, 74, 254
nickel, 210
Nigeria, 73, 211
Nobel Prize, 65
node, 65
North Africa, xiv
North America, viii
North Korea, xiii, 4, 5, 7, 8, 13, 17, 29, 32, 33, 42, 43, 46, 47, 49, 61, 91, 94, 95, 100, 102, 105, 107, 110, 112, 122, 123, 125, 126, 127, 129, 140, 145, 146, 147, 148, 149, 150, 152, 153, 154, 155, 156, 157, 158, 160, 161, 198, 200, 228, 233
Northeast Asia, 3, 5, 7, 8, 12, 48, 94, 102, 104, 110, 111, 122, 129, 132, 140, 145, 146, 156, 158, 159, 160, 161, 163, 177, 201, 271
nuclear program, 4, 127, 140, 152, 156, 233, 236, 250
nuclear talks, 258
nuclear weapons, 74, 82, 95, 102, 123, 125, 152, 230, 233, 251, 256, 258, 273

O

observations, 29
Oceania, viii

OECD, 68
oil, viii, 72, 94, 116, 178, 202, 209, 210, 211, 216, 217, 244, 271
old age, 244
omission, 5, 155
open economy, 18
open markets, 46, 96, 208
openness, 4, 9, 14, 17, 18, 19, 36, 44, 54, 55, 61, 246
opposition parties, 148, 204
optimism, 35, 44, 76, 93, 94
optimists, 10
ores, 253
organised crime, 190
organization, 215
organizations, 235
orientation, 160, 228
oscillation, 99
outline, 122
ownership, 60, 66, 140

P

Pacific, i, iii, vii, viii, ix, xi, xii, xiii, 3, 4, 5, 6, 7, 8, 9, 10, 11, 12, 13, 14, 16, 22, 31, 32, 33, 35, 36, 39, 40, 41, 44, 45, 46, 47, 48, 50, 51, 52, 53, 63, 71, 74, 75, 78, 79, 86, 88, 91, 92, 93, 96, 97, 99, 101, 102, 103, 104, 105, 106, 107, 115, 122, 123, 125, 127, 128, 132, 140, 161, 163, 176, 187, 191, 193, 195, 196, 200, 201, 202, 205, 208, 209, 210, 214, 221, 225, 227, 243, 244, 267, 268, 269, 271, 273, 274, 275, 277, 278, 279, 280, 281, 282, 283
pain, 167, 173
Pakistan, vii, xiv, 9, 13, 19, 24, 26, 27, 30, 35, 40, 42, 43, 45, 50, 65, 74, 81, 82, 83, 86, 87, 146, 185, 199, 202, 209, 211, 212, 213, 218, 219, 225, 227, 228, 229, 230, 231, 232, 233, 234, 235, 236, 237, 238, 239, 240, 241, 252, 259, 271, 272
PAN, 168, 169, 172
paradigm shift, 272
parents, 61, 79, 154
partnership, 45, 97, 127, 128, 129, 130, 138, 198, 199, 214, 216, 218, 233
passive, 200, 208, 228
peace process, 261
Pentagon, 93, 118, 270
per capita income, 74, 172, 178
perceptions, 22, 32, 73, 80, 134, 142, 153, 187, 189, 213
permit, 175
perspective, 5, 6, 8, 45, 56, 76, 77, 78, 84, 113, 116, 158, 160, 181, 203, 233, 261, 279, 280
persuasion, 114
Perth, xiv

Peru, 77
pessimism, 263
pessimists, 246, 247
Philippines, 18, 26, 27, 30, 41, 45, 46, 49, 72, 80, 81, 140, 174, 179, 188, 189, 196, 203, 216, 271, 272
physical health, 40
planning, 99, 159, 203
pleasure, ix, 116
pluralism, 257, 264
PM, 36, 264, 265, 266, 282, 283
Poland, 156
polarity, 220
police, 175, 186, 190, 244, 277, 278
policy reform, 95
political crisis, 188
political instability, vii, 4, 8, 98, 159, 275, 276
political leaders, 96, 234, 275
political legitimacy, 181, 183, 217
political opposition, 109, 185
political participation, 217
political parties, xii, 64, 80, 81, 169, 171, 184, 186, 267
politics, vii, xii, xiii, xiv, 4, 6, 8, 10, 11, 29, 33, 54, 64, 72, 74, 77, 80, 81, 86, 92, 97, 102, 112, 115, 123, 124, 125, 146, 153, 155, 158, 160, 161, 167, 170, 171, 173, 183, 184, 204, 211, 219, 227, 231, 232, 233, 249, 251, 255, 257, 259, 260, 261, 262, 274
polling, 51, 255
pollution, 62, 215
poor, 26, 35, 50, 74, 109, 141, 145, 160, 235, 244, 265, 269, 274, 278
poor performance, 269
population, xiii, 9, 34, 72, 73, 74, 77, 115, 149, 167, 174, 183, 184, 196, 202, 216, 217, 220, 233, 235, 243, 244, 250, 254, 261, 262, 277
population density, 243
ports, 189
poverty, 64, 154, 166, 253, 255
poverty alleviation, 166
power, xii, 4, 5, 8, 9, 11, 14, 15, 33, 34, 36, 40, 41, 42, 44, 45, 48, 53, 54, 55, 56, 57, 58, 59, 60, 61, 62, 63, 64, 65, 66, 72, 75, 81, 84, 91, 92, 100, 101, 102, 103, 104, 105, 110, 111, 114, 115, 116, 121, 123, 125, 126, 128, 129, 130, 133, 134, 136, 141, 145, 146, 147, 157, 165, 170, 171, 172, 173, 176, 177, 183, 199, 208, 209, 210, 213, 216, 218, 219, 220, 228, 229, 239, 244, 252, 255, 257, 259, 262, 263, 267, 270, 271, 274, 275, 279, 280
power relations, 15, 129
pragmatism, 49, 182, 207
prayer, 74
predictability, 99

prediction, 146
pre-emptive attacks, 101
preference, 101, 102, 232, 236, 237
preparation, 130
preparedness, 256
presidency, 92, 93, 94, 99, 110, 111, 112, 114, 168, 169, 170, 171, 269
President Clinton, 103, 106, 128, 231, 269
pressure, 42, 61, 96, 99, 113, 133, 157, 177, 184, 195, 197, 220, 232, 233, 237, 245, 247, 250, 254, 257, 258, 260, 273
pressure groups, 260
prestige, 9, 255, 266
prevention, 110, 127, 215
prices, 176
primacy, 46, 92, 160, 228, 229, 232, 267
principle, 62, 63, 78, 105, 237
prisoners, 186
probability, 82, 230, 248
producers, 58
production, 15, 65, 94, 211, 233
program, viii, 15, 35, 95, 113, 123, 152, 168, 174, 176, 184, 189, 190, 233, 250, 251
proliferation, 41, 49, 51, 92, 94, 100, 103, 104, 122, 127, 130, 136, 137, 139, 188, 199, 209, 234, 244, 247, 263, 280
promoter, 153
propaganda, 157, 237
propagation, 63
proposition, 8
prosperity, 4, 6, 9, 15, 17, 42, 44, 45, 54, 64, 92, 100, 104, 105, 117, 125, 127, 141, 142, 158, 159, 161, 200, 217, 229, 267
psychological health, 41
public goods, 199, 200
public opinion, 123, 153
public support, 57, 172
publishers, 59
punishment, 137
PVS, 79

Q

quality control, 58
quality of life, 104
questioning, 92, 239

R

race, 16, 28, 76, 128
racism, 61
radio, 56

range, viii, xiii, 16, 18, 39, 48, 50, 80, 94, 128, 136, 213, 249, 253, 261
rape, 73
ratings, 178
raw materials, 15, 178
reading, 71, 80, 168, 262
real estate, 273
real terms, 259
realignments, viii
realism, 146, 234, 252
reality, 5, 56, 114, 116, 135, 192, 213, 217, 218
reasoning, 75, 79, 105
recall, 82, 83, 212
reception, 201
reciprocity, 103
recognition, 49, 215, 276
reconciliation, 153, 204, 268
reconstruction, 49, 91, 103, 122, 126, 198, 248
recovery, 26, 78, 95, 96, 146, 165, 166, 174, 176
recruiting, 185
reduction, 103, 104, 151, 154
reductionism, 75
refining, 110, 114
reflection, 234
reforms, 3, 33, 35, 61, 62, 64, 79, 96, 111, 124, 172, 174, 212, 250, 257, 263, 276
refugee camps, 83
refugee status, 277
refugees, 126, 270, 277
regional economies, 97
regional policy, 92, 195
regionalism, 93, 96, 97, 127, 166, 177, 178
regression, 26, 27
regulations, 133, 137, 138, 140
rehabilitation, 198, 272
reinforcement, 5
relationship, 5, 6, 7, 42, 43, 45, 47, 49, 51, 61, 72, 81, 82, 95, 102, 112, 121, 122, 124, 127, 128, 146, 175, 176, 190, 191, 196, 200, 214, 230, 231, 234, 236, 238, 267, 268, 269, 272, 275, 279, 280
relationships, 5, 13, 33, 39, 40, 41, 42, 44, 45, 46, 48, 49, 51, 99, 130, 145, 199, 214, 219
relatives, 154
relevance, 43, 60, 66, 177, 233, 235, 236, 269
reliability, 227, 231
religion, xii, xiv, 64, 71, 72, 76, 79, 81, 135, 183, 185, 232, 270
religiosity, 73, 79, 80, 81
repair, 84, 114, 149, 157
replacement, 111, 168
Republican Party, 98
Republicans, 79
reputation, 64, 65, 110, 165, 203, 269, 277

resentment, 96, 232, 239
reserves, 101, 123, 209, 211
resistance, 47, 58, 64, 65, 82, 98, 99, 140, 200, 245, 247, 255
resolution, 9, 62, 98, 127, 128, 139, 140, 189, 190, 216, 233, 236, 237, 262, 276
resources, 35, 41, 48, 49, 57, 65, 72, 98, 103, 105, 109, 114, 115, 129, 133, 141, 209, 210, 215, 253, 261, 273, 282
responsibility, 47, 74, 99, 125, 142, 159, 209, 210, 215, 216, 229, 274
restructuring, xii, 7, 101, 278
retaliation, 258
retention, 93
retirement, 191
retribution, 234
revenue, 109
rewards, 81
rice, 147
rights, 22, 26, 27, 28, 35, 49, 61, 62, 79, 127, 134, 137, 154, 171, 192, 197, 203, 229, 244, 257, 276
risk, xii, 77, 95, 154, 159, 200, 232, 250, 268, 269, 278
river systems, 215
rods, 73
rubber, 189
rule of law, 15, 16, 34, 127, 130
runoff, 169, 170
rural population, 35
Russia, xiii, 4, 5, 7, 10, 57, 102, 109, 110, 111, 112, 113, 114, 115, 116, 117, 118, 119, 127, 129, 140, 145, 146, 153, 158, 199, 212, 218, 219, 220, 223, 224, 228, 252, 272

S

sacrifice, 60
Saddam Hussein, 113, 244, 271
sales, 7, 42, 58, 59, 60, 100, 134, 189, 215, 251
sanctions, 55, 82, 94, 100, 109, 231, 262
SARS, 41, 44
satellite, 245, 253
satisfaction, viii
Saudi Arabia, 78, 82, 211, 245, 246, 247, 248
savings, 167
school, 33, 39, 64, 83, 112, 149, 156, 157, 185, 186
scores, 17, 22
search, 8, 64, 75, 111, 112, 212, 218, 221, 256
searching, 213
Second World, 64, 121, 145
Secretary of Defense, 49, 50, 100, 101, 107, 228
secularism, 250
securitisation, 210

security, vii, viii, xi, xii, xiii, 4, 5, 6, 7, 8, 9, 14, 15, 16, 29, 36, 39, 40, 41, 42, 43, 44, 45, 46, 48, 49, 50, 51, 71, 91, 92, 93, 95, 96, 97, 98, 99, 101, 102, 103, 104, 105, 109, 110, 111, 112, 113, 121, 122, 123, 124, 125, 126, 127, 128, 129, 130, 136, 137, 140, 147, 148, 149, 151, 152, 153, 155, 161, 173, 174, 175, 176, 179, 182, 183, 185, 186, 187, 189, 190, 191, 192, 195, 196, 198, 199, 200, 202, 203, 207, 209, 210, 211, 212, 213, 214, 215, 216, 217, 218, 219, 220, 221, 228, 232, 238, 246, 247, 249, 250, 252, 253, 255, 256, 258, 259, 260, 261, 262, 263, 267, 269, 270, 272, 274, 275, 276, 277, 279
seizure, 190
selecting, 170
self, 9, 44, 48, 60, 64, 71, 76, 102, 116, 124, 125, 129, 145, 149, 154, 183, 191, 217, 230, 251, 254, 260, 261, 273, 277, 280
self-confidence, 260
self-interest, 9, 277
Senate, 68, 161, 280, 281, 282
sensing, 270
sensitivity, 6, 63, 277, 280
separation, 79, 202
September 11th, 37
series, 59, 85, 105, 110, 125, 139, 155, 161, 174, 200, 216, 217, 220, 221, 246
services, 54, 126, 138
shape, viii, 7, 11, 40, 42, 55, 64, 66, 113, 142, 229, 280
shaping, 43, 56, 103, 134, 141, 142, 158, 159, 160
shares, 7, 140, 173, 185, 267
sharing, 28, 101, 129, 190, 214, 216
shelter, 83, 173
shock, 166, 274
shores, 221
Siberia, 115, 116, 129
sign, 7, 32, 113, 171, 175, 191, 272
signals, 45, 191
silver, 217
similarity, 260
Singapore, xi, 3, 12, 18, 26, 27, 33, 34, 35, 45, 46, 49, 52, 65, 80, 128, 131, 176, 177, 178, 179, 193, 196, 198, 199, 201, 205, 212, 213, 215, 268
sites, 14, 65, 251
skills, 185
slaves, 257
smoothness, 165
snakes, 145
social capital, xiii
social costs, 9, 95, 166
social group, 255
social indicator, 244

social problems, 255
social structure, 255
socialism, 5, 61
software, 64, 65
solidarity, 157, 188, 192, 202, 207, 215
South Africa, 64
South Asia, vii, viii, 9, 17, 20, 24, 26, 27, 30, 34, 35, 45, 65, 73, 81, 82, 199, 202, 212, 213, 222, 223, 224, 225, 229, 230, 231, 232, 233, 235, 236, 238, 241
South Asian Association for Regional Cooperation, 213
South Korea, 3, 5, 6, 9, 10, 11, 17, 22, 24, 26, 42, 45, 46, 47, 49, 54, 57, 61, 67, 68, 91, 93, 94, 95, 96, 101, 102, 110, 112, 115, 116, 121, 122, 123, 124, 128, 137, 145, 146, 147, 148, 149, 150, 151, 152, 153, 154, 155, 156, 157, 158, 159, 160, 161, 163, 164, 166, 201, 256, 263, 272
South Pacific, viii, 5, 45, 267, 273, 274, 275, 277, 278, 279, 280, 281, 282
Southeast Asia, vii, xi, xii, 3, 5, 6, 7, 9, 10, 11, 16, 17, 18, 20, 24, 25, 26, 27, 30, 33, 34, 40, 45, 46, 50, 72, 78, 79, 80, 85, 86, 87, 88, 91, 93, 97, 98, 101, 106, 107, 121, 122, 124, 127, 138, 165, 166, 173, 174, 176, 177, 178, 179, 182, 185, 187, 189, 190, 191, 193, 196, 197, 198, 199, 200, 201, 205, 212, 216, 221, 224, 270, 271, 272
sovereignty, 6, 7, 36, 40, 61, 76, 124, 135, 146, 181, 236, 237, 238, 249, 276, 279
Soviet Union, vii, 3, 4, 5, 9, 16, 82, 91, 92, 109, 112, 115, 156, 181, 189, 209, 230, 273
Spain, 72
spectrum, 121, 256
speculation, vii, 50, 146, 198
speech, 97, 107, 114, 131, 134, 136, 138, 212, 217, 228
speed, 5, 15, 98, 165, 166
spillovers, 51
Sri Lanka, 19, 24, 26, 28, 30, 35, 201, 215
stability, 16, 28, 34, 42, 43, 44, 61, 63, 92, 95, 98, 100, 102, 103, 109, 123, 125, 127, 129, 130, 136, 139, 140, 142, 160, 183, 187, 190, 197, 199, 204, 210, 212, 214, 217, 220, 227, 228, 230, 232, 234, 238, 239, 245, 267, 270, 276, 277, 280
stages, 104, 112
stakeholders, 43, 213
standard of living, 202, 244
standards, 56, 159
stars, 55
statehood, 112
state-owned enterprises, 141
stereotyping, 79
stock, 76

stockpiling, 271
strategies, 5, 7, 9, 16, 92, 100, 102, 103, 133, 209, 238, 239
strength, 53, 55, 63, 76, 82, 91, 102, 113, 171, 183, 267
stress, 64, 256
stretching, 48, 209, 244
structural adjustment, 42
structural changes, 40, 41
structural reforms, 95
structuring, 231
students, 57, 58, 60, 61, 62, 83, 148, 185
subjectivity, 232
sub-Saharan Africa, 244
subsistence, 274
Sudan, 61, 191
sugar, 273
Suharto, 6, 27, 34, 80, 81, 165, 166, 167, 168, 170, 171, 172, 173, 175, 185, 276
suicide, xiii, 77
summer, 250
Sun, 162
supervision, 60, 254
supplements, 252
suppliers, 137, 199, 211, 217
supply, 15, 93, 102, 116, 126, 209, 210, 211
suppression, 62, 244
Supreme Court, 279
surplus, 72, 216
surprise, 74, 101, 196, 203, 252
surveillance, 95, 126, 269
survival, 40, 181, 184, 187
survivors, 272
suspects, 175, 203
sustainable development, 103, 138, 211
Switzerland, 262
sympathy, 64, 114, 188
symptoms, 6
syndrome, 77
synthesis, 114
systems, 15, 33, 53, 56, 58, 62, 76, 148, 166, 181, 185, 228, 253, 278

T

Taiwan, xii, 3, 5, 6, 10, 13, 17, 24, 26, 33, 40, 42, 43, 46, 49, 51, 58, 61, 97, 99, 102, 103, 122, 123, 127, 133, 139, 143, 146, 200, 269
Tajikistan, 110, 140, 217, 218
takeover, 125
Taliban, 65, 73, 74, 75, 82, 83, 87, 101, 102, 184, 196, 239, 270, 271
targets, 173, 174

taxation, 62
teachers, 185, 186
teaching, xii, 61, 186, 261
technology, 3, 10, 43, 49, 57, 58, 64, 65, 100, 101, 135, 137, 198, 213, 214, 215, 233, 250, 251, 256, 257, 258, 259, 261, 263
technology transfer, 135
telecommunications, 3
television, 6, 54, 77, 115, 245, 282
television stations, 115, 245
tension, 140, 152, 167, 199, 211, 213, 232, 238, 239, 251, 255, 269
terrorism, 16, 41, 49, 50, 51, 71, 72, 73, 74, 77, 80, 92, 101, 104, 110, 113, 136, 137, 165, 167, 174, 175, 176, 179, 182, 183, 187, 188, 189, 190, 191, 192, 196, 197, 199, 200, 203, 214, 215, 217, 229, 232, 235, 236, 237, 239, 241, 245, 246, 247, 258, 259, 260, 263, 271, 272
textbooks, 33
Thailand, 6, 16, 18, 25, 27, 30, 45, 46, 49, 81, 95, 96, 166, 176, 177, 188, 195, 196, 197, 198, 199, 200, 201, 202, 203, 205, 214, 215, 268, 271
theory, xiii, 15, 77, 156, 158
thinking, 9, 15, 39, 63, 100, 104, 110, 124, 127, 136, 202, 209, 210, 269
Third World, xi, 11, 77, 86, 183, 208
threat, 4, 29, 32, 39, 46, 47, 53, 58, 72, 99, 100, 103, 104, 105, 110, 113, 123, 124, 126, 129, 133, 141, 146, 152, 155, 158, 160, 165, 170, 171, 173, 174, 182, 183, 185, 187, 189, 192, 195, 197, 198, 200, 208, 229, 230, 232, 235, 239, 244, 245, 257, 259, 260, 261, 263, 270, 271, 272, 273, 277
threatening behavior, 260
threats, 40, 41, 45, 47, 48, 71, 72, 100, 101, 114, 122, 127, 130, 174, 175, 181, 182, 187, 188, 189, 192, 195, 196, 200, 228, 229, 234, 245, 249, 251, 252, 259, 262
thresholds, 140
tides, 178
time, vii, 3, 5, 7, 10, 14, 16, 24, 34, 35, 41, 42, 45, 53, 58, 60, 66, 68, 72, 78, 81, 82, 83, 84, 91, 92, 94, 96, 98, 103, 104, 105, 109, 111, 112, 113, 116, 121, 124, 129, 135, 136, 138, 140, 141, 145, 147, 149, 154, 160, 161, 177, 178, 179, 181, 182, 184, 187, 192, 195, 197, 203, 207, 213, 215, 216, 217, 218, 219, 229, 231, 232, 237, 238, 239, 244, 245, 247, 259, 264, 265, 266, 267, 268, 270, 272, 273, 275, 276, 279
tin, 189, 210
titanium, 210
torture, 73
tourism, 197, 214, 215
tracking, 239, 270

trade, 4, 15, 20, 28, 35, 50, 53, 58, 93, 96, 110, 121, 135, 138, 139, 140, 153, 154, 176, 189, 198, 199, 201, 212, 213, 214, 215, 216, 261, 262, 274
trading, 16, 34, 45, 72, 97, 122, 166, 198, 215, 268, 270, 272
trading bloc, 272
tradition, 33, 60, 80, 84, 135, 148, 171, 246
training, 101, 116, 148, 175, 176, 185, 186, 190, 192, 196, 230, 244
traits, 11, 74
trajectory, 30, 178, 211
transformation, 13, 34, 35, 36, 50, 99, 101, 127, 166, 168, 171, 172, 173, 178, 184
transformations, 14, 177, 178, 221, 273
transistor, 56
transition, xi, 7, 34, 50, 75, 81, 84, 114, 167, 172, 178, 234
transition period, 172
transitions, 15
transmission, 232
transnational corporations, 138
transparency, 15, 16, 22, 24, 28, 35, 96, 127, 181
transport, 215, 221
transportation, 126, 190
traumatic events, 177
trend, 17, 18, 102, 135, 137, 210, 211, 218, 230, 255
trial, 176, 188
trust, 160, 203, 256, 260
trustworthiness, 57
tungsten, 210
turbulence, 93
Turkey, 216, 245, 252, 255, 259, 261, 262
Turkmenistan, 217, 219, 252
turnout, 255

U

UK, 126, 210, 239, 269
UN, 66, 98, 116, 125, 126, 135, 136, 138, 139, 140, 143, 213, 235, 237, 240, 251, 257, 264, 268, 271, 276, 277
uncertainty, 8, 10, 109, 125, 209
unemployment, 33, 254
UNESCO, xiv
uniform, 13
unilateralism, 103, 124, 212, 234, 237, 238, 258
United Kingdom, xi, 201
United Nations, 57, 58, 62, 68, 91, 98, 103, 125, 127, 129, 135, 138, 143, 144, 173, 175, 188, 190, 191, 232, 244
United States, vii, viii, 4, 5, 8, 10, 16, 40, 41, 45, 46, 48, 49, 50, 51, 56, 63, 82, 83, 84, 87, 91, 92, 94, 95, 96, 97, 100, 102, 103, 104, 105, 106, 107,

109, 111, 112, 113, 114, 116, 122, 123, 124, 126, 128, 129, 130, 131, 133, 140, 141, 143, 144, 145, 146, 148, 150, 151, 153, 156, 158, 160, 161, 163, 166, 173, 174, 175, 181, 182, 183, 186, 187, 188, 189, 190, 191, 192, 209, 210, 217, 218, 219, 223, 227, 228, 229, 230, 231, 232, 233, 235, 236, 238, 239, 240, 241, 248, 259, 267, 268, 269, 270, 275, 277
Universal Declaration of Human Rights, 66
universe, 59
universities, xi, xiii
uranium, 250, 251, 258, 263
USSR, 91, 275
Uzbekistan, 110, 114, 140, 217

V

validity, 76
values, 54, 55, 56, 59, 60, 61, 62, 63, 65, 66, 71, 72, 76, 78, 80, 91, 92, 96, 127, 130, 135, 154, 160, 184, 187, 246, 249, 263
Vanuatu, 275
variable, 262, 264
variables, 42, 43, 153, 195
variance, 189
vein, 138
vessels, 126, 176
victimisation, 271
victims, 217
Vietnam, 5, 6, 18, 20, 25, 27, 30, 32, 45, 77, 115, 118, 140, 198, 214, 276, 277
village, 74, 186
violence, xi, 16, 35, 64, 72, 73, 74, 75, 77, 81, 84, 154, 171, 174, 195, 197, 202, 203, 250, 277
vision, 8, 62, 71, 97, 103, 110, 122, 127, 156, 159, 160, 161, 213, 231, 245, 256
vocabulary, 136
voice, vii, 44, 156, 170, 171, 178, 188, 277
voters, 147, 148, 149, 170, 172
voting, 149, 170
vulnerability, 102, 105, 109, 176, 196, 255, 275, 280

W

wages, 74
war, 3, 5, 13, 15, 16, 17, 33, 39, 40, 48, 49, 50, 55, 74, 75, 83, 84, 91, 92, 95, 100, 101, 109, 110, 112, 113, 114, 121, 123, 124, 125, 126, 127, 136, 145, 146, 154, 155, 157, 161, 169, 173, 182, 187, 188, 197, 198, 208, 216, 217, 227, 228, 229, 230, 235, 236, 237, 245, 246, 247, 248, 258, 261, 263, 269, 271, 276

War on Terror, vii, 10, 16, 32, 34, 36, 41, 81, 92, 161, 165, 166, 173, 174, 175, 176, 178, 195, 196, 197, 198, 227, 228, 229, 230, 231, 232, 233, 234, 235, 238, 239, 246, 269, 270, 271, 274
war years, 127
warlords, 82, 83
Washington Consensus, 96
water, 126, 216, 217
water resources, 216, 217
watershed, 125, 165
weakness, 57, 76, 109, 234, 244, 276
wealth, 53, 56, 72, 103, 217, 244, 268
weapons, 41, 47, 48, 51, 82, 92, 93, 123, 127, 130, 136, 137, 179, 185, 186, 190, 197, 198, 228, 233, 237, 248, 258, 275
weapons of mass destruction, 41, 48, 51, 92, 127, 130, 137, 179, 197, 228, 248
wear, 114
web, viii, 69, 125, 143, 154, 161, 240, 246, 254, 264
well-being, 4, 6, 200
Western Europe, 111
White House, 48, 83, 99, 105, 106, 190, 197, 210, 241, 271
wind, 147
winter, 68
withdrawal, 77, 94, 110, 114, 147, 150, 151, 178, 189, 198, 245, 247, 276
witnesses, 254
wives, 154
women, xiii, xiv, 73, 74, 200, 244, 246
words, 47, 77, 112, 128, 135, 137, 184, 234, 246, 258
work, ix, xi, xii, xiii, 14, 39, 45, 47, 49, 54, 58, 60, 61, 65, 74, 80, 102, 103, 104, 111, 134, 135, 136, 138, 140, 149, 170, 177, 190, 220, 221, 260, 273
World Bank, 12, 69, 98, 244
World Health Organization, 104
World Trade Organization, 123, 138, 140, 198
World War I, 123, 145, 146, 161, 183, 271, 273, 276
worldview, 76, 212, 268
worry, 124
writing, 77, 83, 279
WTO, 123, 138, 140, 144, 198

Y

Yemen, 201
yield, 29, 129
young men, 74, 76
yuan, 96